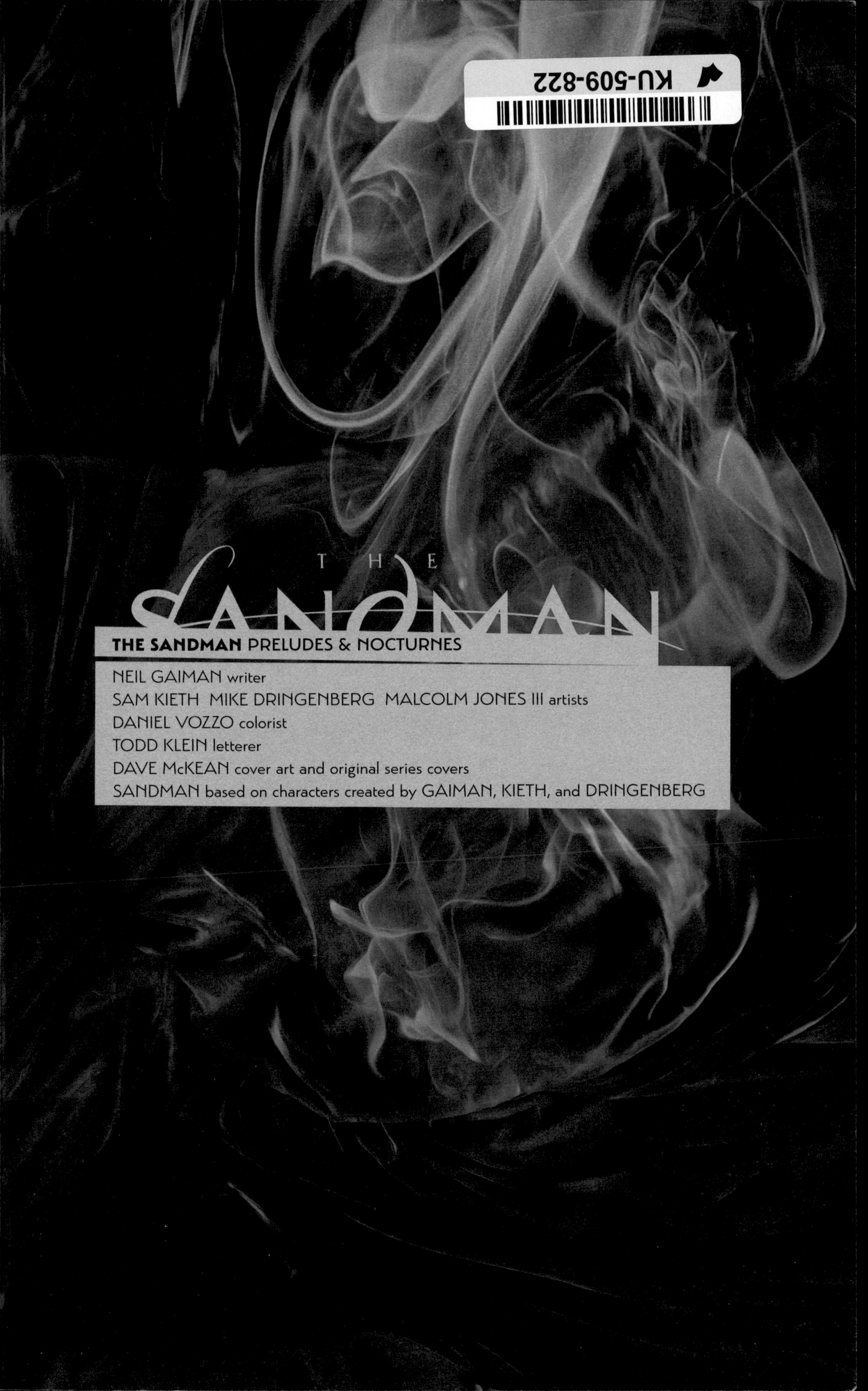
THE SANDMAN
THE SANDMAN PRELUDES & NOCTURNES
NEIL GAIMAN writer
SAM KIETH MIKE DRINGENBERG MALCOLM JONES III artists
DANIEL VOZZO colorist
TODD KLEIN letterer
DAVE McKEAN cover art and original series covers
SANDMAN based on characters created by GAIMAN, KIETH, and DRINGENBERG

Cover design and interior illustrations by DAVE McKEAN.

THE SANDMAN VOL. I: PRELUDES & NOCTURNES

30TH ANNIVERSARY EDITION

Published by DC Comics. Cover, introduction and compilation
Copyright © 2018 DC Comics. Foreword Copyright © 1995
DC Comics. Afterword Copyright © 1991 DC Comics.

Originally published in single magazine form as THE
SANDMAN 1-8. Copyright © 1988, 1989 DC Comics. All
Rights Reserved. All characters, their distinctive likenesses and
related elements featured in this publication are trademarks of
DC Comics. The stories, characters and incidents featured in
this publication are entirely fictional. DC Comics does not read
or accept unsolicited submissions of ideas, stories or artwork.
DC – a WarnerMedia Company.

DC Comics, 2900 West Alameda Ave., Burbank, CA 91505

Printed by LSC Communications, Kendallville, IN, USA.

12/2/19. Third Printing. ISBN: 978-1-4012-8477-0

Library of Congress Cataloging-in-Publication Data is available.

KAREN BERGER Editor – Original Series
ART YOUNG Associate Editor – Original Series
JEB WOODARD Group Editor – Collected Editions
SCOTT NYBAKKEN Editor – Collected Edition
STEVE COOK Design Director – Books
LOUIS PRANDI Publication Design

BOB HARRAS Senior VP – Editor-in-Chief, DC Comics
MARK DOYLE Executive Editor, Vertigo & Black Label

DAN DiDIO Publisher
JIM LEE Publisher & Chief Creative Officer
BOBBIE CHASE VP – New Publishing Initiatives & Talent Development
DON FALLETTI VP – Manufacturing Operations & Workflow Management
LAWRENCE GANEM VP – Talent Services
ALISON GILL Senior VP – Manufacturing & Operations
HANK KANALZ Senior VP – Publishing Strategy & Support Services
DAN MIRON VP – Publishing Operations
NICK J. NAPOLITANO VP – Manufacturing Administration & Design
NANCY SPEARS VP – Sales
MICHELE R. WELLS VP & Executive Editor, Young Reader

INTRODUCTION

I'll admit, I'm at a bit of a loss as to what to do here.

If you've already read THE SANDMAN, what can I tell you that you don't already know, deep in the secret corners of your heart? You know this story is lovely and brilliant and sweet and strange. You know it is beautiful and deep and wry and wondrous. You *know.*

If you've already read this book, you know nothing I can say is as good as what waits for you ahead.

So go. Stop reading this and go.

If you *haven't* read this book, and are, perhaps, standing in a bookstore or a comics shop, wondering if it's worth your time, what I can say to convince you? Should I wax rhapsodic? Get lyrical and grandiose? Reference some of the story's funnier jokes so I seem more clever than I really am?

No. I love this book too much. I don't want to spoil its secrets or steal its thunder.

So let me tell you the simple truth. No hyperbole. THE SANDMAN changed my life.

It's not often you get to say that and mean it. But it's true.

If that's not enough to convince you...I guess all that's left is for me to tell you a story or two. Because that's what I do.

Stories are important, after all...

***

I came to comics late in life. I can't tell you why. I was a voracious reader as a kid, going through pretty much every picture book in the local library until I finally started chapter books around age nine. Then I read a novel or two a day until I finished high school.

Even as I slouched through college, comics simply weren't on my radar. Didn't occur to me to read them. Didn't occur to me that they might be worth reading. I had a couple thousand fantasy and sci-fi novels under my belt, and my classes were exposing me to Shakespeare and Chaucer, Sanskrit theater and the Harlem Renaissance poets. I read Roethke and Frost and Brooks and Baldwin.

But comics? That was like...*Garfield*, right? And superheroes? I didn't spare any thought for them, and when I did, I assumed they were (and I'm ashamed to write this now) silly bullshit for kids.

I was well into my twenties when, at a weekend-long party, I sat down in a quiet corner and idly picked up a copy of THE DARK KNIGHT RETURNS. I read the whole thing straight through, completely lost in it, deaf to the riot and welter around me.

Hours later I hunted down the person who had brought the book. I shook it at them, angry and incredulous, demanding: "Is it all as good as this?"

"Oh, no," he said sadly. "But some of it is close."

First he gave me WATCHMEN, and it floored me despite the fact that I didn't know superhero mythology from a hole in the ground.

Next came THE SANDMAN. And it was unlike any story I'd ever read. In any genre. In any medium. I remember thinking, "Can you do this? Can you have

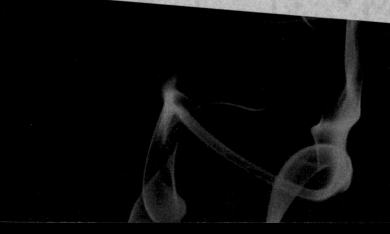

Odin and angels and faeries and witches and...just every-thing? All at once? In the same story? Is this allowed?"

It lit me up inside. I wouldn't shut up about it. I'd give it to people and say, "You have to read this! It's like Shakespeare!"

I blush a little now, remembering that. It's not the best comparison. It's just that back then, Shakespeare was the best thing I'd ever read.

The truth is, Shakespeare wishes he wrote some-thing this good.

***

But let's back up a bit. I'd prefer to be fully honest here. I didn't feel that way about SANDMAN immediately. Not right out of the gate.

I read this first graphic novel and liked it well enough. PRELUDES & NOCTURNES is lovely. It intro-duces the world, the characters, there's a nice little plot. Tension. Mystery. Hero's journey. Mythic underpinning. Descent to the underworld. Vengeance. Recovery of self. Got my RDA of all manner of awesome here. Cool.

Then I kept reading, and the storytelling got looser. But I was still happy. Shakespeare shows up. I dig that. And there's faerie tales. And...What? Are we in Africa now? Wait, is someone telling a story about a story *inside* a story? Okay. That's cool. I guess this series is more like a bunch of different stories? But they're all interesting, so who really cares if they don't really have much to do with one another...

Then I kept reading, and there was a little plotline. And a new character or two. And...and...hold on. Wait. Does all this fit together? Has it all fit together from the beginning?

Has everything been leading to an ending?

Oh. Oh lord. I never knew a story could be like this.

***

I reread this series in grad school, and it comforted me at a time when I desperately needed comfort. The next semester I used a section of it during the single, brief, shining semester I got to teach ancient literature.

THE SANDMAN changed the way that I thought about stories. It taught me that a plot can be gentle and maundering without being broken. It showed me the delight of a wandering way, of the seemingly innocuous stray detail. It showed me the power of melancholy. It showed me that a story about stories is not just possible, but appealing.

THE SANDMAN broadened my horizons. There were gay characters. Trans characters. Queer characters. And for the most part, it really wasn't that big a deal for the people in the story. Nobody really seemed to care that much. For a small-town boy from Wisconsin in the '90s, that was important. I didn't have much of that in my life, and I was a better person for being exposed to it.

About four years ago I reread the series again and was surprised at how much I had remembered and forgotten. It made me cry. It always makes me cry, though not when anything tragic happens, and never because I am sad.

I've played the oldest game with my children (from issue #4): if I come to them and say, "I am a wolf, strong-jawed, fierce hunter," they will easily counter with something like, "I am a snake, poison-biting." They are naturals at it, though their tactics are occasionally unorthodox, as my elder son (age eight) likes to be-come a giant squid, and my younger (four) insists that he can have rocket boots.

I have bought, at my best count, nine complete copies of the series, most of them as gifts. Some be-cause I could not bear to go without reading the story again. And a few simply because they were beautiful...

I reread the series again, just now, before writing this introduction. And the story unfolded inside me like a flower. I know so much more about comics than I did 20 years ago, and I marvel at the craft displayed on these pages. There is so much story, so easy, so clear, so clean, so wonderful...

And I read these stories, and I cry, and I cannot for the life of me tell you why...

***

What you're holding here is something special. THE SANDMAN is, in my opinion, the finest comic book ever written.

If you've read it before, welcome back. Welcome home. Trust me when I say that there are still surprises here for you to find.

If you're here for the first time...? Oh, sweet human child, come play. I envy your first steps along this wind-ing way. One piece of advice: do stray. Taste the fruit. Oh, trust me. Stay.

—Patrick Rothfuss
July 2018

FOREWORD

SANDMAN never lived up to my initial expectations. If it had, it wouldn't be the benchmark series it is today. Instead, it turned into something I never imagined: one of the best comics works ever produced.

Now, don't get me wrong. It's not that I didn't think the series had potential. The initial proposal is long gone, but my hazy memory recalls interesting characters, an intriguing, imaginative atmosphere and some hints at future storylines. It was evident that Neil Gaiman was a good "idea man," but whether he could execute those concepts was another story.

Back in 1987, Neil was a new writer to comics who had submitted a short SWAMP THING story to me a couple of years earlier. Journalism was his background and, like a good reporter, he hounded me every few months about that Swamp Thing tale. It wasn't until we first met in London during my first scouting mission for British talent that I realized that this was the same persistent but polite British guy who'd been bugging me all this time. It was at that meeting that Neil pitched the BLACK ORCHID miniseries, a SANDMAN series and a series featuring John Constantine, among a host of others. The Sandman was already spoken for in the Justice Society of America, and Constantine was on his way to being developed by Jamie Delano. It was decided that BLACK ORCHID made the most sense for us to see a proper proposal. Soon after we accepted Neil's final proposal, he and the silent, young and formidably talented Dave McKean began work.

BLACK ORCHID was the second comics work that Neil had done. Like his first work, *Violent Cases*, it was technically solid but maybe, in a way, too precise. The craft was there, but there was a distance to Neil's writing that kept me from getting emotionally involved with the characters. However, there was enough of a spark in his work that we wanted to see if it would ignite with another project. That project would turn out to be a new Sandman series starring an entirely new character.

I've edited many start-up titles in my time, and THE SANDMAN, like most others, went through its share of birth and growth pains. In rereading the first storyline of the series, I was struck by a dichotomy. On the one hand, the first seven issues were a simple quest tale about the once-captive ruler of the dreamworld, featuring known DC characters and their haunts in known roles. Revenge, battle, quest fulfilled. Conventional stuff? Perhaps. On the other hand, the opening story also introduced a mysterious and powerful yet harebrained bunch of occultists and hangers-on, a bizarre "sleeping sickness" that affected seemingly random people—in an ambitious tale that took these characters through several decades of strange and tumultuous changes. Conventional stuff? Not at all. Still, in the hands of a different writer, the seeds that were planted in this fertile story ground could have borne a B-level fantasy/horror title.

As the series branched out in unexpected directions, THE SANDMAN developed into one of the most atypical books in comics. For me, the turning point was issue #8, "The Sound of Her Wings." It wasn't just the appearance of the adorable and ultimately pragmatic Death trying to cheer up her morose younger brother. Nor was it the fact that the too-familiar faces of DC characters were nowhere in sight. It was the element of humanity and interpersonal relationships that started coming through in Neil's work. Ironically enough, the catalyst for this emotional resonance was a character that traditionally represents the antithesis of all this.

The artists on PRELUDES & NOCTURNES— Sam Kieth, Mike Dringenberg and Malcolm Jones III— provided the right atmosphere for Morpheus' haunting origin story. Like Neil, they were relatively new to comics and were evolving their own distinctive styles. Sam did wonderful portrayals of Cain and Abel, and his visceral renditions of Hell and its gruesome inhabitants were truly horrifying. Mike, most notably, created the perky goth visual for Death, and his interpretation of Morpheus is probably one of the best ever done. Malcolm's illustrative line work brought a cohesive and definitive look to the overall series.

The covers for this first storyline (and all future ones) were illustrated, constructed and assembled by Dave McKean. An extraordinarily gifted artist at the ripe old age of 22, Dave was fresh out of art school when he worked on BLACK ORCHID. He's been most innovative on the SANDMAN covers, experimenting in different styles and techniques since the early portrait covers, complete with odd artifacts tucked away in the frames. Conceptually, Dave has been breaking with convention from the start. I still vividly remember his talking me into the idea of not having Sandman on every cover. (Believe me, it was a big deal back then.)

This first volume of the SANDMAN series is very much a work in progress; that of a talented writer who eventually honed and refined his skills and progressively developed his initial concept—a series about dreams: personal, nocturnal and imaginary—and expanded it in ways that produced some classically modern and unforgettable stories.

Those stories to come—collected in THE DOLL'S HOUSE, SEASON OF MISTS, A GAME OF YOU, FABLES AND REFLECTIONS, BRIEF LIVES, WORLDS' END, THE KINDLY ONES and THE WAKE—represent a wealth of narrative riches. There are the many tales that revolve around Morpheus—his dysfunctional pantheonic family the Endless, his lovers, his enemies, his kingdom and his personal and far-reaching conflicts—though there are also a great number of tales where the Sandman is featured as a cameo player, or even sometimes not at all. It is in these stories (some of my favorites: "Soft Places," "Ramadan," "A Tale of Two Cities" and "Cerements"), where Neil's love of mythology, historical figures and classical literature is woven into his own personal dream lore.

Like the landmark series before it—THE DARK KNIGHT RETURNS, WATCHMEN and V FOR VENDETTA—THE SANDMAN's appeal has transcended the traditional comic market. And there's good reason for that. Ultimately, Neil Gaiman loves to tell stories, and the stories he tells are timeless, resonant and universal. His work on THE SANDMAN appeals to people from different walks of life, attracting a constellation of readers who normally don't inhabit the same literary orbit. THE SANDMAN also has a disproportionate number of women who read the series, probably the most of any mainstream comic. In a medium that is still widely occupied by males, that in itself is a major achievement.

THE SANDMAN's popularity and success helped me to make an argument for forming a new imprint in 1992. I'd wanted to create a separate line of comics that would provide a place for the provocative and personal visions of comics' best talent. THE SANDMAN, along with a number of other highly regarded titles, formed the core of DC's newly formed Vertigo imprint. THE SANDMAN's draw and reach both inside and outside

of the comics market played an integral part in Vertigo's
positioning and image.

I knew early on that Neil had an ending for THE
SANDMAN in sight, and as much as I would've loved
for him to stay on indefinitely, it makes the only sense in
the world to have a writer complete his work and see it
through to its end, especially on a book that has achieved
what it has. In the six years since its publication, THE
SANDMAN has won more industry awards than any
other comics series. It can also claim to its credit a World
Fantasy Award for best short story ("A Midsummer
Night's Dream") and an impressive list of quotes and
introductions that includes Norman Mailer, Stephen King
and Tori Amos.

Neil's strength at creating singular and compelling
characters is no more evident than in the Endless, who
have proved to be just as popular as the Dream King
himself. Each of the Endless will have their story told,
which Neil and Chris Bachalo began with DEATH: THE
HIGH COST OF LIVING and continued in DEATH:
THE TIME OF YOUR LIFE. Soon after the end of
THE SANDMAN, its influence would be felt in THE
DREAMING, a new monthly title that didn't feature
Morpheus or his siblings but highlighted many of the
supernatural and horror characters that Neil used in THE
SANDMAN. Just as important, it left room for writers to
explore and create new dreaming territory, denizens and
dreamers alike.

It's been a poignant and strange feeling, writing this
foreword to the first volume of the SANDMAN stories,
now that the monthly series is winding down to its
conclusion. It's interesting seeing the end of this complex
and masterful epic saga while reexamining its more simple
beginnings. Yet the foundation was strong in those early
tales, firmly rooting the series and lining it with a potential
that would sprout rich and fantastic worlds—a potential
that took seed and blossomed into a phenomenon.

As I said in my opening, I never expected THE
SANDMAN to become the landmark series that it has.
But if there's anything to learn from one's expectations, it
is that it's wonderful to be more than pleasantly surprised.

See you in your dreams.

—**Karen Berger**
Founder, Vertigo
January 1995

For Dave Dickson: oldest friend.
—Neil Gaiman

To my wife Kathy, my pal Tim, and to everyone in jail.
—Sam Kieth

To friends and lovers. To Sam, Malcolm and Neil; may your talents never dim.
You made working on this book an indescribable pleasure. To Karen, Tom and
Art (without whom this book would not have been possible), thanks for the
time and your super-human patience. Special thanks to Beth, Matte, Sigal, the
incomparable Barbara Brandt (a.k.a. Victoria), Rachel, Sean F., Shawn S., Mimi,
Gigi, Heather, Yann, Brantski, Mai Li, Bernie Wrightson (for Cain and Abel)
and, as ever, to Cinnamon.
—Mike Dringenberg

To Little Malcolm.
—Malcolm Jones III

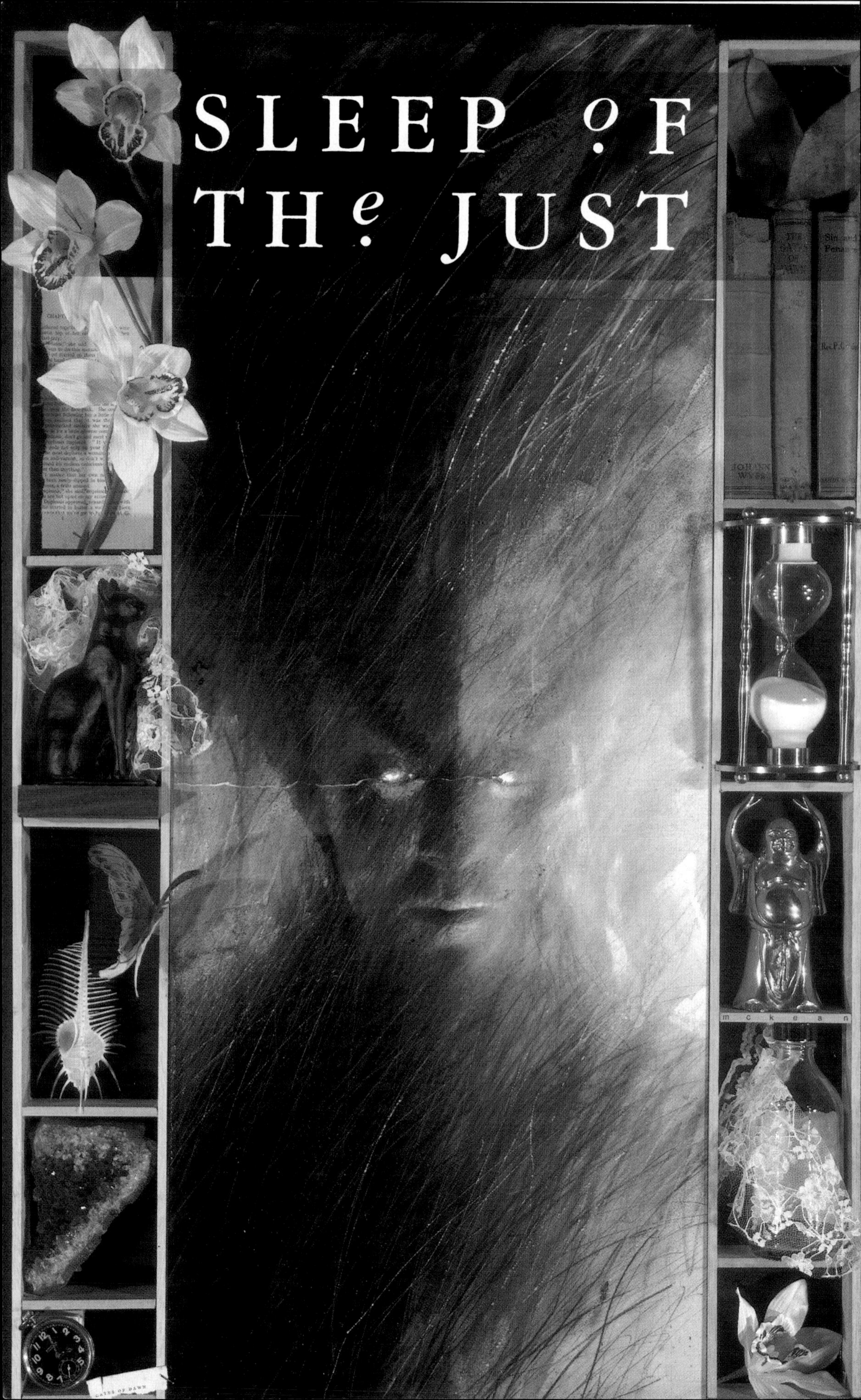
SLEEP OF
THE JUST
mckean

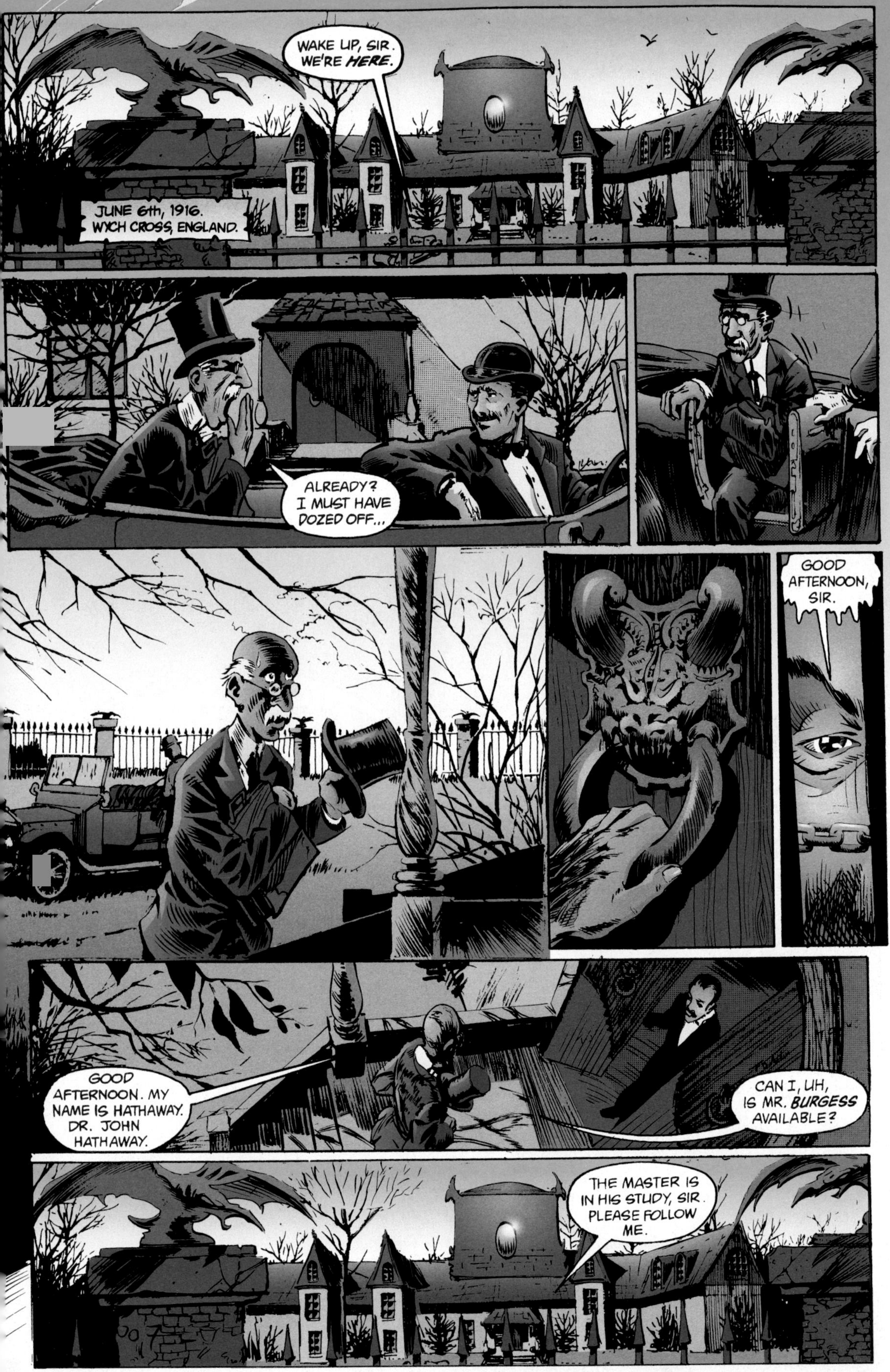
WAKE UP, SIR. WE'RE HERE.
JUNE 6th, 1916. WYCH CROSS, ENGLAND.
ALREADY? I MUST HAVE DOZED OFF...
GOOD AFTERNOON, SIR.
GOOD AFTERNOON. MY NAME IS HATHAWAY. DR. JOHN HATHAWAY.
CAN I, UH, IS MR. BURGESS AVAILABLE?
THE MASTER IS IN HIS STUDY, SIR. PLEASE FOLLOW ME.

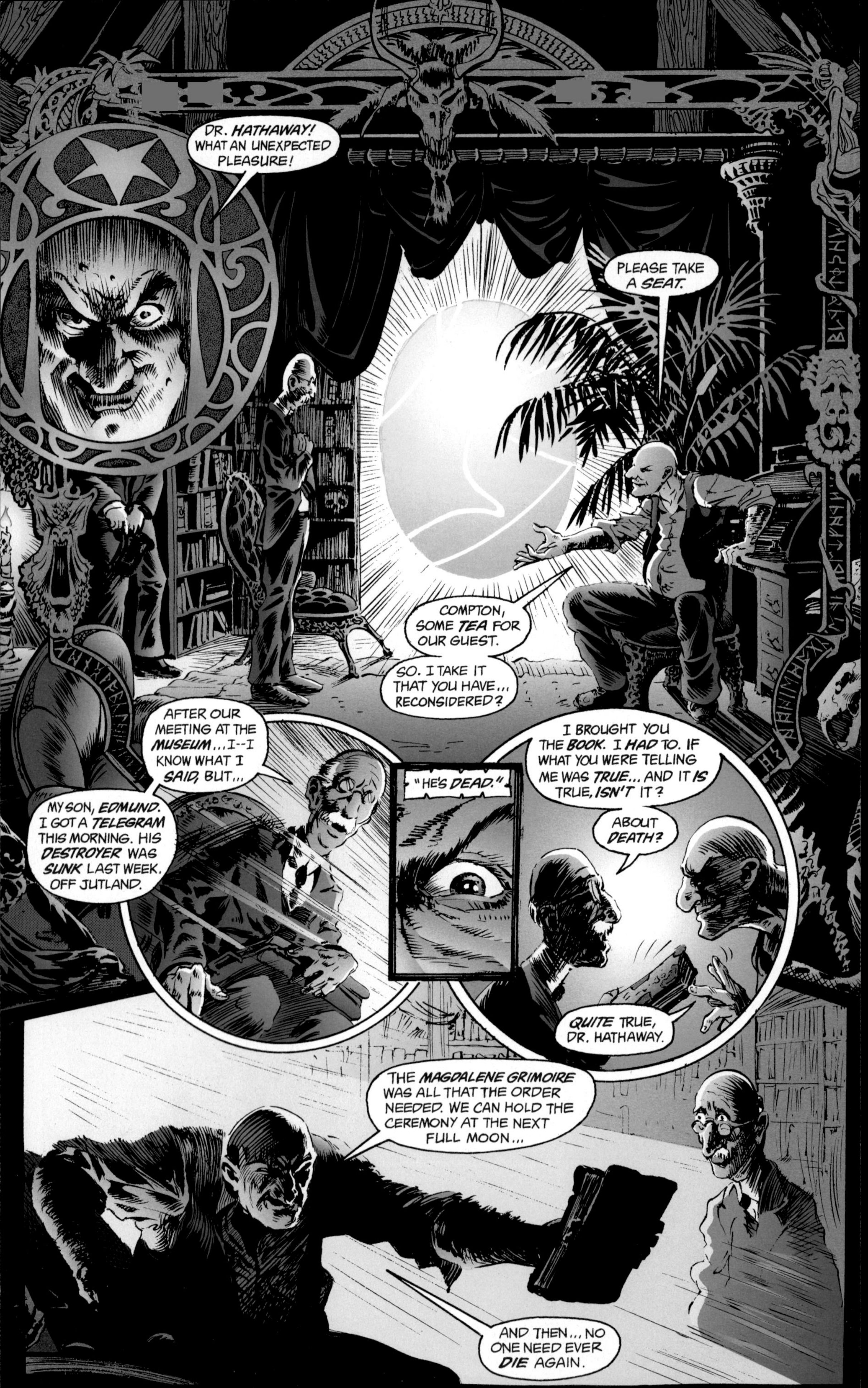
DR. HATHAWAY! WHAT AN UNEXPECTED PLEASURE!
PLEASE TAKE A SEAT.
COMPTON, SOME TEA FOR OUR GUEST.
SO. I TAKE IT THAT YOU HAVE... RECONSIDERED?
AFTER OUR MEETING AT THE MUSEUM... I--I KNOW WHAT I SAID, BUT...
MY SON, EDMUND. I GOT A TELEGRAM THIS MORNING. HIS DESTROYER WAS SUNK LAST WEEK. OFF JUTLAND.
"HE'S DEAD."
I BROUGHT YOU THE BOOK. I HAD TO. IF WHAT YOU WERE TELLING ME WAS TRUE... AND IT IS TRUE, ISN'T IT?
ABOUT DEATH?
QUITE TRUE, DR. HATHAWAY.
THE MAGDALENE GRIMOIRE WAS ALL THAT THE ORDER NEEDED. WE CAN HOLD THE CEREMONY AT THE NEXT FULL MOON...
AND THEN... NO ONE NEED EVER DIE AGAIN.

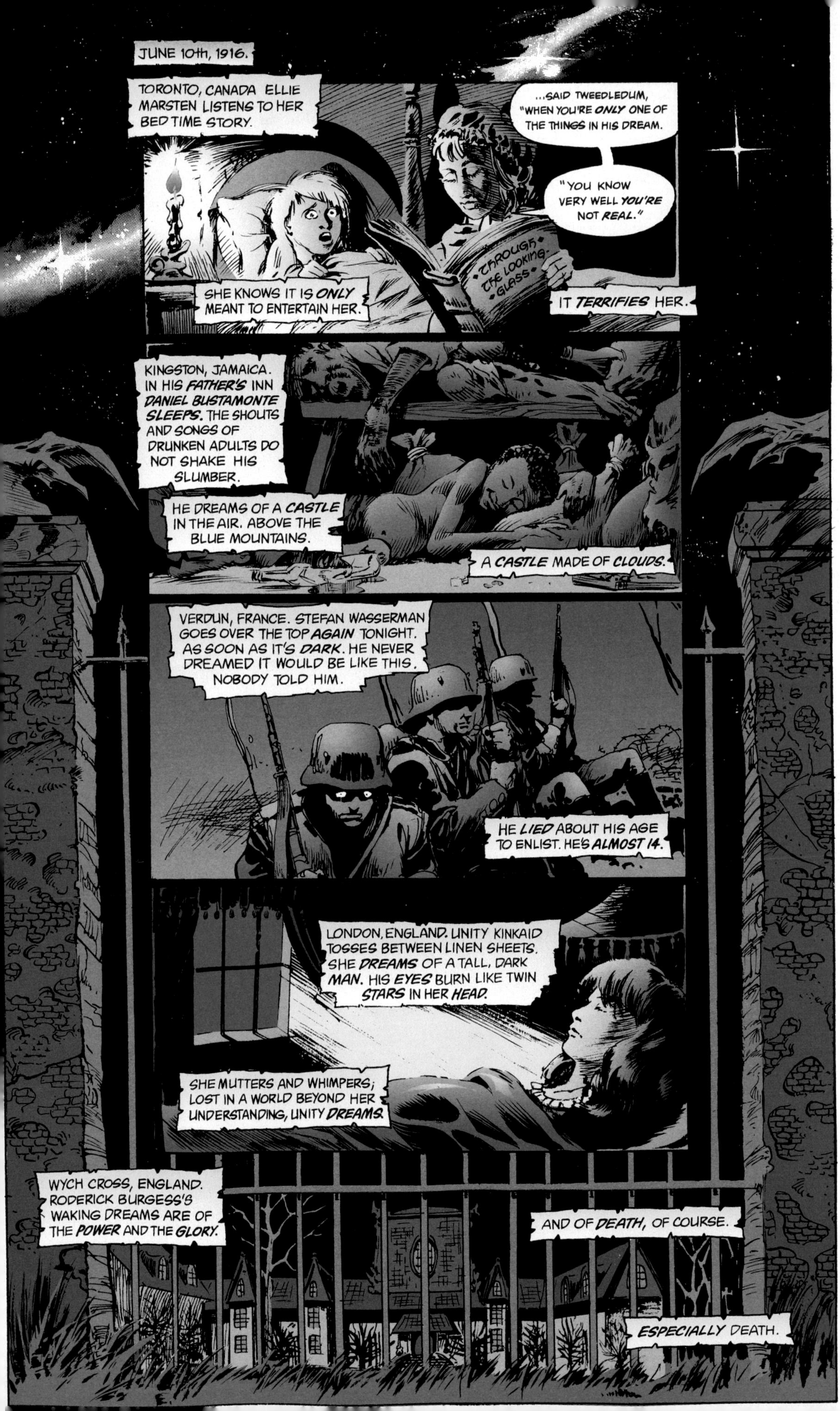
JUNE 10th, 1916.
TORONTO, CANADA ELLIE MARSTEN LISTENS TO HER BED TIME STORY.
...SAID TWEEDLEDUM, "WHEN YOU'RE ONLY ONE OF THE THINGS IN HIS DREAM.
"YOU KNOW VERY WELL YOU'RE NOT REAL."
THROUGH THE LOOKING-GLASS
SHE KNOWS IT IS ONLY MEANT TO ENTERTAIN HER.
IT TERRIFIES HER.
KINGSTON, JAMAICA. IN HIS FATHER'S INN DANIEL BUSTAMONTE SLEEPS. THE SHOUTS AND SONGS OF DRUNKEN ADULTS DO NOT SHAKE HIS SLUMBER.
HE DREAMS OF A CASTLE IN THE AIR. ABOVE THE BLUE MOUNTAINS.
A CASTLE MADE OF CLOUDS.
VERDUN, FRANCE. STEFAN WASSERMAN GOES OVER THE TOP AGAIN TONIGHT. AS SOON AS IT'S DARK. HE NEVER DREAMED IT WOULD BE LIKE THIS. NOBODY TOLD HIM.
HE LIED ABOUT HIS AGE TO ENLIST. HE'S ALMOST 14.
LONDON, ENGLAND. UNITY KINKAID TOSSES BETWEEN LINEN SHEETS. SHE DREAMS OF A TALL, DARK MAN. HIS EYES BURN LIKE TWIN STARS IN HER HEAD.
SHE MUTTERS AND WHIMPERS; LOST IN A WORLD BEYOND HER UNDERSTANDING, UNITY DREAMS.
WYCH CROSS, ENGLAND. RODERICK BURGESS'S WAKING DREAMS ARE OF THE POWER AND THE GLORY.
AND OF DEATH, OF COURSE.
ESPECIALLY DEATH.

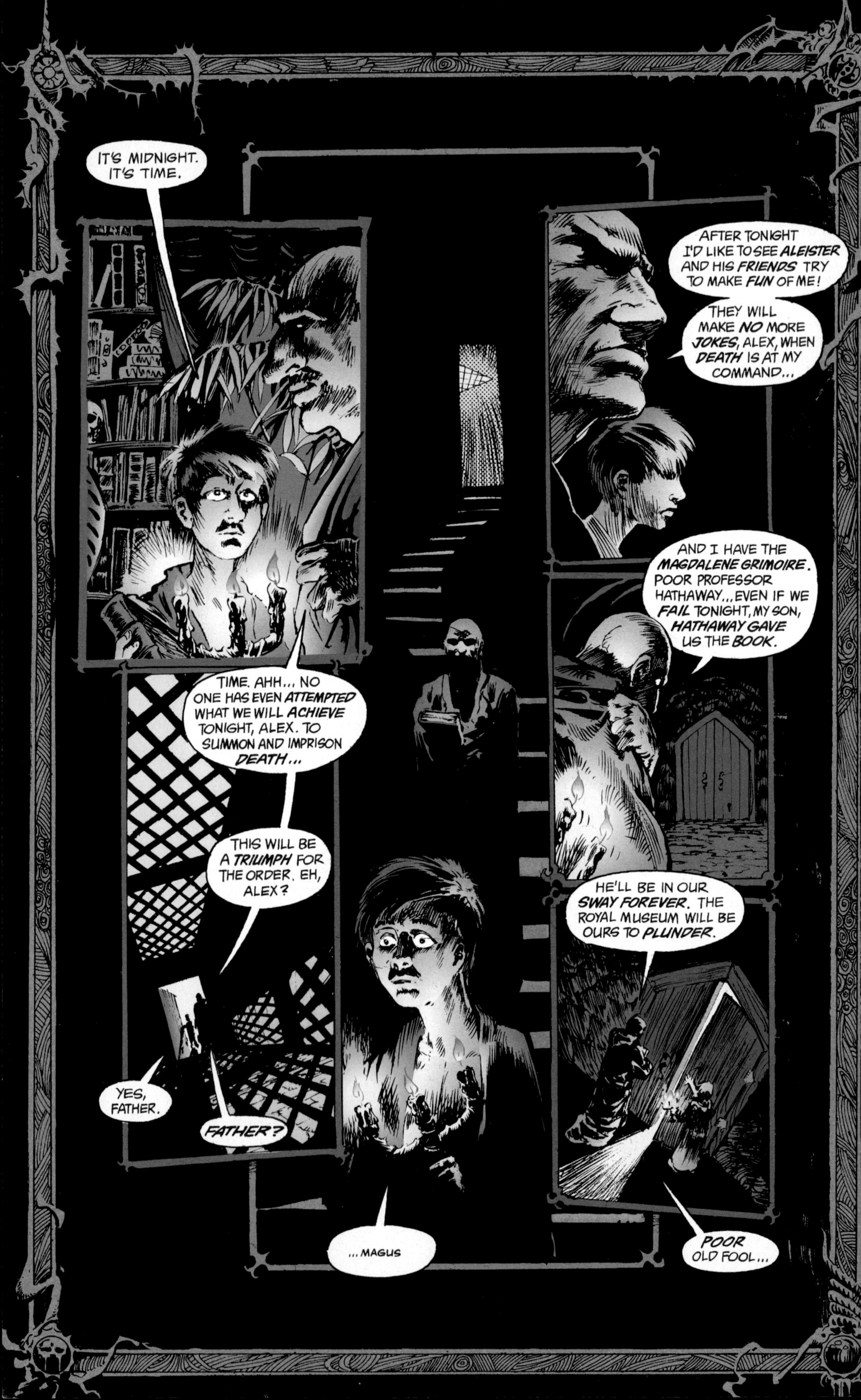
IT'S MIDNIGHT. IT'S TIME.
TIME. AHH... NO ONE HAS EVEN ATTEMPTED WHAT WE WILL ACHIEVE TONIGHT, ALEX. TO SUMMON AND IMPRISON DEATH...
THIS WILL BE A TRIUMPH FOR THE ORDER. EH, ALEX?
YES, FATHER.
FATHER?
...MAGUS
AFTER TONIGHT I'D LIKE TO SEE ALEISTER AND HIS FRIENDS TRY TO MAKE FUN OF ME!
THEY WILL MAKE NO MORE JOKES, ALEX, WHEN DEATH IS AT MY COMMAND...
AND I HAVE THE MAGDALENE GRIMOIRE. POOR PROFESSOR HATHAWAY... EVEN IF WE FAIL TONIGHT, MY SON, HATHAWAY GAVE US THE BOOK.
HE'LL BE IN OUR SWAY FOREVER. THE ROYAL MUSEUM WILL BE OURS TO PLUNDER.
POOR OLD FOOL...

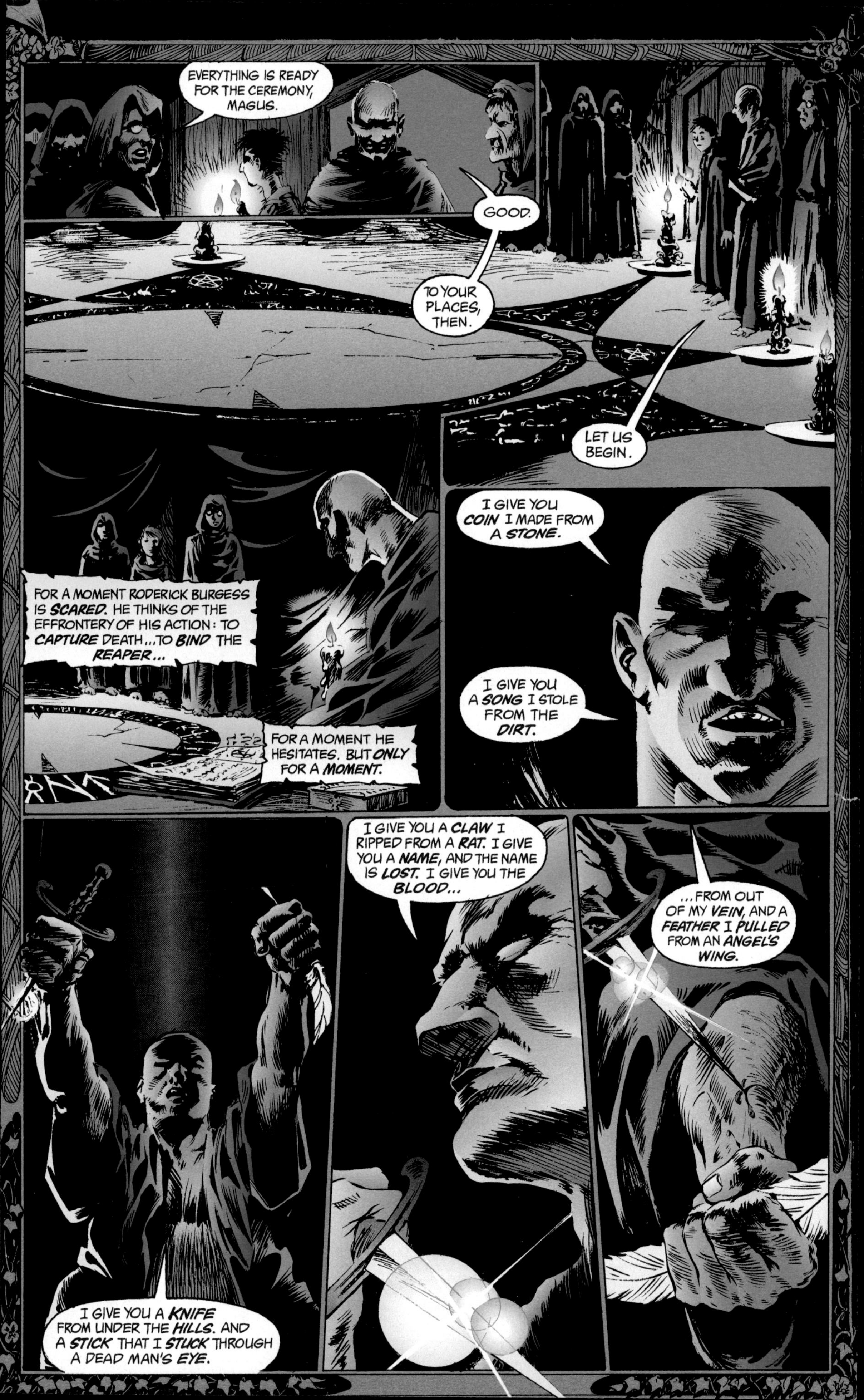
EVERYTHING IS READY FOR THE CEREMONY, MAGUS.
GOOD.
TO YOUR PLACES, THEN.
LET US BEGIN.
FOR A MOMENT RODERICK BURGESS IS SCARED. HE THINKS OF THE EFFRONTERY OF HIS ACTION: TO CAPTURE DEATH...TO BIND THE REAPER...
FOR A MOMENT HE HESITATES. BUT ONLY FOR A MOMENT.
I GIVE YOU COIN I MADE FROM A STONE.
I GIVE YOU A SONG I STOLE FROM THE DIRT.
I GIVE YOU A KNIFE FROM UNDER THE HILLS. AND A STICK THAT I STUCK THROUGH A DEAD MAN'S EYE.
I GIVE YOU A CLAW I RIPPED FROM A RAT. I GIVE YOU A NAME, AND THE NAME IS LOST. I GIVE YOU THE BLOOD...
...FROM OUT OF MY VEIN, AND A FEATHER I PULLED FROM AN ANGEL'S WING.

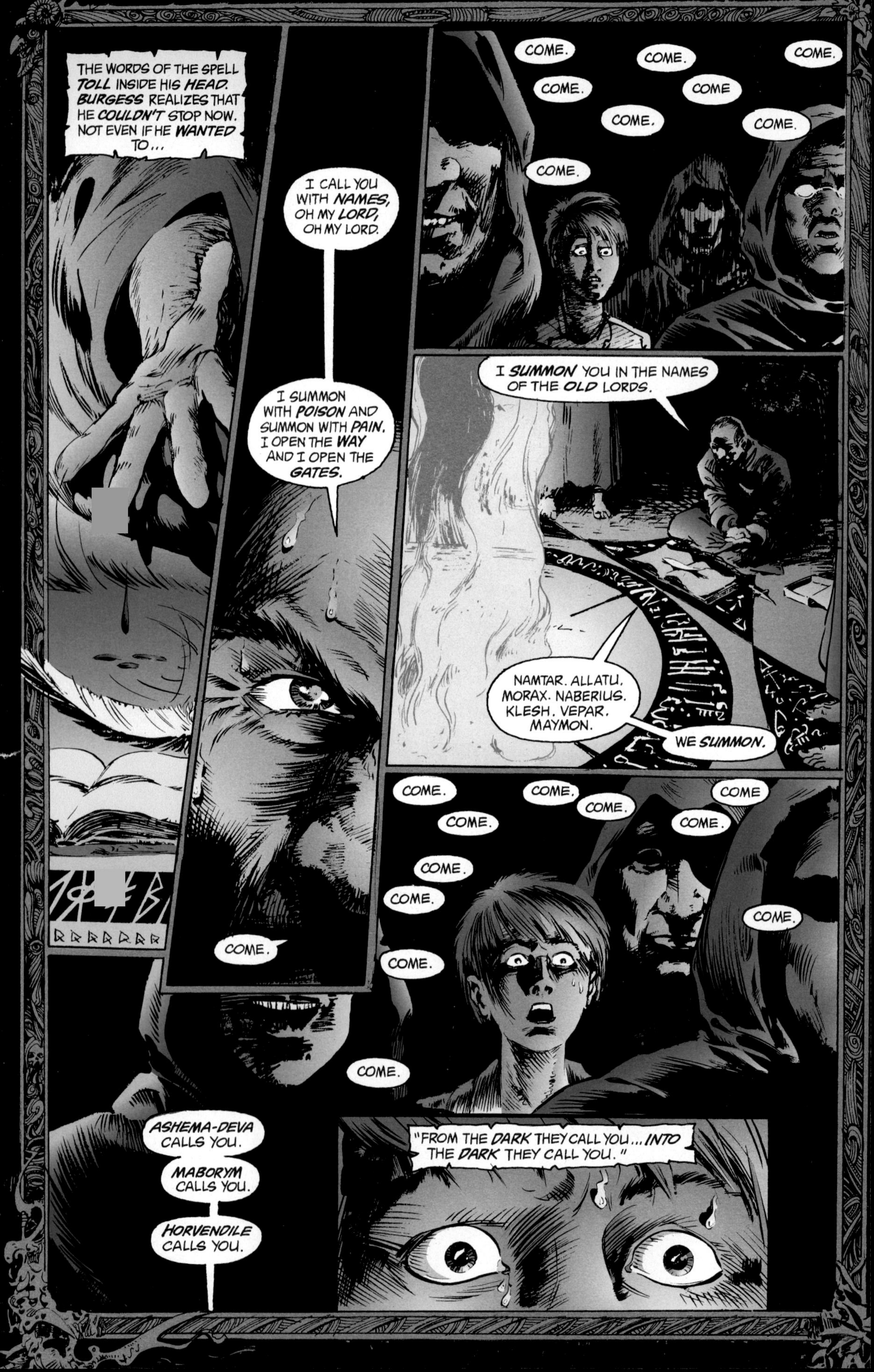
THE WORDS OF THE SPELL TOLL INSIDE HIS HEAD. BURGESS REALIZES THAT HE COULDN'T STOP NOW. NOT EVEN IF HE WANTED TO...
I CALL YOU WITH NAMES, OH MY LORD, OH MY LORD.
I SUMMON WITH POISON AND SUMMON WITH PAIN. I OPEN THE WAY AND I OPEN THE GATES.
COME.
COME.
COME.
COME.
COME
COME.
COME.
COME.
I SUMMON YOU IN THE NAMES OF THE OLD LORDS.
NAMTAR. ALLATU. MORAX. NABERIUS. KLESH. VEPAR. MAYMON.
WE SUMMON.
COME.
COME.
COME.
COME.
COME.
COME
COME.
COME.
COME.
COME.
COME.
COME.
COME.
ASHEMA-DEVA CALLS YOU.
MABORYM CALLS YOU.
HORVENDILE CALLS YOU.
"FROM THE DARK THEY CALL YOU... INTO THE DARK THEY CALL YOU."

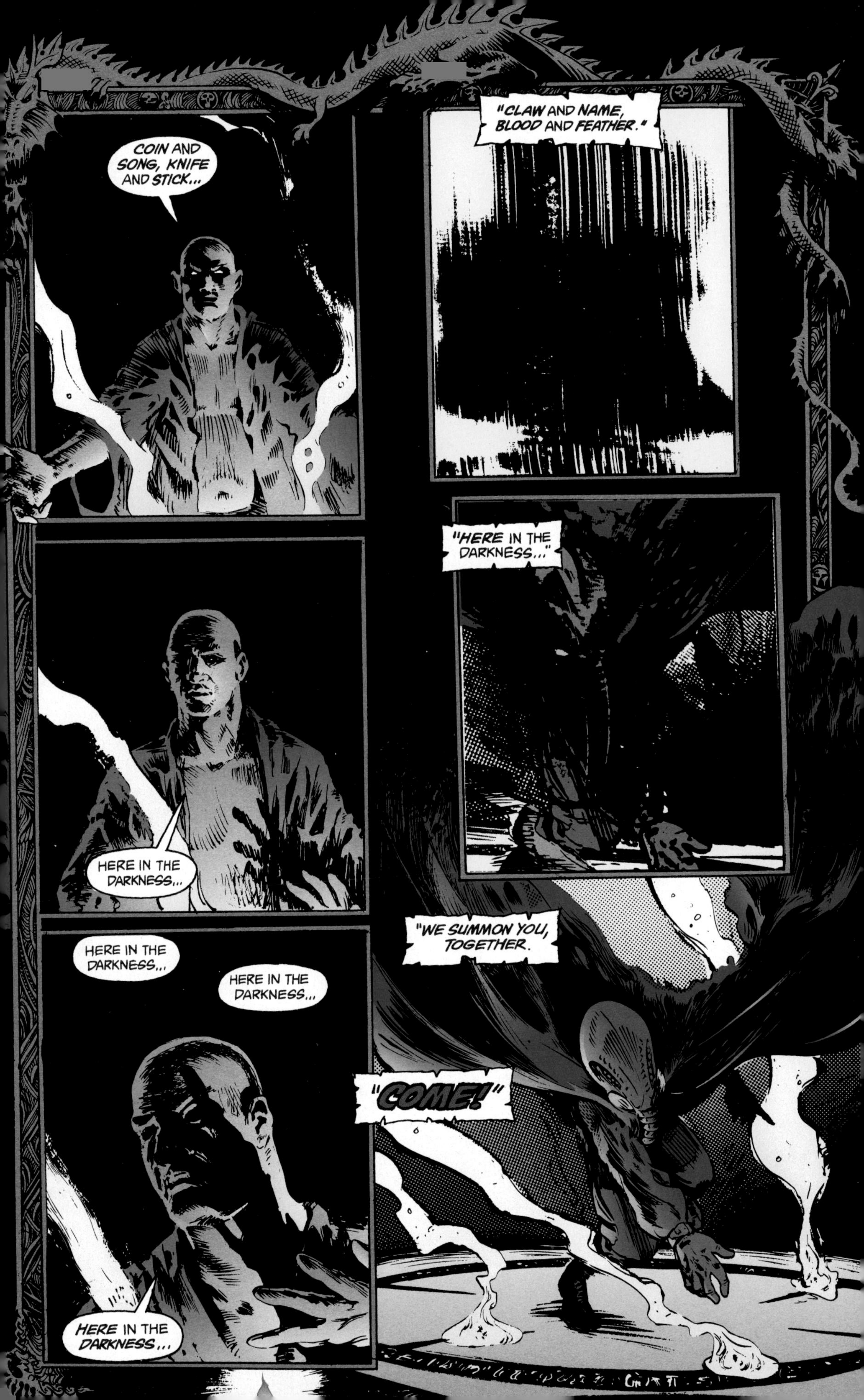
COIN AND SONG, KNIFE AND STICK...
"CLAW AND NAME, BLOOD AND FEATHER."
HERE IN THE DARKNESS...
"HERE IN THE DARKNESS..."
HERE IN THE DARKNESS...
HERE IN THE DARKNESS...
HERE IN THE DARKNESS...
"WE SUMMON YOU, TOGETHER.
"COME!"

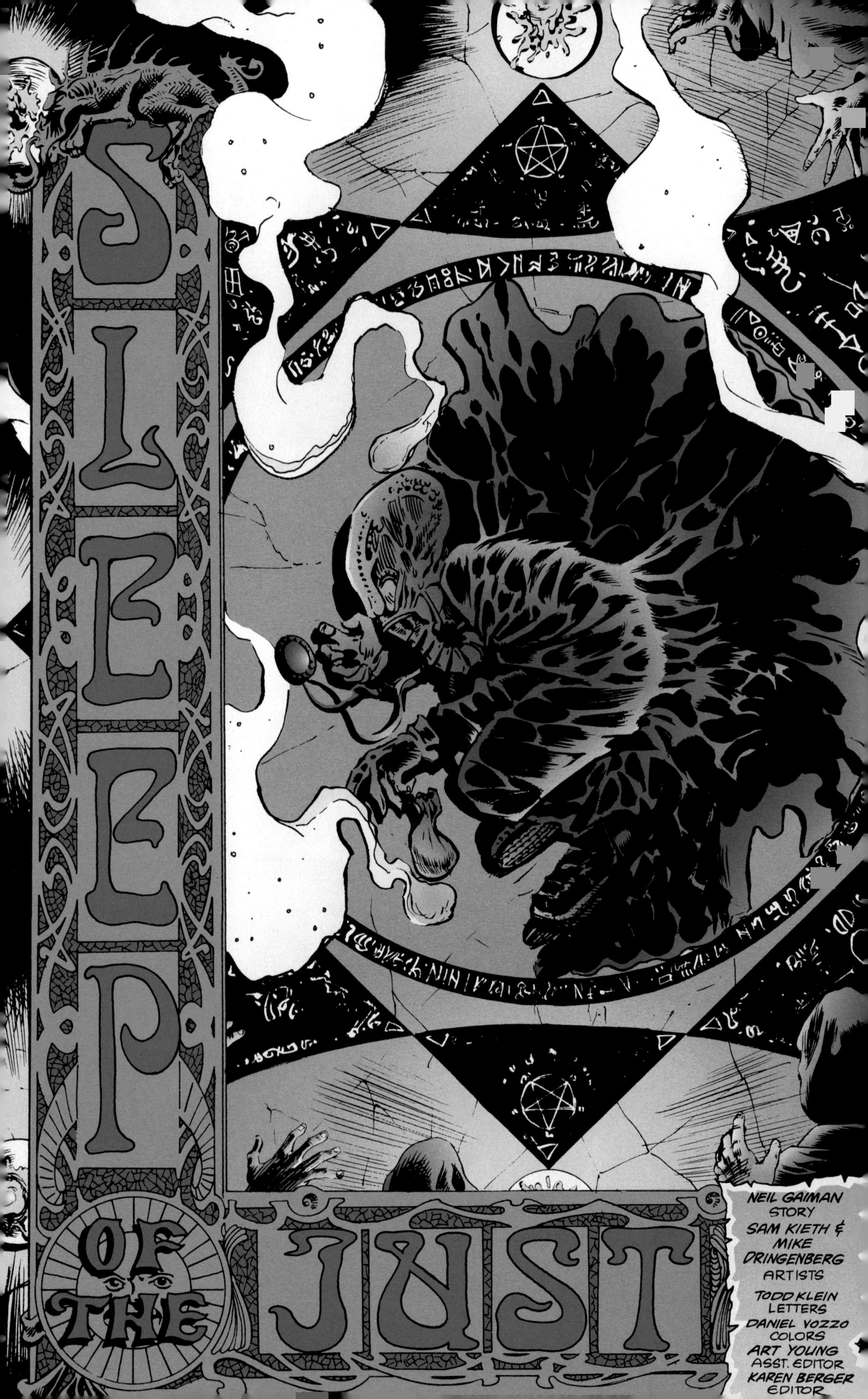
SLEEP
OF THE
JUST
NEIL GAIMAN
STORY
SAM KIETH &
MIKE
DRINGENBERG
ARTISTS
TODD KLEIN
LETTERS
DANIEL VOZZO
COLORS
ART YOUNG
ASST. EDITOR
KAREN BERGER
EDITOR

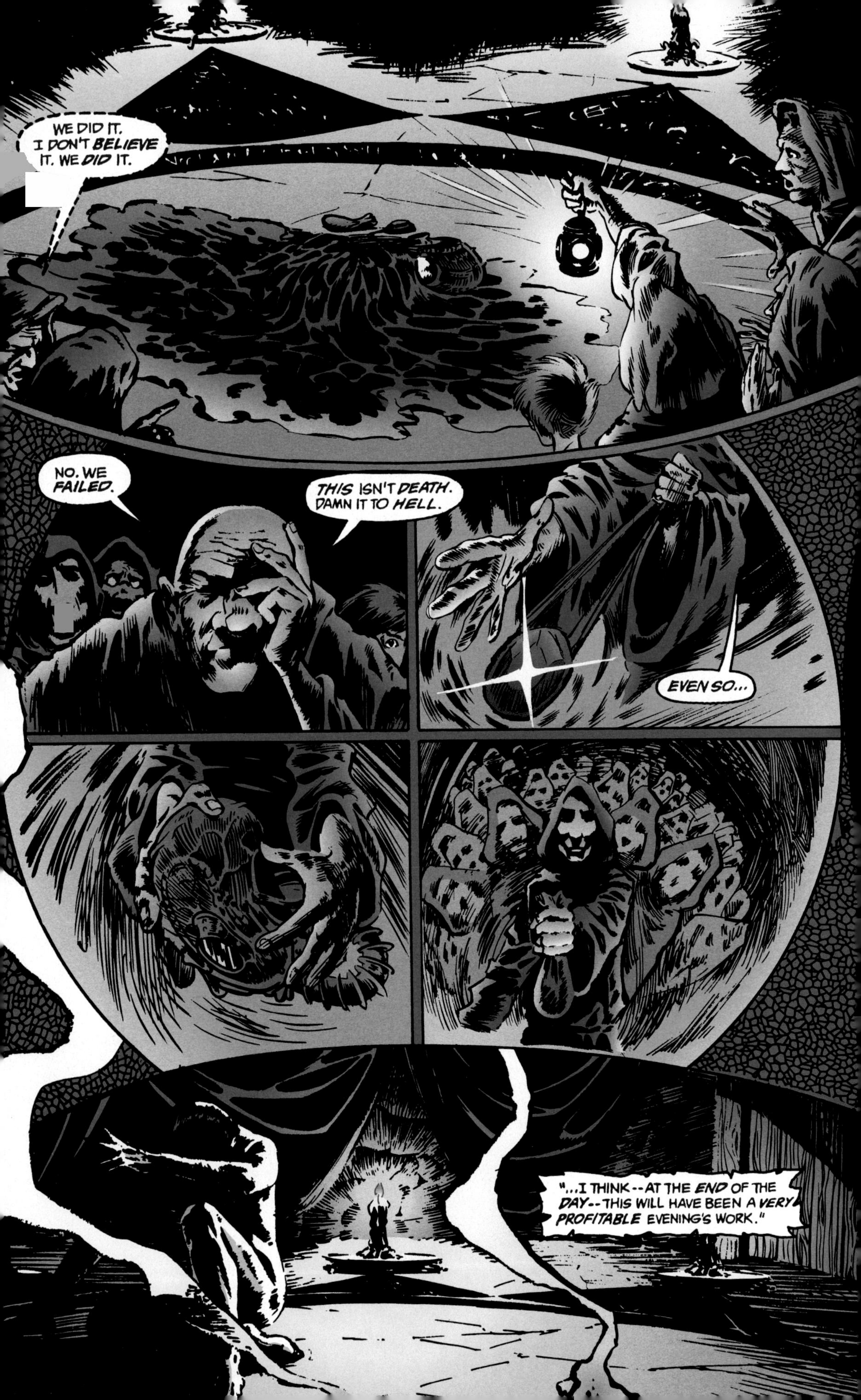
WE DID IT. I DON'T BELIEVE IT. WE DID IT.
NO. WE FAILED.
THIS ISN'T DEATH. DAMN IT TO HELL.
EVEN SO...
"...I THINK--AT THE END OF THE DAY--THIS WILL HAVE BEEN A VERY PROFITABLE EVENING'S WORK."

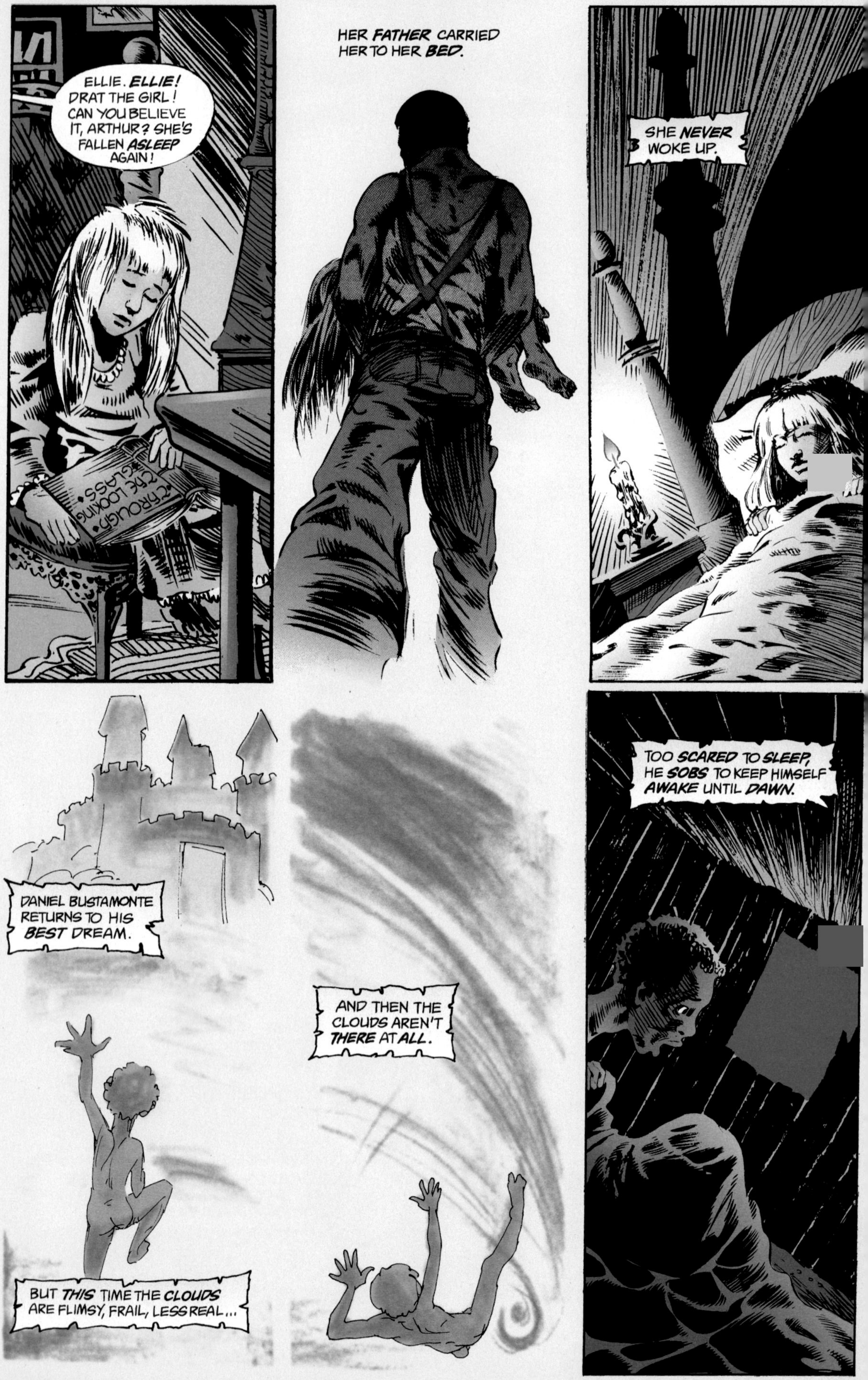
ELLIE. ELLIE! DRAT THE GIRL! CAN YOU BELIEVE IT, ARTHUR? SHE'S FALLEN ASLEEP AGAIN!
THROUGH THE LOOKING GLASS
HER FATHER CARRIED HER TO HER BED.
SHE NEVER WOKE UP.
DANIEL BUSTAMONTE RETURNS TO HIS BEST DREAM.
BUT THIS TIME THE CLOUDS ARE FLIMSY, FRAIL, LESS REAL...
AND THEN THE CLOUDS AREN'T THERE AT ALL.
TOO SCARED TO SLEEP, HE SOBS TO KEEP HIMSELF AWAKE UNTIL DAWN.

STEFAN'S CASE IS *NEW* TO THE DOCTORS. THEY THOUGHT THEY'D SEEN *EVERY* FORM OF *SHELL-SHOCK*.

HOW LONG CAN A BOY GO WITHOUT *SLEEPING?* WHEN DO THE *NIGHTMARES* SNEAK *OUT* INTO THE DAYLIGHT?

THE *MORPHINE* IS PROVING *USELESS*.

IT'S *SAD*.

STEFAN WASSERMAN WENT OVER THE *TOP*.

UNITY KINKAID FINDS IT HARDER AND HARDER TO STAY *AWAKE*.

SHE NOW SLEEPS FOR ALMOST TWENTY HOURS A DAY.

SHE USED TO *DREAM*; TO *SHIFT* IN HER SLEEP, MUTTERING AND SIGHING, *LOCKED* IN HALF-REMEMBERED *FANTASIES*...

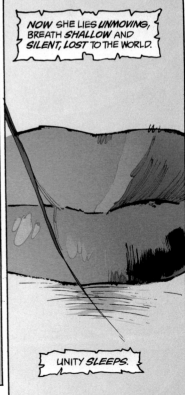

NOW SHE LIES *UNMOVING*, BREATH *SHALLOW* AND *SILENT*, *LOST* TO THE WORLD.

UNITY *SLEEPS*.

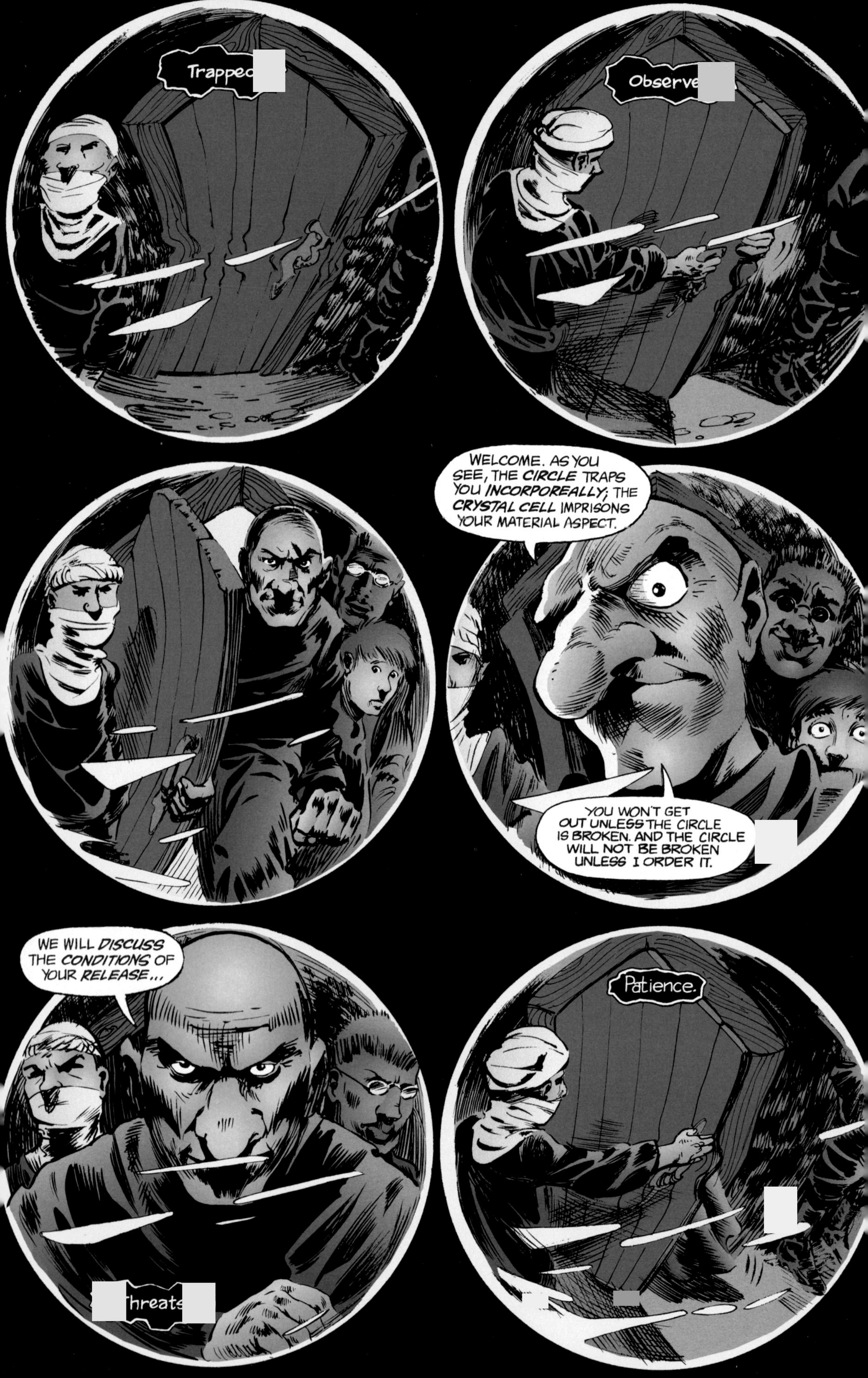
WELCOME. AS YOU SEE, THE CIRCLE TRAPS YOU INCORPOREALLY; THE CRYSTAL CELL IMPRISONS YOUR MATERIAL ASPECT.
YOU WON'T GET OUT UNLESS THE CIRCLE IS BROKEN. AND THE CIRCLE WILL NOT BE BROKEN UNLESS I ORDER IT.
WE WILL DISCUSS THE CONDITIONS OF YOUR RELEASE...
Patience.

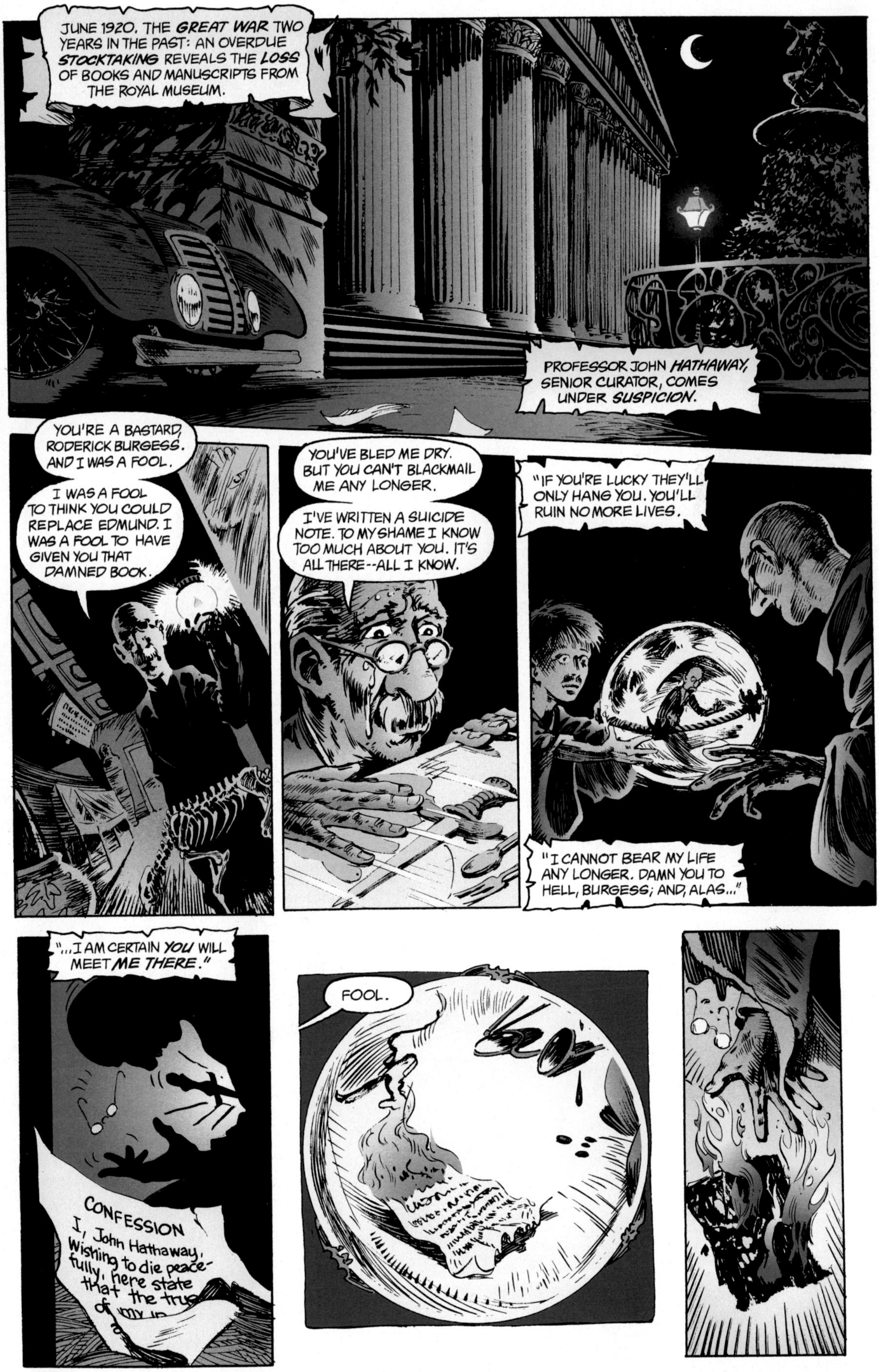
JUNE 1920. THE GREAT WAR TWO YEARS IN THE PAST: AN OVERDUE STOCKTAKING REVEALS THE LOSS OF BOOKS AND MANUSCRIPTS FROM THE ROYAL MUSEUM.
PROFESSOR JOHN HATHAWAY, SENIOR CURATOR, COMES UNDER SUSPICION.
YOU'RE A BASTARD, RODERICK BURGESS. AND I WAS A FOOL.
I WAS A FOOL TO THINK YOU COULD REPLACE EDMUND. I WAS A FOOL TO HAVE GIVEN YOU THAT DAMNED BOOK.
YOU'VE BLED ME DRY. BUT YOU CAN'T BLACKMAIL ME ANY LONGER.
I'VE WRITTEN A SUICIDE NOTE. TO MY SHAME I KNOW TOO MUCH ABOUT YOU. IT'S ALL THERE--ALL I KNOW.
"IF YOU'RE LUCKY THEY'LL ONLY HANG YOU. YOU'LL RUIN NO MORE LIVES.
"I CANNOT BEAR MY LIFE ANY LONGER. DAMN YOU TO HELL, BURGESS; AND, ALAS..."
"...I AM CERTAIN YOU WILL MEET ME THERE."
CONFESSION
I, John Hathaway,
Wishing to die peace-
fully, here state
that the
FOOL.

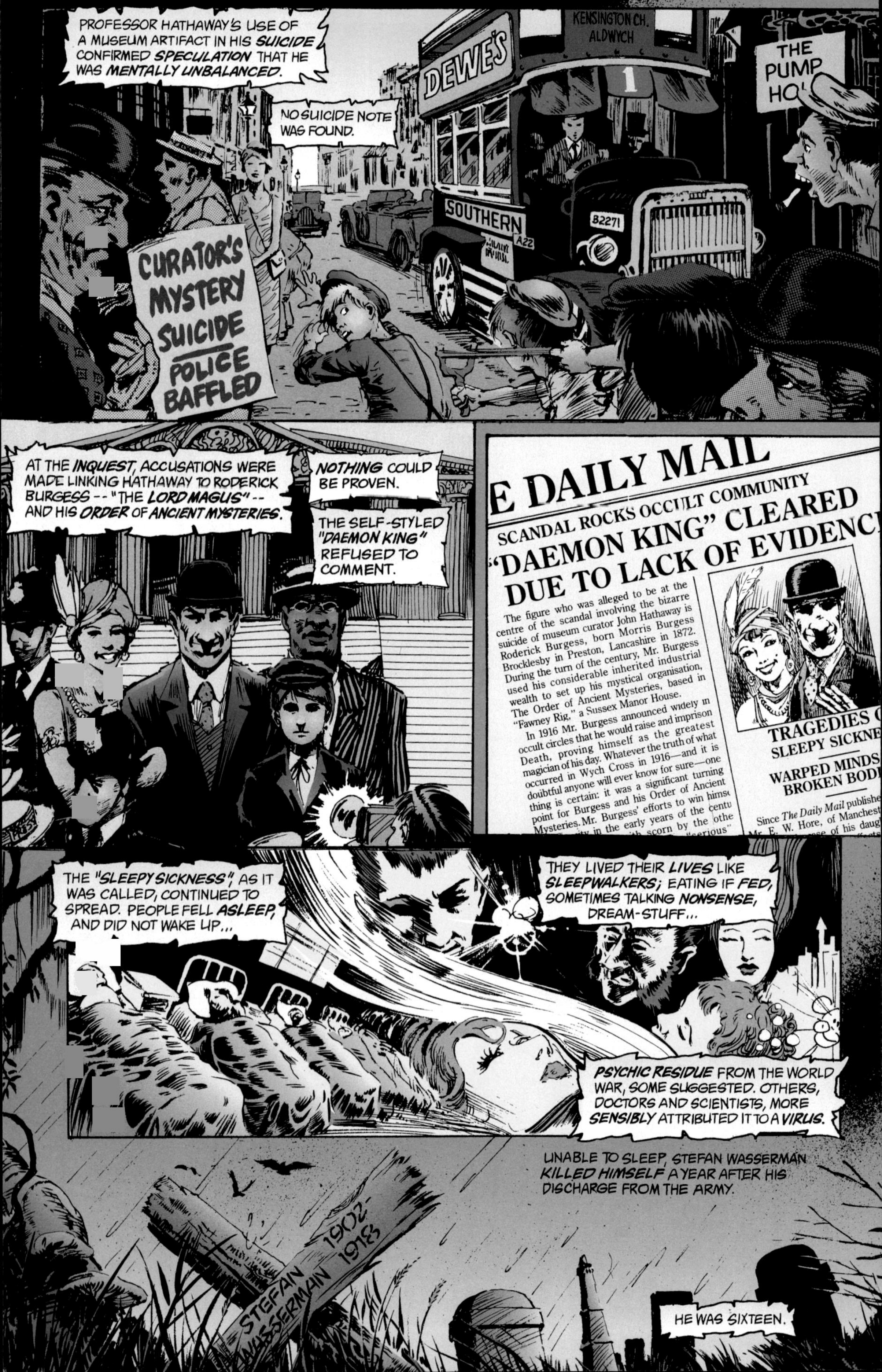
PROFESSOR HATHAWAY'S USE OF A MUSEUM ARTIFACT IN HIS SUICIDE CONFIRMED SPECULATION THAT HE WAS MENTALLY UNBALANCED.
NO SUICIDE NOTE WAS FOUND.
KENSINGTON CH. ALDWYCH
DEWE'S
1
SOUTHERN
B2271
A22
THE PUMP HO
CURATOR'S MYSTERY SUICIDE
POLICE BAFFLED
AT THE INQUEST, ACCUSATIONS WERE MADE LINKING HATHAWAY TO RODERICK BURGESS -- "THE LORD MAGUS" -- AND HIS ORDER OF ANCIENT MYSTERIES.
NOTHING COULD BE PROVEN.
THE SELF-STYLED "DAEMON KING" REFUSED TO COMMENT.
E DAILY MAIL
SCANDAL ROCKS OCCULT COMMUNITY
"DAEMON KING" CLEARED DUE TO LACK OF EVIDENC
The figure who was alleged to be at the centre of the scandal involving the bizarre suicide of museum curator John Hathaway is Roderick Burgess, born Morris Burgess Brocklesby in Preston, Lancashire in 1872. During the turn of the century, Mr. Burgess used his considerable inherited industrial wealth to set up his mystical organisation, The Order of Ancient Mysteries, based in "Fawney Rig," a Sussex Manor House.
In 1916 Mr. Burgess announced widely in occult circles that he would raise and imprison Death, proving himself as the greatest magician of his day. Whatever the truth of what occurred in Wych Cross in 1916—and it is doubtful anyone will ever know for sure—one thing is certain: it was a significant turning point for Burgess and his Order of Ancient Mysteries. Mr. Burgess' efforts to win himse
in the early years of the centu
scorn by the othe
"serious"
TRAGEDIES O
SLEEPY SICKNE
WARPED MINDS
BROKEN BODI
Since The Daily Mail publishe
Mr. E. W. Hore, of Manchest
of his daug
THE "SLEEPY SICKNESS", AS IT WAS CALLED, CONTINUED TO SPREAD. PEOPLE FELL ASLEEP, AND DID NOT WAKE UP...
THEY LIVED THEIR LIVES LIKE SLEEPWALKERS; EATING IF FED, SOMETIMES TALKING NONSENSE, DREAM-STUFF...
PSYCHIC RESIDUE FROM THE WORLD WAR, SOME SUGGESTED. OTHERS, DOCTORS AND SCIENTISTS, MORE SENSIBLY ATTRIBUTED IT TO A VIRUS.
UNABLE TO SLEEP, STEFAN WASSERMAN KILLED HIMSELF A YEAR AFTER HIS DISCHARGE FROM THE ARMY.
STEFAN WASSERMAN 1902-1918
HE WAS SIXTEEN.

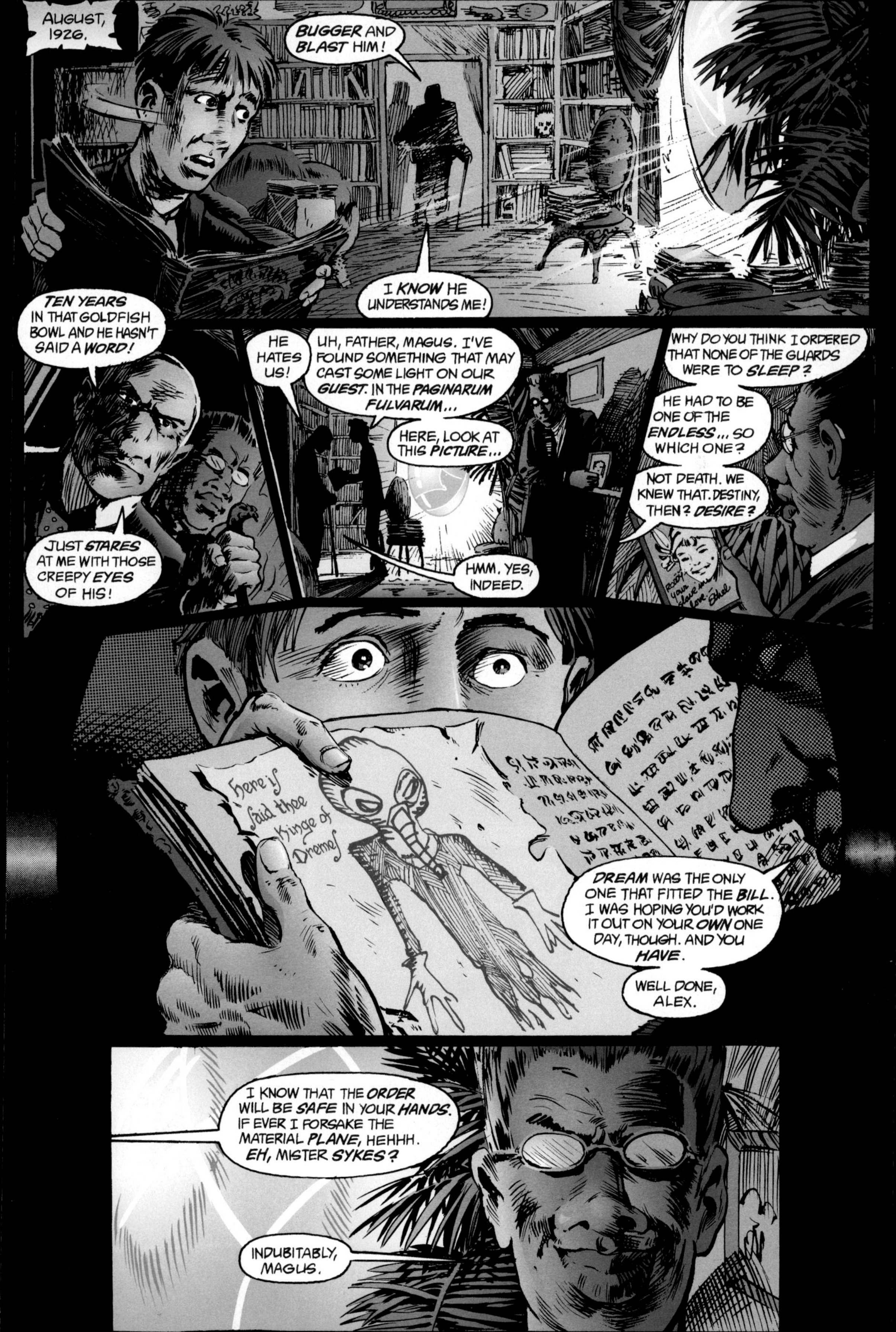
AUGUST, 1926.
BUGGER AND BLAST HIM!
I KNOW HE UNDERSTANDS ME!
TEN YEARS IN THAT GOLDFISH BOWL AND HE HASN'T SAID A WORD!
JUST STARES AT ME WITH THOSE CREEPY EYES OF HIS!
HE HATES US!
UH, FATHER, MAGUS. I'VE FOUND SOMETHING THAT MAY CAST SOME LIGHT ON OUR GUEST. IN THE PAGINARUM FULVARUM...
HERE, LOOK AT THIS PICTURE...
HMM. YES, INDEED.
WHY DO YOU THINK I ORDERED THAT NONE OF THE GUARDS WERE TO SLEEP?
HE HAD TO BE ONE OF THE ENDLESS... SO WHICH ONE?
NOT DEATH. WE KNEW THAT. DESTINY, THEN? DESIRE?
Here is said thee Kinge of Dremes
DREAM WAS THE ONLY ONE THAT FITTED THE BILL. I WAS HOPING YOU'D WORK IT OUT ON YOUR OWN ONE DAY, THOUGH. AND YOU HAVE.
WELL DONE, ALEX.
I KNOW THAT THE ORDER WILL BE SAFE IN YOUR HANDS. IF EVER I FORSAKE THE MATERIAL PLANE, HEHHH. EH, MISTER SYKES?
INDUBITABLY, MAGUS.

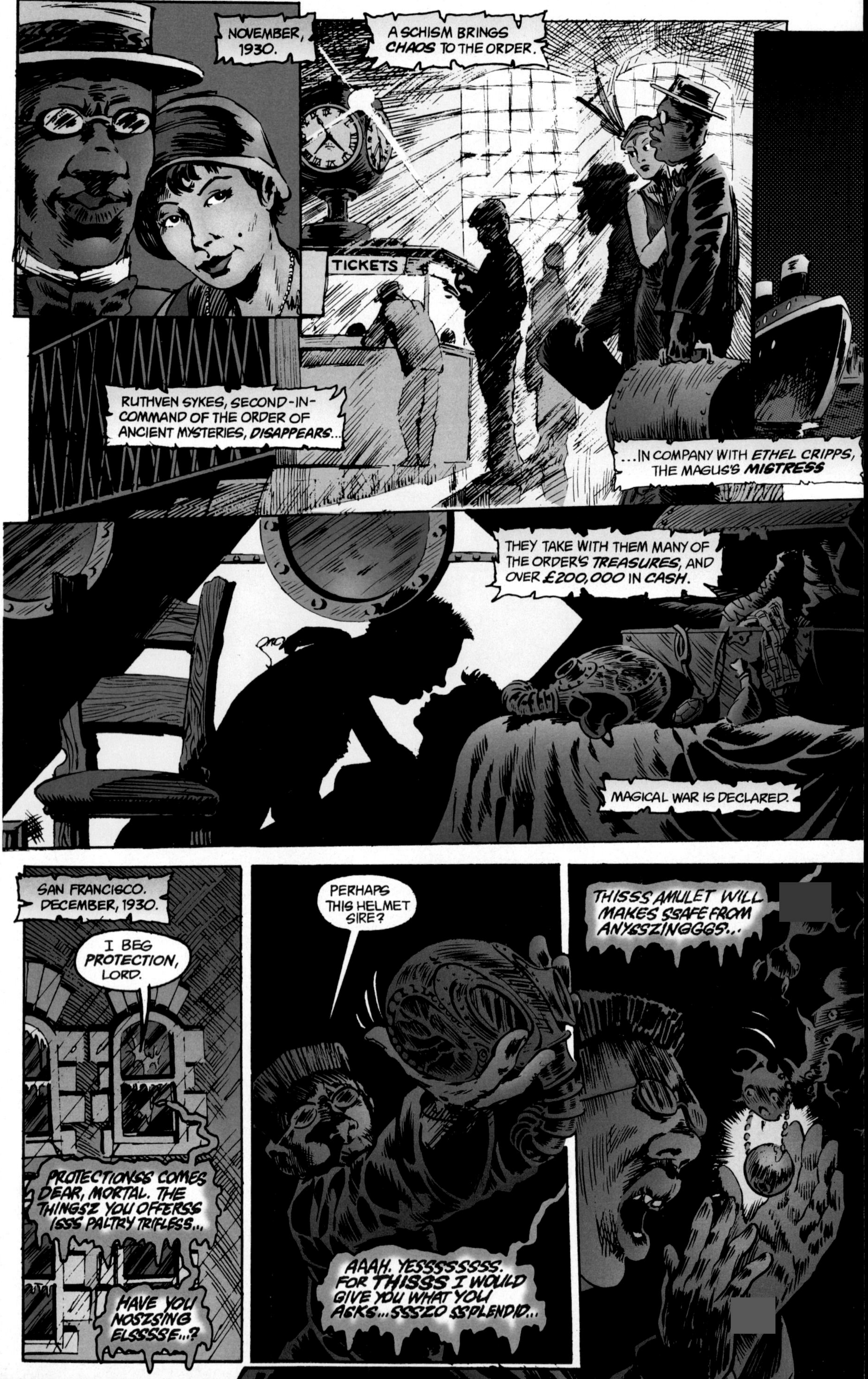
NOVEMBER, 1930.
A SCHISM BRINGS CHAOS TO THE ORDER.
TICKETS
RUTHVEN SYKES, SECOND-IN-COMMAND OF THE ORDER OF ANCIENT MYSTERIES, DISAPPEARS...
...IN COMPANY WITH ETHEL CRIPPS, THE MAGUS'S MISTRESS
THEY TAKE WITH THEM MANY OF THE ORDER'S TREASURES, AND OVER £200,000 IN CASH.
MAGICAL WAR IS DECLARED.
SAN FRANCISCO. DECEMBER, 1930.
I BEG PROTECTION, LORD.
PROTECTIONSS COMES DEAR, MORTAL. THE THINGSZ YOU OFFERSS ISSS PALTRY TRIFLESS...
HAVE YOU NOSZSING ELSSSSE...?
PERHAPS THIS HELMET SIRE?
AAAH. YESSSSSSSS. FOR THISSS I WOULD GIVE YOU WHAT YOU ASKS... SSSZO SSPLENDID...
THISSS AMULET WILL MAKES SSAFE FROM ANYSSZINGGGS...

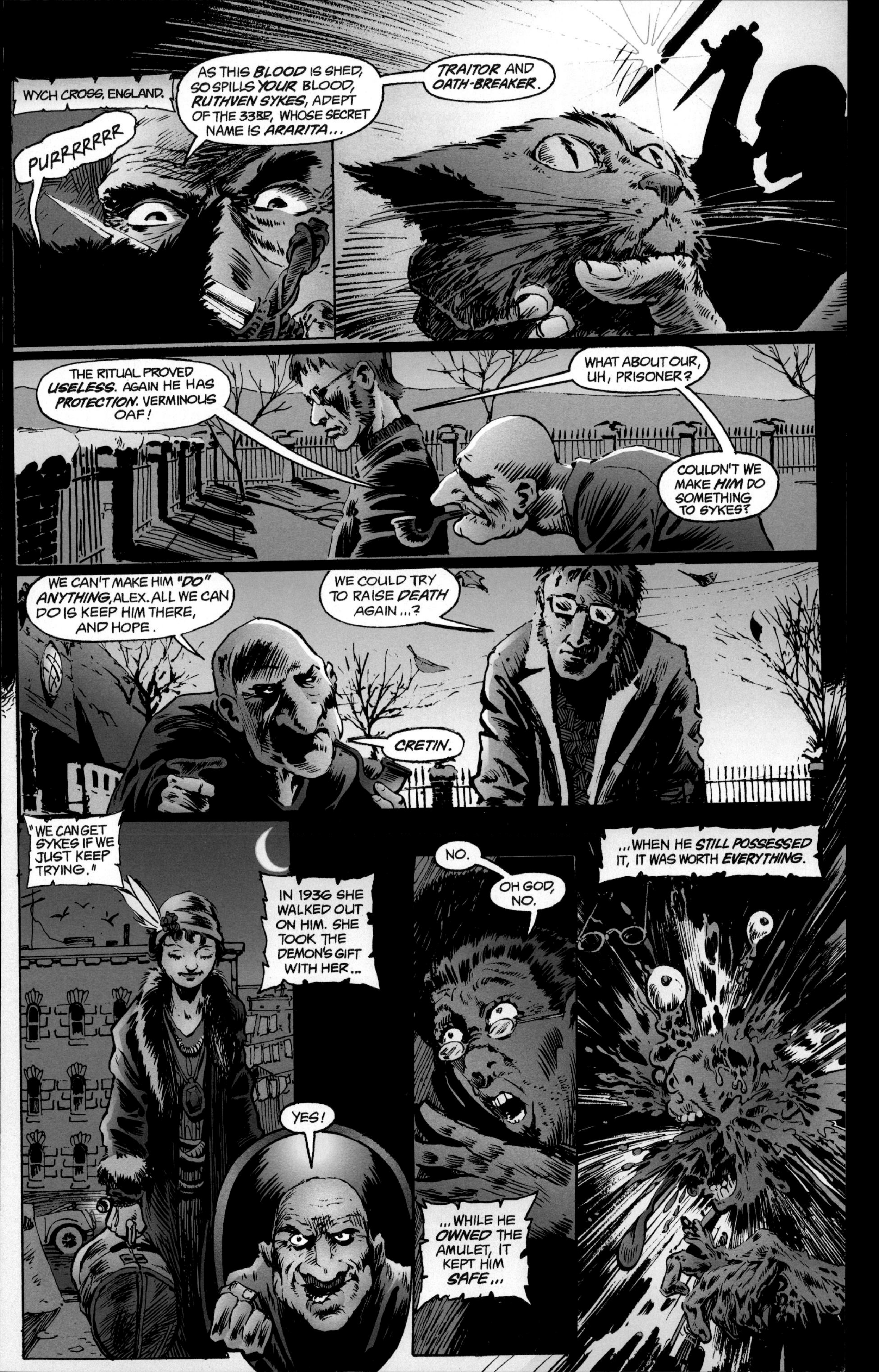
WYCH CROSS, ENGLAND.
AS THIS BLOOD IS SHED, SO SPILLS YOUR BLOOD, RUTHVEN SYKES, ADEPT OF THE 33RD, WHOSE SECRET NAME IS ARARITA...
PURRRRRRR
TRAITOR AND OATH-BREAKER.
THE RITUAL PROVED USELESS. AGAIN HE HAS PROTECTION. VERMINOUS OAF!
WHAT ABOUT OUR, UH, PRISONER?
COULDN'T WE MAKE HIM DO SOMETHING TO SYKES?
WE CAN'T MAKE HIM "DO" ANYTHING, ALEX. ALL WE CAN DO IS KEEP HIM THERE, AND HOPE.
WE COULD TRY TO RAISE DEATH AGAIN...?
CRETIN.
"WE CAN GET SYKES IF WE JUST KEEP TRYING."
IN 1936 SHE WALKED OUT ON HIM. SHE TOOK THE DEMON'S GIFT WITH HER...
YES!
NO.
OH GOD, NO.
...WHILE HE OWNED THE AMULET, IT KEPT HIM SAFE...
...WHEN HE STILL POSSESSED IT, IT WAS WORTH EVERYTHING.

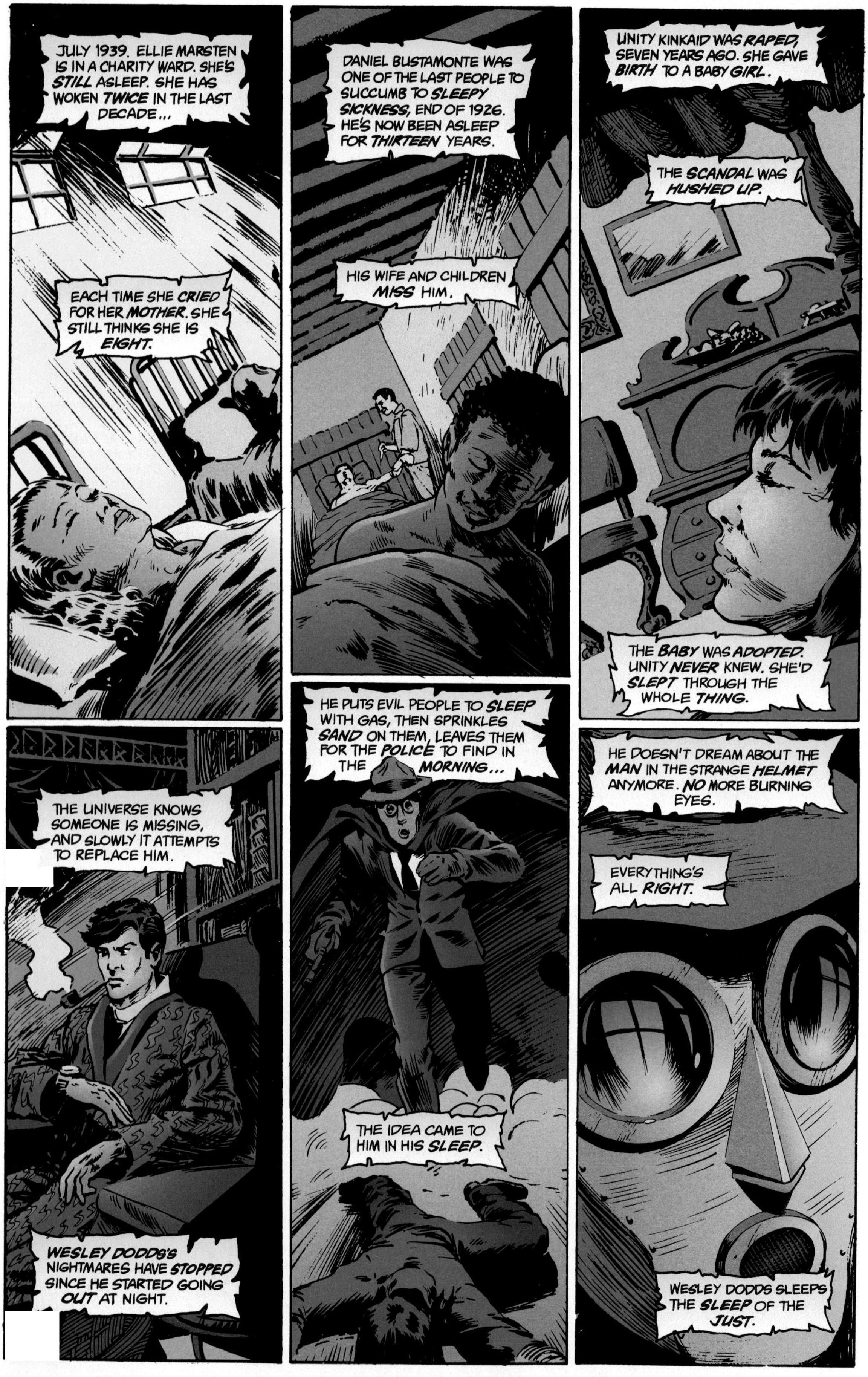
JULY 1939. ELLIE MARSTEN IS IN A CHARITY WARD. SHE'S STILL ASLEEP. SHE HAS WOKEN TWICE IN THE LAST DECADE...
EACH TIME SHE CRIED FOR HER MOTHER. SHE STILL THINKS SHE IS EIGHT.
DANIEL BUSTAMONTE WAS ONE OF THE LAST PEOPLE TO SUCCUMB TO SLEEPY SICKNESS, END OF 1926. HE'S NOW BEEN ASLEEP FOR THIRTEEN YEARS.
HIS WIFE AND CHILDREN MISS HIM.
UNITY KINKAID WAS RAPED, SEVEN YEARS AGO. SHE GAVE BIRTH TO A BABY GIRL.
THE SCANDAL WAS HUSHED UP.
THE BABY WAS ADOPTED. UNITY NEVER KNEW. SHE'D SLEPT THROUGH THE WHOLE THING.
THE UNIVERSE KNOWS SOMEONE IS MISSING, AND SLOWLY IT ATTEMPTS TO REPLACE HIM.
WESLEY DODDS'S NIGHTMARES HAVE STOPPED SINCE HE STARTED GOING OUT AT NIGHT.
HE PUTS EVIL PEOPLE TO SLEEP WITH GAS, THEN SPRINKLES SAND ON THEM, LEAVES THEM FOR THE POLICE TO FIND IN THE MORNING...
THE IDEA CAME TO HIM IN HIS SLEEP.
HE DOESN'T DREAM ABOUT THE MAN IN THE STRANGE HELMET ANYMORE. NO MORE BURNING EYES.
EVERYTHING'S ALL RIGHT.
WESLEY DODDS SLEEPS THE SLEEP OF THE JUST.

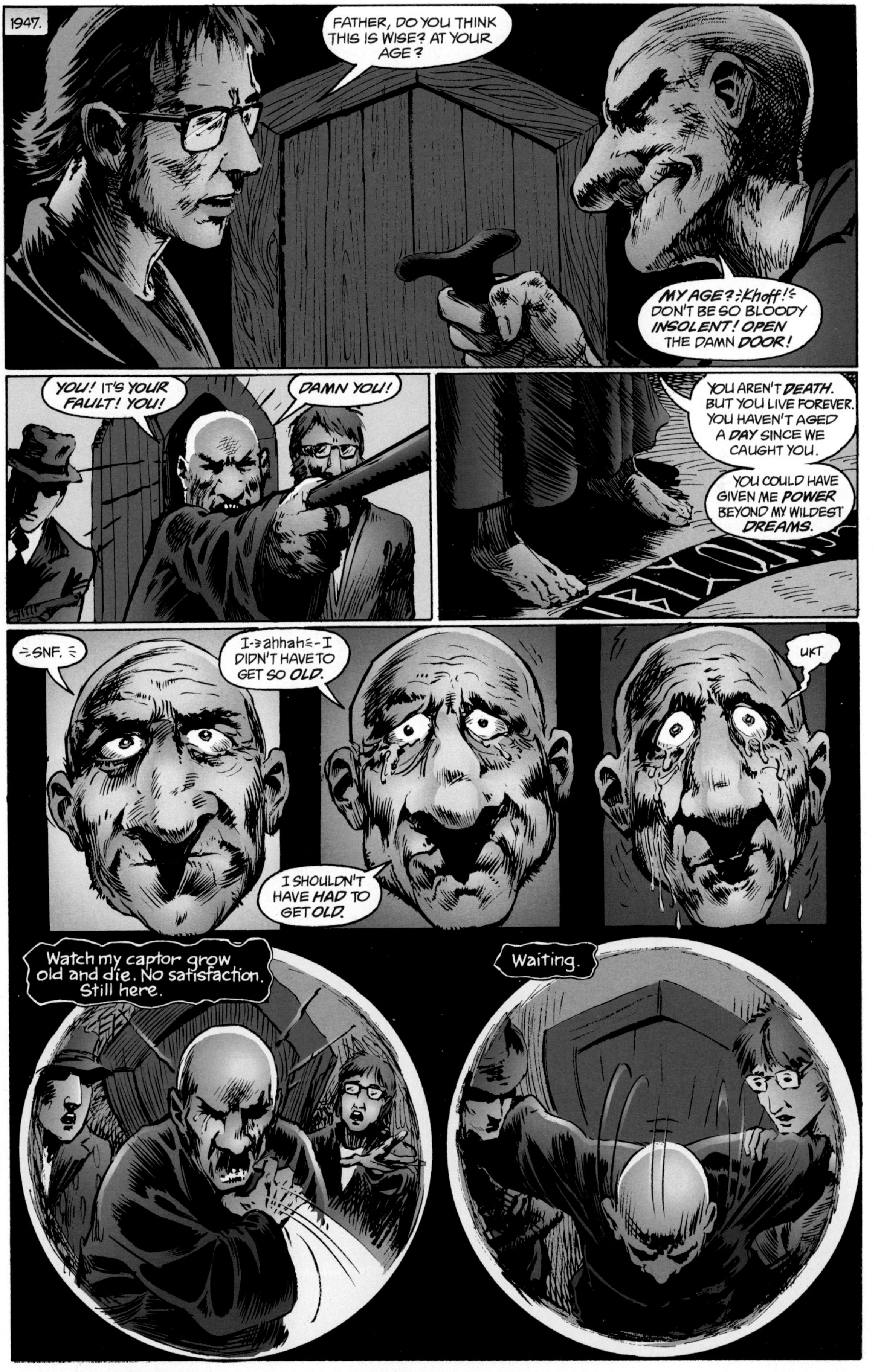
1947.
FATHER, DO YOU THINK THIS IS WISE? AT YOUR AGE?
MY AGE? =Khoff!= DON'T BE SO BLOODY INSOLENT! OPEN THE DAMN DOOR!
YOU! IT'S YOUR FAULT! YOU!
DAMN YOU!
YOU AREN'T DEATH. BUT YOU LIVE FOREVER. YOU HAVEN'T AGED A DAY SINCE WE CAUGHT YOU.
YOU COULD HAVE GIVEN ME POWER BEYOND MY WILDEST DREAMS.
=SNF.=
I-=ahhah=-I DIDN'T HAVE TO GET SO OLD.
I SHOULDN'T HAVE HAD TO GET OLD.
UKT
Watch my captor grow old and die. No satisfaction. Still here.
Waiting.

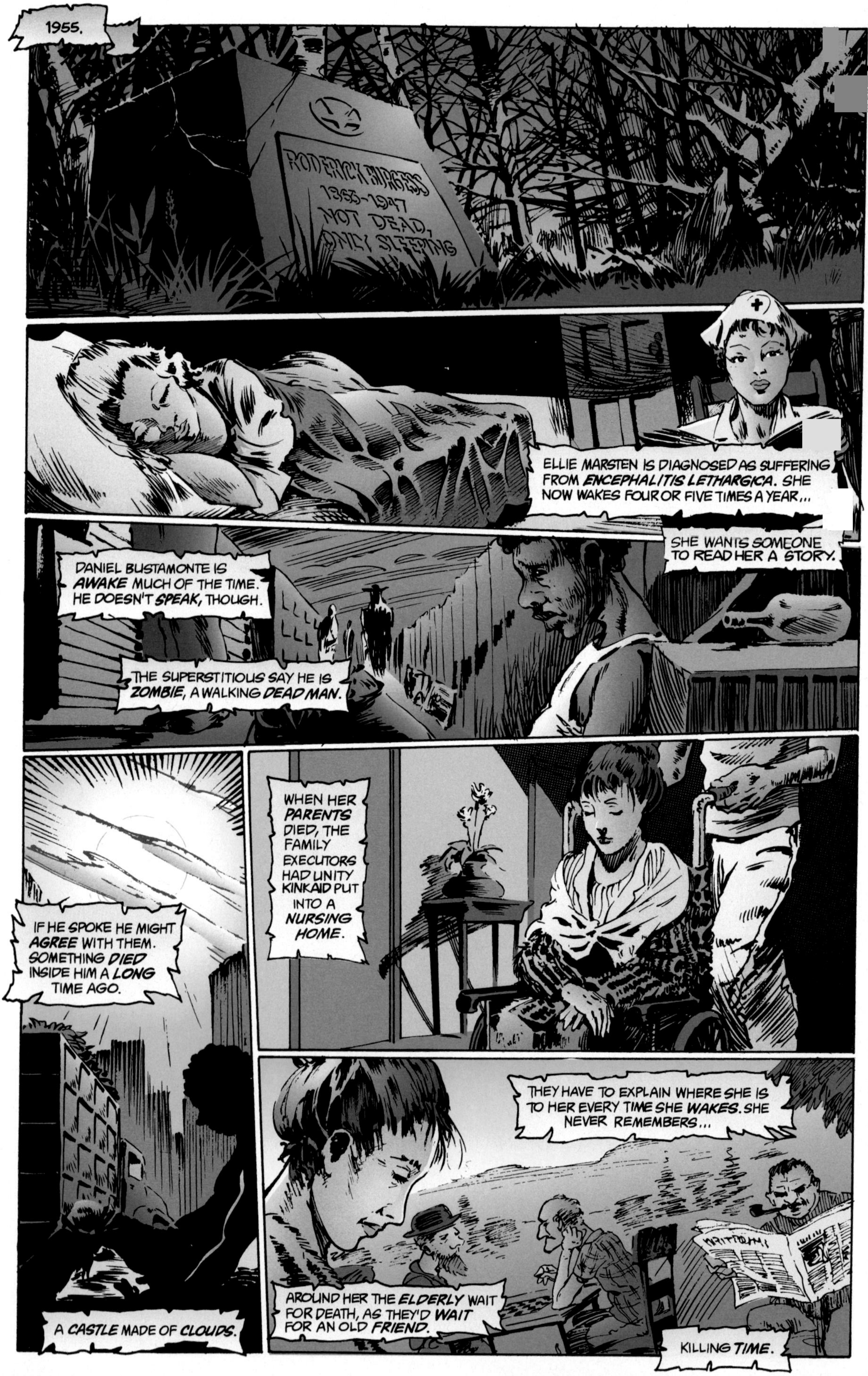
1955.
RODERICK BURGESS
1865-1947
NOT DEAD,
ONLY SLEEPING
ELLIE MARSTEN IS DIAGNOSED AS SUFFERING FROM ENCEPHALITIS LETHARGICA. SHE NOW WAKES FOUR OR FIVE TIMES A YEAR...
SHE WANTS SOMEONE TO READ HER A STORY.
DANIEL BUSTAMONTE IS AWAKE MUCH OF THE TIME. HE DOESN'T SPEAK, THOUGH.
THE SUPERSTITIOUS SAY HE IS ZOMBIE, A WALKING DEAD MAN.
IF HE SPOKE HE MIGHT AGREE WITH THEM. SOMETHING DIED INSIDE HIM A LONG TIME AGO.
WHEN HER PARENTS DIED, THE FAMILY EXECUTORS HAD UNITY KINKAID PUT INTO A NURSING HOME.
A CASTLE MADE OF CLOUDS.
THEY HAVE TO EXPLAIN WHERE SHE IS TO HER EVERY TIME SHE WAKES. SHE NEVER REMEMBERS...
AROUND HER THE ELDERLY WAIT FOR DEATH, AS THEY'D WAIT FOR AN OLD FRIEND.
KILLING TIME.

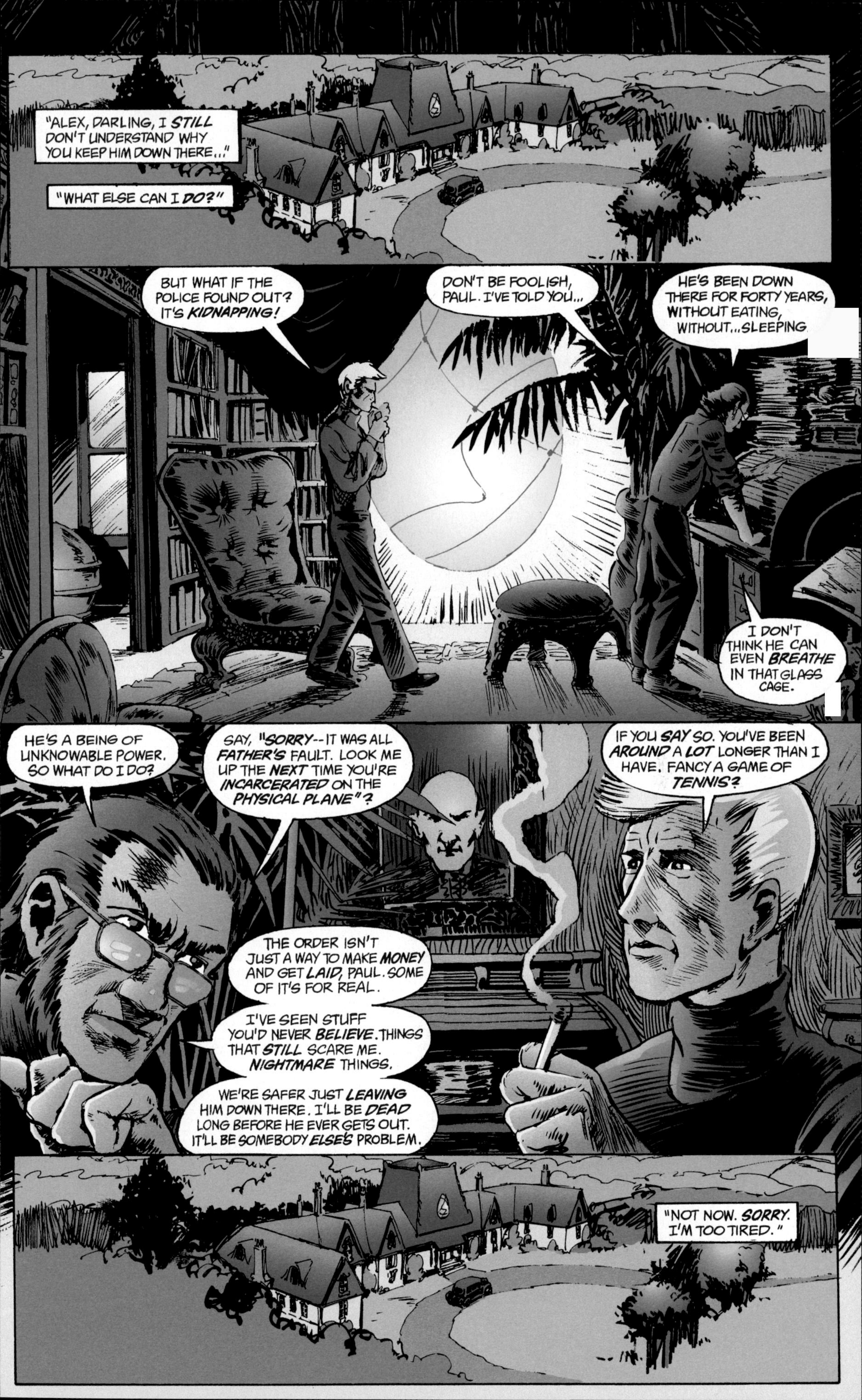
"ALEX, DARLING, I STILL DON'T UNDERSTAND WHY YOU KEEP HIM DOWN THERE..."
"WHAT ELSE CAN I DO?"
BUT WHAT IF THE POLICE FOUND OUT? IT'S KIDNAPPING!
DON'T BE FOOLISH, PAUL. I'VE TOLD YOU...
HE'S BEEN DOWN THERE FOR FORTY YEARS, WITHOUT EATING, WITHOUT...SLEEPING.
I DON'T THINK HE CAN EVEN BREATHE IN THAT GLASS CAGE.
HE'S A BEING OF UNKNOWABLE POWER. SO WHAT DO I DO?
SAY, "SORRY--IT WAS ALL FATHER'S FAULT. LOOK ME UP THE NEXT TIME YOU'RE INCARCERATED ON THE PHYSICAL PLANE"?
IF YOU SAY SO. YOU'VE BEEN AROUND A LOT LONGER THAN I HAVE. FANCY A GAME OF TENNIS?
THE ORDER ISN'T JUST A WAY TO MAKE MONEY AND GET LAID, PAUL. SOME OF IT'S FOR REAL.
I'VE SEEN STUFF YOU'D NEVER BELIEVE. THINGS THAT STILL SCARE ME. NIGHTMARE THINGS.
WE'RE SAFER JUST LEAVING HIM DOWN THERE. I'LL BE DEAD LONG BEFORE HE EVER GETS OUT. IT'LL BE SOMEBODY ELSE'S PROBLEM.
"NOT NOW. SORRY. I'M TOO TIRED."

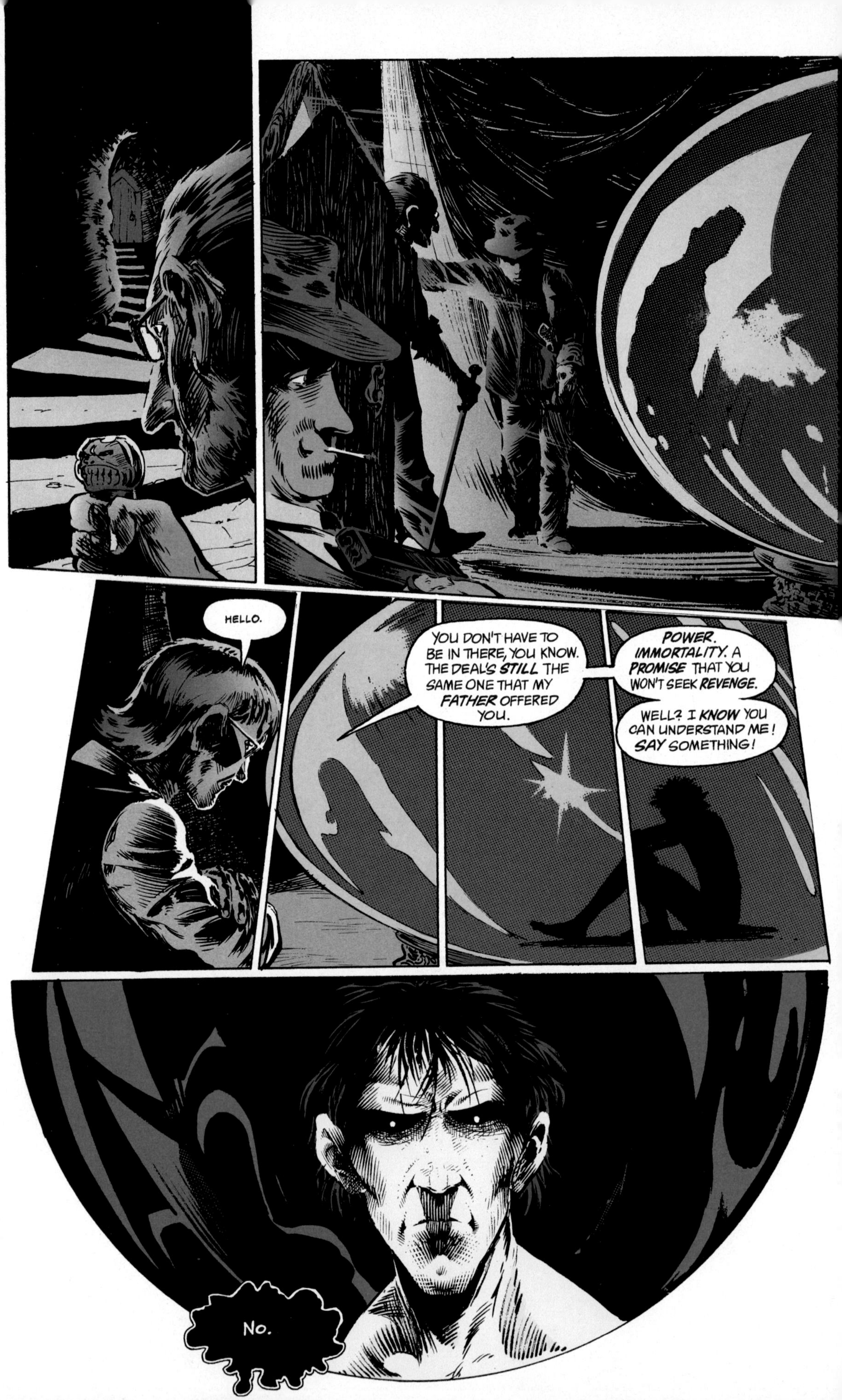
HELLO.
YOU DON'T HAVE TO BE IN THERE, YOU KNOW. THE DEAL'S STILL THE SAME ONE THAT MY FATHER OFFERED YOU.
POWER. IMMORTALITY. A PROMISE THAT YOU WON'T SEEK REVENGE.
WELL? I KNOW YOU CAN UNDERSTAND ME! SAY SOMETHING!
No.

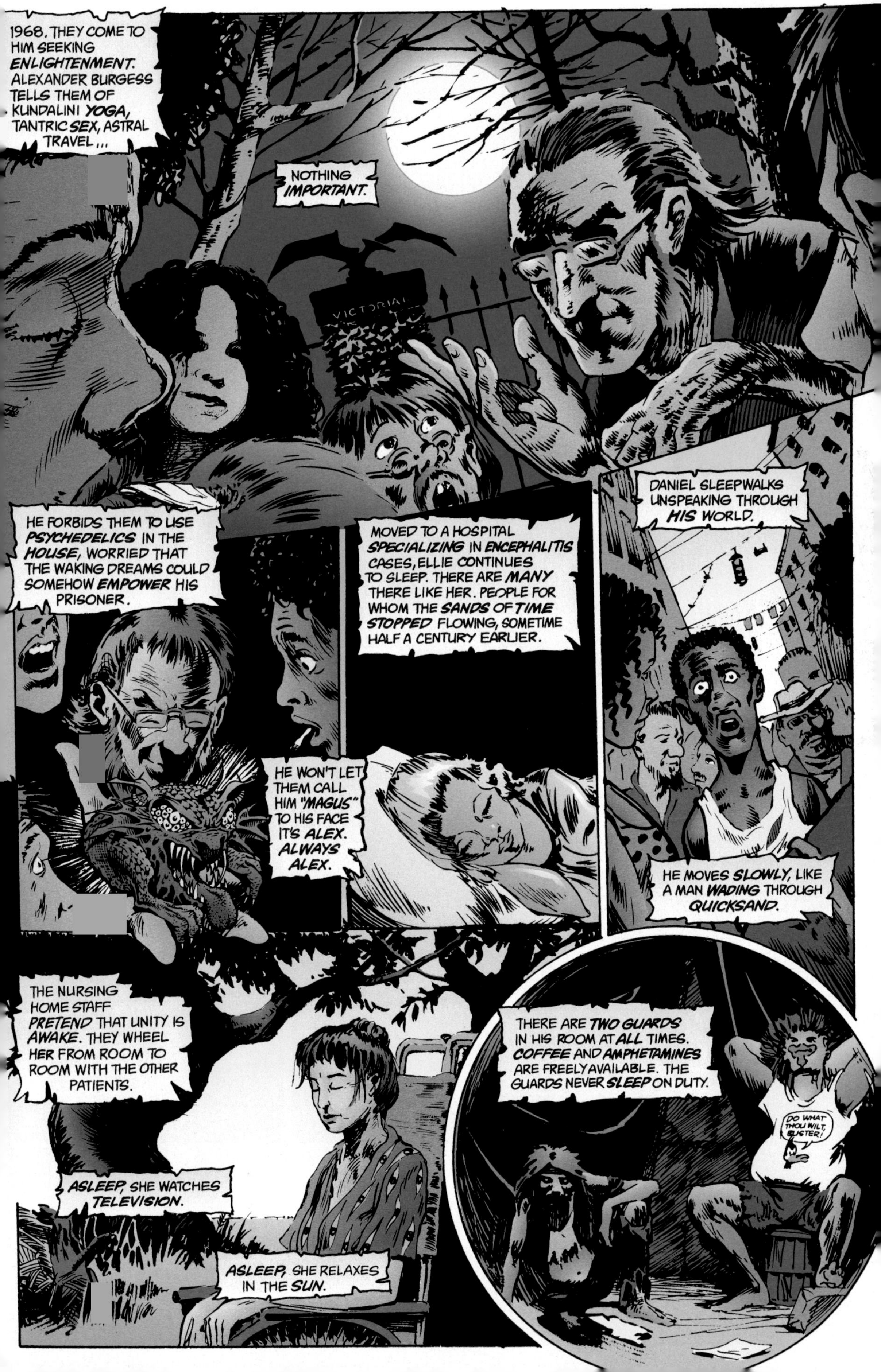
1968. THEY COME TO HIM SEEKING ENLIGHTENMENT. ALEXANDER BURGESS TELLS THEM OF KUNDALINI YOGA, TANTRIC SEX, ASTRAL TRAVEL...
NOTHING IMPORTANT.
HE FORBIDS THEM TO USE PSYCHEDELICS IN THE HOUSE, WORRIED THAT THE WAKING DREAMS COULD SOMEHOW EMPOWER HIS PRISONER.
HE WON'T LET THEM CALL HIM "MAGUS" TO HIS FACE IT'S ALEX. ALWAYS ALEX.
MOVED TO A HOSPITAL SPECIALIZING IN ENCEPHALITIS CASES, ELLIE CONTINUES TO SLEEP. THERE ARE MANY THERE LIKE HER. PEOPLE FOR WHOM THE SANDS OF TIME STOPPED FLOWING, SOMETIME HALF A CENTURY EARLIER.
DANIEL SLEEPWALKS UNSPEAKING THROUGH HIS WORLD.
HE MOVES SLOWLY, LIKE A MAN WADING THROUGH QUICKSAND.
THE NURSING HOME STAFF PRETEND THAT UNITY IS AWAKE. THEY WHEEL HER FROM ROOM TO ROOM WITH THE OTHER PATIENTS.
ASLEEP, SHE WATCHES TELEVISION.
ASLEEP, SHE RELAXES IN THE SUN.
THERE ARE TWO GUARDS IN HIS ROOM AT ALL TIMES. COFFEE AND AMPHETAMINES ARE FREELY AVAILABLE. THE GUARDS NEVER SLEEP ON DUTY.
DO WHAT THOU WILT, BUSTER!

1970.

THE YOUNG PEOPLE HAVE DRIFTED AWAY.

ALEX HANDS OVER THE REINS OF ORGANIZATION TO *PAUL McGUIRE*, HIS LONGTIME PERSONAL *ASSISTANT*.

HE SEES THE ORDER OF ANCIENT MYSTERIES AS AN *EFFICIENT* METHOD OF PARTING THE *CREDULOUS* FROM THEIR *CASH*.

RODERICK BURGESS
1863 - 1947
NOT DEAD,
ONLY SLEEPING

PAUL DOESN'T *BELIEVE* IN MAGIC.

ALEX SPENDS MOST OF HIS TIME IN HIS *STUDY*. HE WROTE A *MEMOIR* ABOUT HIS FATHER; WRITES LETTERS TO *NEWSPAPERS* DEFENDING HIS FATHER'S REPUTATION; IS EDITING A VOLUME OF HIS FATHER'S *LETTERS*.

ONE NIGHT HE *SLASHED* HIS FATHER'S PORTRAIT WITH A *KNIFE*.

ALEX WILL NO LONGER *READ* BOOKS ON *MAGIC*, EXCEPT FOR ONE. THE *LIBER FULVARUM PAGINARUM*, AND HE ONLY READS *ONE* PAGE OF THAT BOOK....

here laid
thee
Kinge of

OVER...

AND OVER...

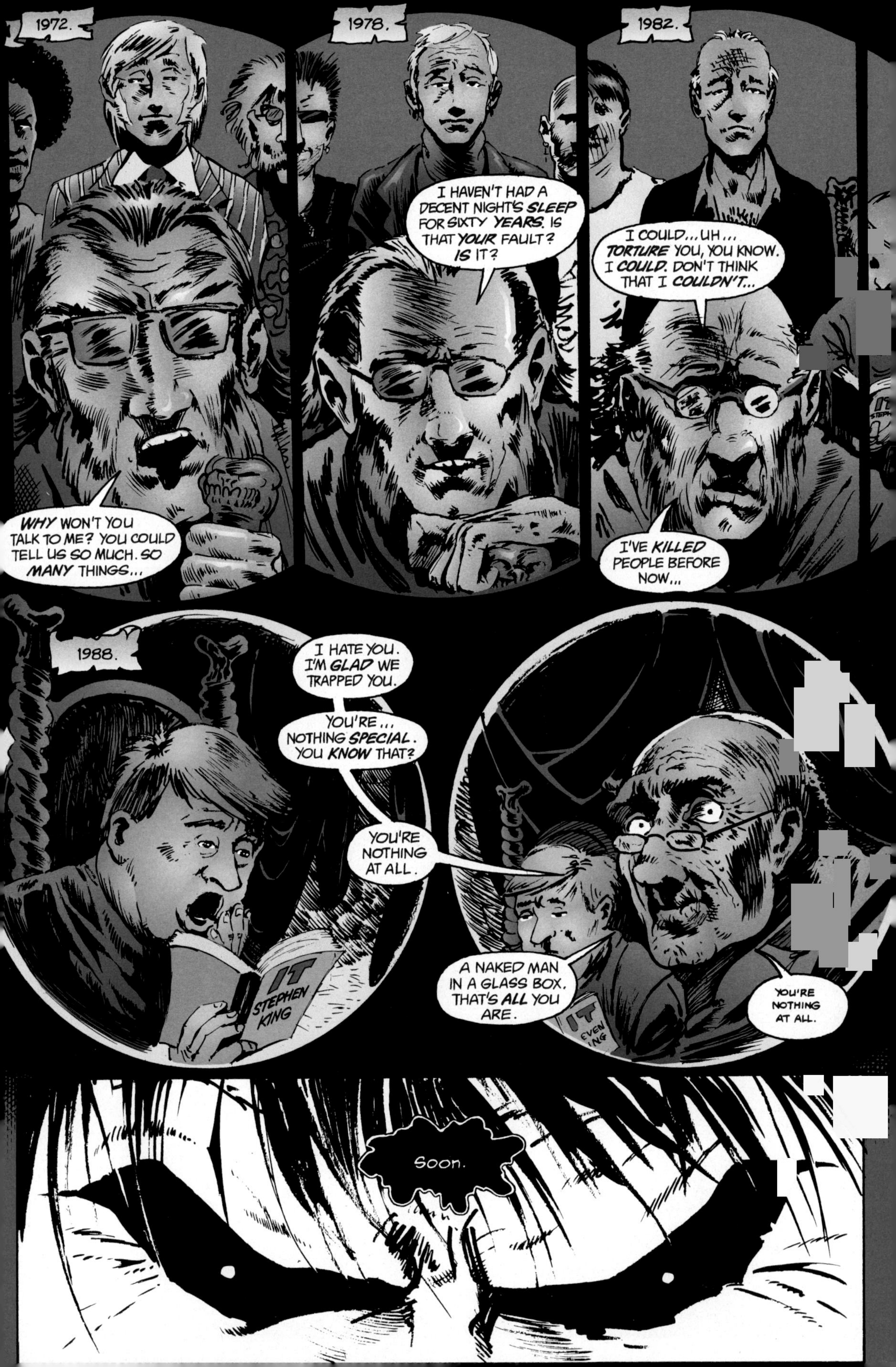
1972.
WHY WON'T YOU TALK TO ME? YOU COULD TELL US SO MUCH. SO MANY THINGS...
1978.
I HAVEN'T HAD A DECENT NIGHT'S SLEEP FOR SIXTY YEARS. IS THAT YOUR FAULT? IS IT?
1982.
I COULD... UH... TORTURE YOU, YOU KNOW. I COULD. DON'T THINK THAT I COULDN'T...
I'VE KILLED PEOPLE BEFORE NOW...
1988.
I HATE YOU. I'M GLAD WE TRAPPED YOU.
YOU'RE... NOTHING SPECIAL. YOU KNOW THAT?
YOU'RE NOTHING AT ALL.
IT
STEPHEN KING
A NAKED MAN IN A GLASS BOX. THAT'S ALL YOU ARE.
YOU'RE NOTHING AT ALL.
Soon.

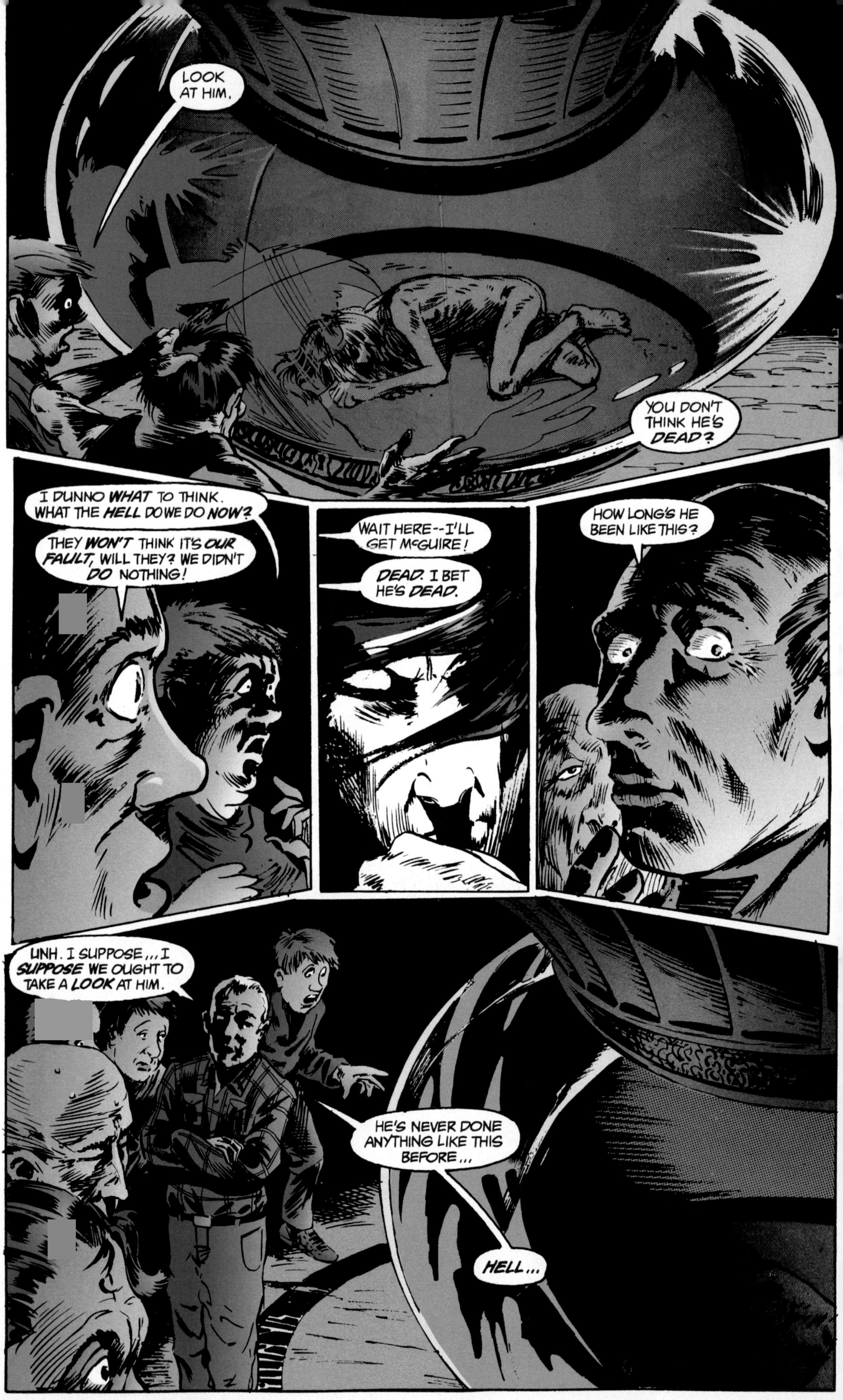
LOOK AT HIM.
YOU DON'T THINK HE'S *DEAD?*
I DUNNO *WHAT* TO THINK. WHAT THE *HELL* DO WE DO *NOW?*
THEY *WON'T* THINK IT'S *OUR FAULT,* WILL THEY? WE DIDN'T *DO* NOTHING!
WAIT HERE--I'LL GET McGUIRE!
DEAD. I BET HE'S *DEAD.*
HOW LONG'S HE BEEN LIKE THIS?
UNH. I SUPPOSE... I *SUPPOSE* WE OUGHT TO TAKE A *LOOK* AT HIM.
HE'S NEVER DONE ANYTHING LIKE THIS BEFORE...
HELL...

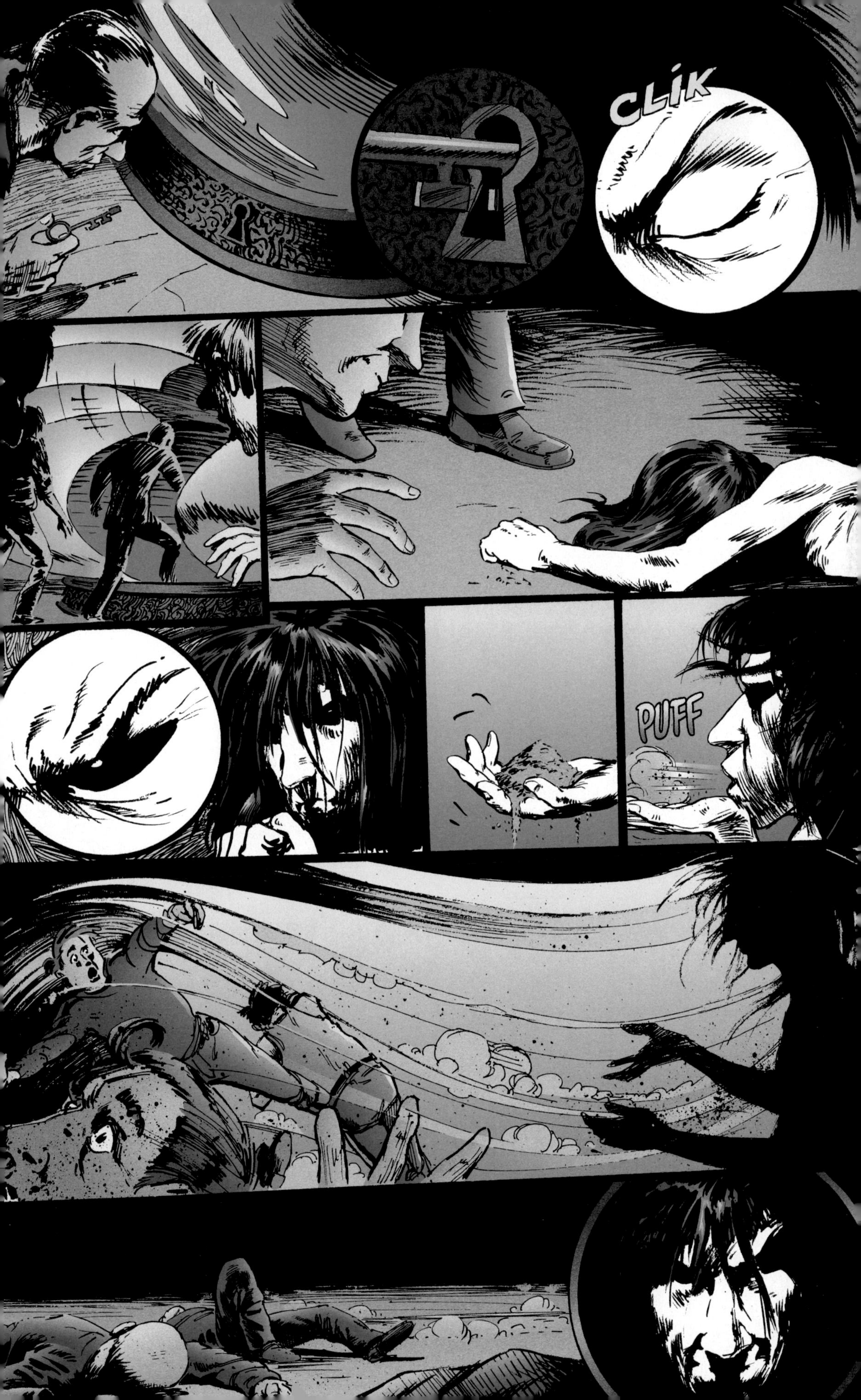
CLIK
PUFF

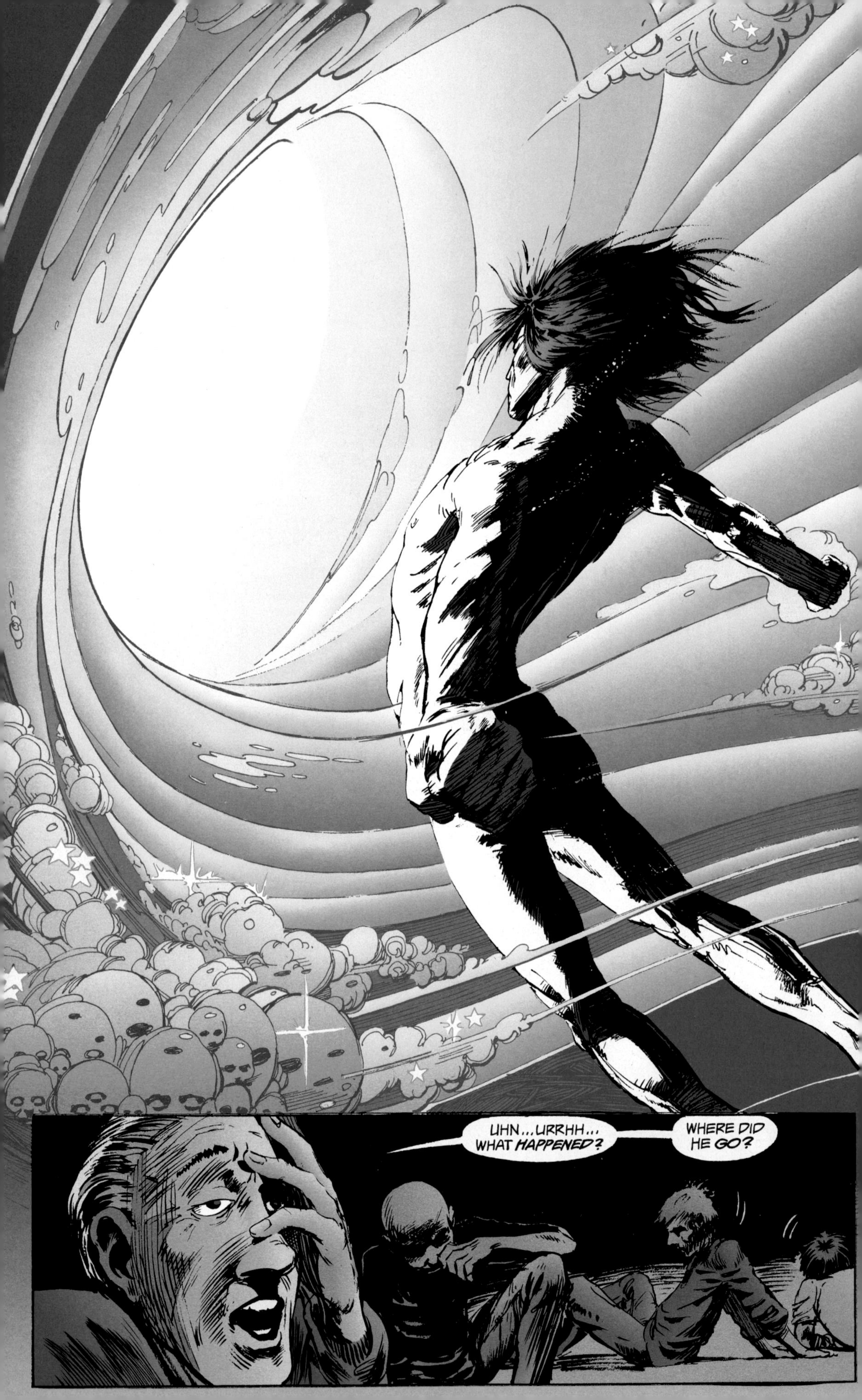
UHN...URRHH... WHAT HAPPENED?
WHERE DID HE GO?

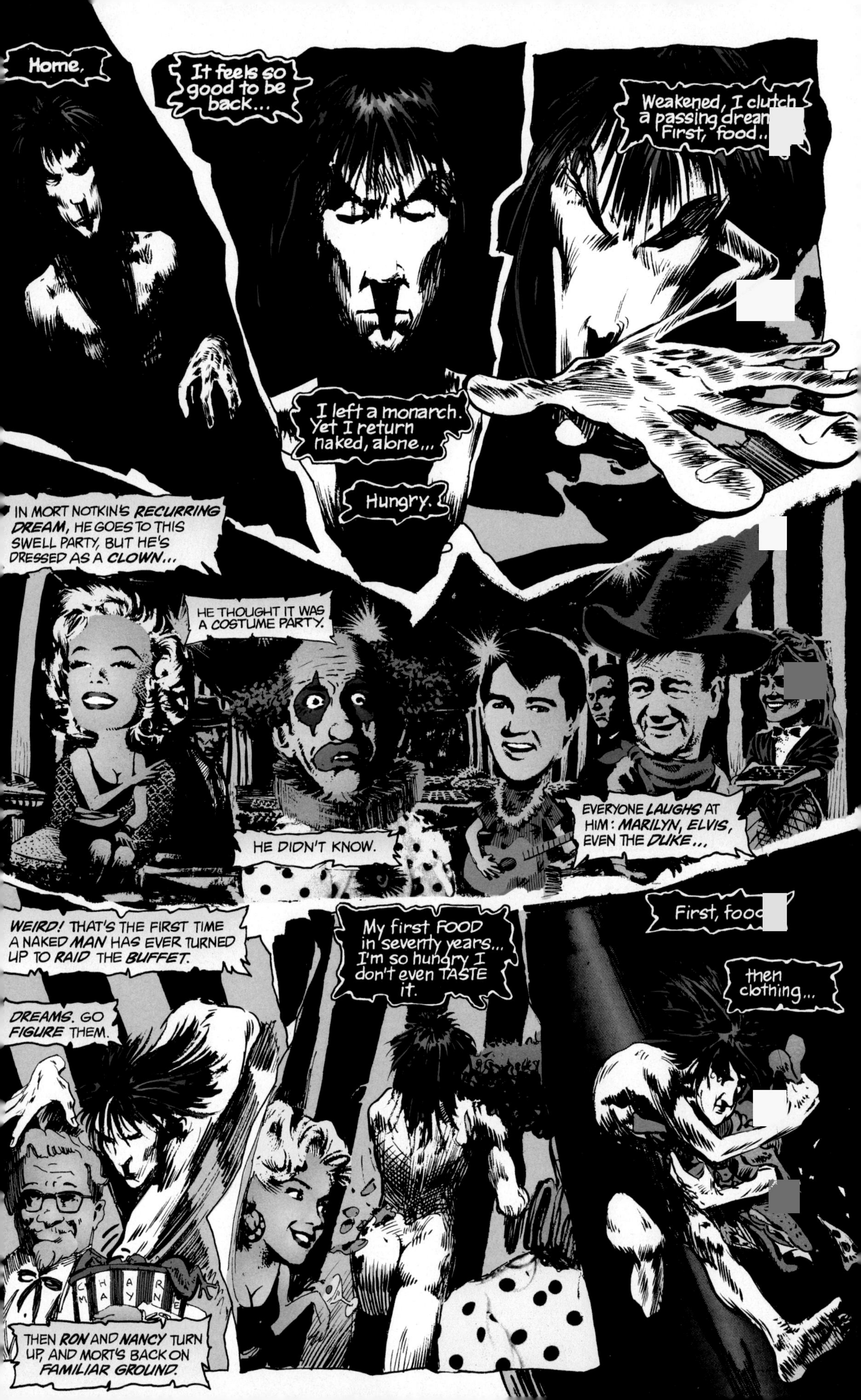
Home,
It feels so good to be back...
Weakened, I clutch a passing drea
First, food..
I left a monarch. Yet I return naked, alone...
Hungry.
IN MORT NOTKIN'S RECURRING DREAM, HE GOES TO THIS SWELL PARTY, BUT HE'S DRESSED AS A CLOWN...
HE THOUGHT IT WAS A COSTUME PARTY.
HE DIDN'T KNOW.
EVERYONE LAUGHS AT HIM: MARILYN, ELVIS, EVEN THE DUKE...
WEIRD! THAT'S THE FIRST TIME A NAKED MAN HAS EVER TURNED UP TO RAID THE BUFFET.
DREAMS. GO FIGURE THEM.
My first FOOD in seventy years... I'm so hungry I don't even TASTE it.
First, foo
then clothing...
THEN RON AND NANCY TURN UP, AND MORT'S BACK ON FAMILIAR GROUND.

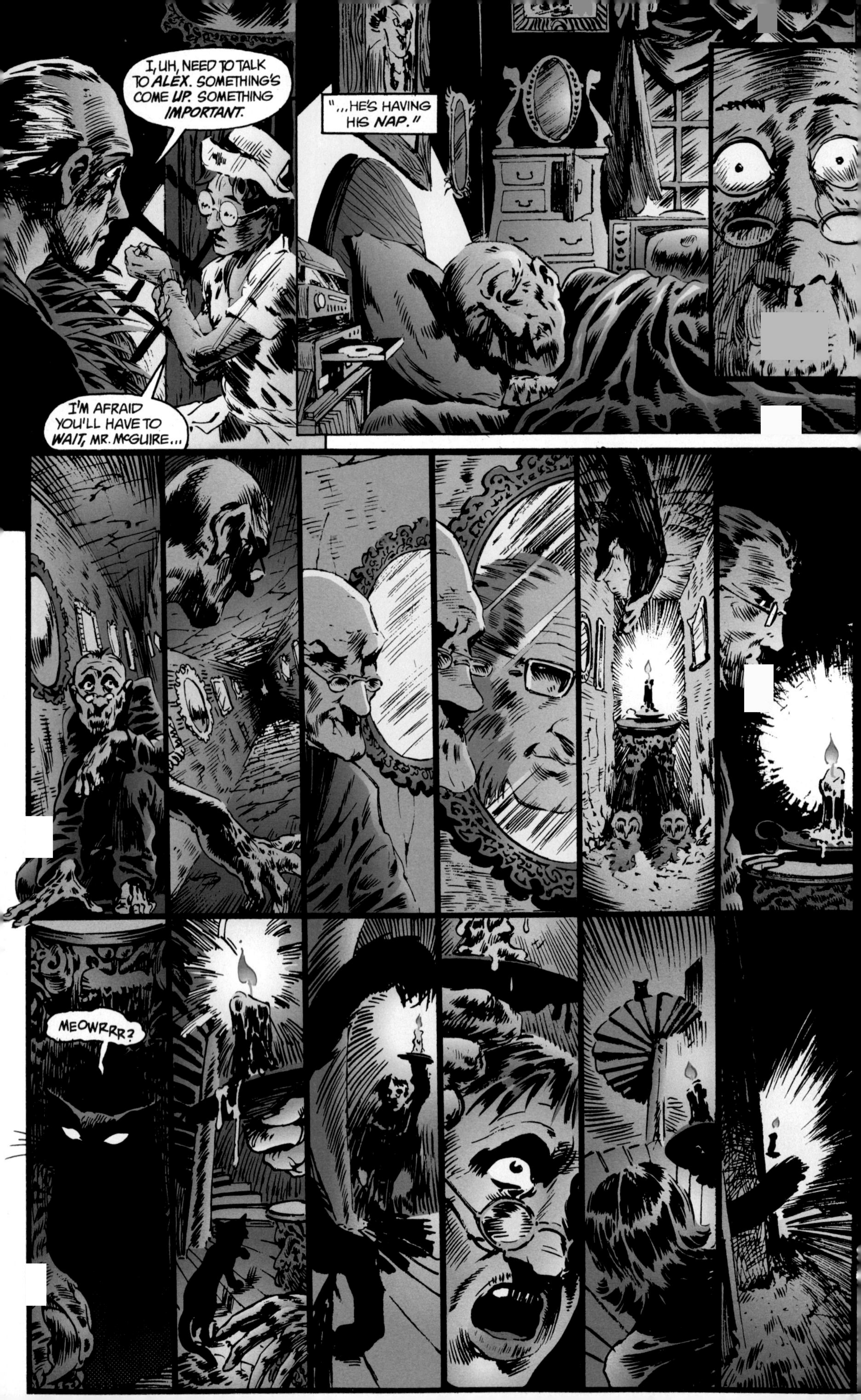
I, UH, NEED TO TALK TO ALEX. SOMETHING'S COME UP. SOMETHING IMPORTANT.
I'M AFRAID YOU'LL HAVE TO WAIT, MR. McGUIRE...
"...HE'S HAVING HIS NAP."
MEOWRRR?

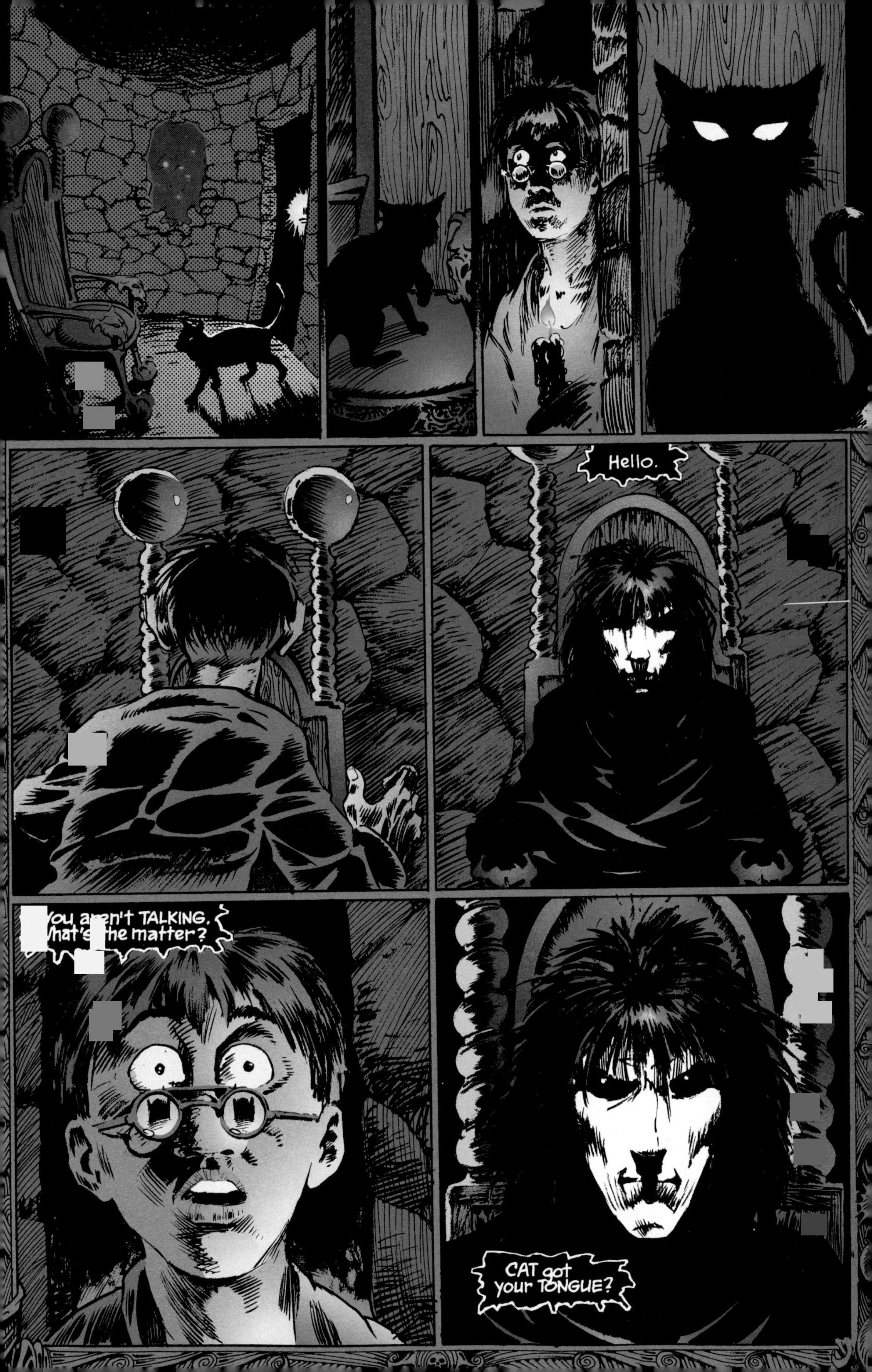
Hello.
You aren't TALKING. What's the matter?
CAT got your TONGUE?

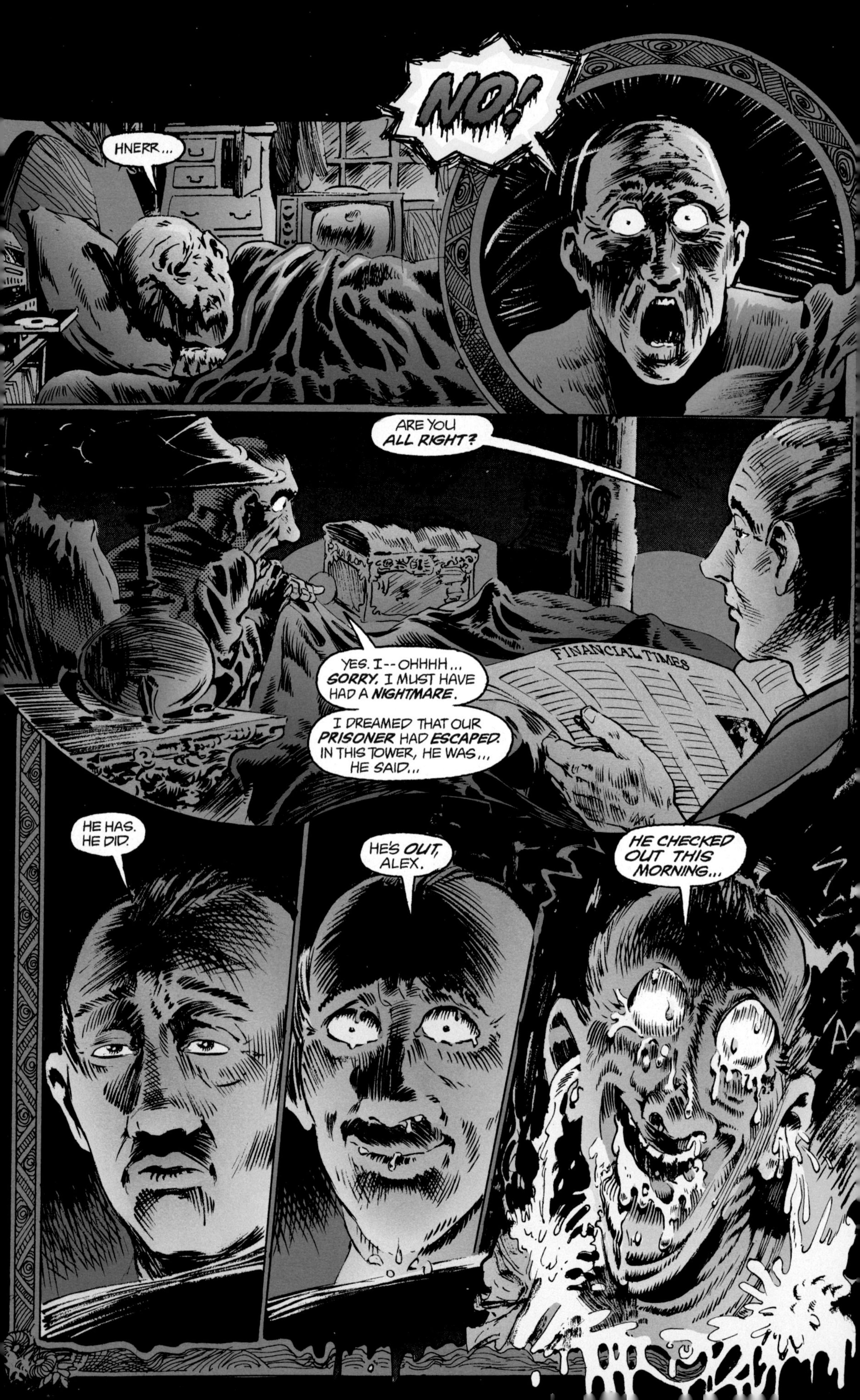
HNERR...
NO!
ARE YOU ALL RIGHT?
YES. I--OHHHH... SORRY. I MUST HAVE HAD A NIGHTMARE.
I DREAMED THAT OUR PRISONER HAD ESCAPED. IN THIS TOWER, HE WAS... HE SAID...
FINANCIAL TIMES
HE HAS. HE DID.
HE'S OUT, ALEX.
HE CHECKED OUT THIS MORNING...

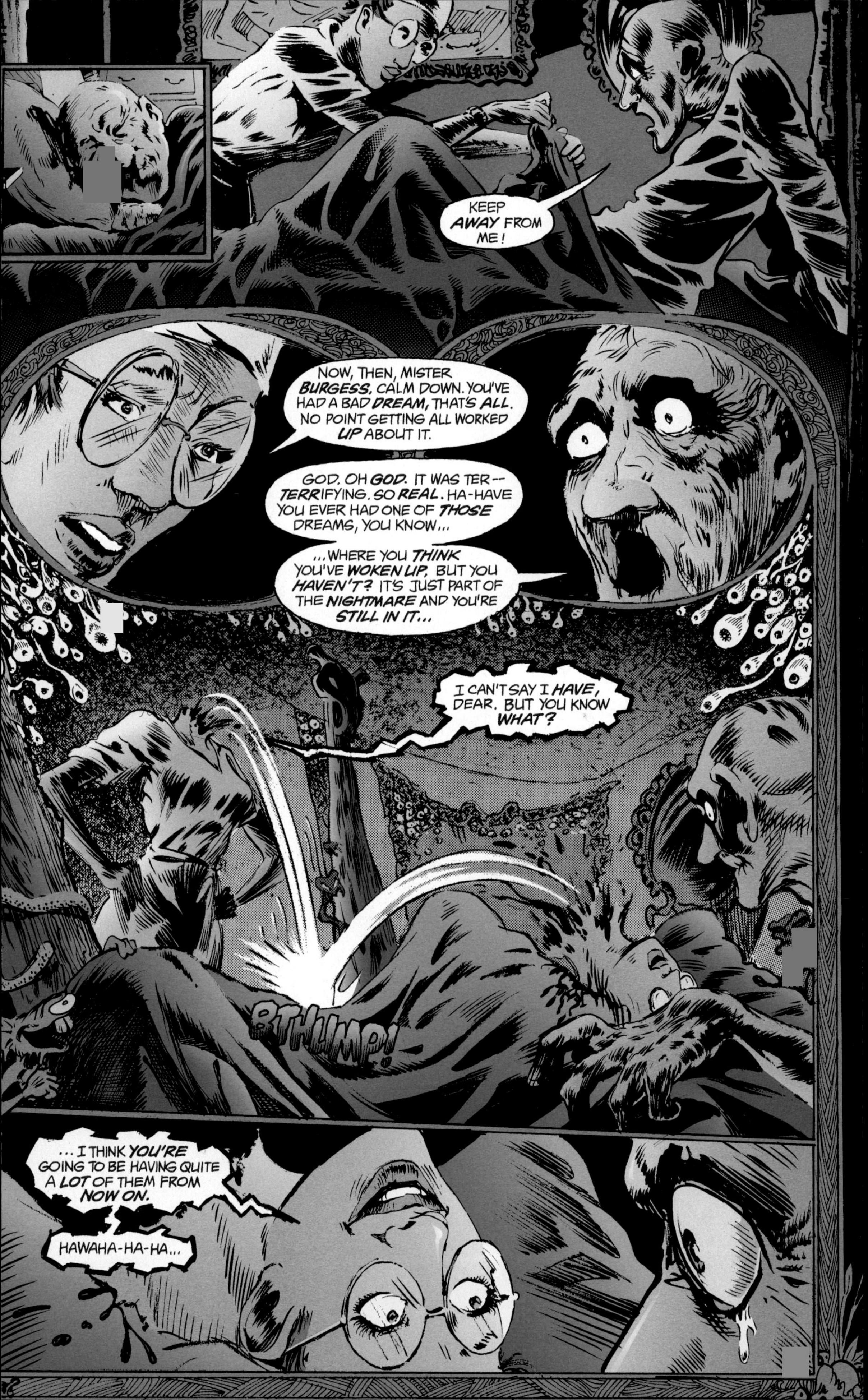
KEEP AWAY FROM ME!
NOW, THEN, MISTER BURGESS. CALM DOWN. YOU'VE HAD A BAD DREAM, THAT'S ALL. NO POINT GETTING ALL WORKED UP ABOUT IT.
GOD. OH GOD. IT WAS TER-- TERRIFYING. SO REAL. HA-HAVE YOU EVER HAD ONE OF THOSE DREAMS, YOU KNOW...
...WHERE YOU THINK YOU'VE WOKEN UP, BUT YOU HAVEN'T? IT'S JUST PART OF THE NIGHTMARE AND YOU'RE STILL IN IT...
I CAN'T SAY I HAVE, DEAR. BUT YOU KNOW WHAT?
BTHUMP!
...I THINK YOU'RE GOING TO BE HAVING QUITE A LOT OF THEM FROM NOW ON.
HAWAHA-HA-HA...

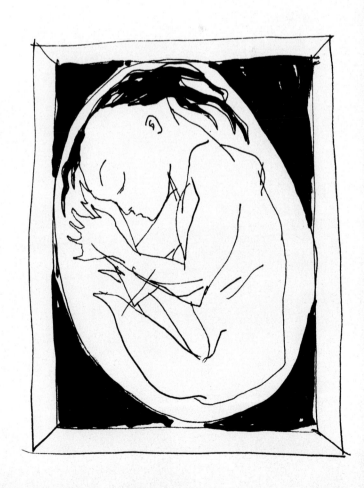

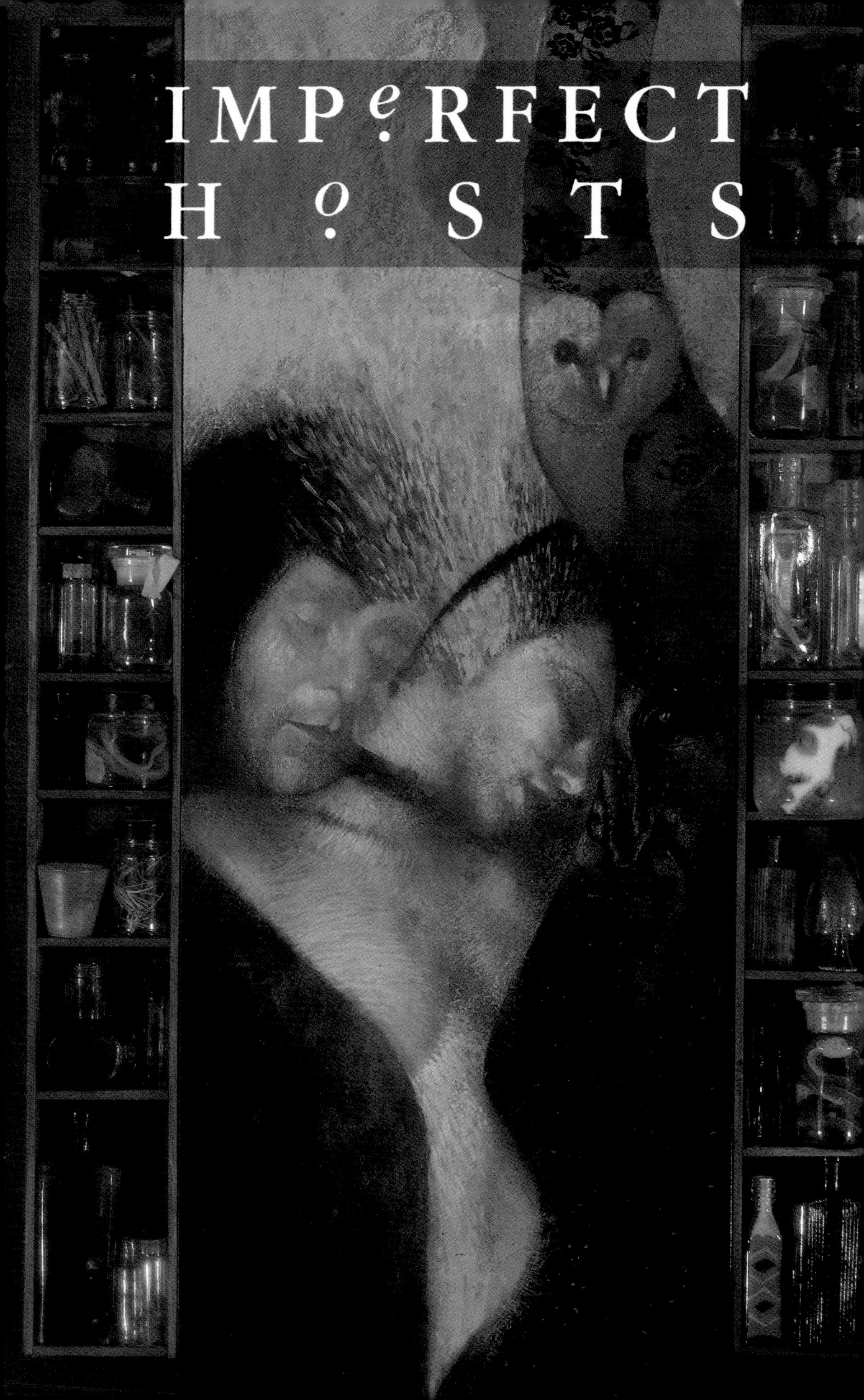
IMPeRFECT
HoSTS

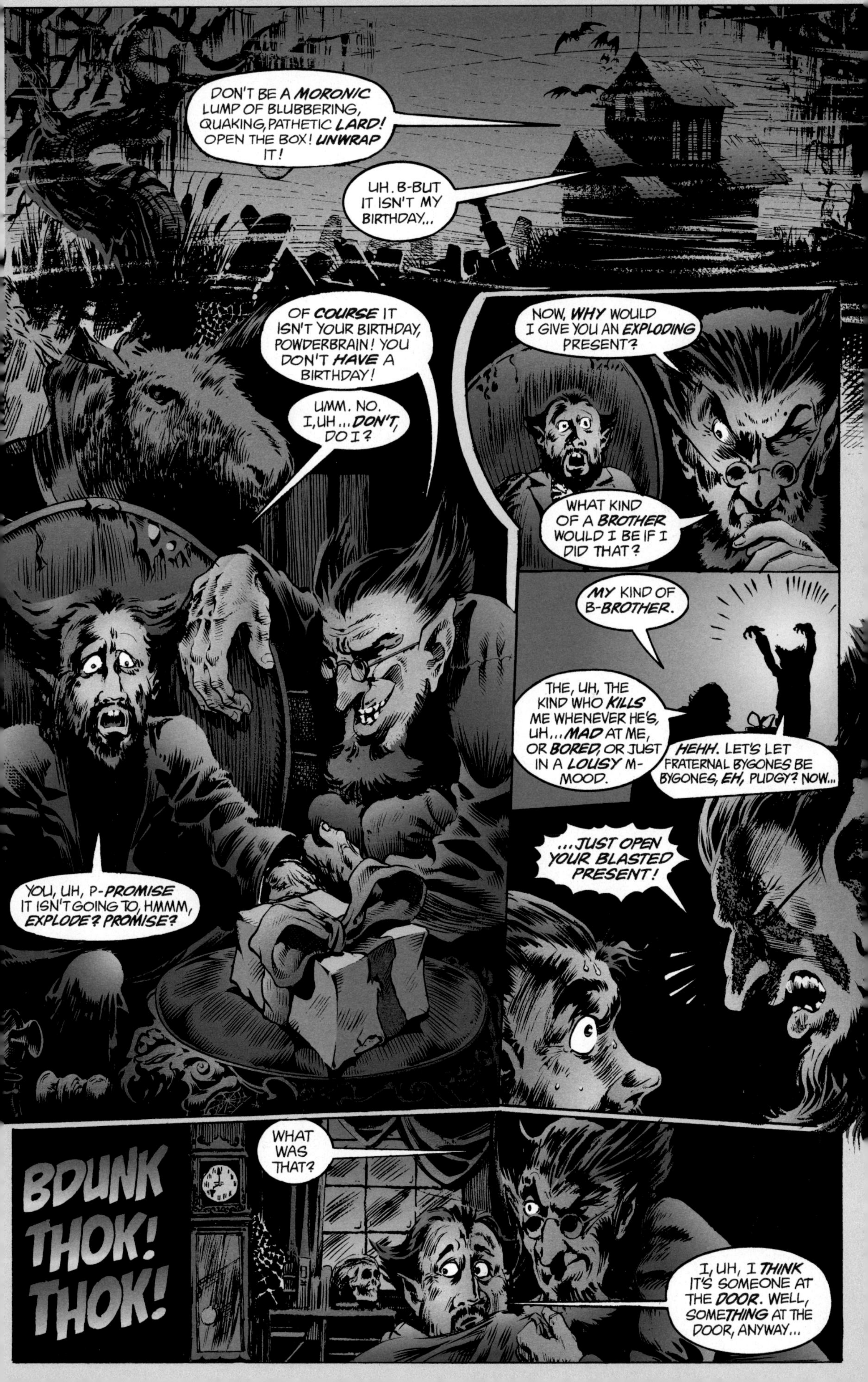
DON'T BE A MORONIC LUMP OF BLUBBERING, QUAKING, PATHETIC LARD! OPEN THE BOX! UNWRAP IT!
UH. B-BUT IT ISN'T MY BIRTHDAY...
OF COURSE IT ISN'T YOUR BIRTHDAY, POWDERBRAIN! YOU DON'T HAVE A BIRTHDAY!
UMM. NO. I, UH... DON'T, DO I?
YOU, UH, P-PROMISE IT ISN'T GOING TO, HMMM, EXPLODE? PROMISE?
NOW, WHY WOULD I GIVE YOU AN EXPLODING PRESENT?
WHAT KIND OF A BROTHER WOULD I BE IF I DID THAT?
MY KIND OF B-BROTHER.
THE, UH, THE KIND WHO KILLS ME WHENEVER HE'S, UH,... MAD AT ME, OR BORED, OR JUST IN A LOUSY M-MOOD.
HEHH. LET'S LET FRATERNAL BYGONES BE BYGONES, EH, PUDGY? NOW...
...JUST OPEN YOUR BLASTED PRESENT!
BDUNK THOK! THOK!
WHAT WAS THAT?
I, UH, I THINK IT'S SOMEONE AT THE DOOR. WELL, SOMETHING AT THE DOOR, ANYWAY...

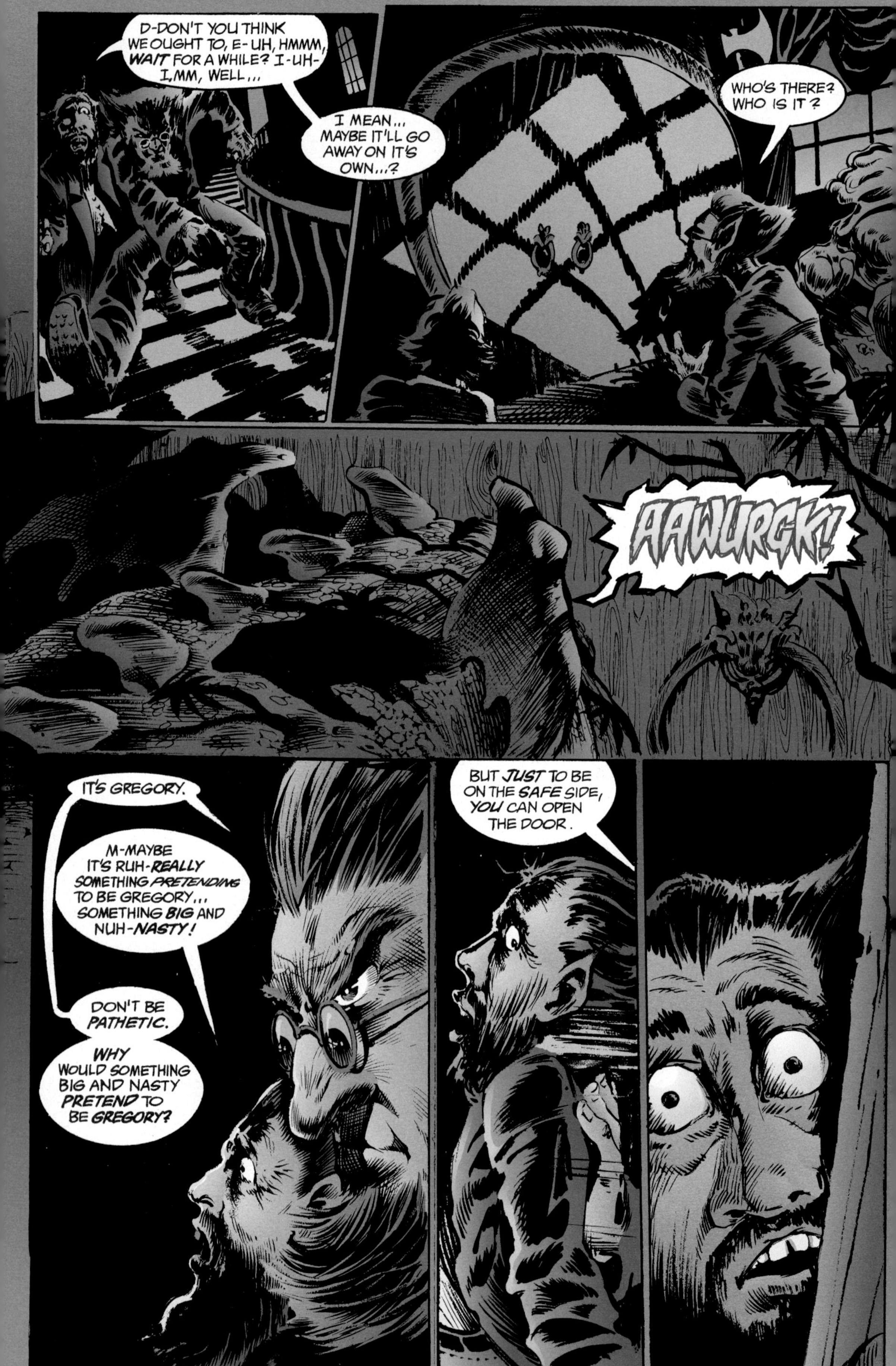
D-DON'T YOU THINK WE OUGHT TO, E- UH, HMMM, WAIT FOR A WHILE? I-UH-I,MM, WELL...
I MEAN... MAYBE IT'LL GO AWAY ON IT'S OWN...?
WHO'S THERE? WHO IS IT?
AAWURGK!
IT'S GREGORY.
M-MAYBE IT'S RUH-REALLY SOMETHING PRETENDING TO BE GREGORY... SOMETHING BIG AND NUH-NASTY!
DON'T BE PATHETIC.
WHY WOULD SOMETHING BIG AND NASTY PRETEND TO BE GREGORY?
BUT JUST TO BE ON THE SAFE SIDE, YOU CAN OPEN THE DOOR.

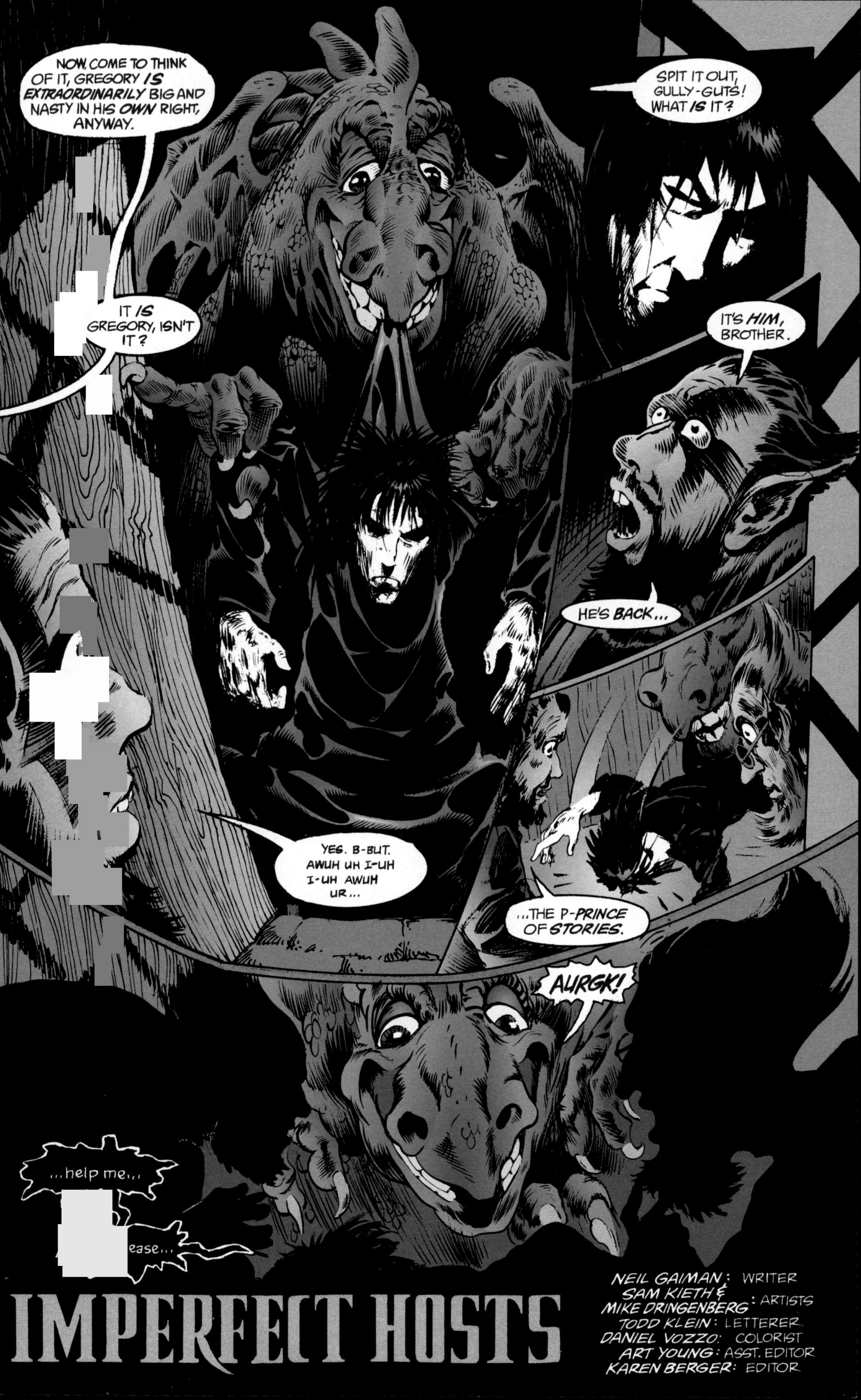

NOW, COME TO THINK OF IT, GREGORY IS EXTRAORDINARILY BIG AND NASTY IN HIS OWN RIGHT, ANYWAY.
IT IS GREGORY, ISN'T IT?
SPIT IT OUT, GULLY-GUTS! WHAT IS IT?
IT'S HIM, BROTHER.
HE'S BACK...
...THE P-PRINCE OF STORIES.
YES. B-BUT. AWUH UH I-UH I-UH AWUH UR...
AURGK!
...help me...
IMPERFECT HOSTS
NEIL GAIMAN: WRITER
SAM KIETH & MIKE DRINGENBERG: ARTISTS
TODD KLEIN: LETTERER
DANIEL VOZZO: COLORIST
ART YOUNG: ASST. EDITOR
KAREN BERGER: EDITOR

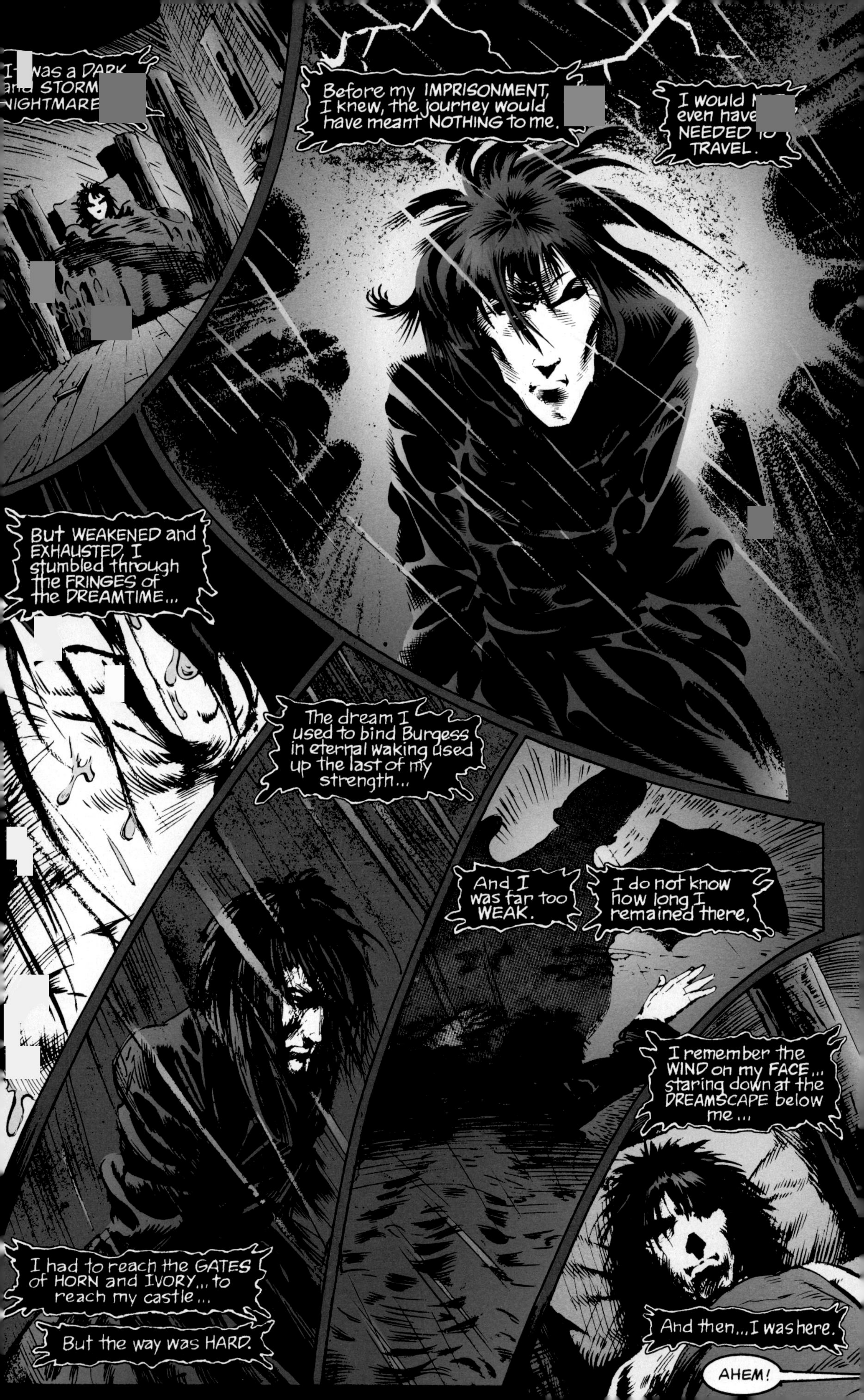

I was a DARK
and STORM
NIGHTMARE
Before my IMPRISONMENT, I knew, the journey would have meant NOTHING to me.
I would
even have
NEEDED
TRAVEL.
But WEAKENED and EXHAUSTED, I stumbled through the FRINGES of the DREAMTIME...
The dream I used to bind Burgess in eternal waking used up the last of my strength...
And I was far too WEAK.
I do not know how long I remained there,
I remember the WIND on my FACE... staring down at the DREAMSCAPE below me...
I had to reach the GATES of HORN and IVORY... to reach my castle...
But the way was HARD.
And then... I was here.
AHEM!

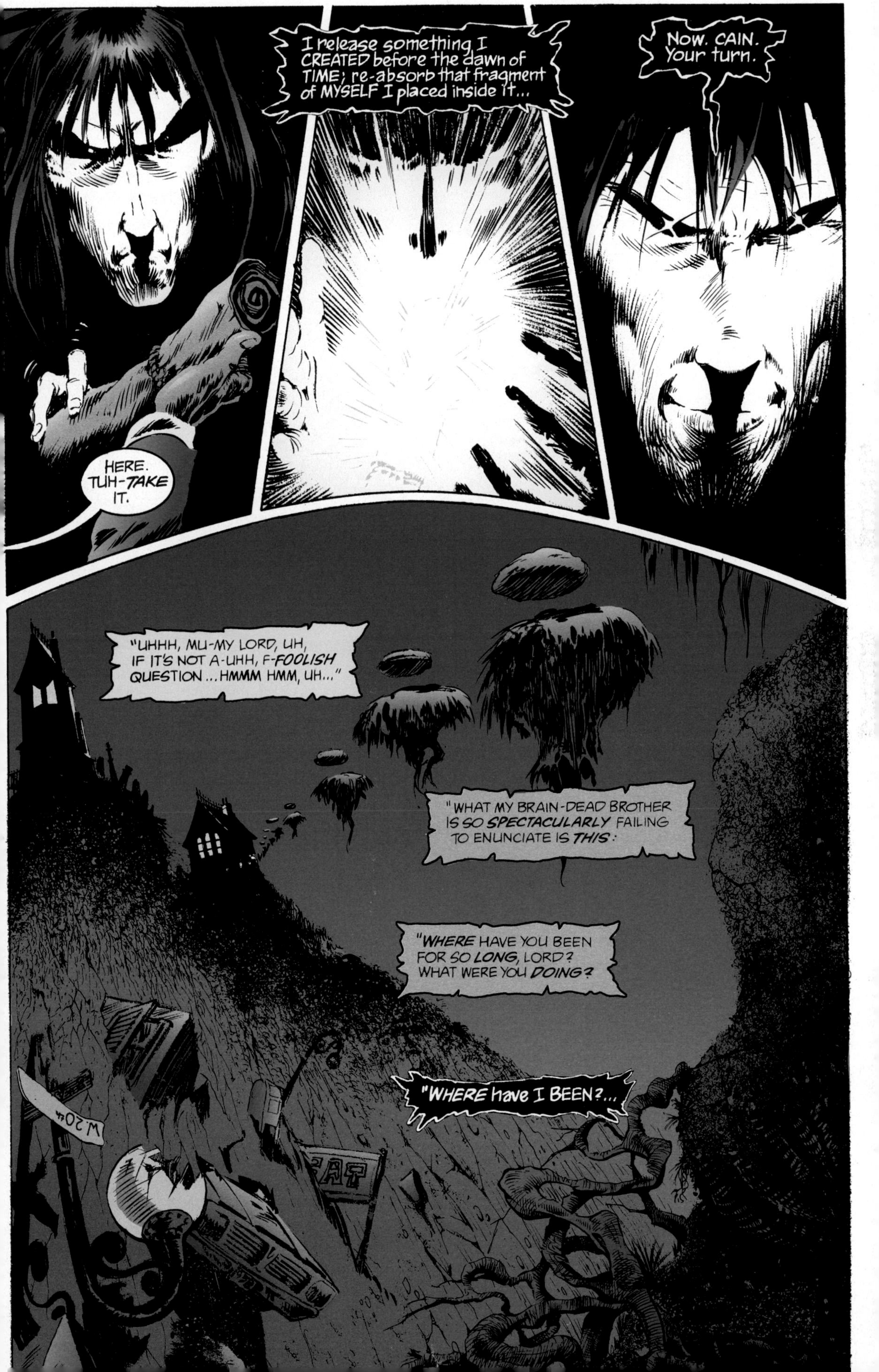
HERE. TUH-TAKE IT.
I release something I CREATED before the dawn of TIME; re-absorb that fragment of MYSELF I placed inside it...
Now. CAIN. Your turn.
"UHHH, MU-MY LORD, UH, IF IT'S NOT A-UHH, F-FOOLISH QUESTION ... HMMM HMM, UH..."
"WHAT MY BRAIN-DEAD BROTHER IS SO SPECTACULARLY FAILING TO ENUNCIATE IS THIS:
"WHERE HAVE YOU BEEN FOR SO LONG, LORD? WHAT WERE YOU DOING?
"WHERE have I BEEN?...

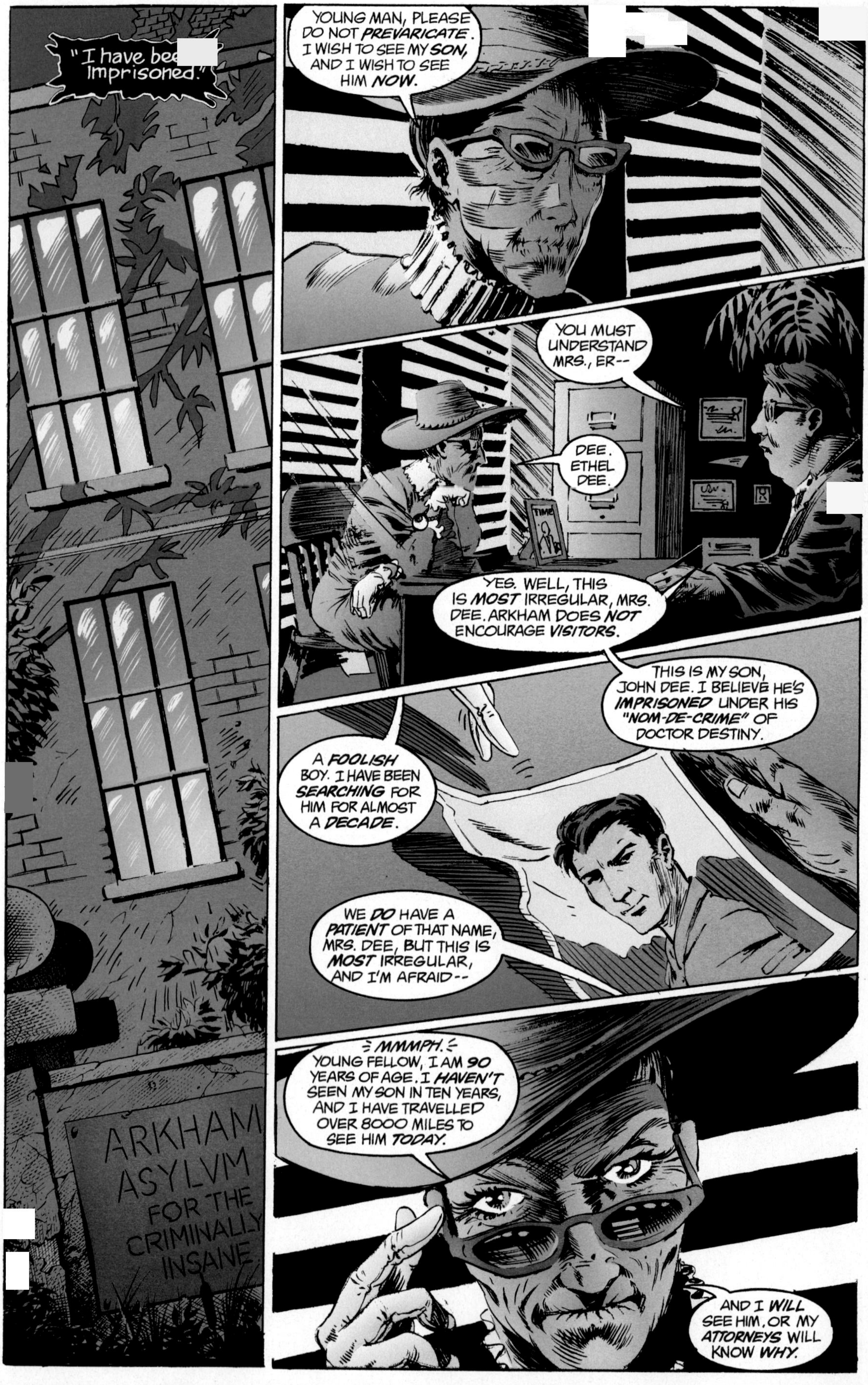

"I have bee imprisoned."
YOUNG MAN, PLEASE DO NOT PREVARICATE. I WISH TO SEE MY SON, AND I WISH TO SEE HIM NOW.
YOU MUST UNDERSTAND MRS., ER--
DEE. ETHEL DEE.
TIME
YES. WELL, THIS IS MOST IRREGULAR, MRS. DEE. ARKHAM DOES NOT ENCOURAGE VISITORS.
THIS IS MY SON, JOHN DEE. I BELIEVE HE'S IMPRISONED UNDER HIS "NOM-DE-CRIME" OF DOCTOR DESTINY.
A FOOLISH BOY. I HAVE BEEN SEARCHING FOR HIM FOR ALMOST A DECADE.
WE DO HAVE A PATIENT OF THAT NAME, MRS. DEE, BUT THIS IS MOST IRREGULAR, AND I'M AFRAID--
MMMPH.
YOUNG FELLOW, I AM 90 YEARS OF AGE. I HAVEN'T SEEN MY SON IN TEN YEARS, AND I HAVE TRAVELLED OVER 8000 MILES TO SEE HIM TODAY.
AND I WILL SEE HIM, OR MY ATTORNEYS WILL KNOW WHY.
ARKHAM ASYLVM FOR THE CRIMINALLY INSANE

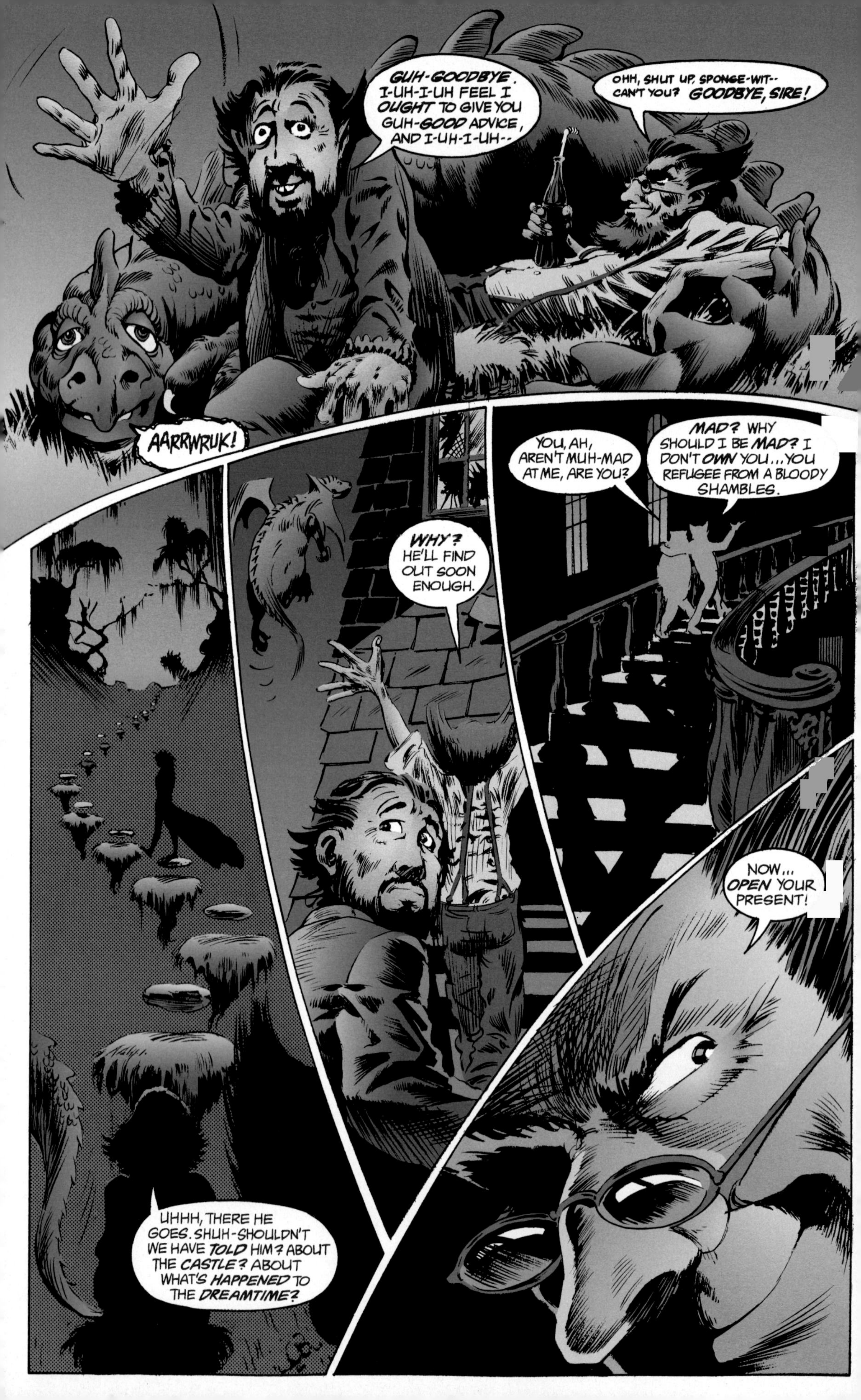
GUH-GOODBYE. I-UH-I-UH FEEL I OUGHT TO GIVE YOU GUH-GOOD ADVICE, AND I-UH-I-UH--
OHH, SHUT UP, SPONGE-WIT--CAN'T YOU? GOODBYE, SIRE!
AARRWRUK!
WHY? HE'LL FIND OUT SOON ENOUGH.
YOU, AH, AREN'T MUH-MAD AT ME, ARE YOU?
MAD? WHY SHOULD I BE MAD? I DON'T OWN YOU...YOU REFUGEE FROM A BLOODY SHAMBLES.
UHHH, THERE HE GOES. SHUH-SHOULDN'T WE HAVE TOLD HIM? ABOUT THE CASTLE? ABOUT WHAT'S HAPPENED TO THE DREAMTIME?
NOW... OPEN YOUR PRESENT!

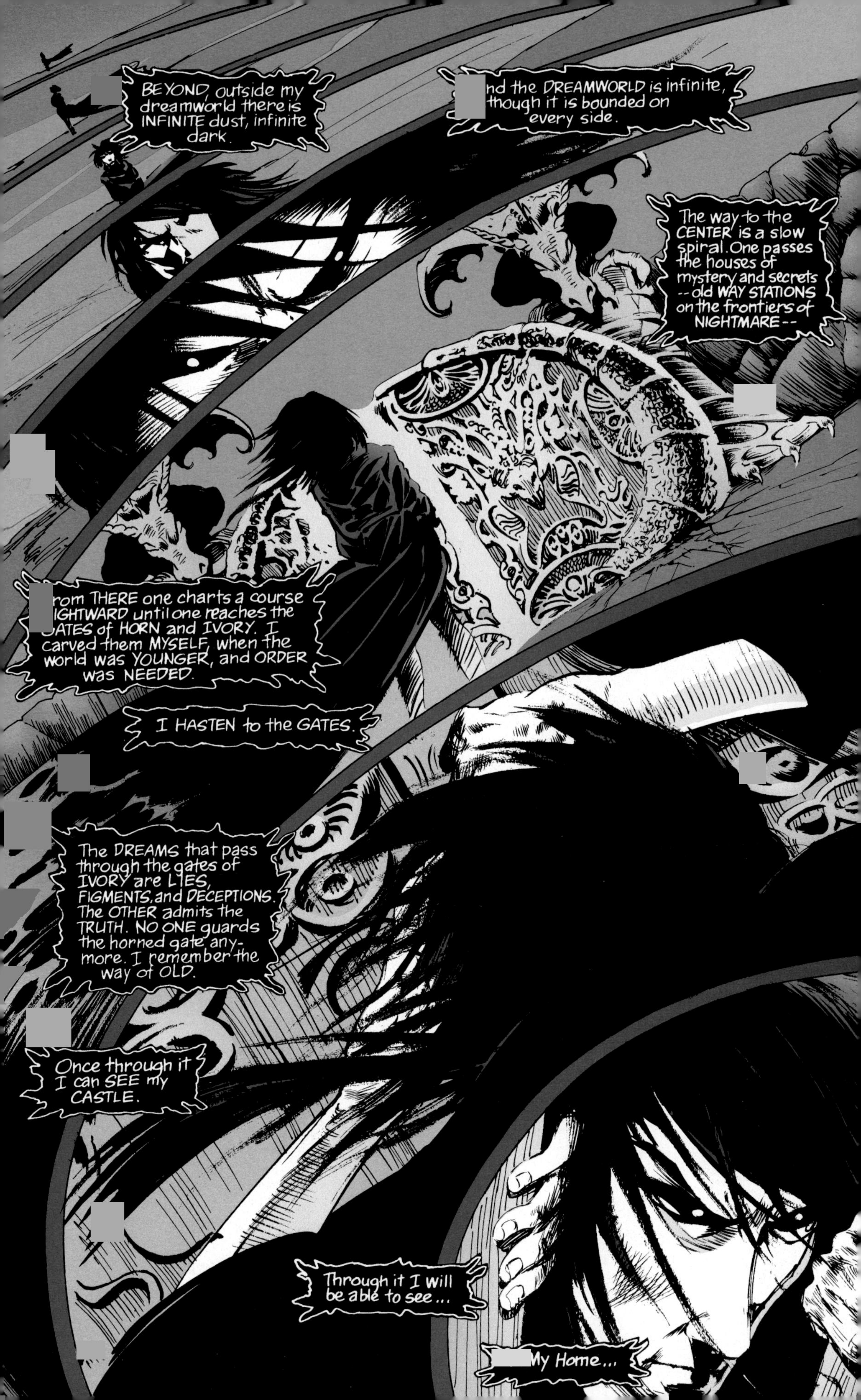

BEYOND, outside my dreamworld there is INFINITE dust, infinite dark.
nd the DREAMWORLD is infinite, though it is bounded on every side.
The way to the CENTER is a slow spiral. One passes the houses of mystery and secrets --old WAY STATIONS on the frontiers of NIGHTMARE--
rom THERE one charts a course IGHTWARD until one reaches the ATES of HORN and IVORY. I carved them MYSELF, when the world was YOUNGER, and ORDER was NEEDED.
I HASTEN to the GATES.
The DREAMS that pass through the gates of IVORY are LIES, FIGMENTS, and DECEPTIONS. The OTHER admits the TRUTH. NO ONE guards the horned gate any-more. I remember the way of OLD.
Once through it I can SEE my CASTLE.
Through it I will be able to see...
My Home...

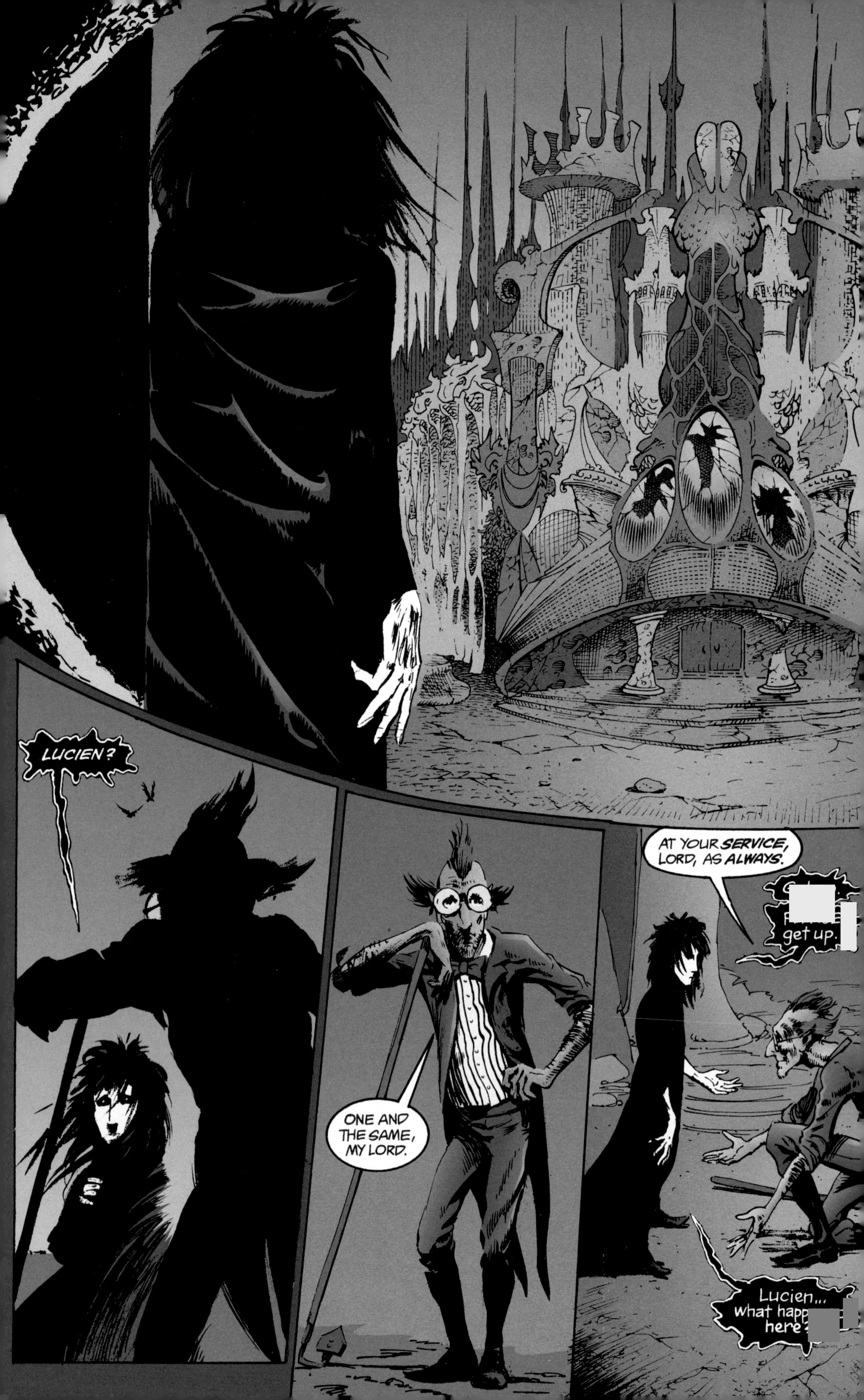
LUCIEN?
ONE AND THE SAME, MY LORD.
AT YOUR SERVICE, LORD, AS ALWAYS.
get up.
Lucien... what happ here?

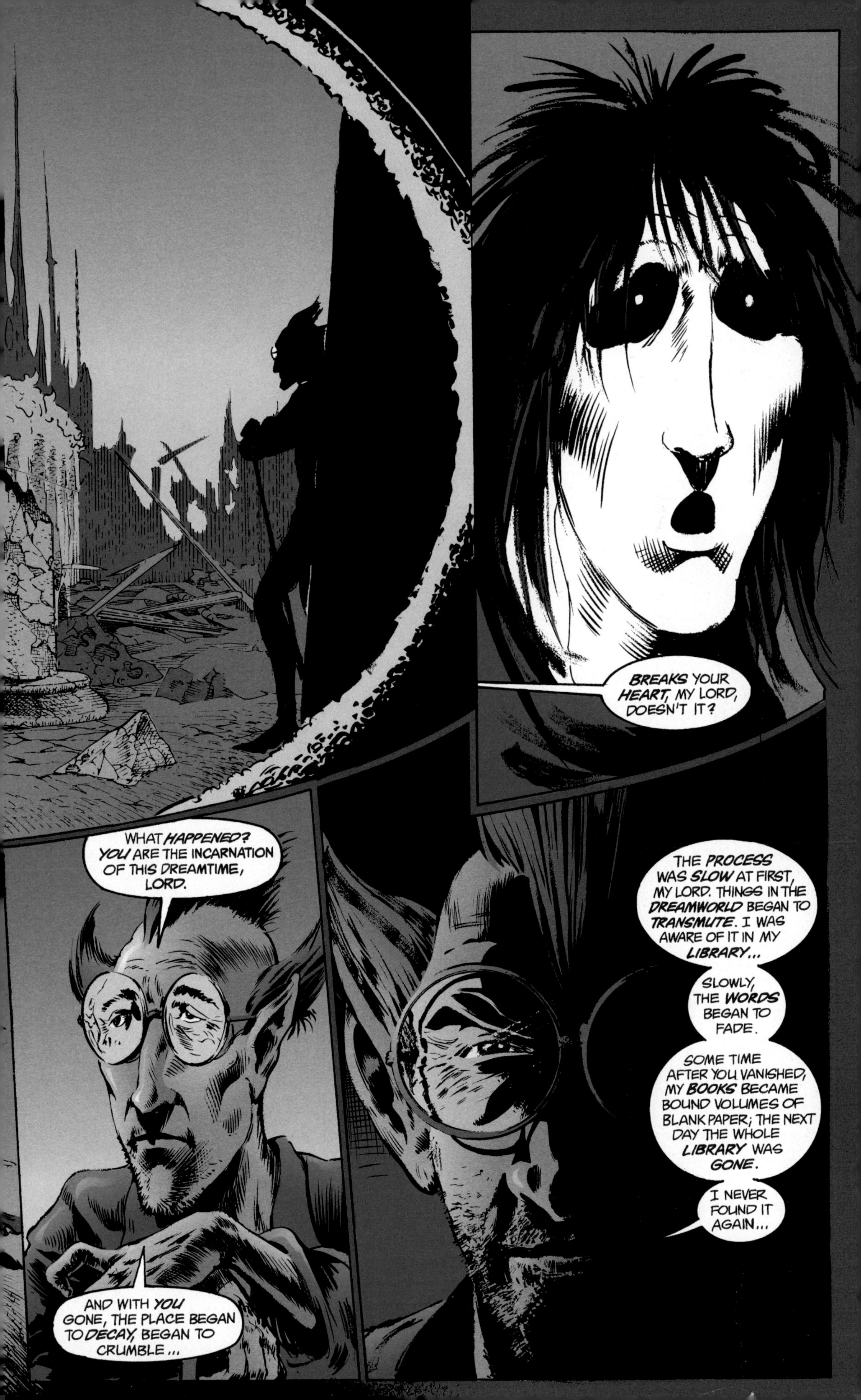
BREAKS YOUR HEART, MY LORD, DOESN'T IT?
WHAT HAPPENED? YOU ARE THE INCARNATION OF THIS DREAMTIME, LORD.
AND WITH YOU GONE, THE PLACE BEGAN TO DECAY, BEGAN TO CRUMBLE...
THE PROCESS WAS SLOW AT FIRST, MY LORD. THINGS IN THE DREAMWORLD BEGAN TO TRANSMUTE. I WAS AWARE OF IT IN MY LIBRARY...
SLOWLY, THE WORDS BEGAN TO FADE.
SOME TIME AFTER YOU VANISHED, MY BOOKS BECAME BOUND VOLUMES OF BLANK PAPER; THE NEXT DAY THE WHOLE LIBRARY WAS GONE.
I NEVER FOUND IT AGAIN...

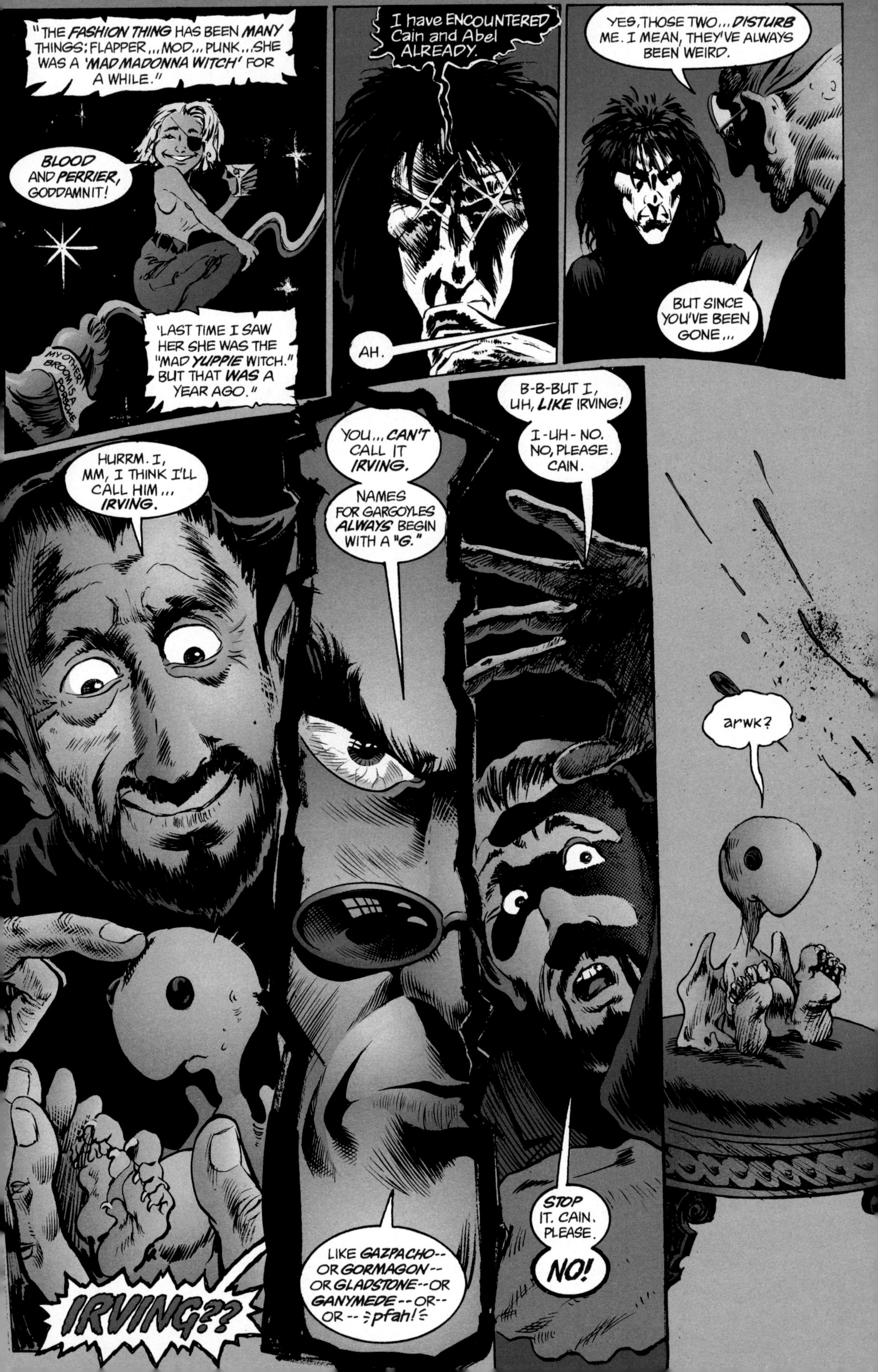
"THE FASHION THING HAS BEEN MANY THINGS: FLAPPER... MOD... PUNK... SHE WAS A 'MAD MADONNA WITCH' FOR A WHILE."
BLOOD AND PERRIER, GODDAMNIT!
'LAST TIME I SAW HER SHE WAS THE "MAD YUPPIE WITCH." BUT THAT WAS A YEAR AGO."
MY OTHER BROOM IS A PORSCHE
I have ENCOUNTERED Cain and Abel ALREADY.
AH.
YES, THOSE TWO... DISTURB ME. I MEAN, THEY'VE ALWAYS BEEN WEIRD.
BUT SINCE YOU'VE BEEN GONE...
HURRM. I, MM, I THINK I'LL CALL HIM... IRVING.
IRVING??
YOU... CAN'T CALL IT IRVING.
NAMES FOR GARGOYLES ALWAYS BEGIN WITH A "G."
LIKE GAZPACHO-- OR GORMAGON-- OR GLADSTONE--OR GANYMEDE--OR-- OR-- pfah!
B-B-BUT I, UH, LIKE IRVING!
I-UH-NO. NO, PLEASE. CAIN.
STOP IT. CAIN. PLEASE.
NO!
arwk?

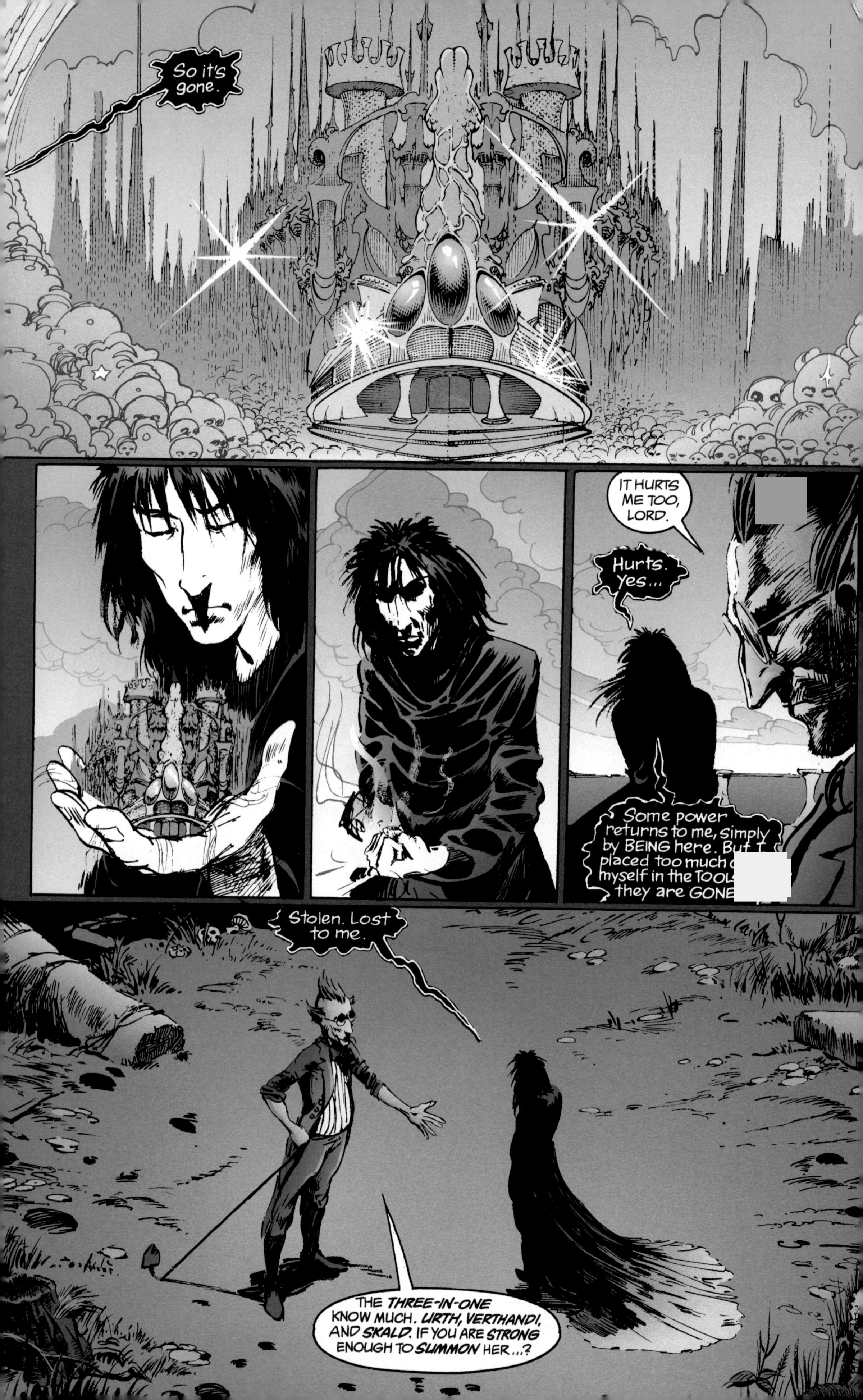
So it's gone.
IT HURTS ME TOO, LORD.
Hurts. Yes...
Some power returns to me, simply by BEING here. But I placed too much o myself in the TOOLS they are GONE
Stolen. Lost to me.
THE THREE-IN-ONE KNOW MUCH. URTH, VERTHANDI, AND SKALD. IF YOU ARE STRONG ENOUGH TO SUMMON HER...?

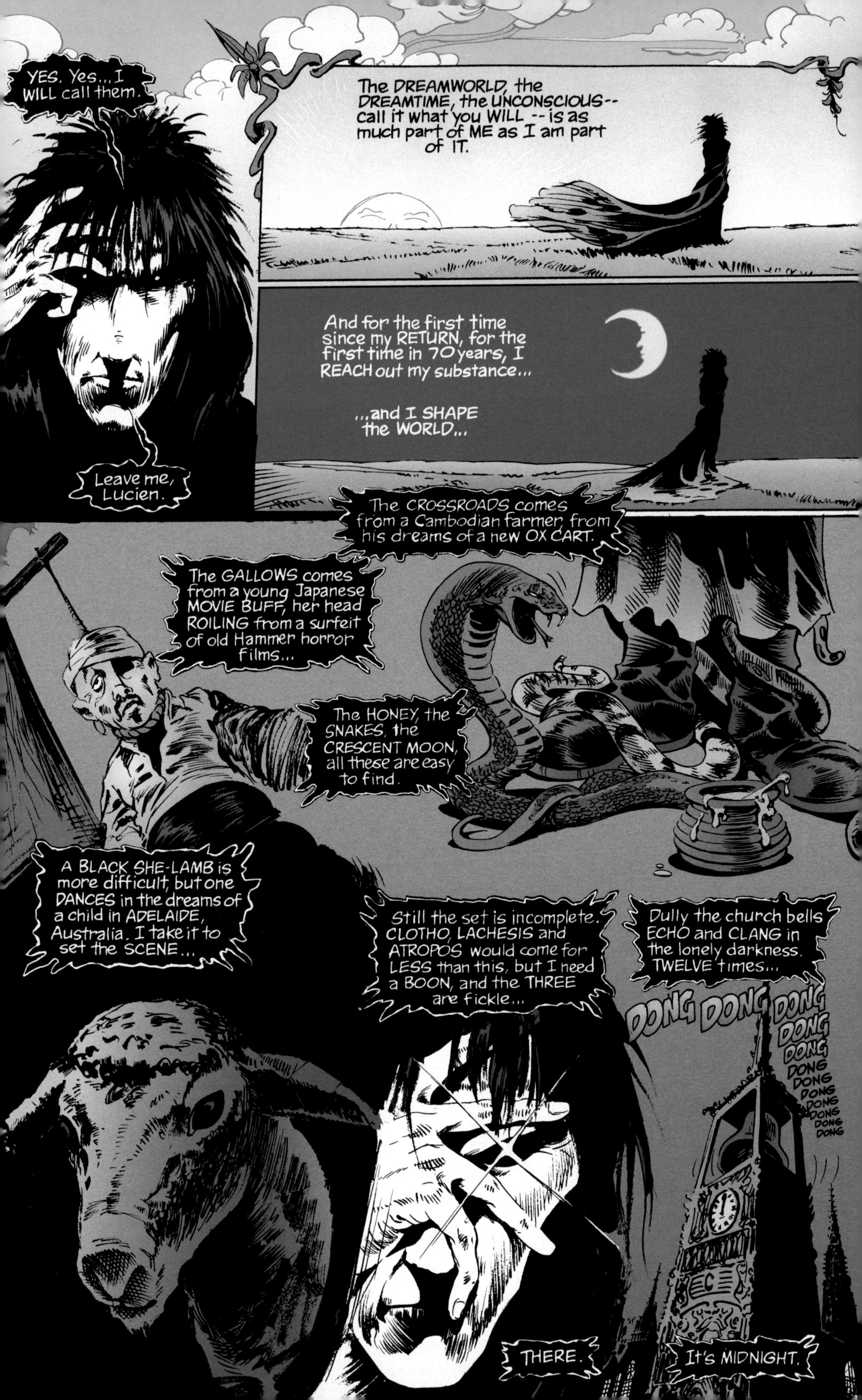
YES. Yes... I WILL call them.
The DREAMWORLD, the DREAMTIME, the UNCONSCIOUS-- call it what you WILL --is as much part of ME as I am part of IT.
And for the first time since my RETURN, for the first time in 70 years, I REACH out my substance...
...and I SHAPE the WORLD...
Leave me, Lucien.
The CROSSROADS comes from a Cambodian farmer, from his dreams of a new OX CART.
The GALLOWS comes from a young Japanese MOVIE BUFF, her head ROILING from a surfeit of old Hammer horror films...
The HONEY, the SNAKES, the CRESCENT MOON, all these are easy to find.
A BLACK SHE-LAMB is more difficult, but one DANCES in the dreams of a child in ADELAIDE, Australia. I take it to set the SCENE...
Still the set is incomplete. CLOTHO, LACHESIS and ATROPOS would come for LESS than this, but I need a BOON, and the THREE are fickle...
Dully the church bells ECHO and CLANG in the lonely darkness. TWELVE times...
DONG DONG DONG DONG DONG DONG DONG DONG DONG DONG DONG DONG
THERE.
It's MIDNIGHT.

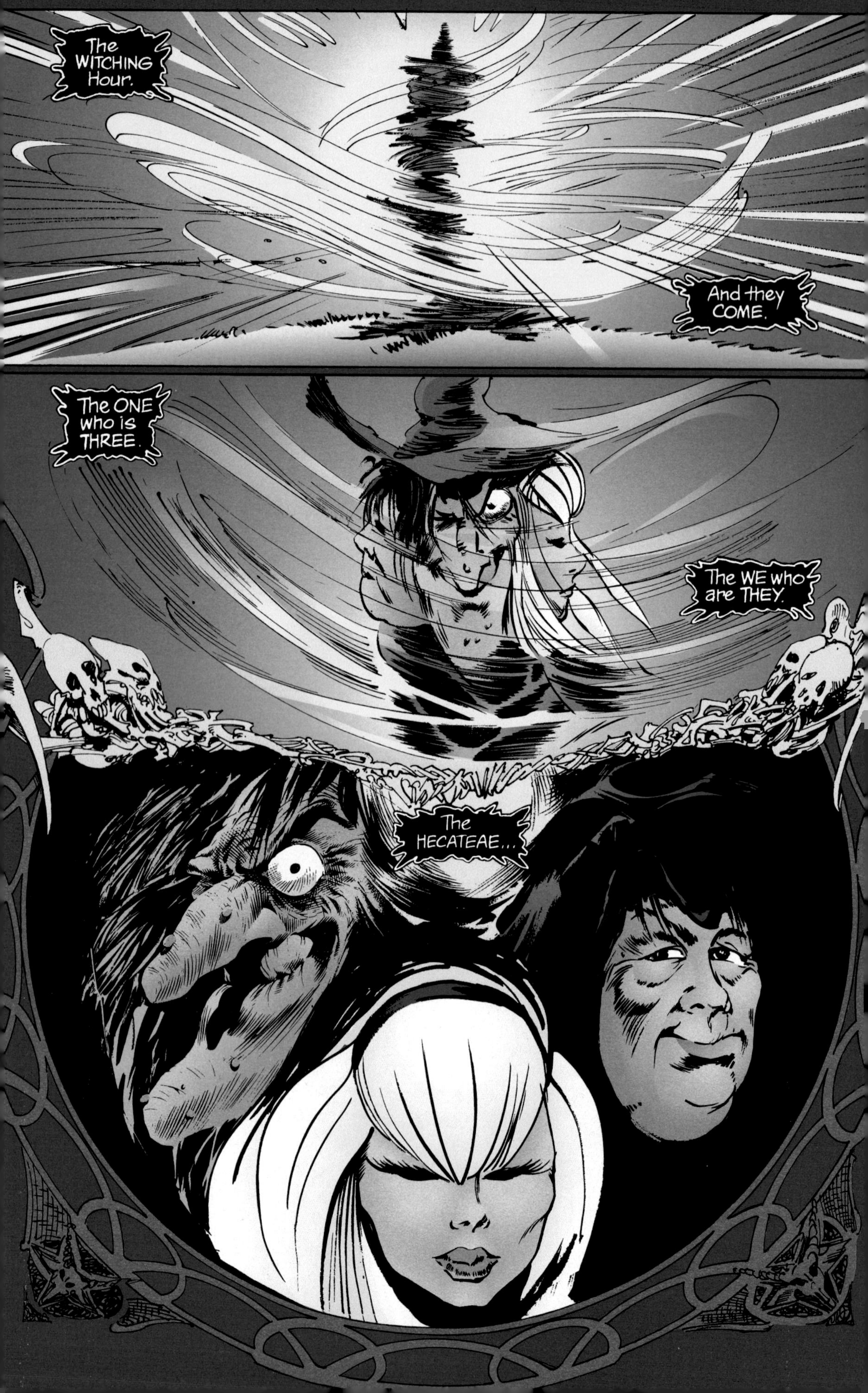
The WITCHING Hour.
And they COME.
The ONE who is THREE.
The WE who are THEY.
The HECATEAE...

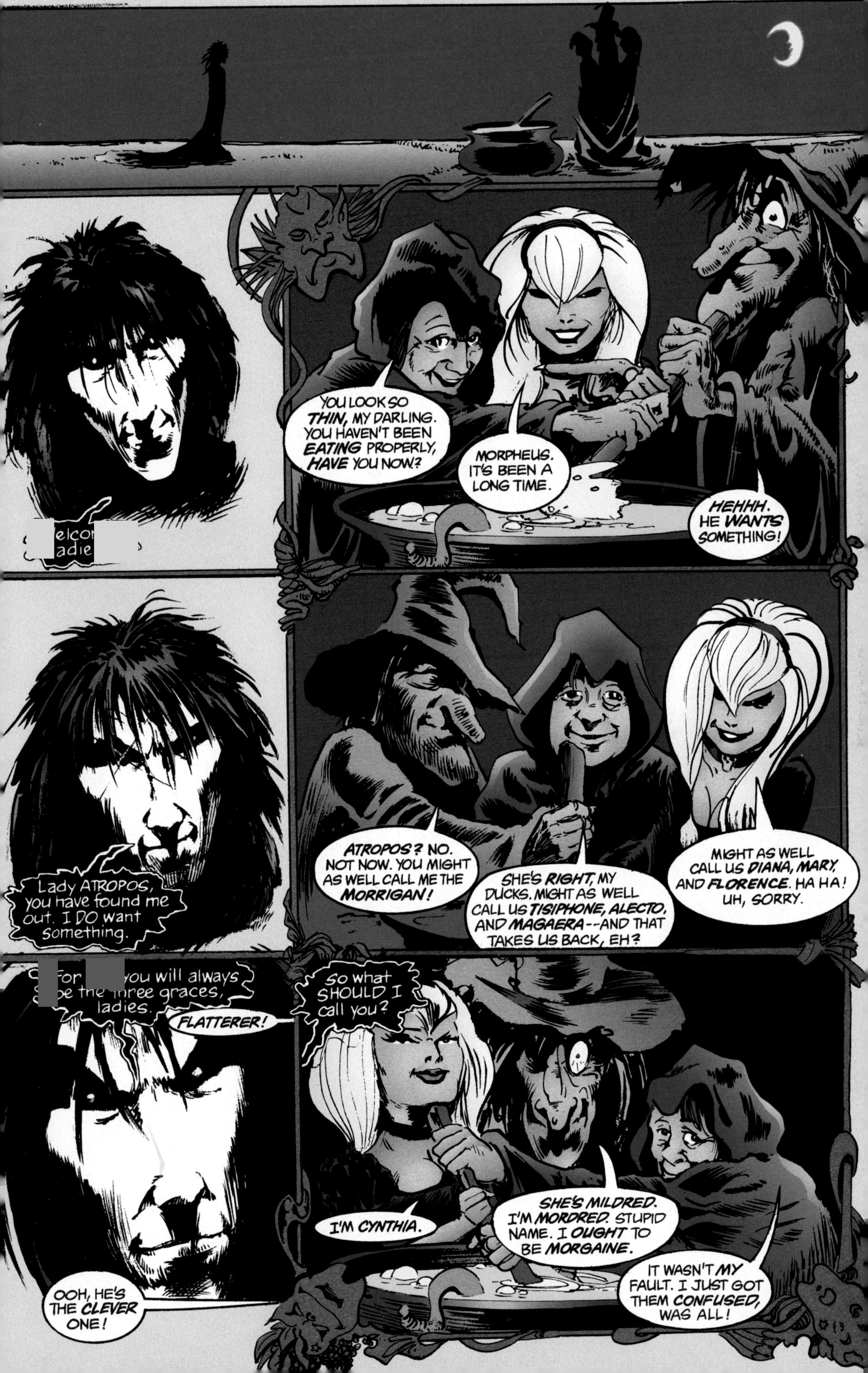

[redacted]elcom[redacted]
[redacted]adie[redacted]
YOU LOOK SO THIN, MY DARLING. YOU HAVEN'T BEEN EATING PROPERLY, HAVE YOU NOW?
MORPHEUS. IT'S BEEN A LONG TIME.
HEHHH. HE WANTS SOMETHING!
Lady ATROPOS, you have found me out. I DO want something.
ATROPOS? NO. NOT NOW. YOU MIGHT AS WELL CALL ME THE MORRIGAN!
SHE'S RIGHT, MY DUCKS. MIGHT AS WELL CALL US TISIPHONE, ALECTO, AND MAGAERA--AND THAT TAKES US BACK, EH?
MIGHT AS WELL CALL US DIANA, MARY, AND FLORENCE. HA HA! UH, SORRY.
[redacted]For[redacted]you will always [redacted]be the three graces, ladies.
FLATTERER!
So what SHOULD I call you?
I'M CYNTHIA.
SHE'S MILDRED. I'M MORDRED. STUPID NAME. I OUGHT TO BE MORGAINE.
IT WASN'T MY FAULT. I JUST GOT THEM CONFUSED, WAS ALL!
OOH, HE'S THE CLEVER ONE!

"MA[...], there was a POUCH of SAND. It was stolen from me."

"I SEE. Then you question, ALL-MOTH[...] My HELM -- what happened to it?"

"CRONE. A final question for you My STONE, my DREAMSTONE, my RUBY MOONSTONE. Who has THAT now?"

"TRADED WITH A DEMON, my DOVE, MANY YEARS AGO. LONG GONE FROM THE MORTAL PLANE."

"HEE! YOUR GEM PASSED THROUGH A MOTHER TO A SON WHO TAPPED ITS DREAM MAGICKS FOR HIS OWN ENDS...

"UNTIL IT--AND HIS DREAMS-- WERE TAKEN AWAY FROM HIM, BY THE SUPERHUMANS.

"ASK THE LEAGUE OF JUSTICE ABOUT ITS PRESENT WHEREABOUTS."

"AN ENGLISHMAN, JOHN CONSTANTINE. HE WAS THE LAST TO PURCHASE YOUR POUCH."

"WHICH demon?"

"He has it STILL?"

"ONE QUESTION, my HONEYSUCKLE, and ONE ANSWER."

"ONE QUESTION, ONE ANSWER. THE RULES, MY LORD."

"But where--? No, one answer only I know...."

"Thank you, weird sisters."

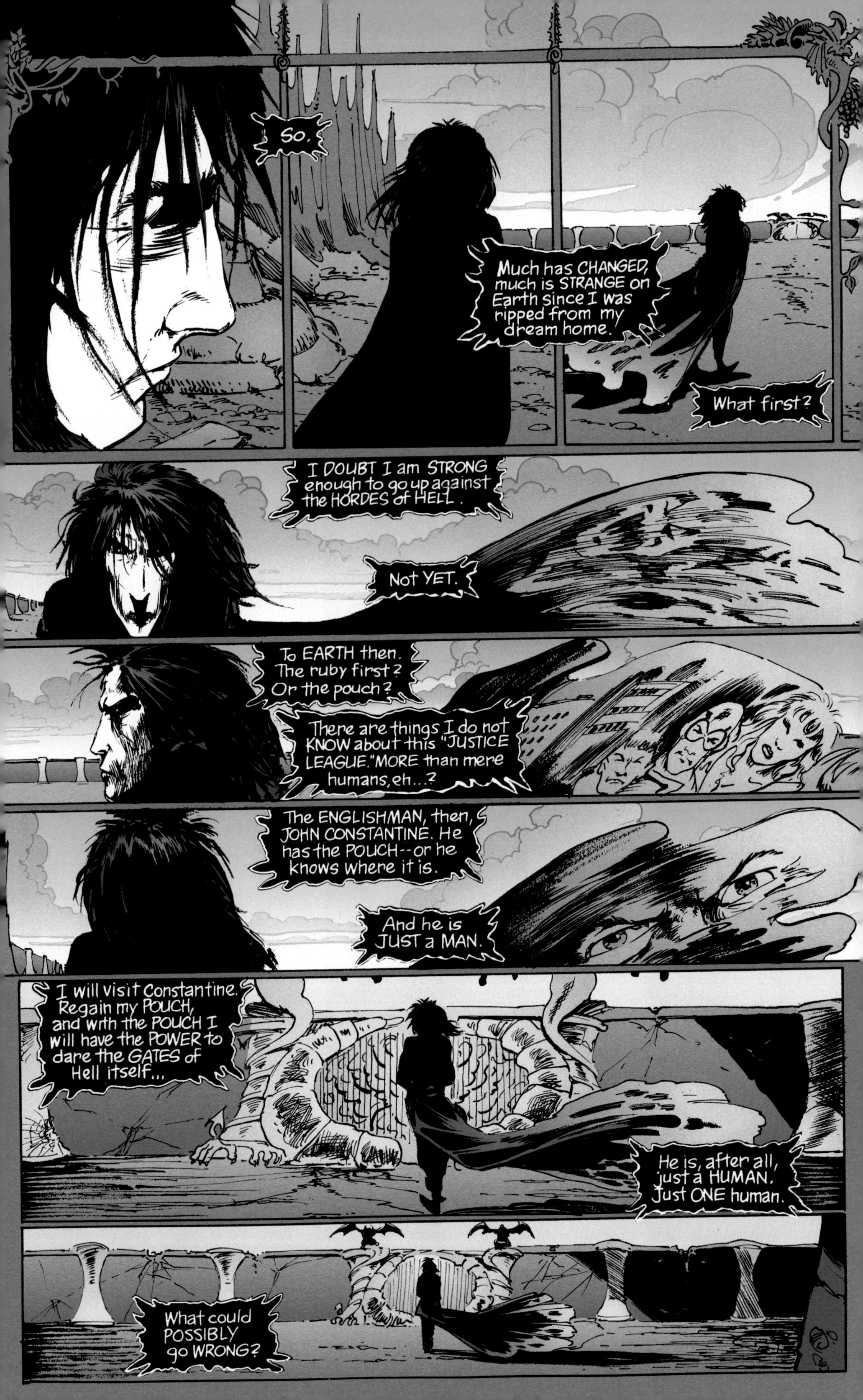
So.
Much has CHANGED, much is STRANGE on Earth since I was ripped from my dream home.
What first?
I DOUBT I am STRONG enough to go up against the HORDES of HELL.
Not YET.
To EARTH then. The ruby first? Or the pouch?
There are things I do not KNOW about this "JUSTICE LEAGUE." MORE than mere humans, eh...?
The ENGLISHMAN, then, JOHN CONSTANTINE. He has the POUCH--or he knows where it is.
And he is JUST a MAN.
I will visit Constantine. Regain my POUCH, and with the POUCH I will have the POWER to dare the GATES of Hell itself...
He is, after all, just a HUMAN. Just ONE human.
What could POSSIBLY go WRONG?

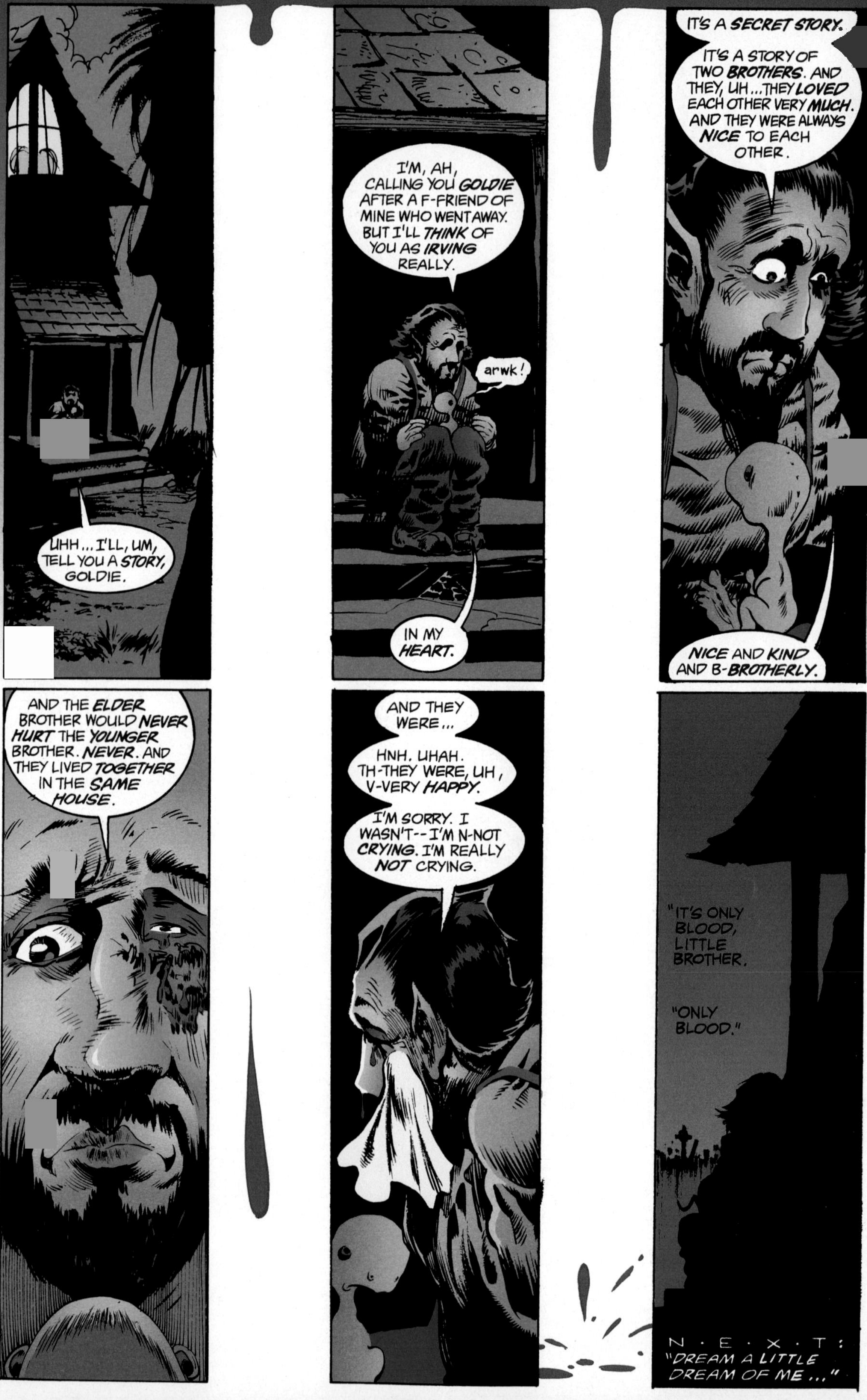
UHH... I'LL, UM, TELL YOU A STORY, GOLDIE.
I'M, AH, CALLING YOU GOLDIE AFTER A F-FRIEND OF MINE WHO WENT AWAY. BUT I'LL THINK OF YOU AS IRVING REALLY.
arwk!
IN MY HEART.
IT'S A SECRET STORY.
IT'S A STORY OF TWO BROTHERS. AND THEY, UH... THEY LOVED EACH OTHER VERY MUCH. AND THEY WERE ALWAYS NICE TO EACH OTHER.
NICE AND KIND AND B-BROTHERLY.
AND THE ELDER BROTHER WOULD NEVER HURT THE YOUNGER BROTHER. NEVER. AND THEY LIVED TOGETHER IN THE SAME HOUSE.
AND THEY WERE...
HNH. UHAH. TH-THEY WERE, UH, V-VERY HAPPY.
I'M SORRY. I WASN'T--I'M N-NOT CRYING. I'M REALLY NOT CRYING.
"IT'S ONLY BLOOD, LITTLE BROTHER.
"ONLY BLOOD."
N · E · X · T: "DREAM A LITTLE DREAM OF ME..."

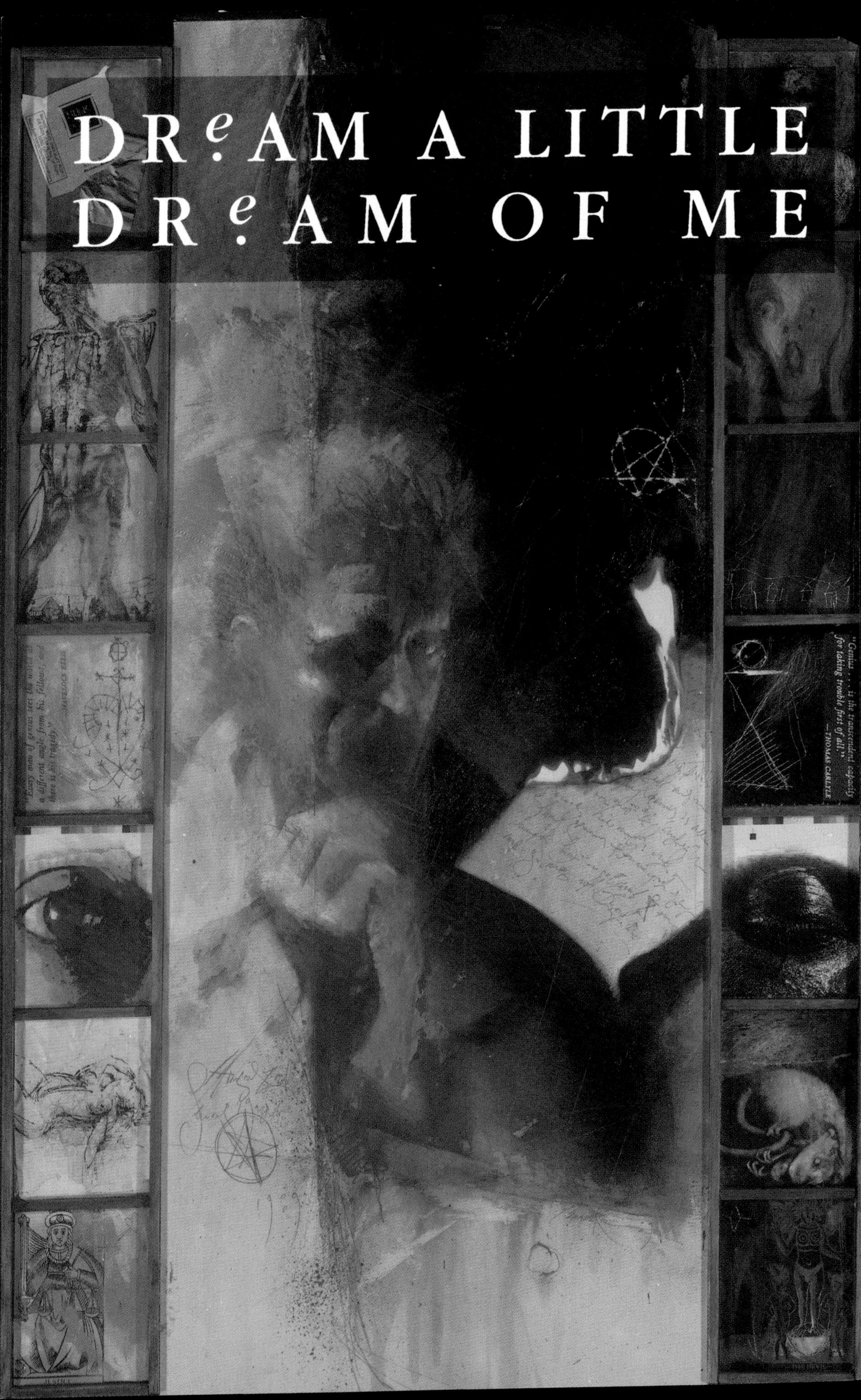
DREAM A LITTLE
DREAM OF ME
"Genius . . . is the transcendent capacity for taking trouble first of all."
—THOMAS CARLYLE

ONE. TWO. THREE. FOUR...

HER *NIPPLES* ARE HARD AND DARK AND SHRUNKEN ON BREASTS LIKE EMPTY POUCHES.

HER *HAIR* COMES OUT IN *CLUMPS* WHEN SHE MOVES. SHE *TRIES* NOT TO MOVE TOO MUCH.

HER *SKIN* IS FLAKING, INFECTED AND INFLAMED. *BEDSORES* COVER HER *BACK* AND LEGS.

TWENTY-EIGHT. TWENTY-NINE. THIRTY...

RADIO 1

ZAPPA

HER FINGERNAILS GREW LONG AND BRITTLE; THEN THEY BROKE OFF. THE RAGGED NAILS RIP HER SKIN WHEN SHE *SCRATCHES*.

HER STOMACH *SHRANK*, THEN *BLOATED*. THEN IT *SHRANK* AGAIN. HUNGER SUBSIDED TO A LOW *NAGGING* IN THE BACK OF HER MIND.

IT'S *OK*. IT GOES AWAY.

LIKE THE *PAIN* GOES AWAY. LIKE *EVERYTHING* GOES AWAY WHEN THE *DREAMS* COME.

...SHE FEELS *REALITY* EBBING *BACK*.

DELAY THE *PLEASURE*.

DELAY THE *DREAMS*.

WILL SHE *DISSOLVE* IT IN HER MOUTH? *BREATHE* IT? *RUB* IT INTO HER *SKIN*?

NINETY-SIX. NINETY-SEVEN. NINETY-EIGHT...

SIXTY-FIVE. SIXTY-SIX...

SHE'LL *WAIT*.

IT *DOESN'T MATTER*.

SHE'S *COUNTING* TO A *HUNDRED*.

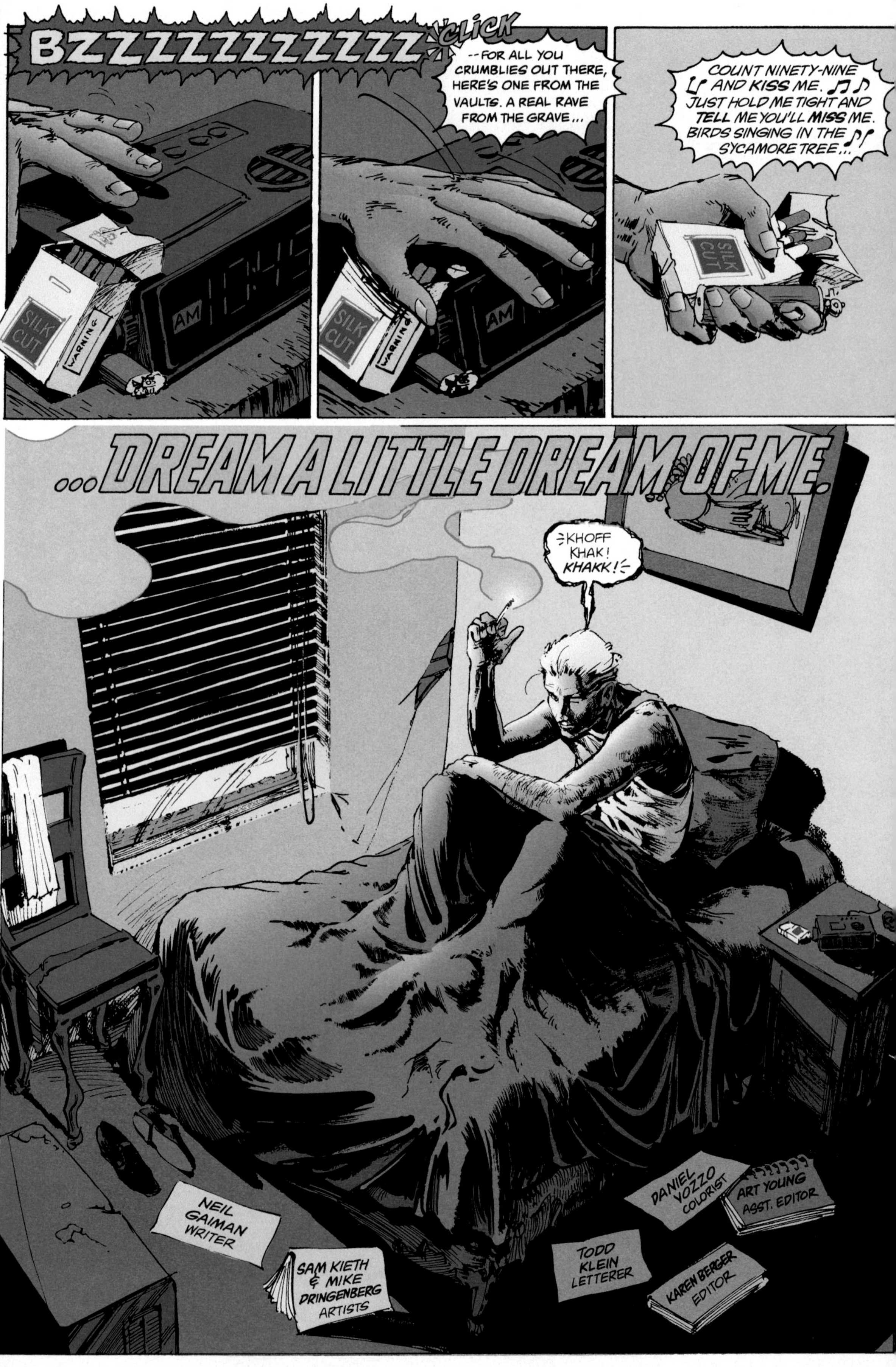
BZZZZZZZZZZZZ
CLICK
--FOR ALL YOU CRUMBLIES OUT THERE, HERE'S ONE FROM THE VAULTS. A REAL RAVE FROM THE GRAVE...
SILK CUT
WARNING
AM
COUNT NINETY-NINE AND KISS ME. JUST HOLD ME TIGHT AND TELL ME YOU'LL MISS ME. BIRDS SINGING IN THE SYCAMORE TREE...
...DREAM A LITTLE DREAM OF ME.
KHOFF KHAK! KHAKK!
NEIL GAIMAN WRITER
SAM KIETH & MIKE DRINGENBERG ARTISTS
DANIEL VOZZO COLORIST
ART YOUNG ASST. EDITOR
TODD KLEIN LETTERER
KAREN BERGER EDITOR

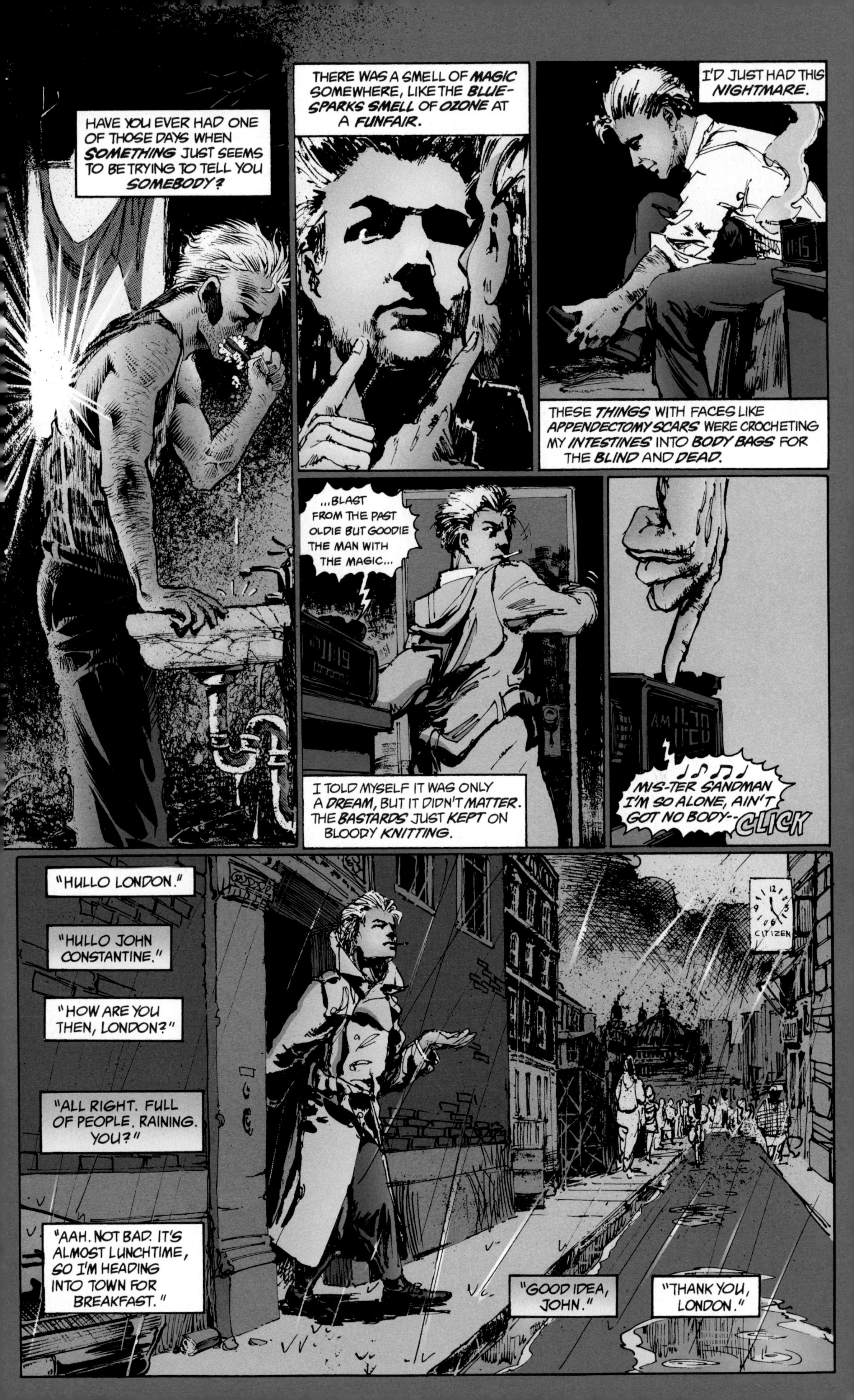

HAVE YOU EVER HAD ONE OF THOSE DAYS WHEN SOMETHING JUST SEEMS TO BE TRYING TO TELL YOU SOMEBODY?
THERE WAS A SMELL OF MAGIC SOMEWHERE, LIKE THE BLUE-SPARKS SMELL OF OZONE AT A FUNFAIR.
I'D JUST HAD THIS NIGHTMARE.
THESE THINGS WITH FACES LIKE APPENDECTOMY SCARS WERE CROCHETING MY INTESTINES INTO BODY BAGS FOR THE BLIND AND DEAD.
...BLAST FROM THE PAST OLDIE BUT GOODIE THE MAN WITH THE MAGIC...
I TOLD MYSELF IT WAS ONLY A DREAM, BUT IT DIDN'T MATTER. THE BASTARDS JUST KEPT ON BLOODY KNITTING.
AM 11:20
MIS-TER SANDMAN I'M SO ALONE, AIN'T GOT NO BODY--
CLICK
"HULLO LONDON."
"HULLO JOHN CONSTANTINE."
"HOW ARE YOU THEN, LONDON?"
"ALL RIGHT. FULL OF PEOPLE. RAINING. YOU?"
"AAH. NOT BAD. IT'S ALMOST LUNCHTIME, SO I'M HEADING INTO TOWN FOR BREAKFAST."
"GOOD IDEA, JOHN."
"THANK YOU, LONDON."
CITIZEN

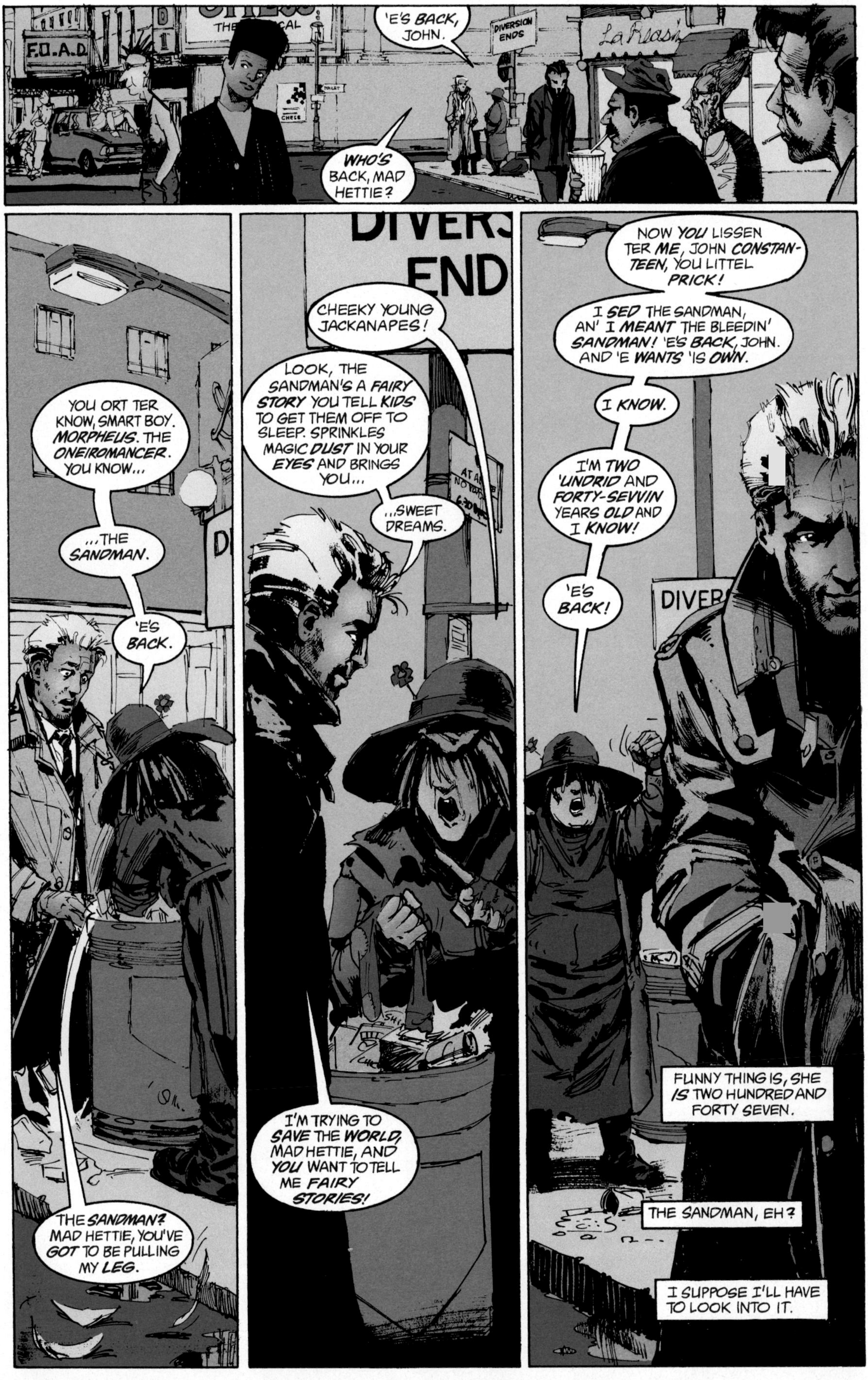

'E'S BACK, JOHN.
DIVERSION ENDS
WHO'S BACK, MAD HETTIE?
YOU ORT TER KNOW, SMART BOY. MORPHEUS. THE ONEIROMANCER. YOU KNOW...
...THE SANDMAN.
'E'S BACK.
THE SANDMAN? MAD HETTIE, YOU'VE GOT TO BE PULLING MY LEG.
CHEEKY YOUNG JACKANAPES!
LOOK, THE SANDMAN'S A FAIRY STORY YOU TELL KIDS TO GET THEM OFF TO SLEEP. SPRINKLES MAGIC DUST IN YOUR EYES AND BRINGS YOU...
...SWEET DREAMS.
I'M TRYING TO SAVE THE WORLD, MAD HETTIE, AND YOU WANT TO TELL ME FAIRY STORIES!
NOW YOU LISSEN TER ME, JOHN CONSTAN-TEEN, YOU LITTEL PRICK!
I SED THE SANDMAN, AN' I MEANT THE BLEEDIN' SANDMAN! 'E'S BACK, JOHN. AND 'E WANTS 'IS OWN.
I KNOW.
I'M TWO 'UNDRID AND FORTY-SEVVIN YEARS OLD AND I KNOW!
'E'S BACK!
FUNNY THING IS, SHE IS TWO HUNDRED AND FORTY SEVEN.
THE SANDMAN, EH?
I SUPPOSE I'LL HAVE TO LOOK INTO IT.

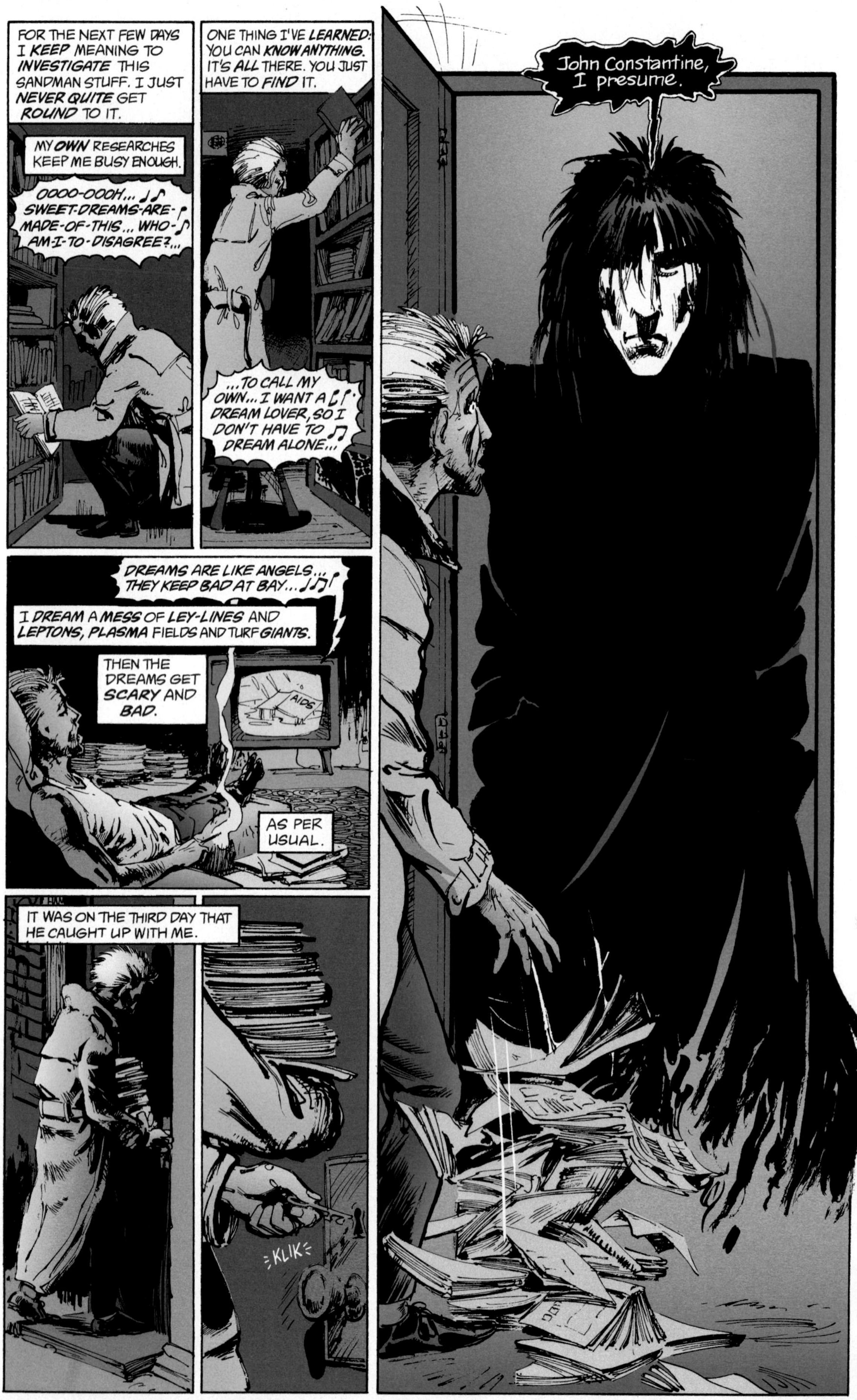

FOR THE NEXT FEW DAYS I KEEP MEANING TO INVESTIGATE THIS SANDMAN STUFF. I JUST NEVER QUITE GET ROUND TO IT.
MY OWN RESEARCHES KEEP ME BUSY ENOUGH.
OOOO-OOOH... SWEET-DREAMS-ARE-MADE-OF-THIS... WHO-AM-I-TO-DISAGREE?...
ONE THING I'VE LEARNED: YOU CAN KNOW ANYTHING. IT'S ALL THERE. YOU JUST HAVE TO FIND IT.
...TO CALL MY OWN... I WANT A DREAM LOVER, SO I DON'T HAVE TO DREAM ALONE...
DREAMS ARE LIKE ANGELS... THEY KEEP BAD AT BAY...
I DREAM A MESS OF LEY-LINES AND LEPTONS, PLASMA FIELDS AND TURF GIANTS.
THEN THE DREAMS GET SCARY AND BAD.
AIDS
AS PER USUAL.
IT WAS ON THE THIRD DAY THAT HE CAUGHT UP WITH ME.
KLIK
John Constantine, I presume.

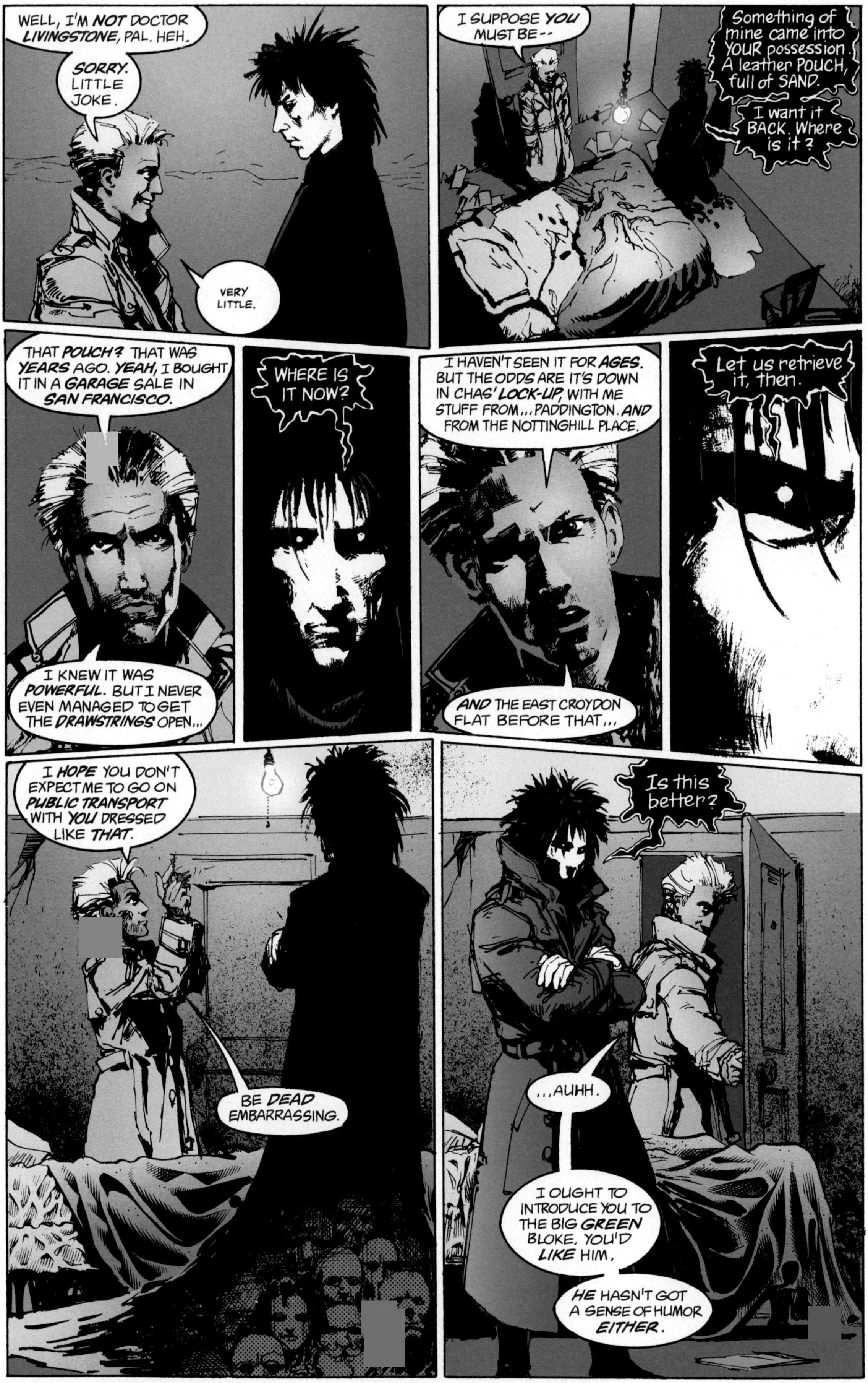
WELL, I'M NOT DOCTOR LIVINGSTONE, PAL. HEH.
SORRY. LITTLE JOKE.
VERY LITTLE.
I SUPPOSE YOU MUST BE--
Something of mine came into YOUR possession. A leather POUCH, full of SAND.
I want it BACK. Where is it?
THAT POUCH? THAT WAS YEARS AGO. YEAH, I BOUGHT IT IN A GARAGE SALE IN SAN FRANCISCO.
I KNEW IT WAS POWERFUL. BUT I NEVER EVEN MANAGED TO GET THE DRAWSTRINGS OPEN...
WHERE IS IT NOW?
I HAVEN'T SEEN IT FOR AGES. BUT THE ODDS ARE IT'S DOWN IN CHAS' LOCK-UP, WITH ME STUFF FROM... PADDINGTON. AND FROM THE NOTTINGHILL PLACE.
AND THE EAST CROYDON FLAT BEFORE THAT...
Let us retrieve it, then.
I HOPE YOU DON'T EXPECT ME TO GO ON PUBLIC TRANSPORT WITH YOU DRESSED LIKE THAT.
BE DEAD EMBARRASSING.
Is this better?
...AUHH.
I OUGHT TO INTRODUCE YOU TO THE BIG GREEN BLOKE. YOU'D LIKE HIM.
HE HASN'T GOT A SENSE OF HUMOR EITHER.

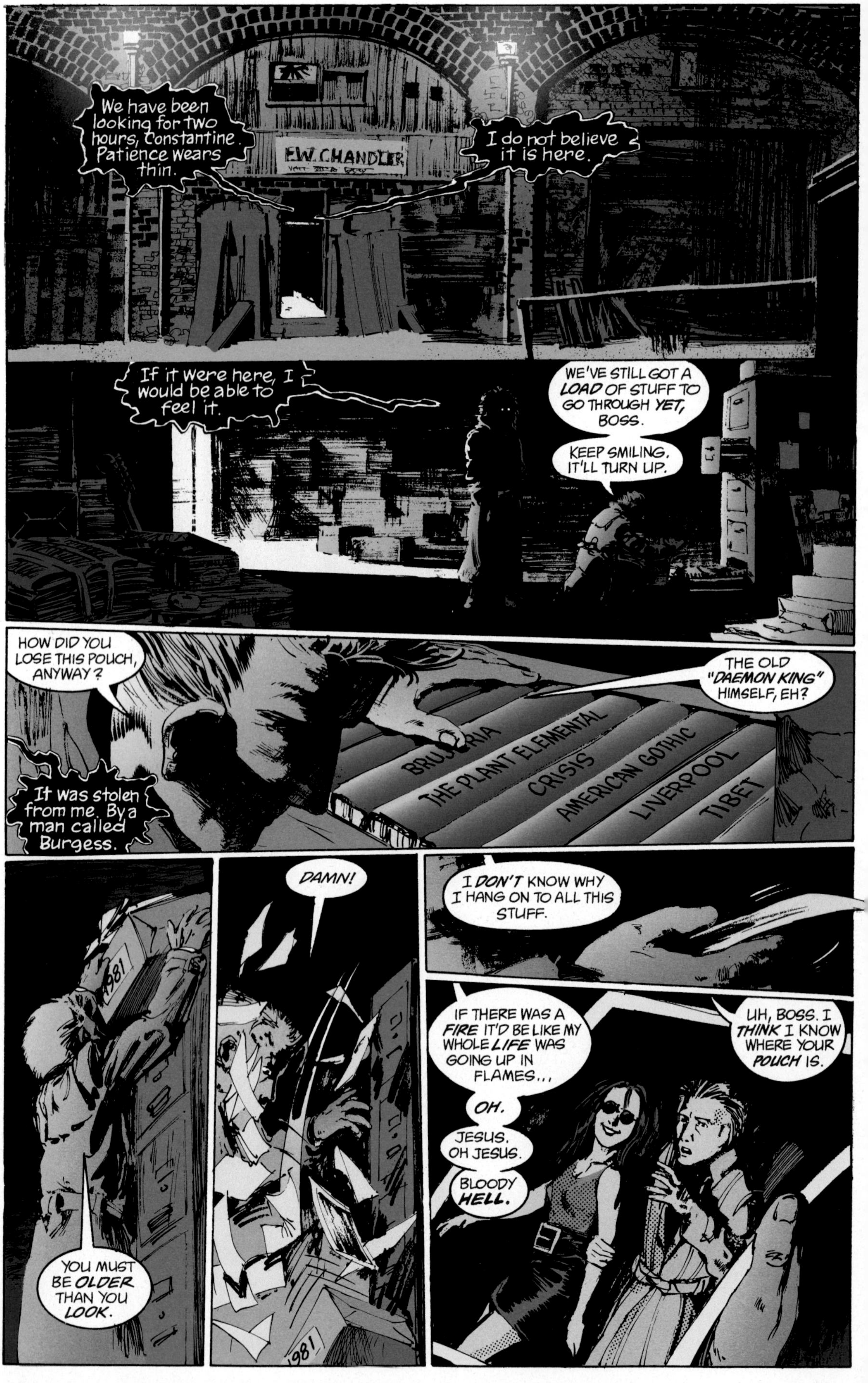

F.W. CHANDLER
We have been looking for two hours, Constantine. Patience wears thin.
I do not believe it is here.
If it were here, I would be able to feel it.
WE'VE STILL GOT A LOAD OF STUFF TO GO THROUGH YET, BOSS.
KEEP SMILING. IT'LL TURN UP.
HOW DID YOU LOSE THIS POUCH, ANYWAY?
It was stolen from me. By a man called Burgess.
THE OLD "DAEMON KING" HIMSELF, EH?
BRUJERIA
THE PLANT ELEMENTAL
CRISIS
AMERICAN GOTHIC
LIVERPOOL
TIBET
1981
YOU MUST BE OLDER THAN YOU LOOK.
DAMN!
1981
I DON'T KNOW WHY I HANG ON TO ALL THIS STUFF.
IF THERE WAS A FIRE IT'D BE LIKE MY WHOLE LIFE WAS GOING UP IN FLAMES...
UH, BOSS. I THINK I KNOW WHERE YOUR POUCH IS.
OH.
JESUS. OH JESUS.
BLOODY HELL.

RACHEL WAS *ALWAYS* PLAYING WITH THE *POUCH*. KEPT GOING ON AT ME TO TRY TO OPEN IT.

SHE'D ASK ME, WHAT'S THE POINT OF *HAVING* SOMETHING *MAGIC* IF YOU DON'T *USE* IT?

I KNEW THE *ANSWER*. BUT I KNEW SHE'D *NEVER* UNDERSTAND.

WELL, THERE'S NO *ANSWER*. AND IT'S *LOCKED, BOLTED* AND *ALARMED*.

LET'S GO ROUND THE *BACK*, WE CAN *SMASH* A WINDOW, GET IN *THAT* WAY...

No.

We go in by the FRONT door.

KREEK

IT SMELLS *STRANGE*. PART OF IT REMINDS ME OF THE MONTH I WORKED FOR AN *UNDERTAKER*; ALL *FLESH* AND *FORMALDEHYDE*.

'S *WEIRD*: SMELLS ARE A HOTLINE TO *MEMORY*.

NAW, I'LL STICK AROUND. I'M INTRIGUED.

ANYWAY, I WAS *FOND* OF RACHEL ONCE. SHE WAS, YOU KNOW, THE *GIRL* OF MY *DREAMS*.

Constantine... This place is not SAFE for you.

Things are free in this house that should NOT be loose on Earth.

not stay here.

FOR A *WHILE*.

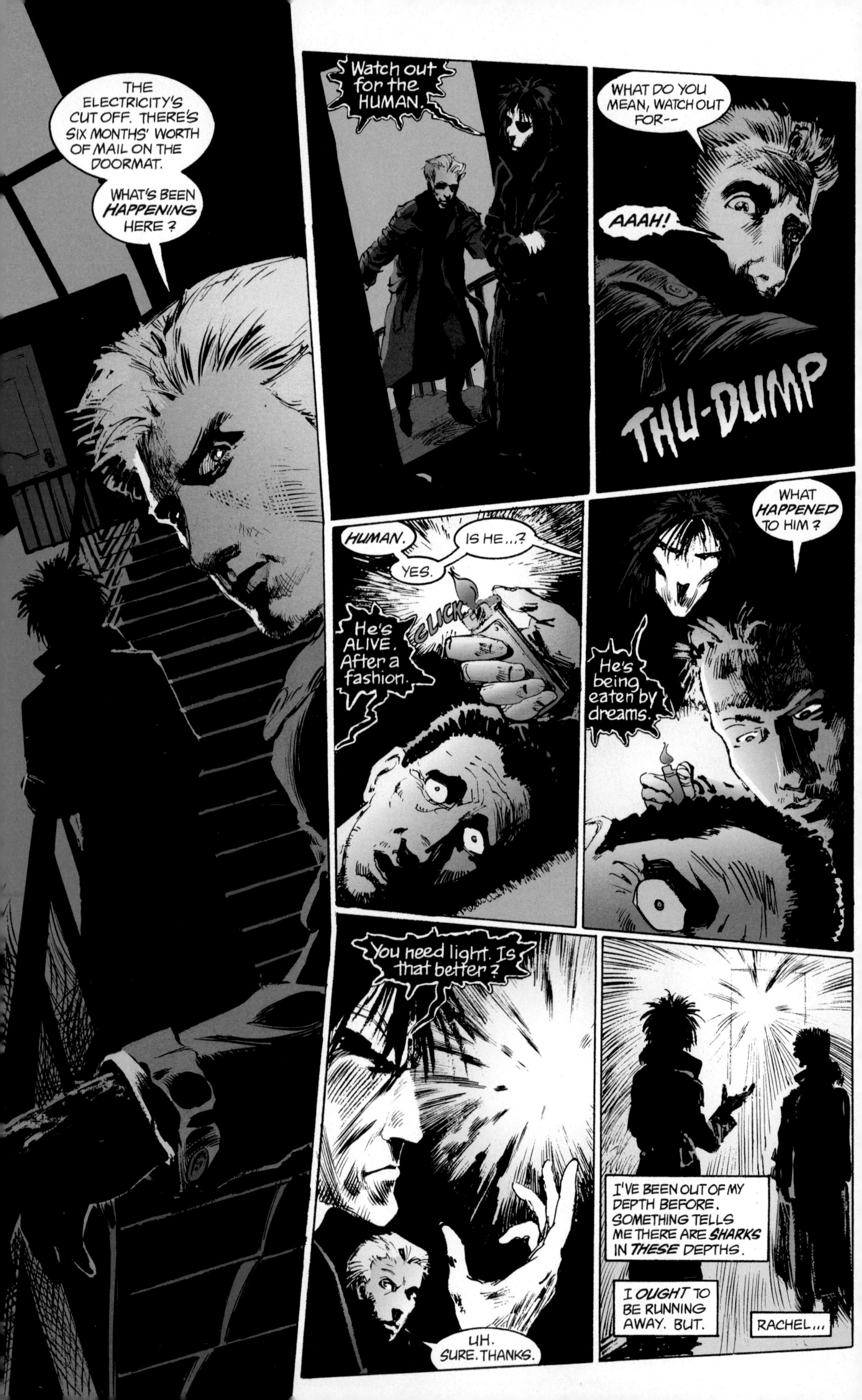
THE ELECTRICITY'S CUT OFF. THERE'S SIX MONTHS' WORTH OF MAIL ON THE DOORMAT.
WHAT'S BEEN *HAPPENING* HERE?
Watch out for the HUMAN.
WHAT DO YOU MEAN, WATCH OUT FOR--
AAAH!
THU-DUMP
HUMAN.
IS HE...?
YES.
CLICK
He's ALIVE. After a fashion.
WHAT *HAPPENED* TO HIM?
He's being eaten by dreams.
You need light. Is that better?
UH. SURE. THANKS.
I'VE BEEN OUT OF MY DEPTH BEFORE. SOMETHING TELLS ME THERE ARE *SHARKS* IN *THESE* DEPTHS.
I *OUGHT* TO BE RUNNING AWAY. BUT.
RACHEL...

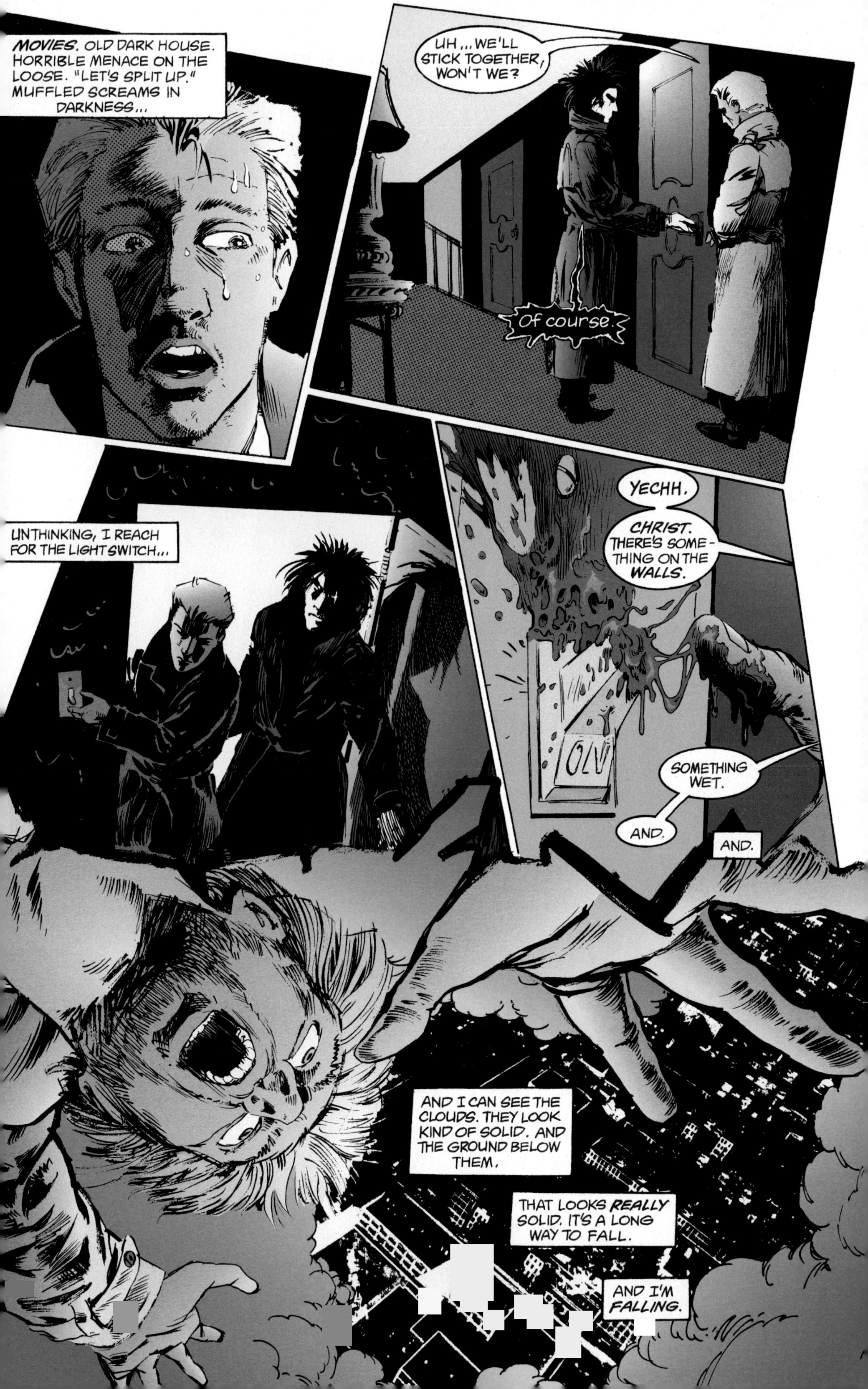
MOVIES. OLD DARK HOUSE. HORRIBLE MENACE ON THE LOOSE. "LET'S SPLIT UP." MUFFLED SCREAMS IN DARKNESS...
UH...WE'LL STICK TOGETHER, WON'T WE?
Of course.
UNTHINKING, I REACH FOR THE LIGHTSWITCH...
YECHH.
CHRIST. THERE'S SOMETHING ON THE WALLS.
SOMETHING WET.
AND.
AND.
AND I CAN SEE THE CLOUDS. THEY LOOK KIND OF SOLID. AND THE GROUND BELOW THEM.
THAT LOOKS REALLY SOLID. IT'S A LONG WAY TO FALL.
AND I'M FALLING.

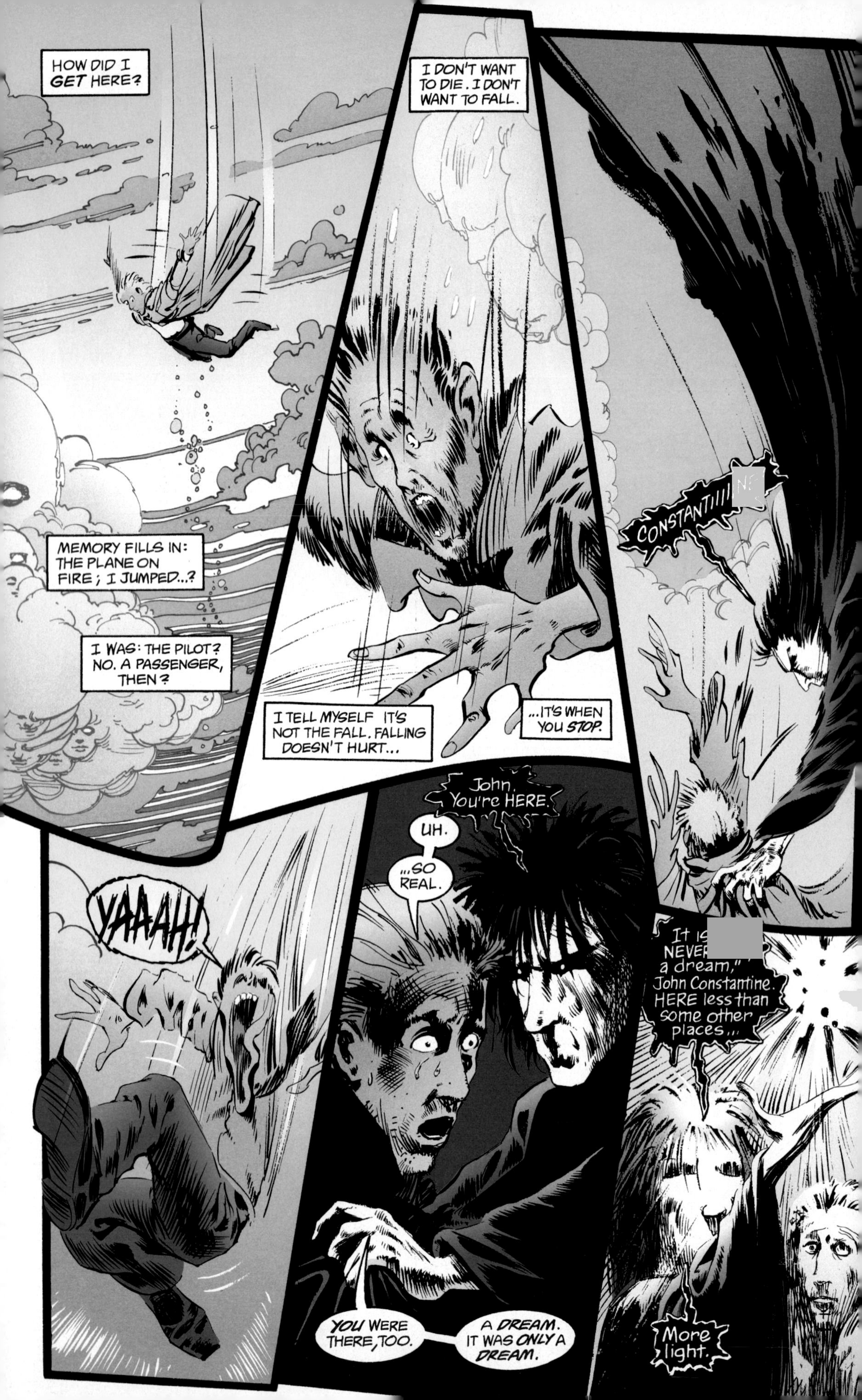

HOW DID I GET HERE?
I DON'T WANT TO DIE. I DON'T WANT TO FALL.
MEMORY FILLS IN: THE PLANE ON FIRE; I JUMPED...?
I WAS: THE PILOT? NO. A PASSENGER, THEN?
I TELL MYSELF IT'S NOT THE FALL. FALLING DOESN'T HURT...
...IT'S WHEN YOU STOP.
CONSTANT!!!!!
YAAAH!
John. You're HERE.
UH.
...SO REAL.
YOU WERE THERE, TOO.
A DREAM. IT WAS ONLY A DREAM.
It i
NEVE
a dream," John Constantine. HERE less than some other places...
More light.

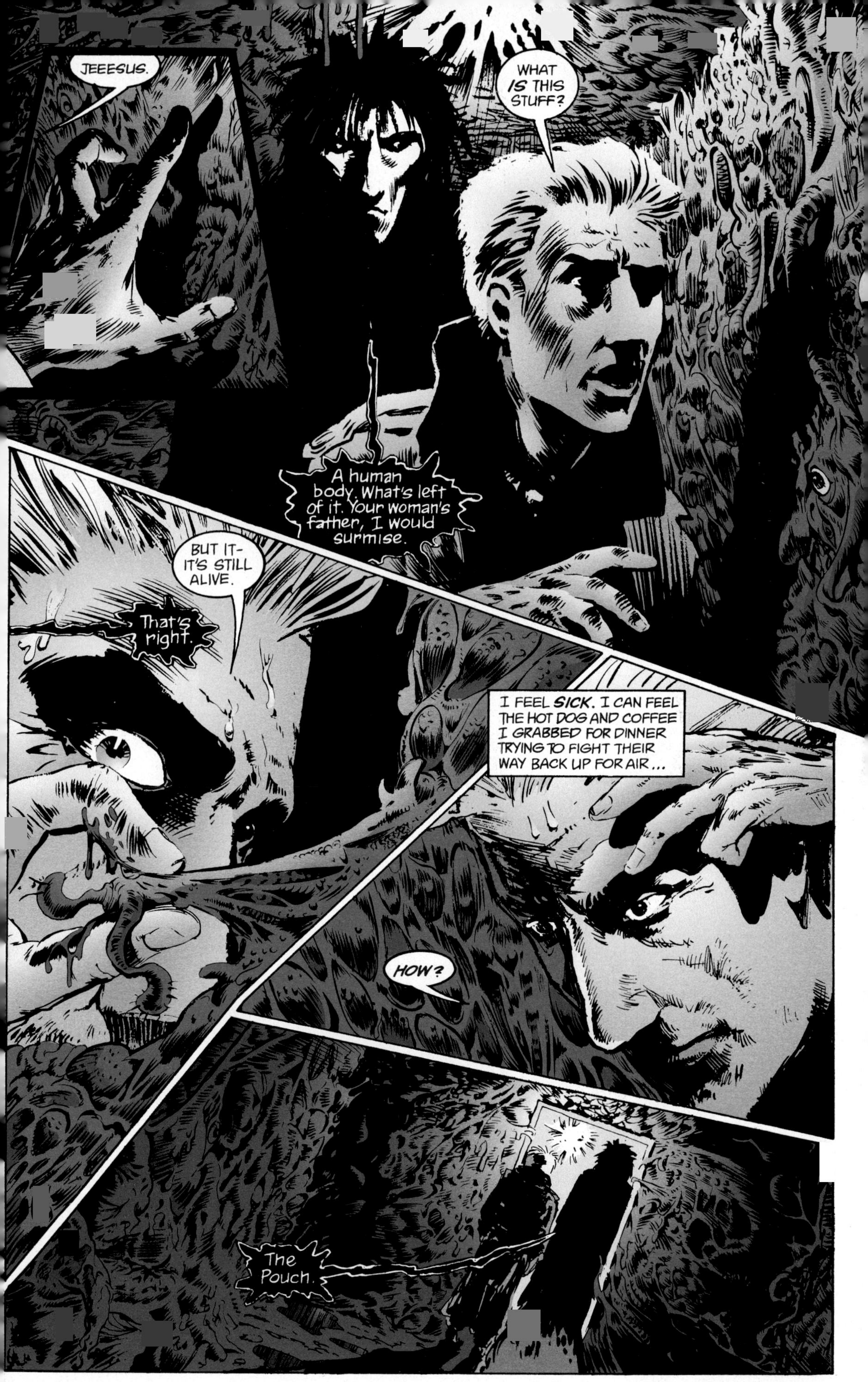
JEEESUS.
WHAT IS THIS STUFF?
A human body. What's left of it. Your woman's father, I would surmise.
BUT IT- IT'S STILL ALIVE.
That's right.
I FEEL SICK. I CAN FEEL THE HOT DOG AND COFFEE I GRABBED FOR DINNER TRYING TO FIGHT THEIR WAY BACK UP FOR AIR...
HOW?
The Pouch.

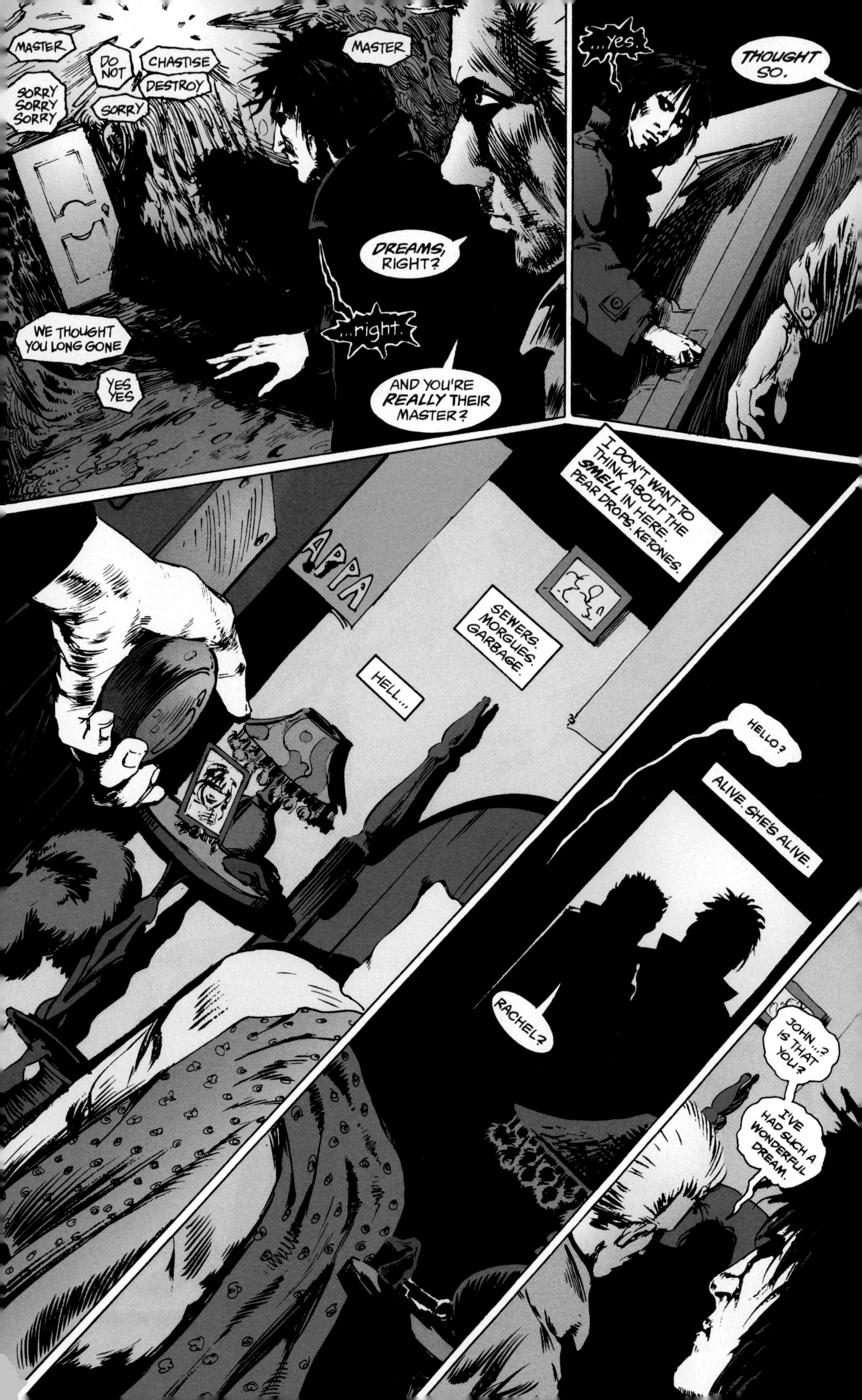
MASTER
DO NOT
CHASTISE
DESTROY
SORRY SORRY SORRY
SORRY
MASTER
DREAMS, RIGHT?
...right.
WE THOUGHT YOU LONG GONE
YES YES
AND YOU'RE REALLY THEIR MASTER?
...yes.
THOUGHT SO.
I DON'T WANT TO THINK ABOUT THE SMELL IN HERE. PEAR DROPS. KETONES.
SEWERS. MORGUES. GARBAGE.
HELL...
HELLO?
ALIVE. SHE'S ALIVE.
RACHEL?
JOHN...? IS THAT YOU?
I'VE HAD SUCH A WONDERFUL DREAM.

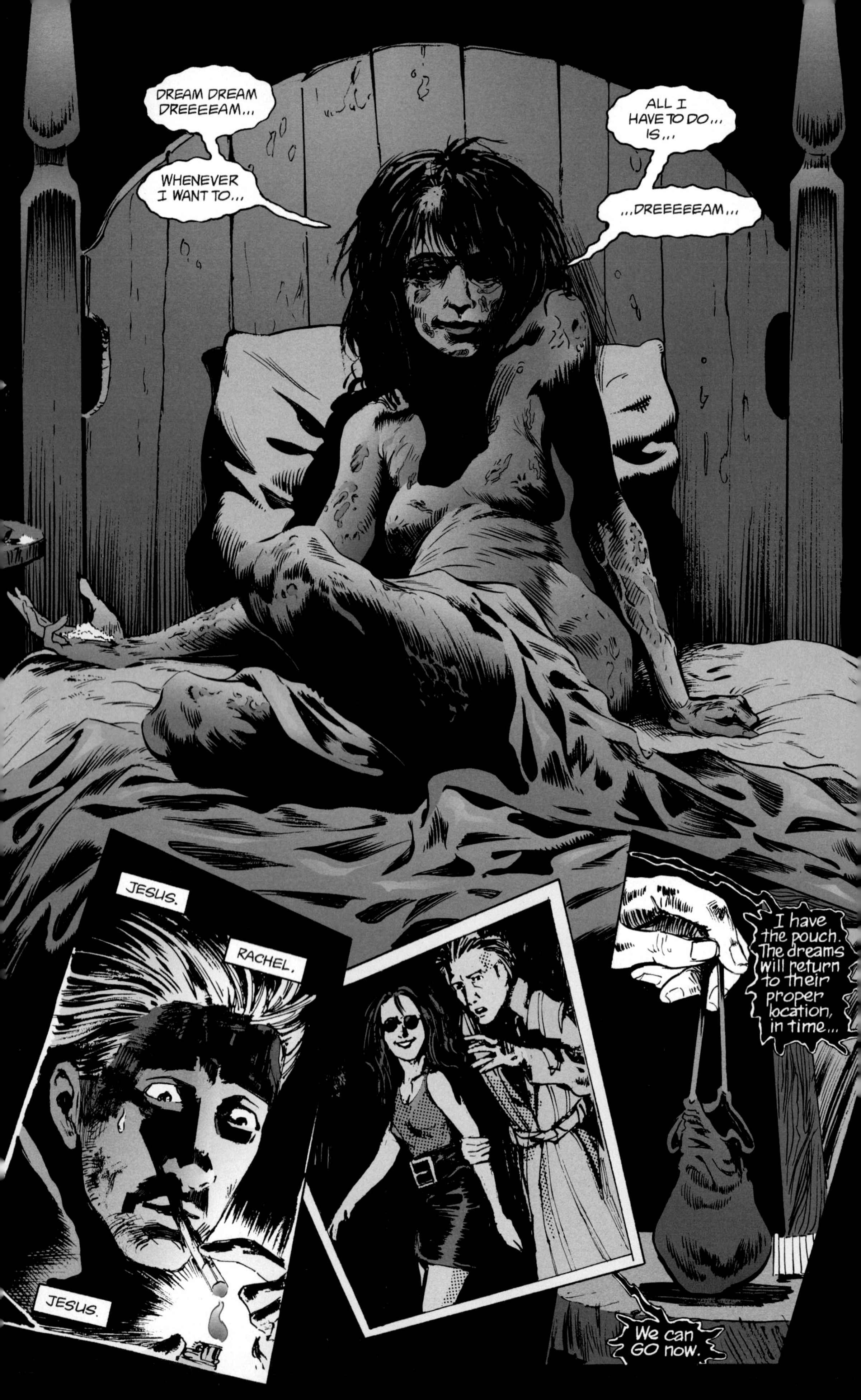
DREAM DREAM DREEEEAM...
WHENEVER I WANT TO...
ALL I HAVE TO DO... IS...
...DREEEEEAM...
JESUS.
RACHEL.
JESUS.
I have the pouch. The dreams will return to their proper location, in time...
We can GO now.

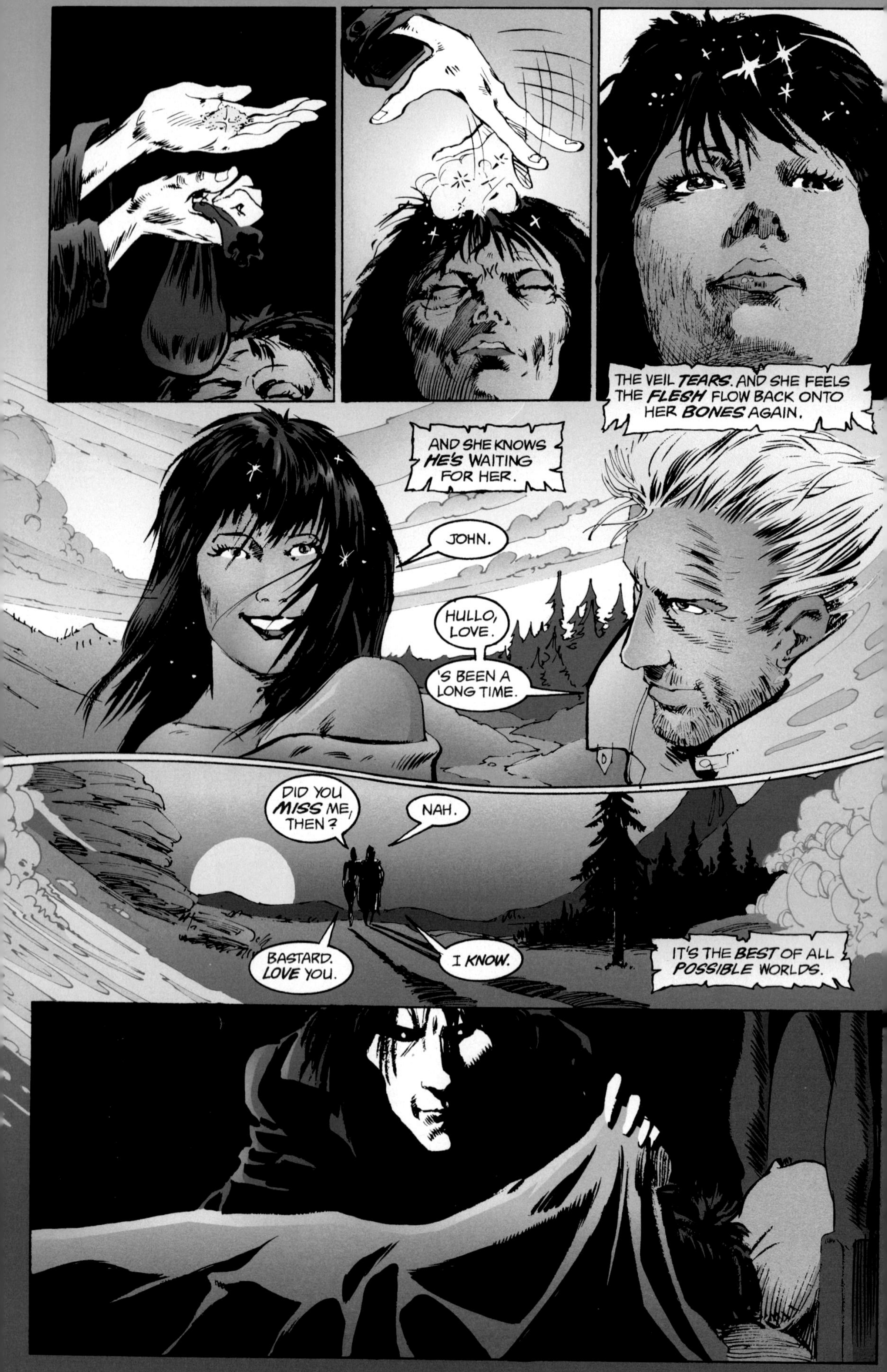
THE VEIL TEARS. AND SHE FEELS THE FLESH FLOW BACK ONTO HER BONES AGAIN.
AND SHE KNOWS HE'S WAITING FOR HER.
JOHN.
HULLO, LOVE.
'S BEEN A LONG TIME.
DID YOU MISS ME, THEN?
NAH.
BASTARD. LOVE YOU.
I KNOW.
IT'S THE BEST OF ALL POSSIBLE WORLDS.

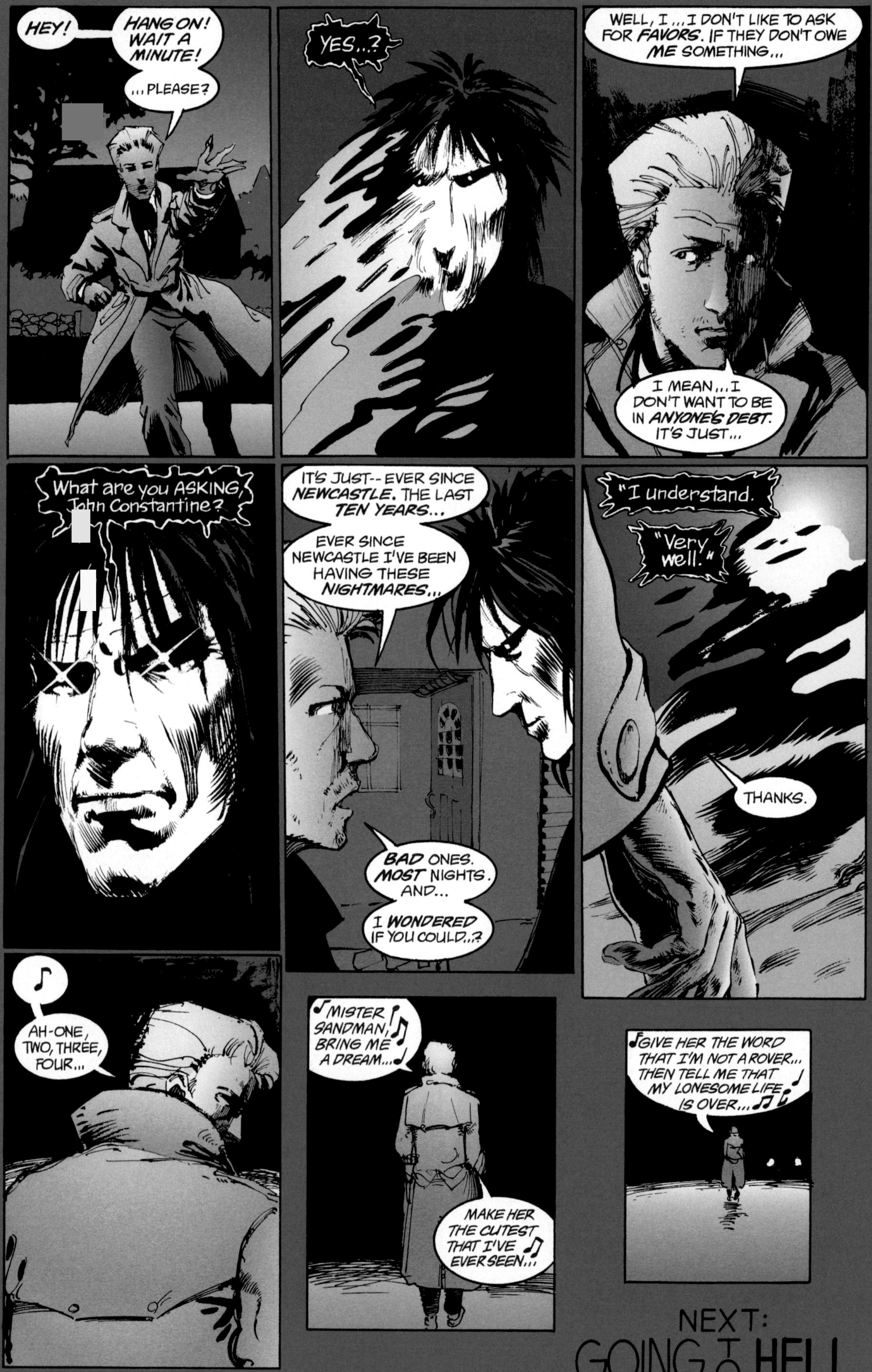
HEY!
HANG ON! WAIT A MINUTE!
...PLEASE?
YES...?
WELL, I...I DON'T LIKE TO ASK FOR FAVORS. IF THEY DON'T OWE ME SOMETHING...
I MEAN...I DON'T WANT TO BE IN ANYONE'S DEBT. IT'S JUST...
What are you ASKING, John Constantine?
IT'S JUST-- EVER SINCE NEWCASTLE. THE LAST TEN YEARS...
EVER SINCE NEWCASTLE I'VE BEEN HAVING THESE NIGHTMARES...
BAD ONES. MOST NIGHTS. AND...
I WONDERED IF YOU COULD...?
"I understand.
"Very well."
THANKS.
♪
AH-ONE, TWO, THREE, FOUR...
♪MISTER SANDMAN, BRING ME A DREAM...♪
MAKE HER THE CUTEST THAT I'VE EVER SEEN...♪
♪GIVE HER THE WORD THAT I'M NOT A ROVER... THEN TELL ME THAT MY LONESOME LIFE IS OVER...♪
NEXT:
GOING TO HELL

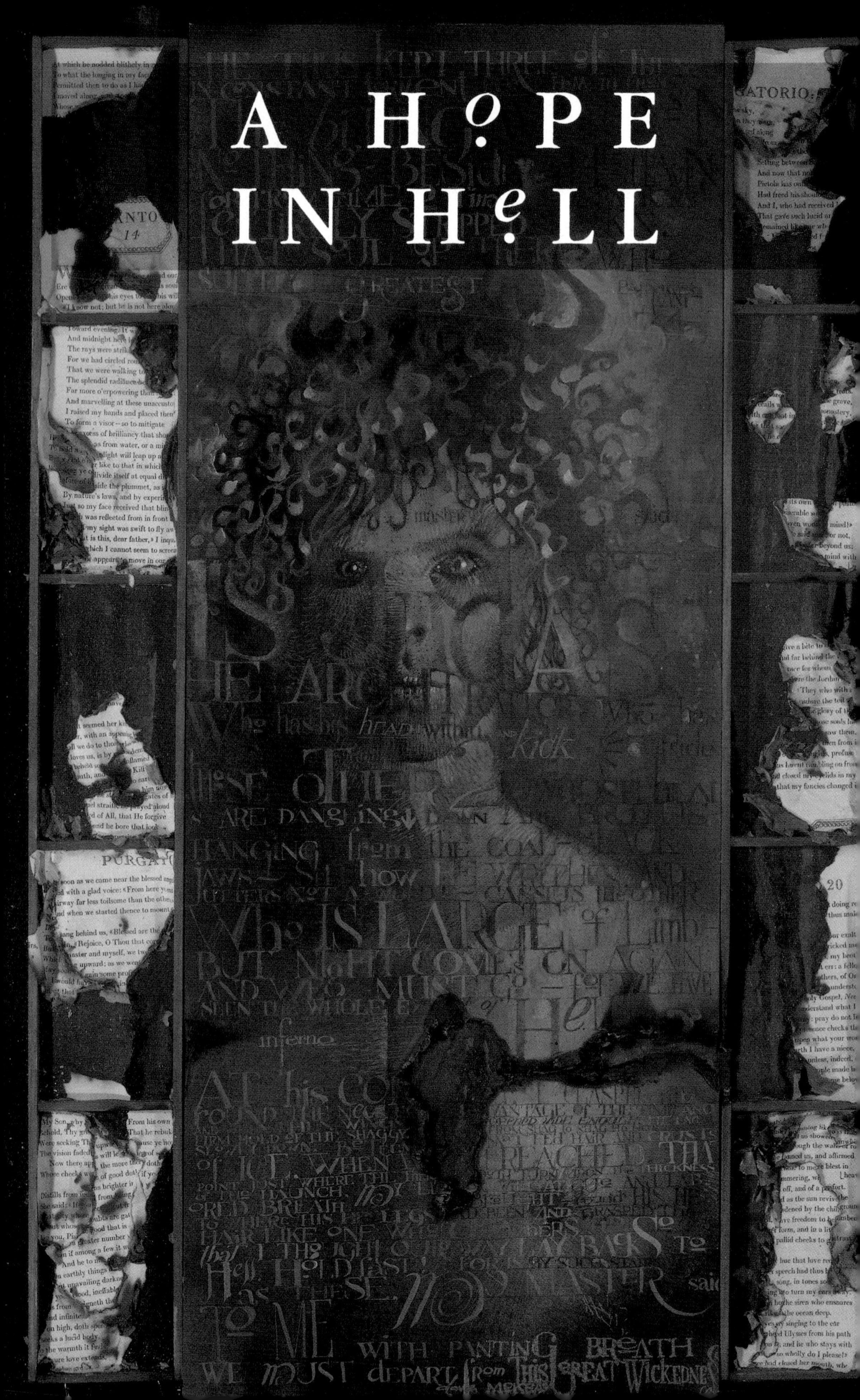
A HOPE
IN HELL

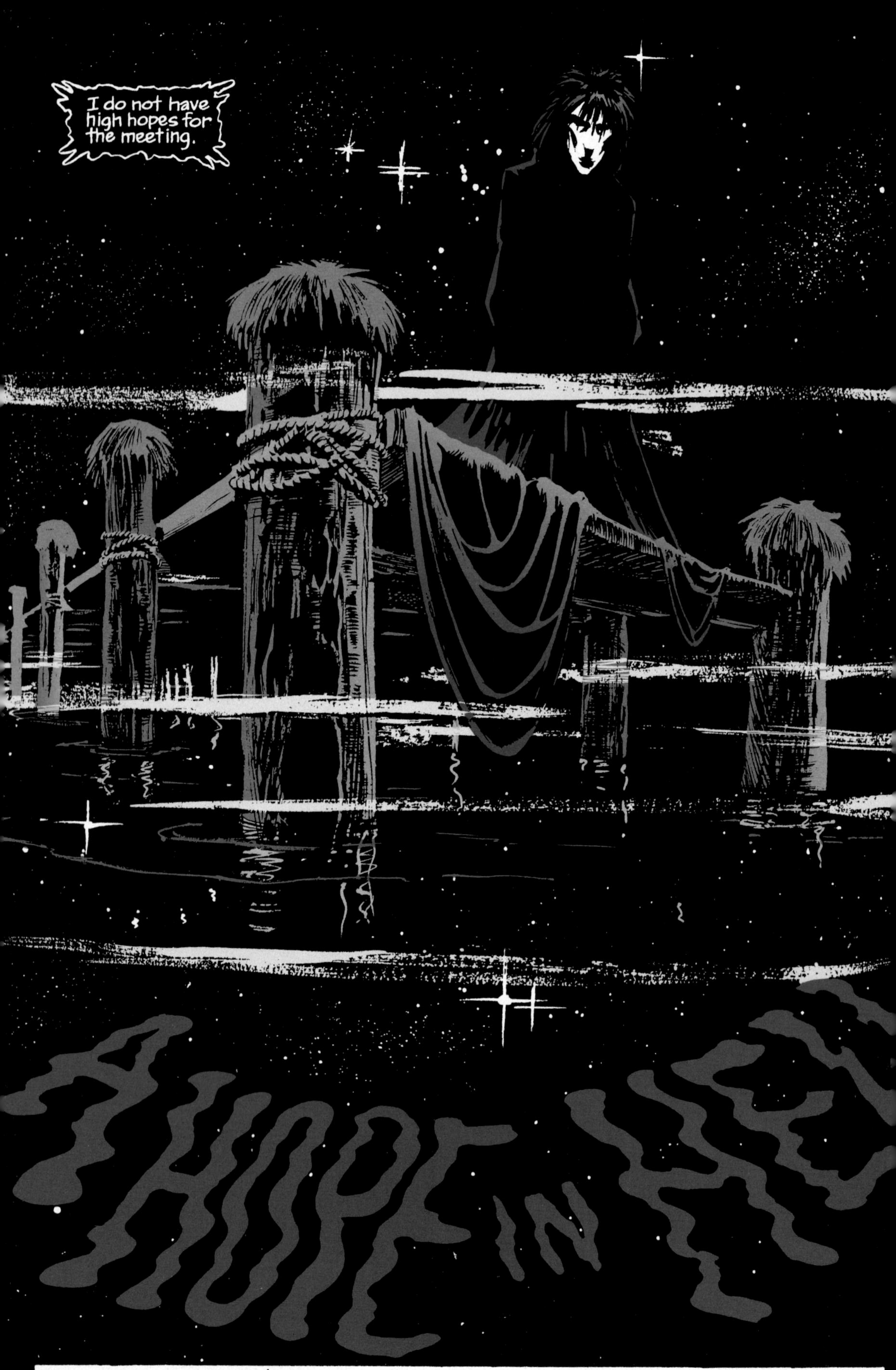

I do not have high hopes for the meeting.
A HOPE IN

NEIL GAIMAN WRITER · SAM KIETH & MIKE DRINGENBERG ARTISTS · DANIEL VOZZO COLORIST · TODD KLEIN LETTERER · ART YOUNG ASST. EDITOR · KAREN BERGER EDITOR

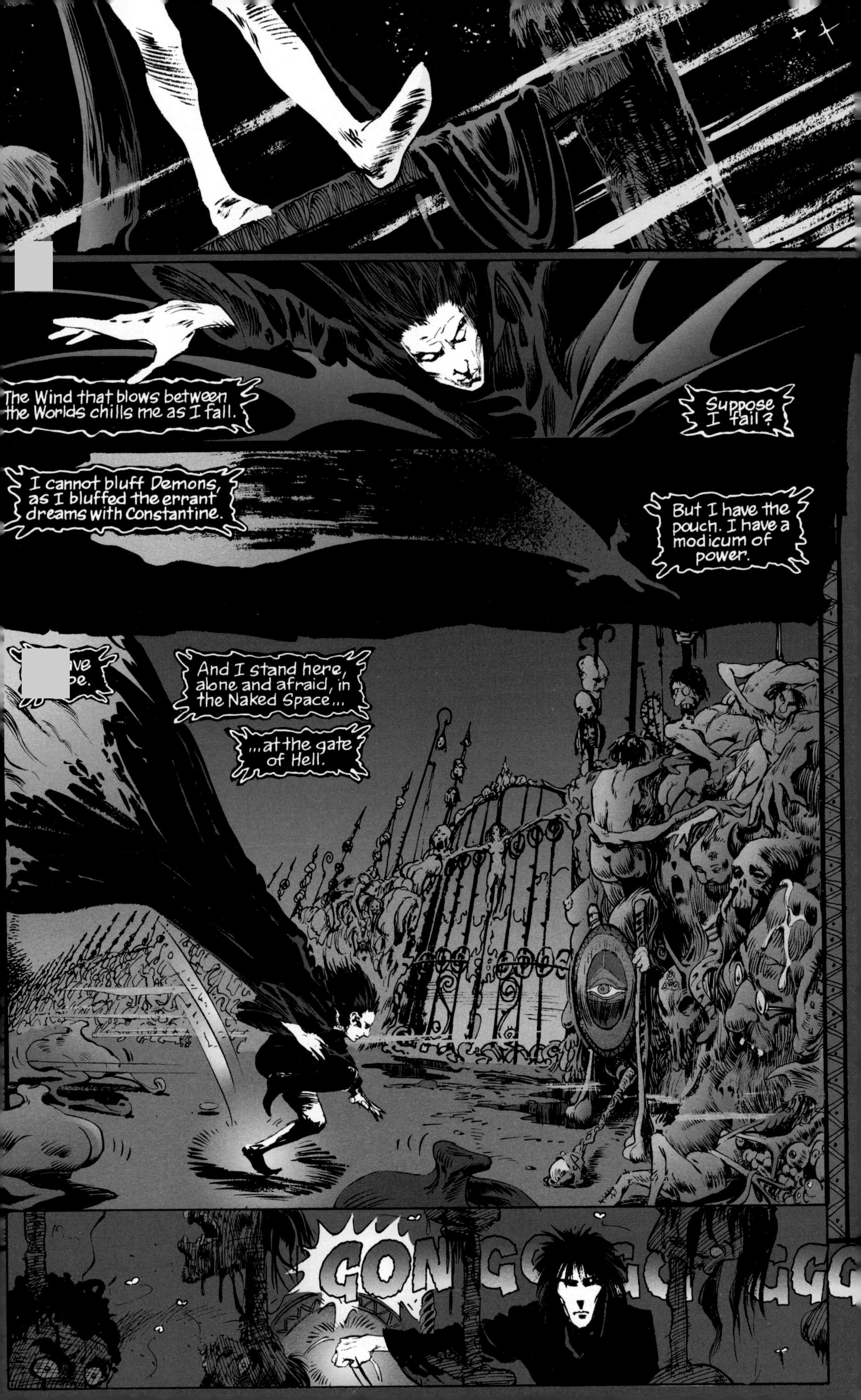

The Wind that blows between the Worlds chills me as I fall.
Suppose I fail?
I cannot bluff Demons, as I bluffed the errant dreams with Constantine.
But I have the pouch. I have a modicum of power.
And I stand here, alone and afraid, in the Naked Space...
...at the gate of Hell.
GON

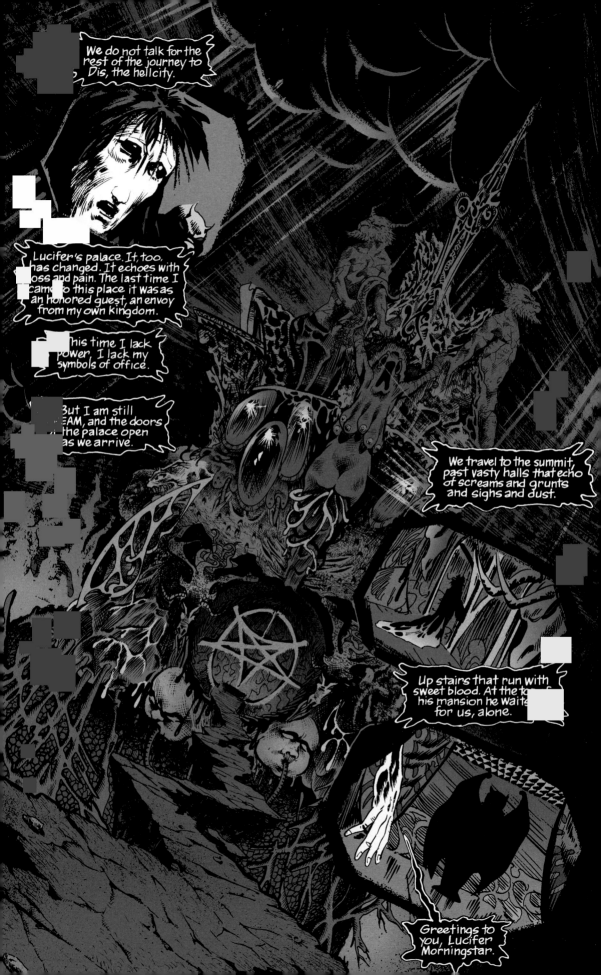

We do not talk for the rest of the journey to Dis, the hellcity.

Lucifer's palace. It, too, has changed. It echoes with loss and pain. The last time I came to this place it was as an honored guest, an envoy from my own kingdom.

This time I lack power, I lack my symbols of office.

But I am still DREAM, and the doors of the palace open as we arrive.

We travel to the summit, past vasty halls that echo of screams and grunts and sighs and dust.

Up stairs that run with sweet blood. At the top of his mansion he waits for us, alone.

Greetings to you, Lucifer Morningstar.

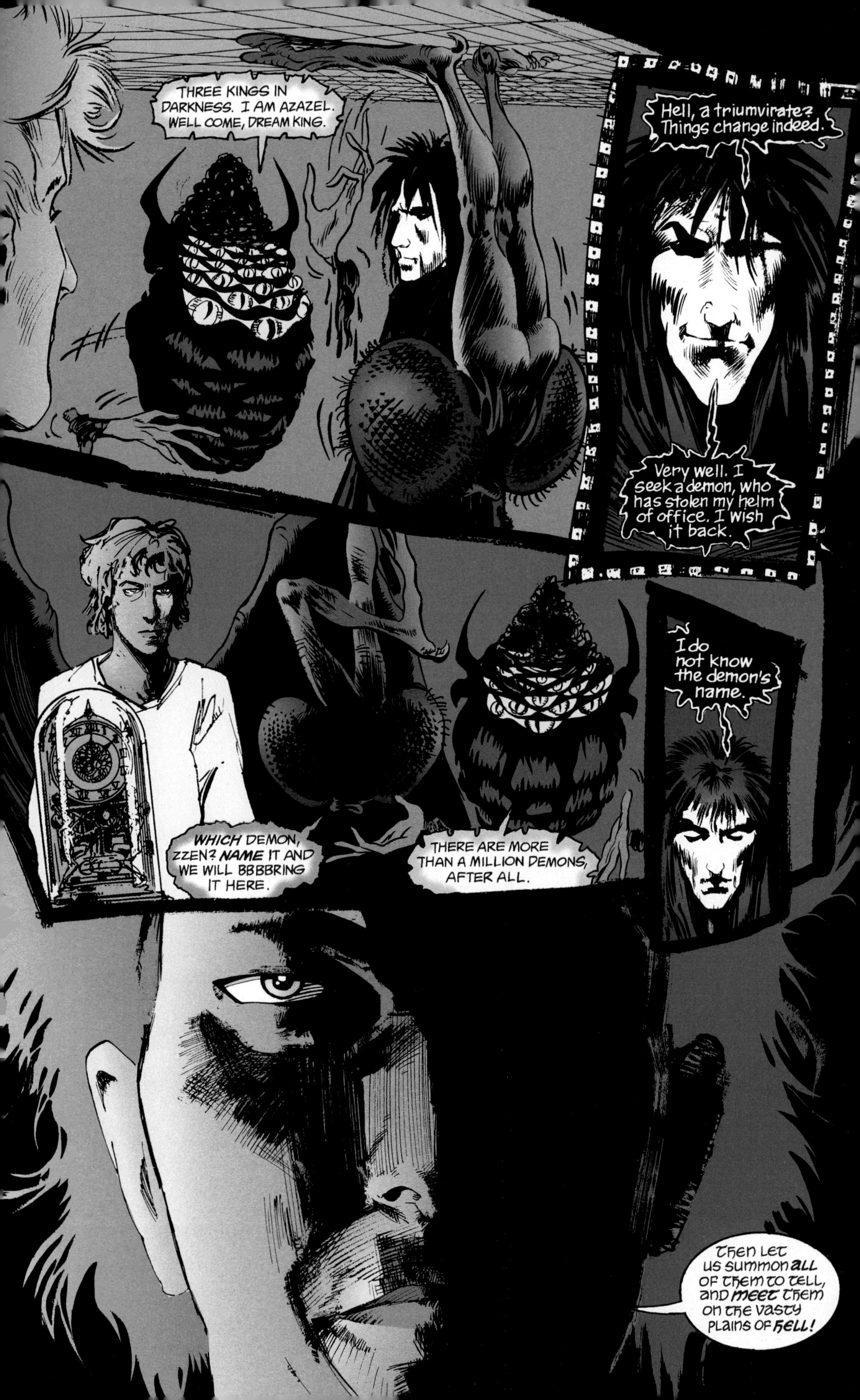
THREE KINGS IN DARKNESS. I AM AZAZEL. WELL COME, DREAM KING.
Hell, a triumvirate? Things change indeed.
Very well. I seek a demon, who has stolen my helm of office. I wish it back.
WHICH DEMON, ZZEN? NAME IT AND WE WILL BBBBRING IT HERE.
THERE ARE MORE THAN A MILLION DEMONS, AFTER ALL.
I do not know the demon's name.
Then let us summon ALL of them to tell, and MEET them on the vasty plains of HELL!

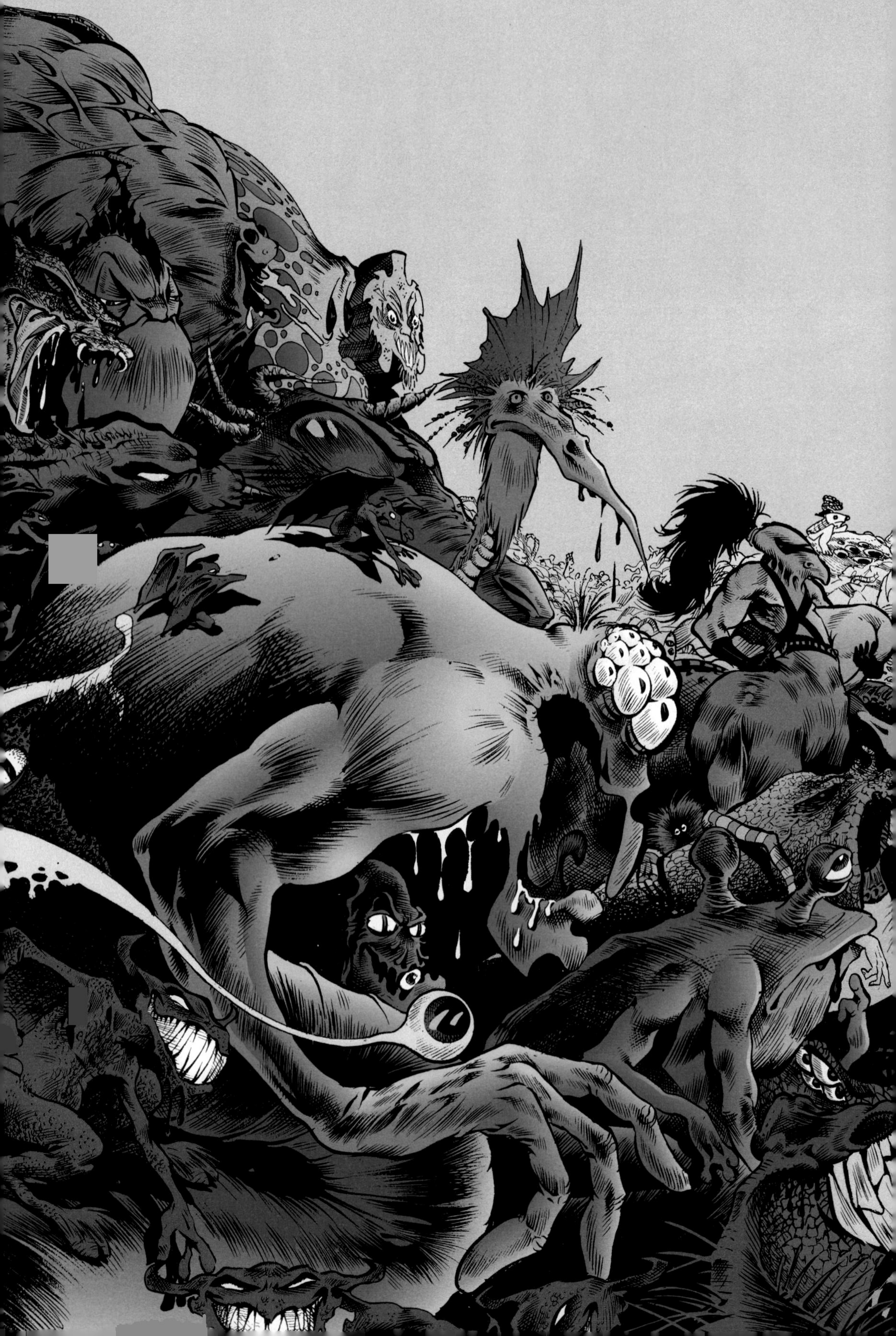

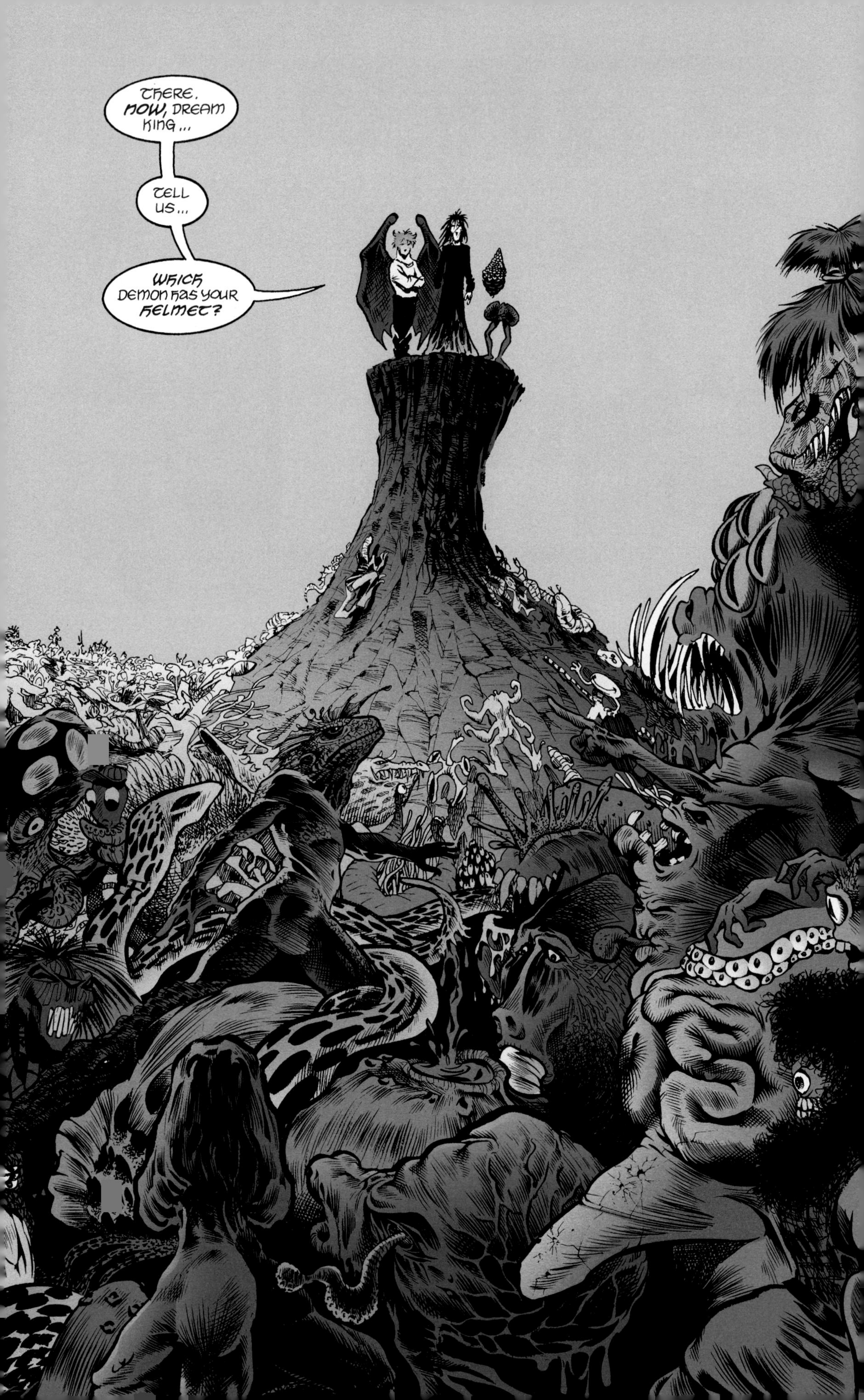
THERE. NOW, DREAM KING...
TELL US...
WHICH DEMON HAS YOUR HELMET?

I look at the demons. Some I recognize from nightmares. Others have passed through the dreamworld in the past. But there are so many...

One of you has my helm; my mask of pure dream. I crafted it myself, from the bones of a dead god. It is one of my tools...

Ah.

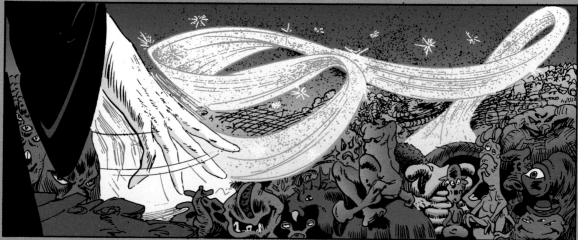

That one.

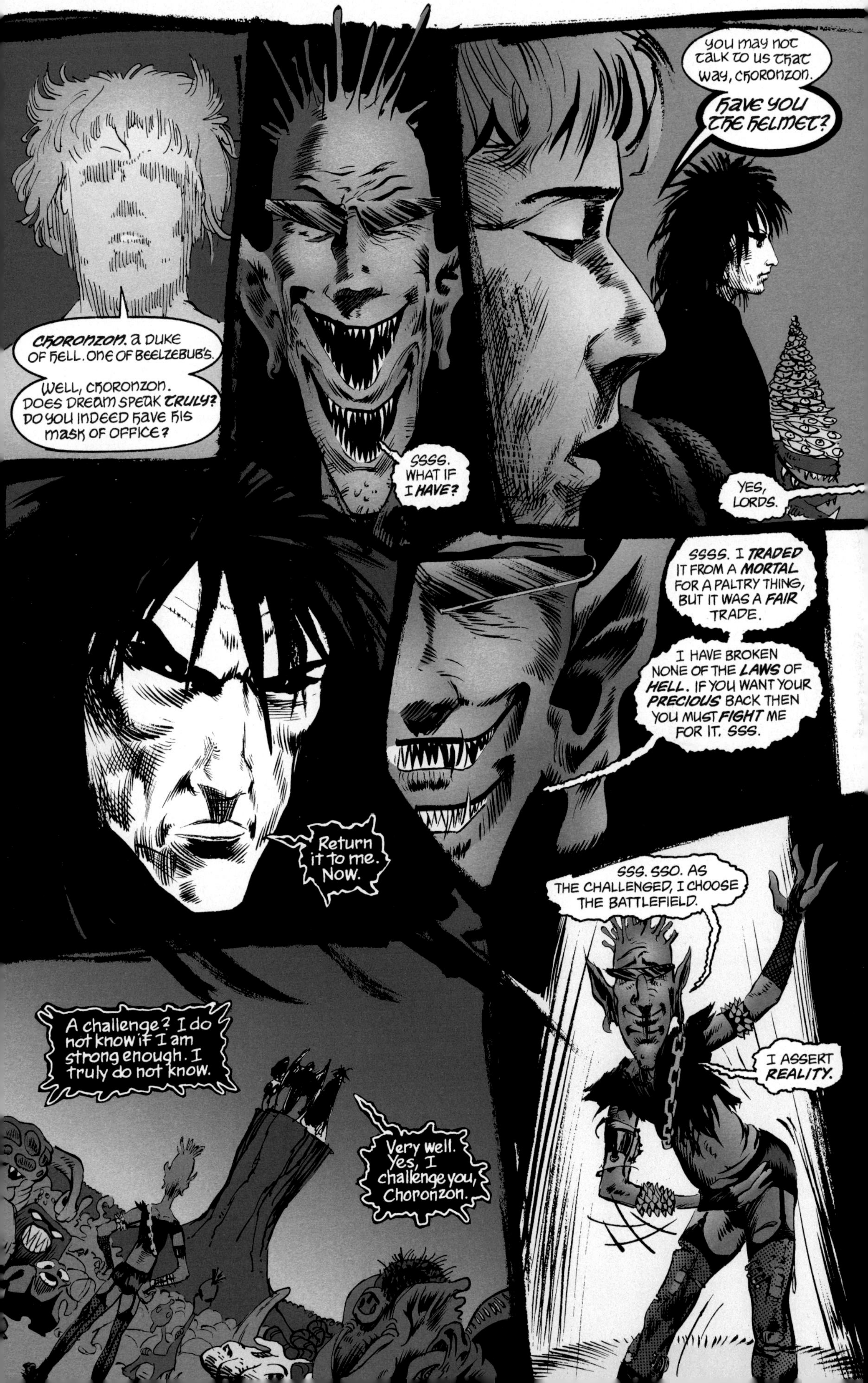
CHORONZON. A DUKE OF HELL. ONE OF BEELZEBUB'S.
WELL, CHORONZON. DOES DREAM SPEAK TRULY? DO YOU INDEED HAVE HIS MASK OF OFFICE?
SSSS. WHAT IF I HAVE?
YOU MAY NOT TALK TO US THAT WAY, CHORONZON.
HAVE YOU THE HELMET?
YES, LORDS.
SSSS. I TRADED IT FROM A MORTAL FOR A PALTRY THING, BUT IT WAS A FAIR TRADE.
I HAVE BROKEN NONE OF THE LAWS OF HELL. IF YOU WANT YOUR PRECIOUS BACK THEN YOU MUST FIGHT ME FOR IT. SSS.
Return it to me. Now.
A challenge? I do not know if I am strong enough. I truly do not know.
Very well. Yes, I challenge you, Choronzon.
SSS. SSO. AS THE CHALLENGED, I CHOOSE THE BATTLEFIELD.
I ASSERT REALITY.

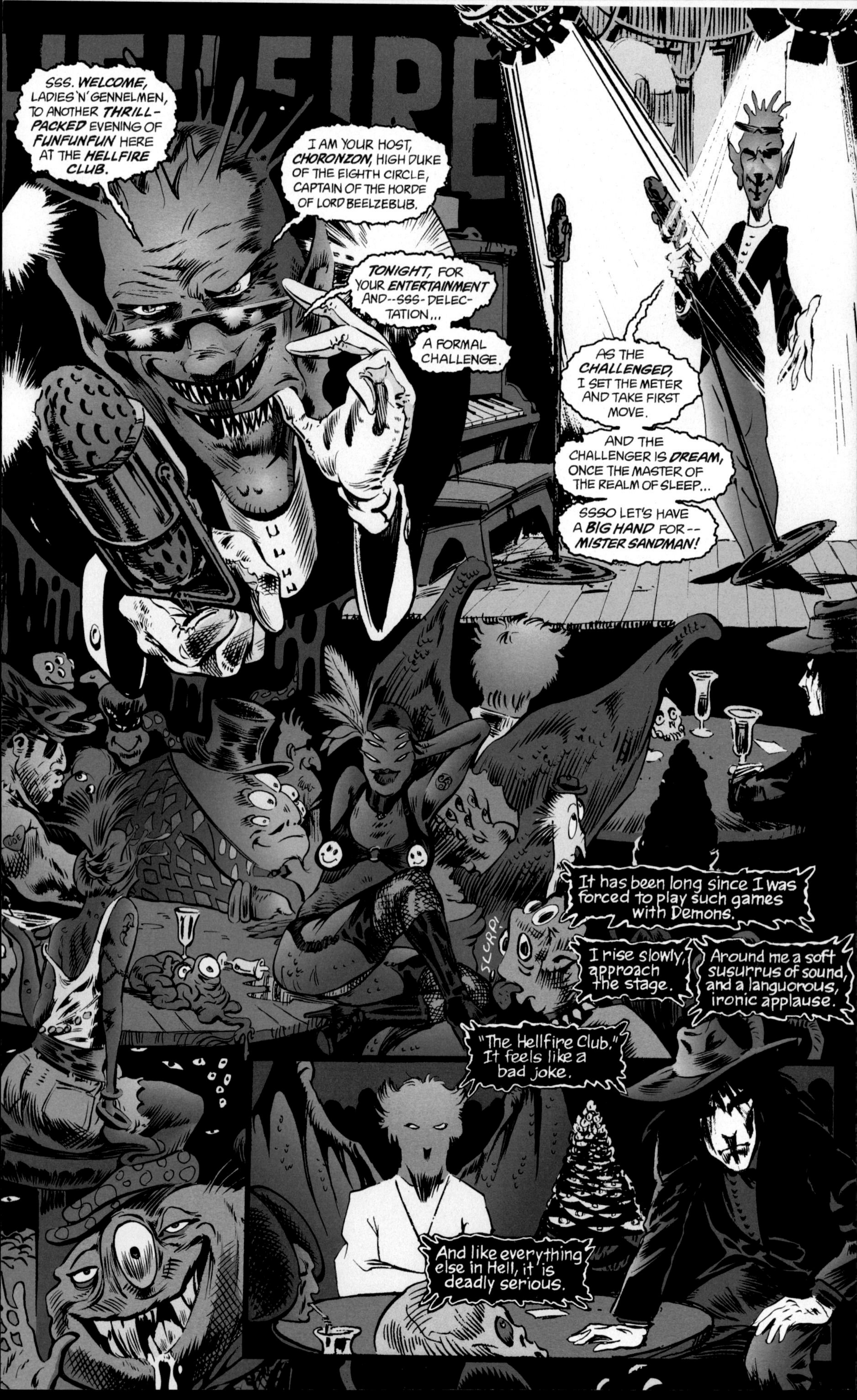
HELLFIRE
SSS. WELCOME, LADIES 'N' GENNELMEN, TO ANOTHER THRILL-PACKED EVENING OF FUNFUNFUN HERE AT THE HELLFIRE CLUB.
I AM YOUR HOST, CHORONZON, HIGH DUKE OF THE EIGHTH CIRCLE, CAPTAIN OF THE HORDE OF LORD BEELZEBUB.
TONIGHT, FOR YOUR ENTERTAINMENT AND--SSS-DELECTATION...
A FORMAL CHALLENGE.
AS THE CHALLENGED, I SET THE METER AND TAKE FIRST MOVE.
AND THE CHALLENGER IS DREAM, ONCE THE MASTER OF THE REALM OF SLEEP...
SSSO LET'S HAVE A BIG HAND FOR--MISTER SANDMAN!
It has been long since I was forced to play such games with Demons.
SLURP!
I rise slowly, approach the stage.
Around me a soft susurrus of sound, and a languorous, ironic applause.
"The Hellfire Club." It feels like a bad joke.
And like everything else in Hell, it is deadly serious.

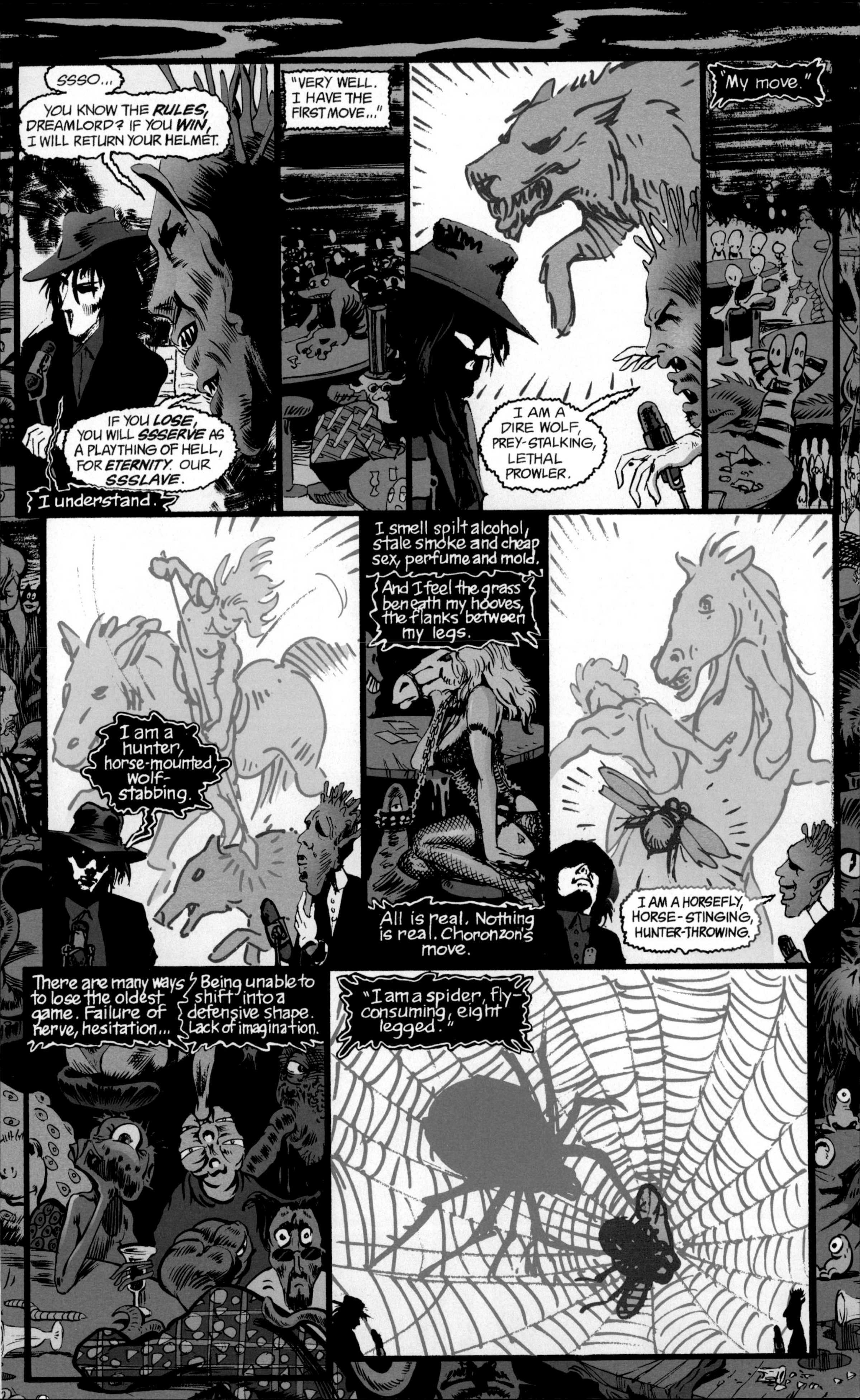

SSSO...
YOU KNOW THE RULES, DREAMLORD? IF YOU WIN, I WILL RETURN YOUR HELMET.
IF YOU LOSE, YOU WILL SSSERVE AS A PLAYTHING OF HELL, FOR ETERNITY. OUR SSSLAVE.
I understand.
"VERY WELL. I HAVE THE FIRST MOVE..."
I AM A DIRE WOLF, PREY-STALKING, LETHAL PROWLER.
"My move."
I am a hunter, horse-mounted, wolf-stabbing.
I smell spilt alcohol, stale smoke and cheap sex, perfume and mold.
And I feel the grass beneath my hooves, the flanks between my legs.
All is real. Nothing is real. Choronzon's move.
I AM A HORSEFLY, HORSE-STINGING, HUNTER-THROWING.
There are many ways to lose the oldest game. Failure of nerve, hesitation...
Being unable to shift into a defensive shape. Lack of imagination.
"I am a spider, fly-consuming, eight legged."

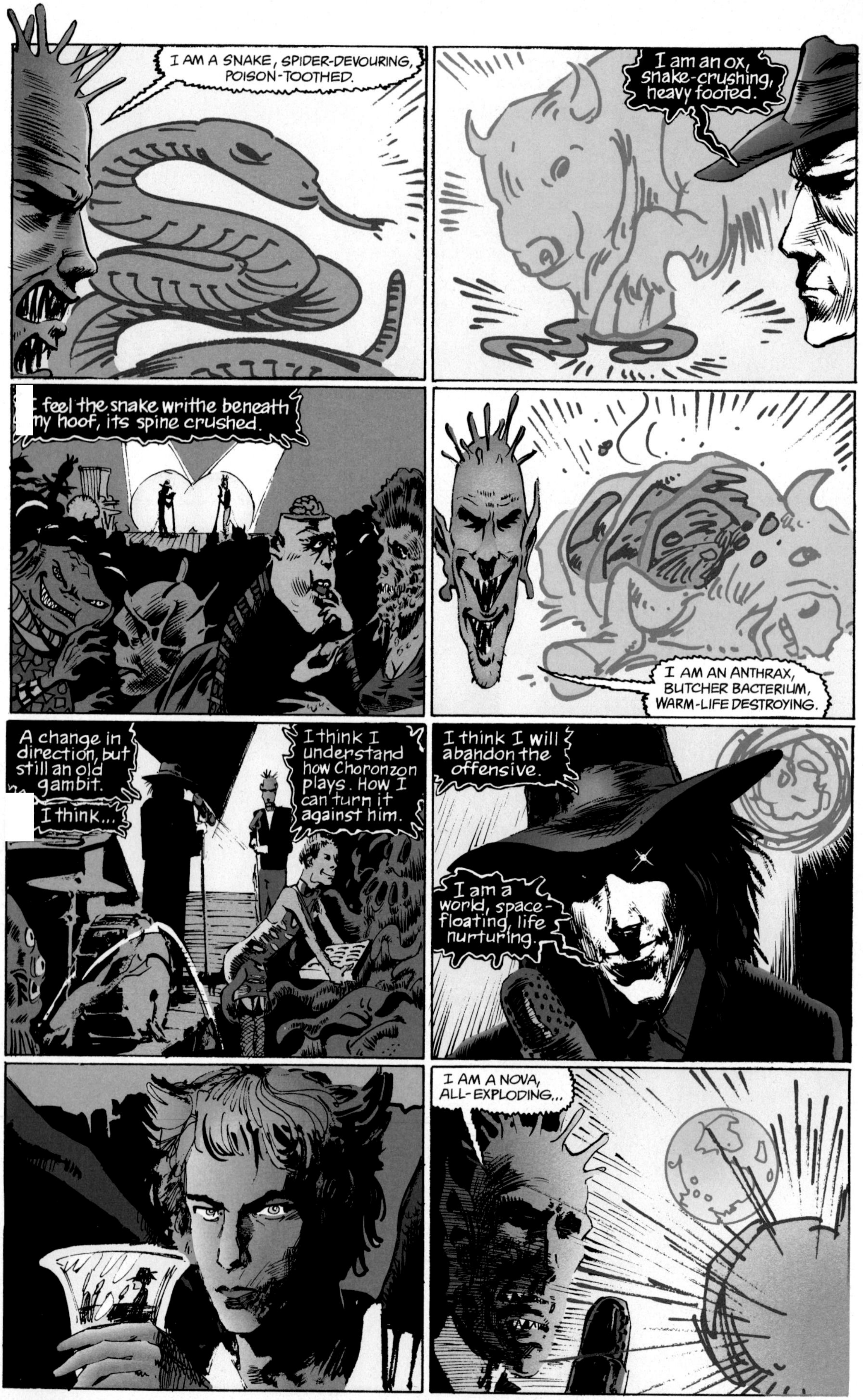
I AM A SNAKE, SPIDER-DEVOURING, POISON-TOOTHED.
I am an ox, snake-crushing, heavy footed.
I feel the snake writhe beneath my hoof, its spine crushed.
I AM AN ANTHRAX, BUTCHER BACTERIUM, WARM-LIFE DESTROYING.
A change in direction, but still an old gambit.
I think...
I think I understand how Choronzon plays. How I can turn it against him.
I think I will abandon the offensive.
I am a world, space-floating, life nurturing.
I AM A NOVA, ALL-EXPLODING...

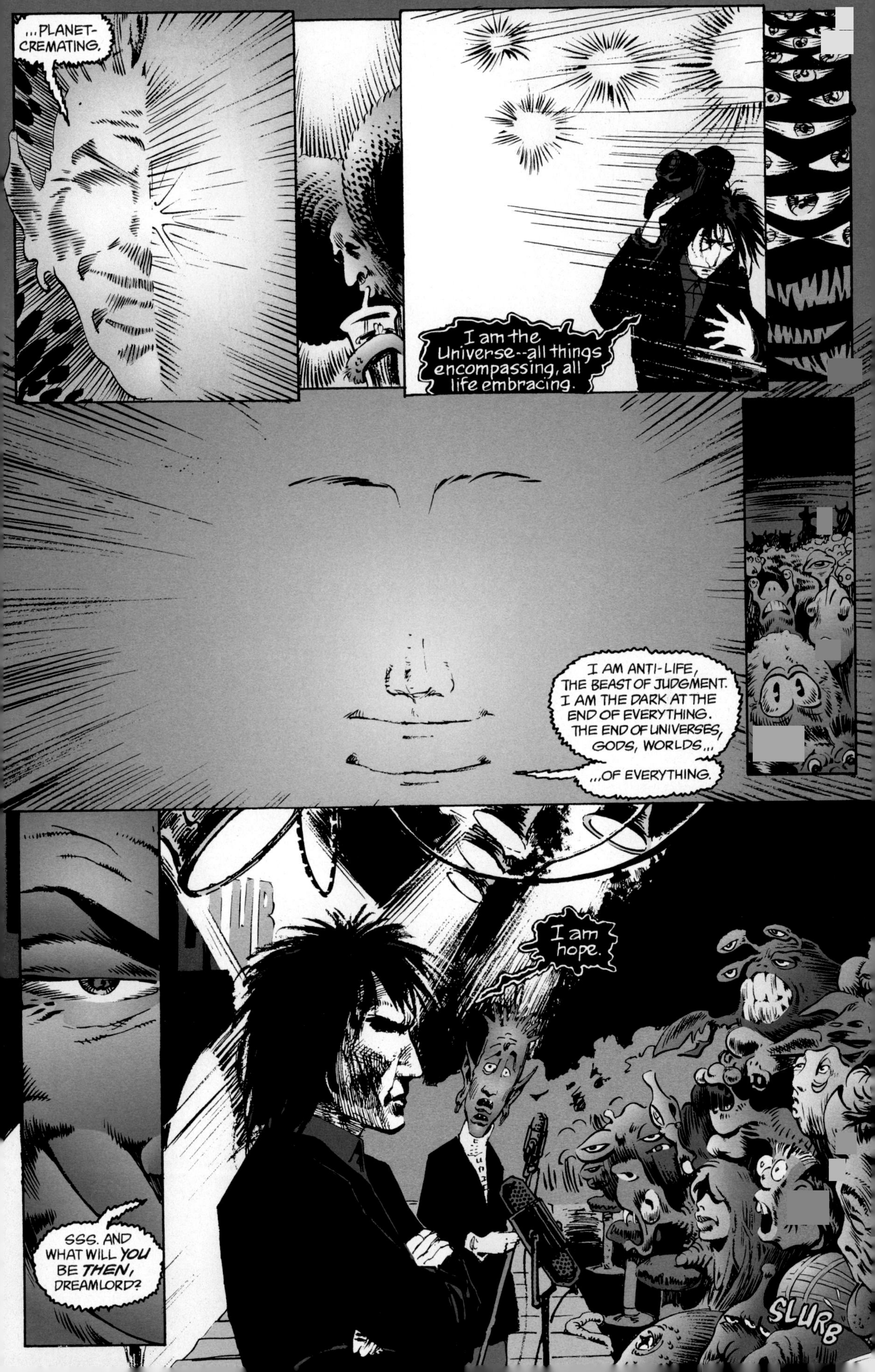

...PLANET-CREMATING.
I am the Universe--all things encompassing, all life embracing.
I AM ANTI-LIFE, THE BEAST OF JUDGMENT. I AM THE DARK AT THE END OF EVERYTHING. THE END OF UNIVERSES, GODS, WORLDS...
...OF EVERYTHING.
I am hope.
SSS. AND WHAT WILL YOU BE THEN, DREAMLORD?
SLURB

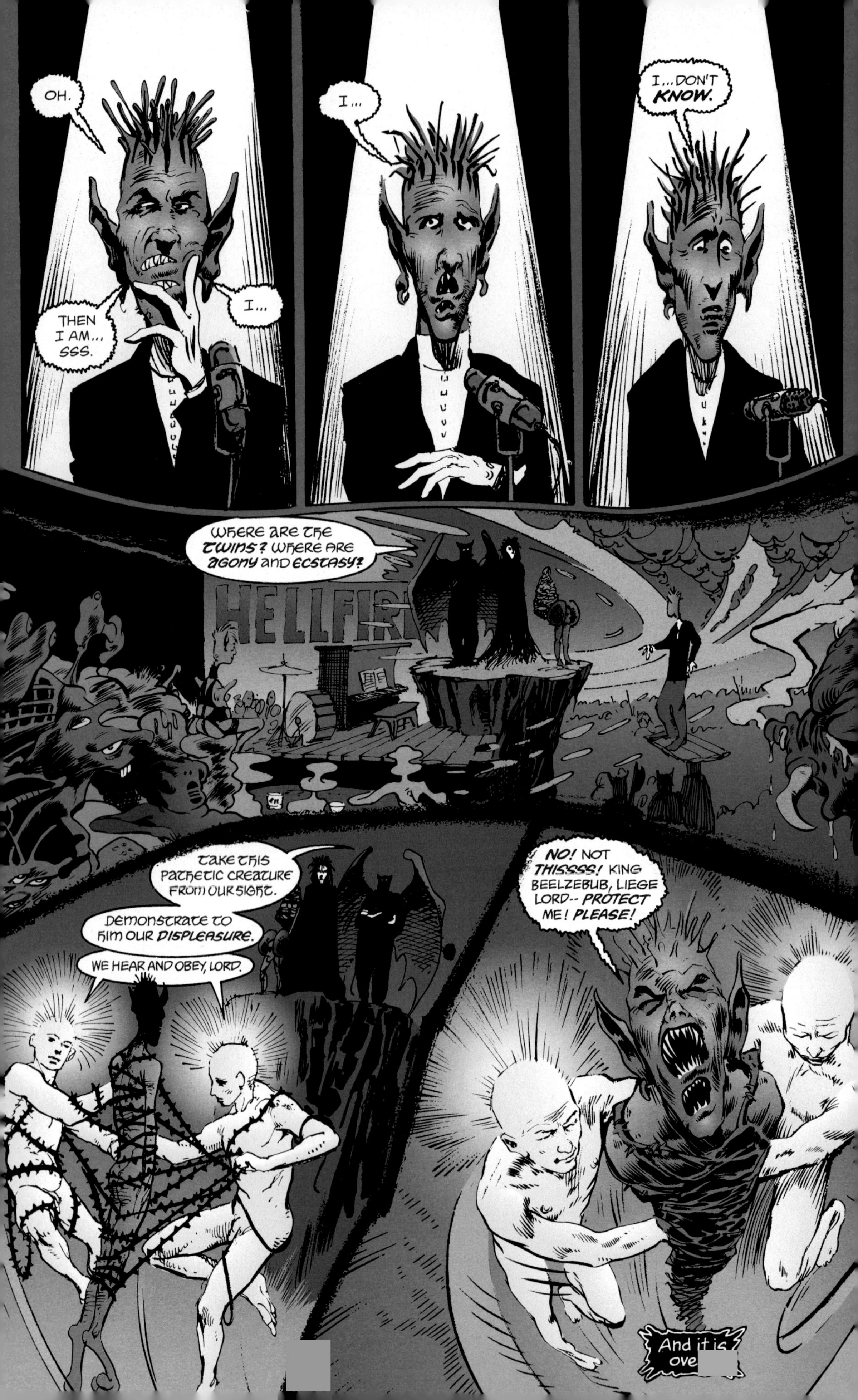
OH.
THEN I AM... SSS.
I...
I...
I...DON'T *KNOW.*
WHERE ARE THE *TWINS?* WHERE ARE *AGONY* AND *ECSTASY?*
HELLFIRE
TAKE THIS PATHETIC CREATURE FROM OUR SIGHT.
DEMONSTRATE TO HIM OUR *DISPLEASURE.*
WE HEAR AND OBEY, LORD.
NO! NOT *THISSSS!* KING BEELZEBUB, LIEGE LORD-- *PROTECT* ME! *PLEASE!*
And it is ove

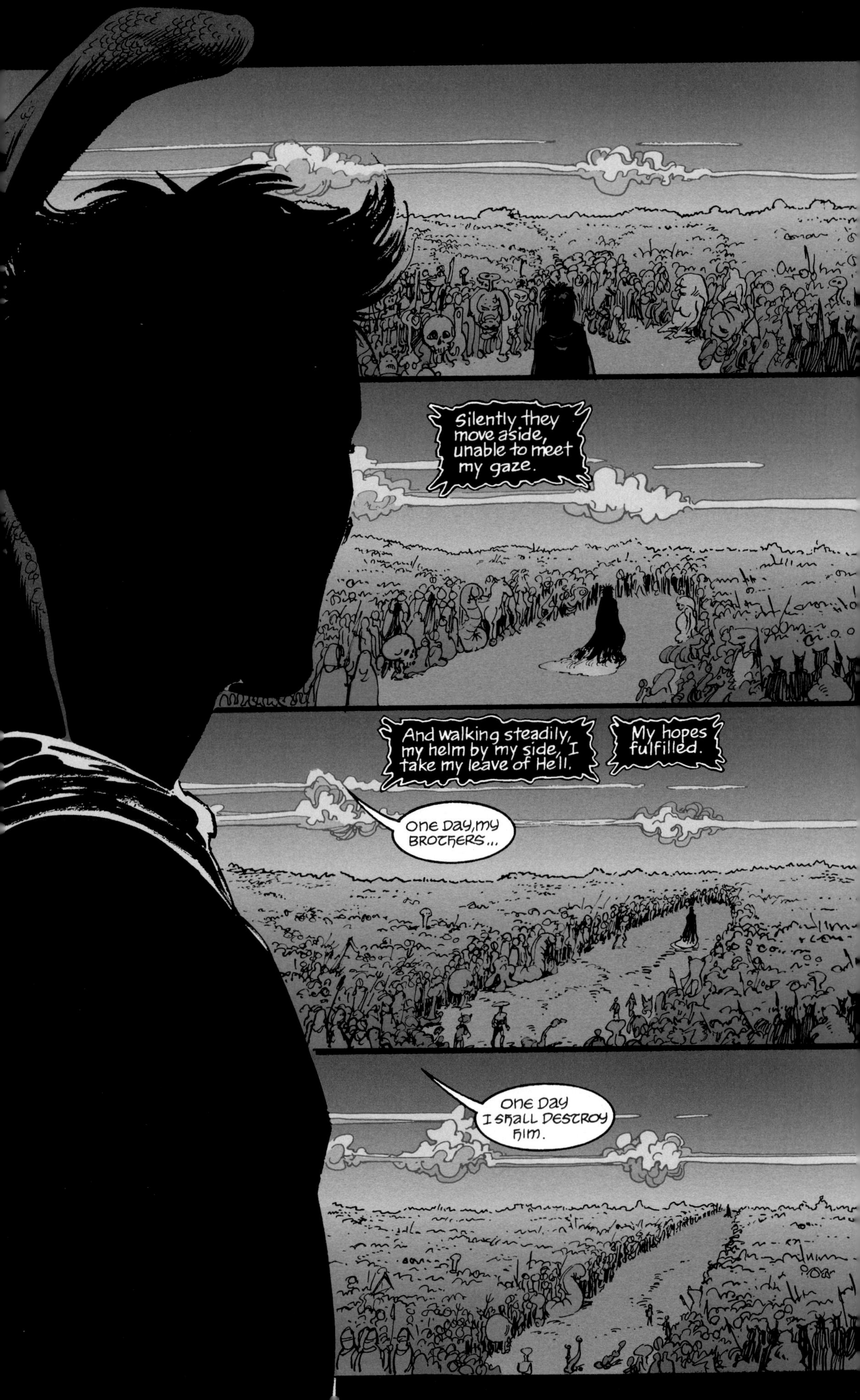
Silently they move aside, unable to meet my gaze.
And walking steadily, my helm by my side, I take my leave of Hell.
My hopes fulfilled.
One day, my brothers...
One day I shall destroy him.

EPILOGUE

ARKHAM ASYLVM

HUNTOON SEZ TO TELL YOU YOUR *MOTHER'S* CROAKED. SHE'S *DEAD*.

SEEMS SHE WANTED YOU TO HAVE THIS. *CATCH!*

CLINK

HEY--*DEE, DES*TINY, WHAT*EVER* YOUR NAME IS!

'FRAID I'VE GOT SOME *BAD NEWS* FOR YOU, GEEK!

THANK YOU ... MOTHER.

IT'S JUST WHAT I ALWAYS WANTED.

NEXT: *MONSTERS & MIRACLES*

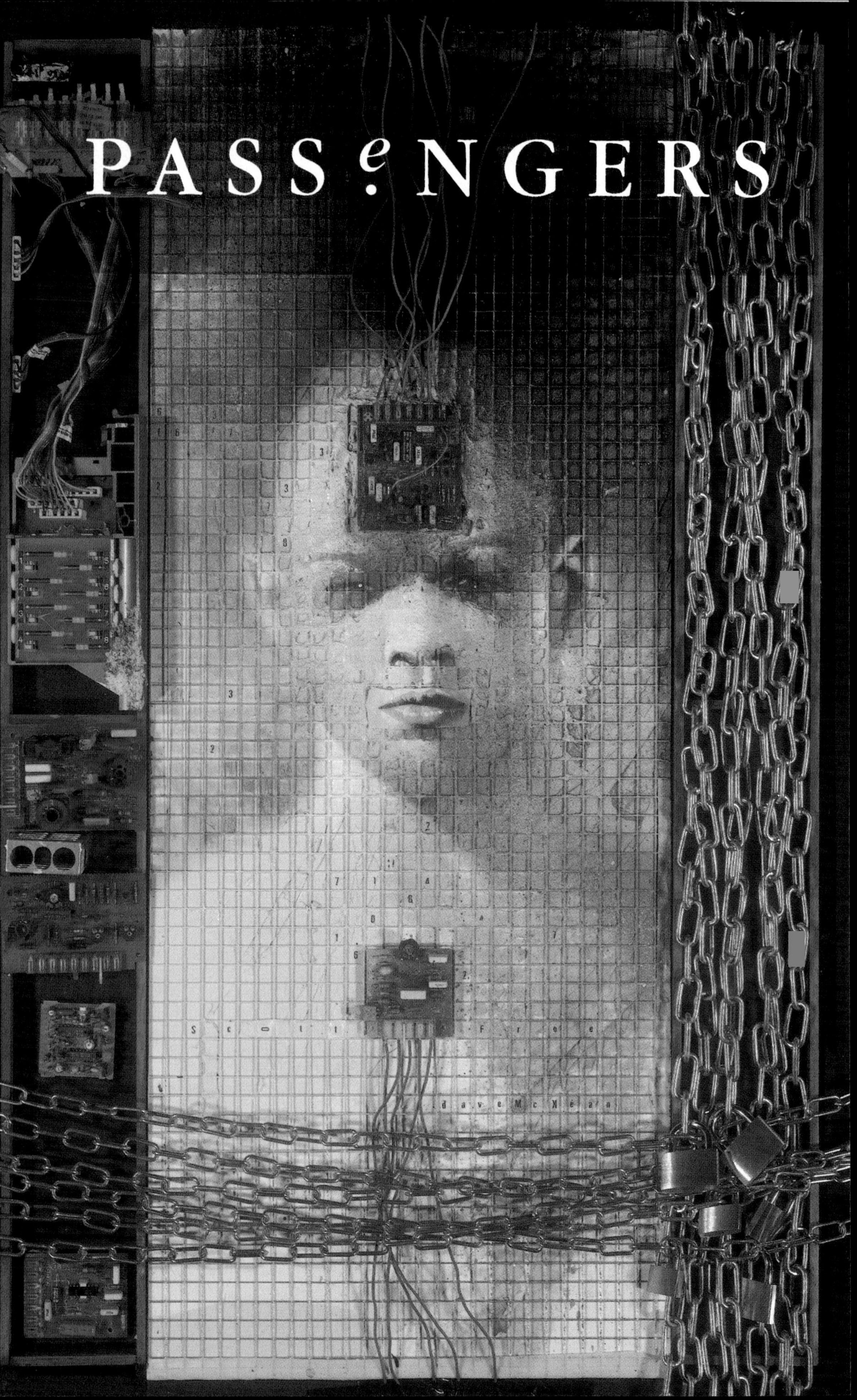
PASSeNGERS
Scott Free
daveMcKean

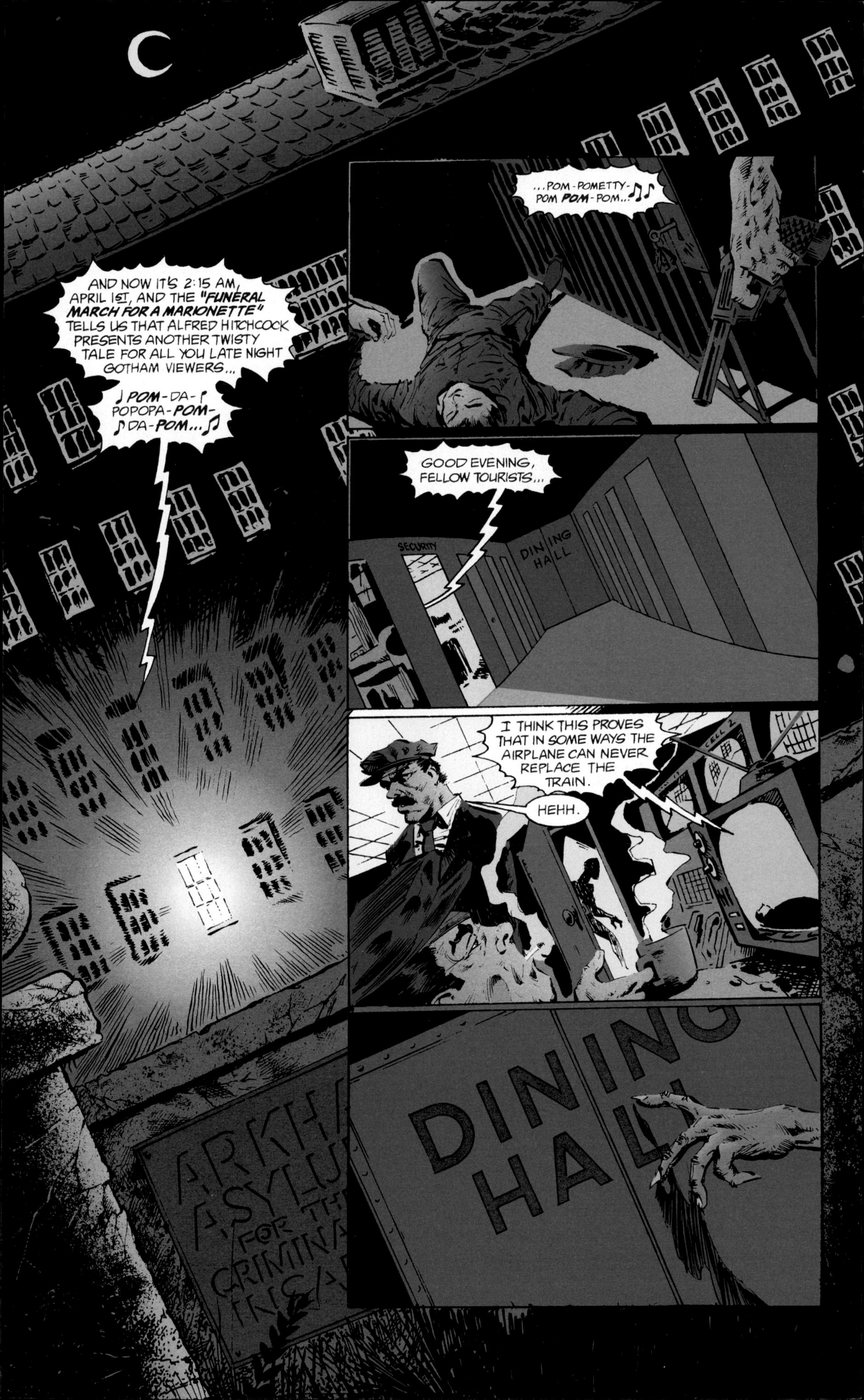
AND NOW IT'S 2:15 AM, APRIL 1ST, AND THE "FUNERAL MARCH FOR A MARIONETTE" TELLS US THAT ALFRED HITCHCOCK PRESENTS ANOTHER TWISTY TALE FOR ALL YOU LATE NIGHT GOTHAM VIEWERS...
♩POM-DA-♪ POPOPA-POM-♪DA-POM...♫
...POM-POMETTY-POM POM-POM...♫♪
GOOD EVENING, FELLOW TOURISTS...
SECURITY
DINING HALL
I THINK THIS PROVES THAT IN SOME WAYS THE AIRPLANE CAN NEVER REPLACE THE TRAIN.
HEHH.
DINING HALL

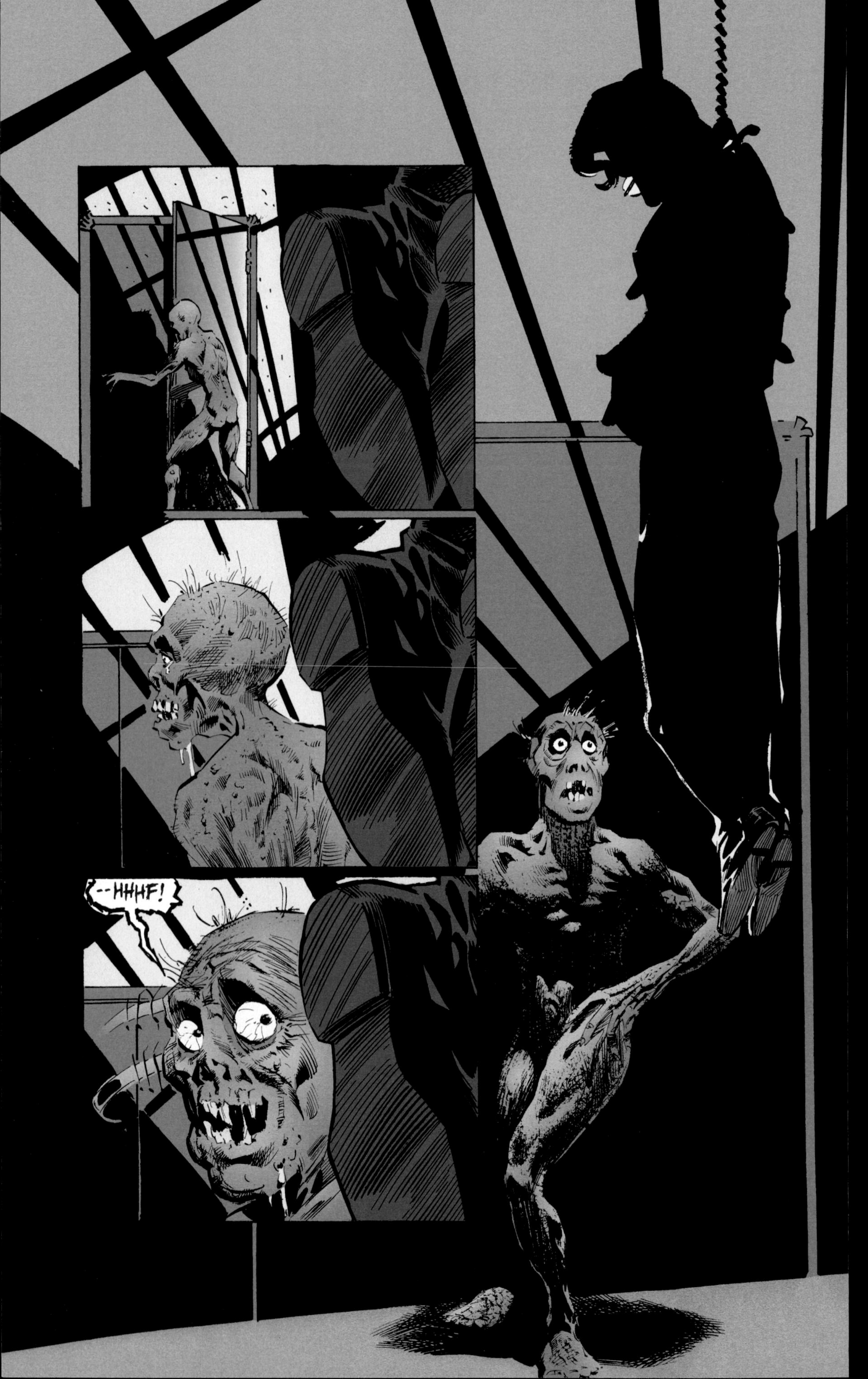
--HHHF!

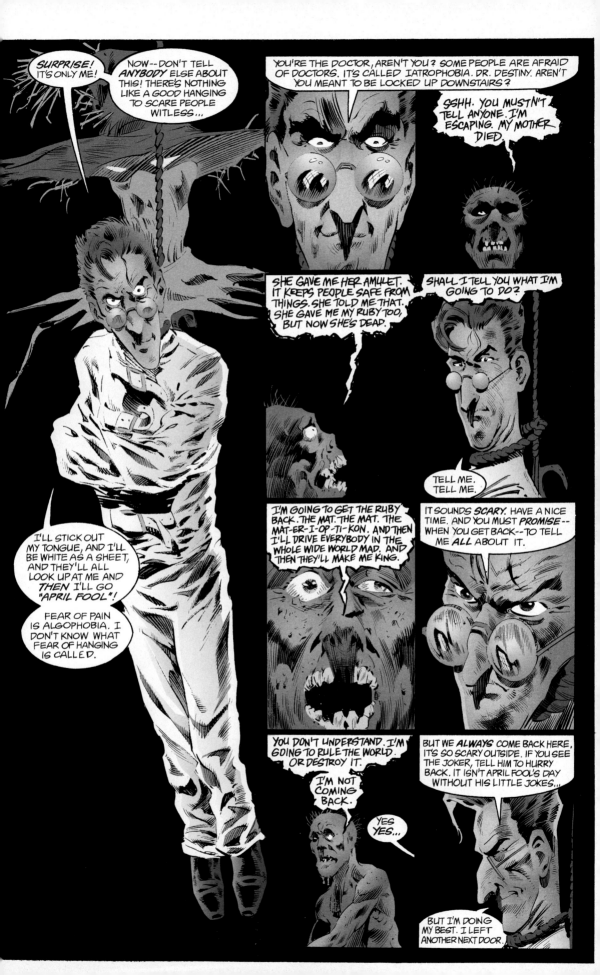

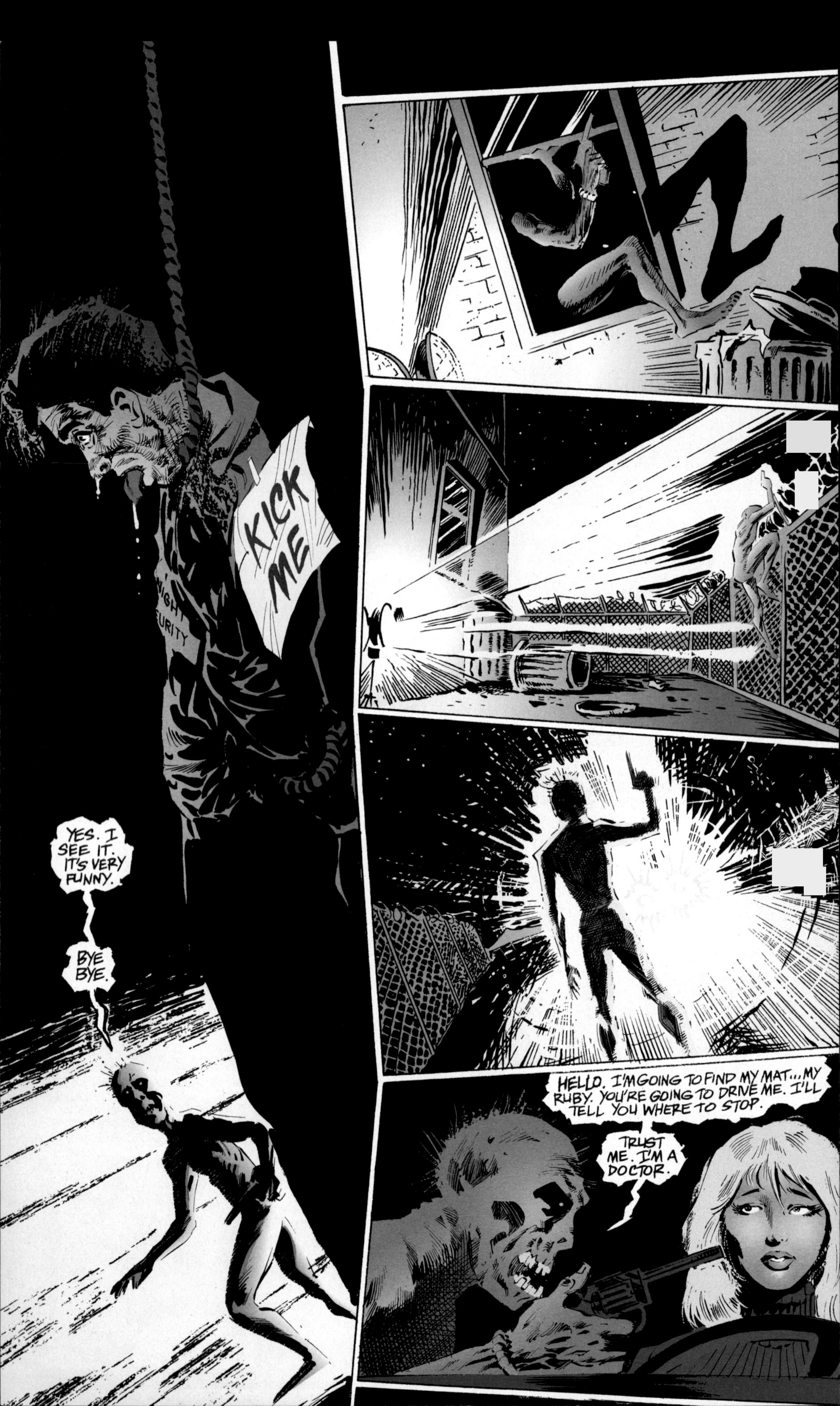
KICK ME
YES. I SEE IT. IT'S VERY FUNNY.
BYE BYE.
HELLO. I'M GOING TO FIND MY MAT... MY RUBY. YOU'RE GOING TO DRIVE ME. I'LL TELL YOU WHERE TO STOP.
TRUST ME. I'M A DOCTOR.

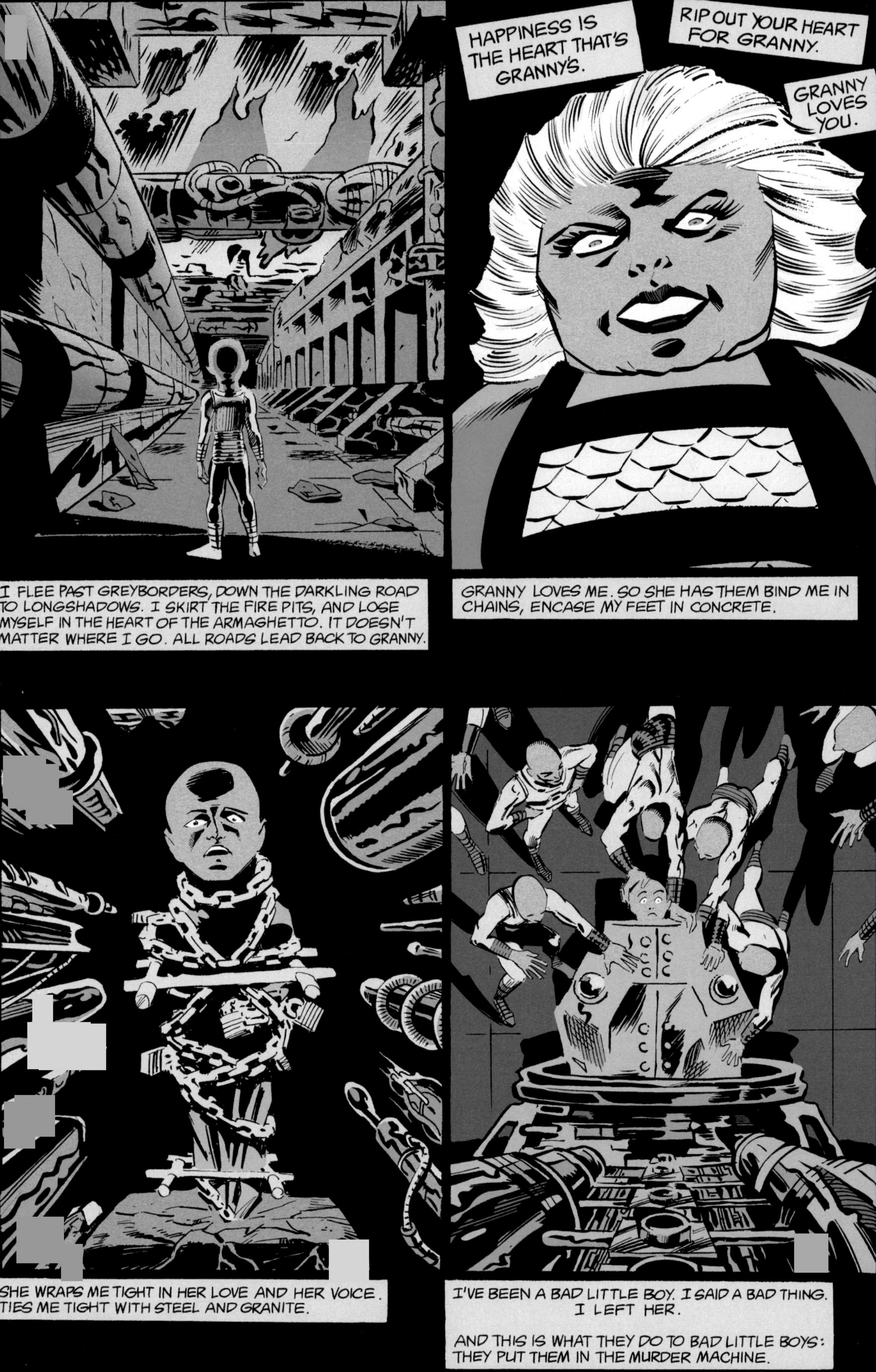
I FLEE PAST GREYBORDERS, DOWN THE DARKLING ROAD TO LONGSHADOWS. I SKIRT THE FIRE PITS, AND LOSE MYSELF IN THE HEART OF THE ARMAGHETTO. IT DOESN'T MATTER WHERE I GO. ALL ROADS LEAD BACK TO GRANNY.
HAPPINESS IS THE HEART THAT'S GRANNY'S.
RIP OUT YOUR HEART FOR GRANNY.
GRANNY LOVES YOU.
GRANNY LOVES ME. SO SHE HAS THEM BIND ME IN CHAINS, ENCASE MY FEET IN CONCRETE.
SHE WRAPS ME TIGHT IN HER LOVE AND HER VOICE. TIES ME TIGHT WITH STEEL AND GRANITE.
I'VE BEEN A BAD LITTLE BOY. I SAID A BAD THING. I LEFT HER.
AND THIS IS WHAT THEY DO TO BAD LITTLE BOYS: THEY PUT THEM IN THE MURDER MACHINE.

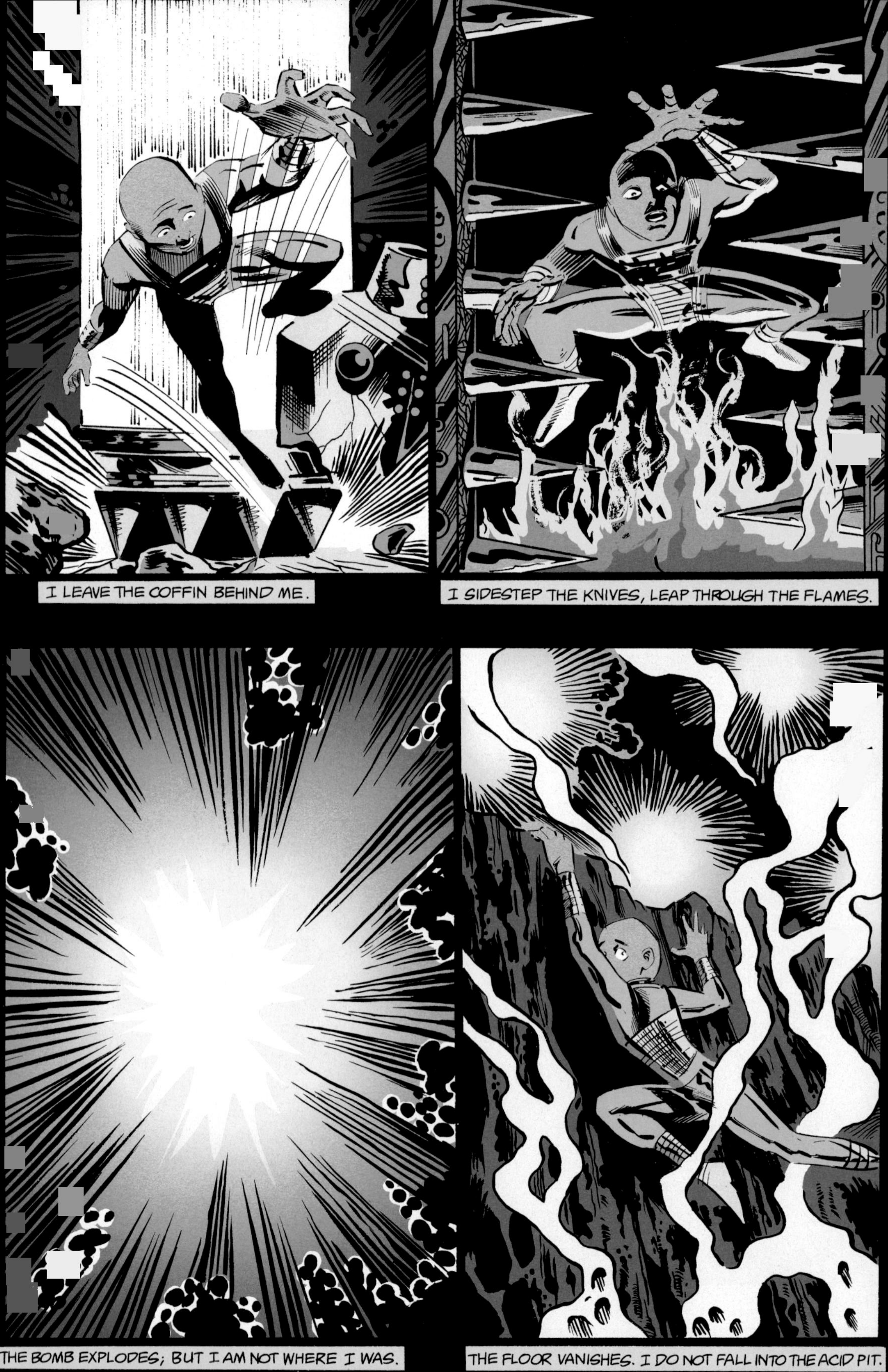
I LEAVE THE COFFIN BEHIND ME.
I SIDESTEP THE KNIVES, LEAP THROUGH THE FLAMES.
THE BOMB EXPLODES; BUT I AM NOT WHERE I WAS.
THE FLOOR VANISHES. I DO NOT FALL INTO THE ACID PIT.

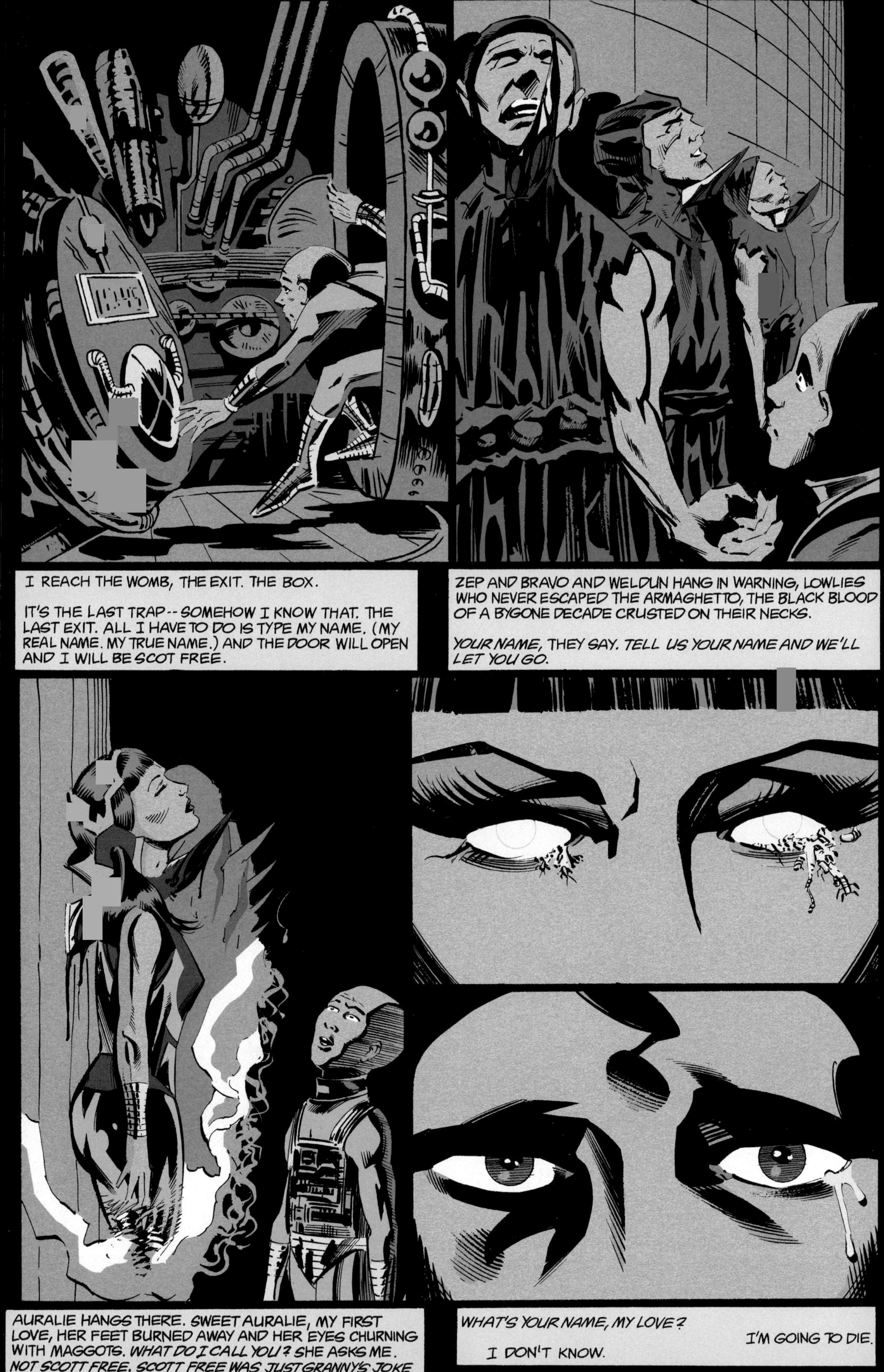
I REACH THE WOMB, THE EXIT. THE BOX.
IT'S THE LAST TRAP -- SOMEHOW I KNOW THAT. THE LAST EXIT. ALL I HAVE TO DO IS TYPE MY NAME. (MY REAL NAME. MY TRUE NAME.) AND THE DOOR WILL OPEN AND I WILL BE SCOT FREE.
ZEP AND BRAVO AND WELDUN HANG IN WARNING, LOWLIES WHO NEVER ESCAPED THE ARMAGHETTO, THE BLACK BLOOD OF A BYGONE DECADE CRUSTED ON THEIR NECKS.
YOUR NAME, THEY SAY. TELL US YOUR NAME AND WE'LL LET YOU GO.
AURALIE HANGS THERE. SWEET AURALIE, MY FIRST LOVE, HER FEET BURNED AWAY AND HER EYES CHURNING WITH MAGGOTS. WHAT DO I CALL YOU? SHE ASKS ME. NOT SCOTT FREE. SCOTT FREE WAS JUST GRANNY'S JOKE
WHAT'S YOUR NAME, MY LOVE?
I DON'T KNOW.
I'M GOING TO DIE.

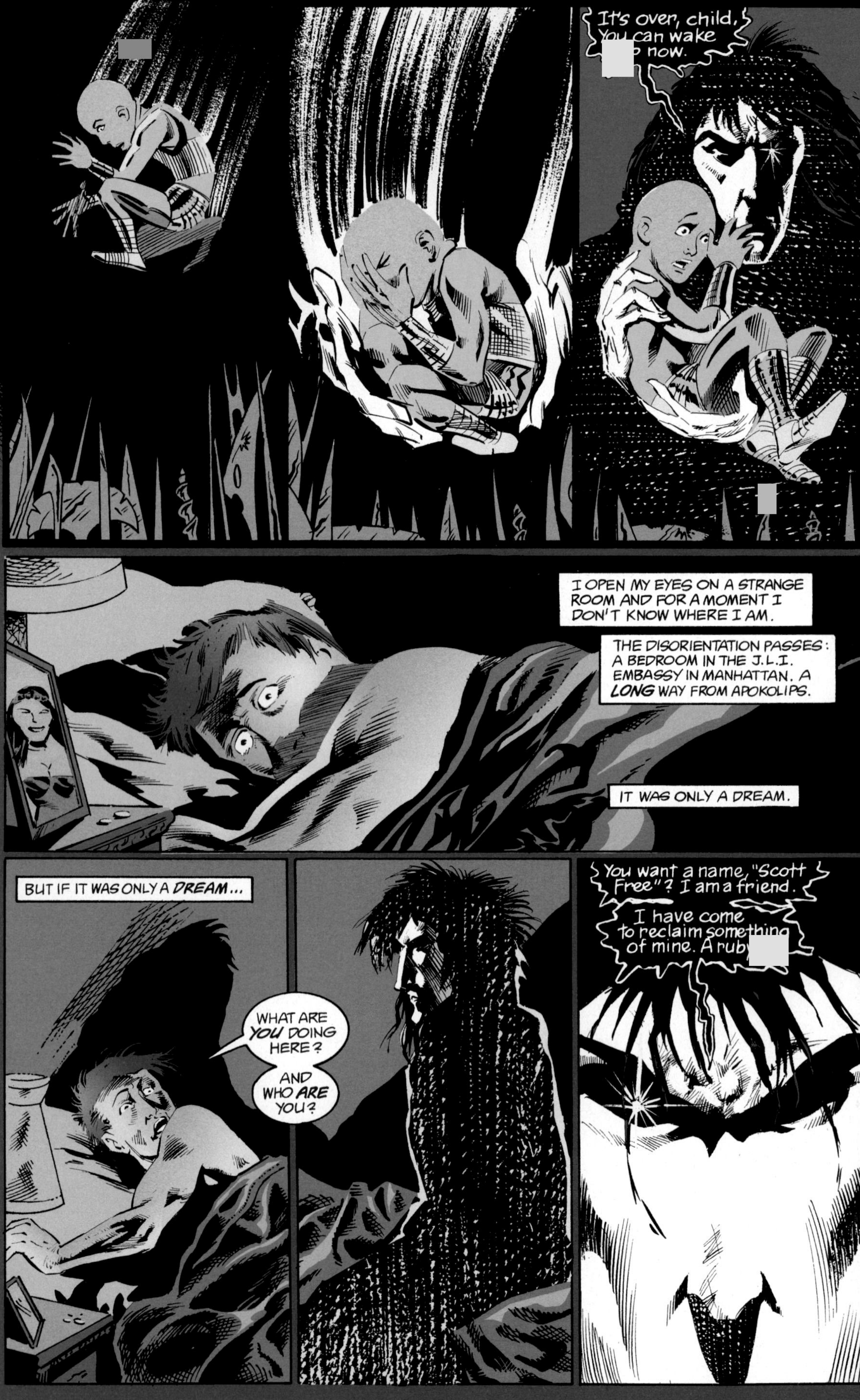

It's over, child, You can wake
now.
I OPEN MY EYES ON A STRANGE ROOM AND FOR A MOMENT I DON'T KNOW WHERE I AM.
THE DISORIENTATION PASSES: A BEDROOM IN THE J.L.I. EMBASSY IN MANHATTAN. A LONG WAY FROM APOKOLIPS.
IT WAS ONLY A DREAM.
BUT IF IT WAS ONLY A DREAM...
WHAT ARE YOU DOING HERE?
AND WHO ARE YOU?
You want a name, "Scott Free"? I am a friend.
I have come to reclaim something of mine. A rub

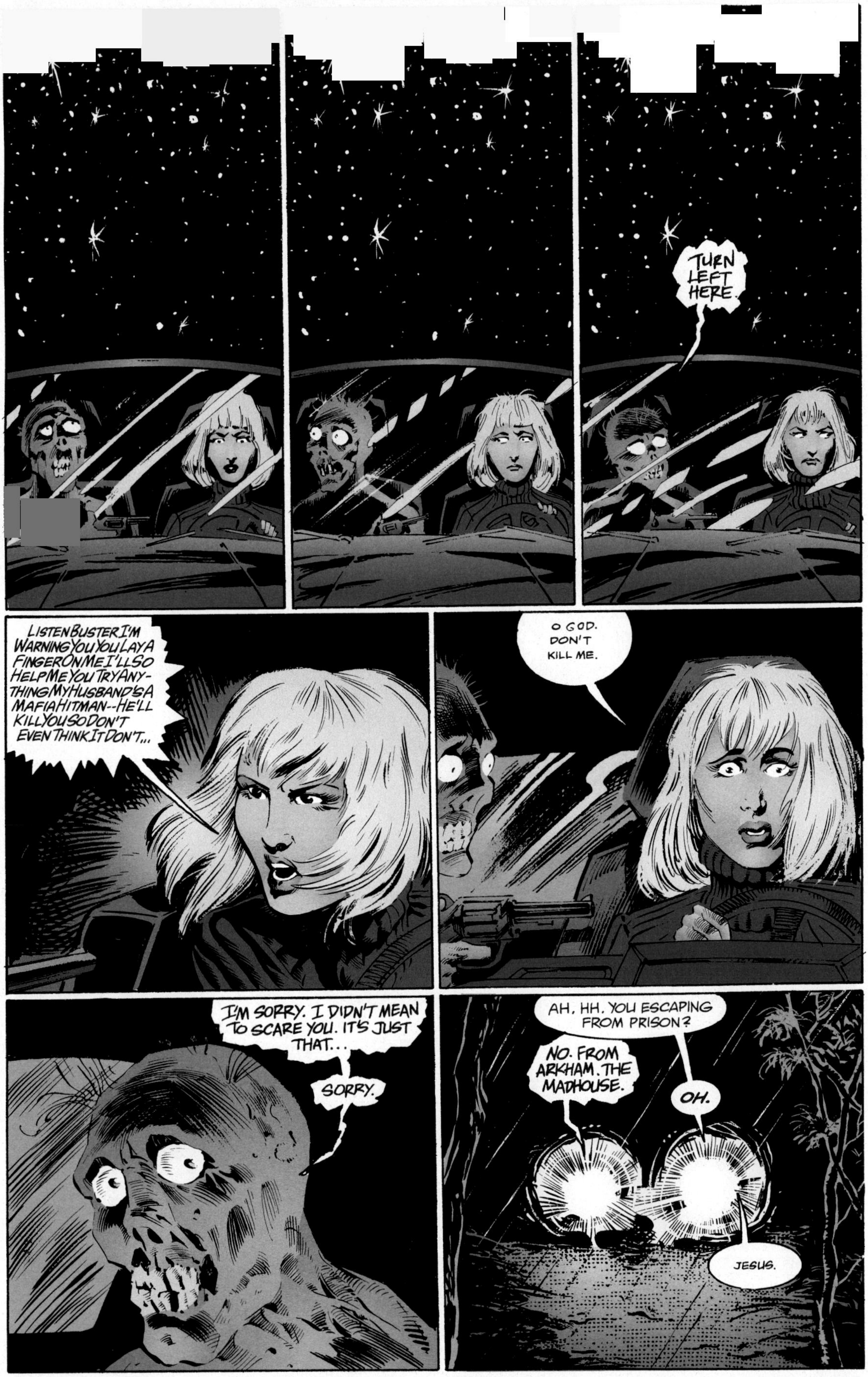
TURN LEFT HERE.
LISTEN BUSTER I'M WARNING YOU YOU LAY A FINGER ON ME I'LL SO HELP ME YOU TRY ANY-THING MY HUSBAND'S A MAFIA HITMAN--HE'LL KILL YOU SO DON'T EVEN THINK IT DON'T...
O GOD. DON'T KILL ME.
I'M SORRY. I DIDN'T MEAN TO SCARE YOU. IT'S JUST THAT...
SORRY.
AH, HH. YOU ESCAPING FROM PRISON?
NO. FROM ARKHAM. THE MADHOUSE.
OH.
JESUS.

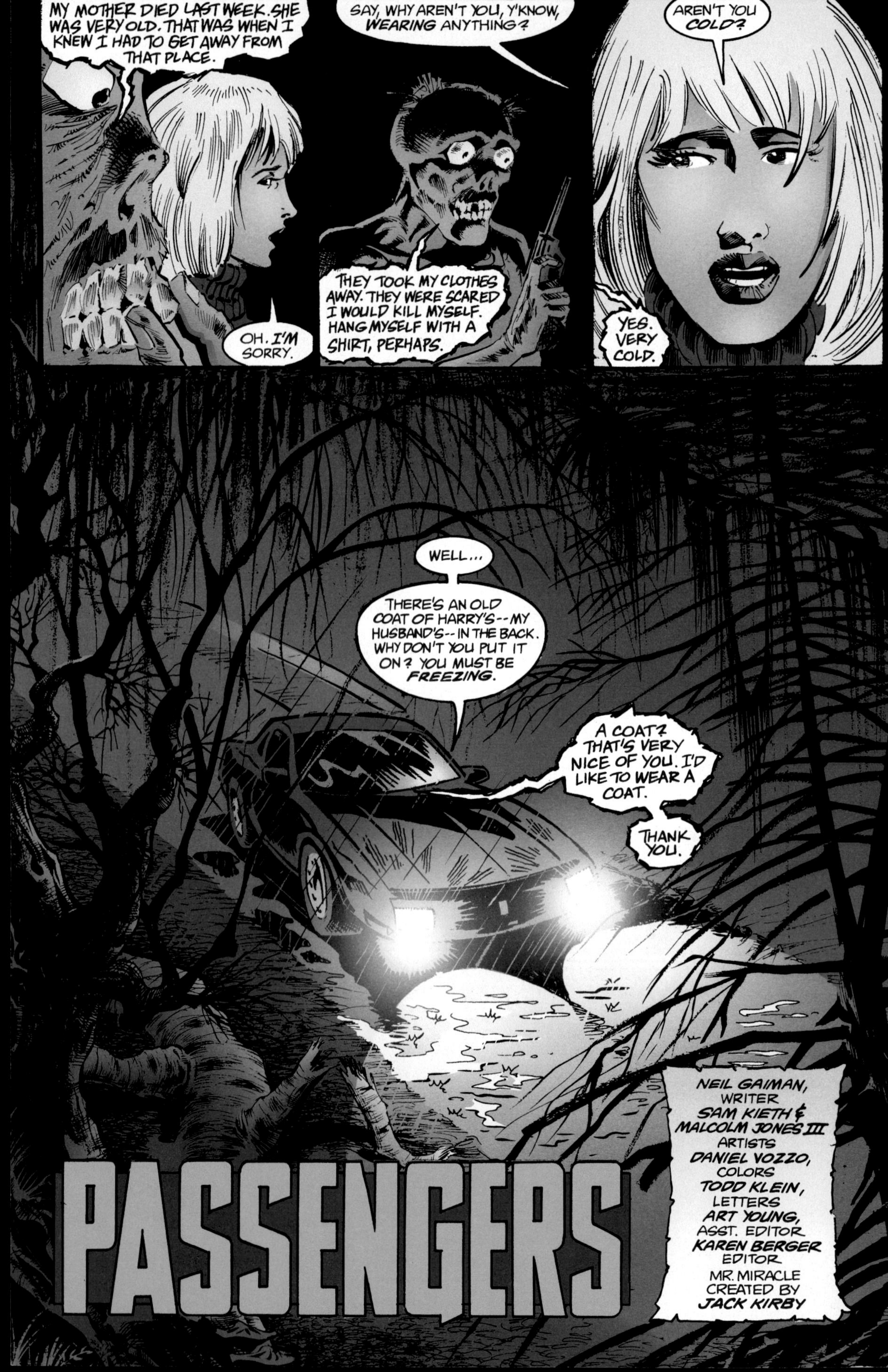

MY MOTHER DIED LAST WEEK. SHE WAS VERY OLD. THAT WAS WHEN I KNEW I HAD TO GET AWAY FROM THAT PLACE.
OH. I'M SORRY.
SAY, WHY AREN'T YOU, Y'KNOW, WEARING ANYTHING?
THEY TOOK MY CLOTHES AWAY. THEY WERE SCARED I WOULD KILL MYSELF. HANG MYSELF WITH A SHIRT, PERHAPS.
AREN'T YOU COLD?
YES. VERY COLD.
WELL...
THERE'S AN OLD COAT OF HARRY'S--MY HUSBAND'S--IN THE BACK. WHY DON'T YOU PUT IT ON? YOU MUST BE FREEZING.
A COAT? THAT'S VERY NICE OF YOU. I'D LIKE TO WEAR A COAT.
THANK YOU.
PASSENGERS
NEIL GAIMAN, WRITER
SAM KIETH & MALCOLM JONES III ARTISTS
DANIEL VOZZO, COLORS
TODD KLEIN, LETTERS
ART YOUNG, ASST. EDITOR
KAREN BERGER EDITOR
MR. MIRACLE CREATED BY JACK KIRBY

OK. I'VE SEARCHED THE OLD JUSTICE LEAGUE OF AMERICA FILES, AND I *THINK* WE'VE FOUND IT.

SHOULD BE UP ON THE SCREENS ANY SECOND.

THERE YOU GO. TAKEN FROM SOME *PSYCHO* CALLING HIMSELF "DOCTOR DESTINY." HE WAS USING IT TO AFFECT PEOPLE'S *DREAMS* -- MAKE NIGHTMARES REAL, THAT KIND OF THING.

IT WAS KEPT IN THE *TROPHY* ROOM ON THE *SATELLITE.*

SPACE JUNK. DESTROYED.

And my *ruby?*

Where is this satellite?

COULD HAVE BEEN DESTROYED. COULD HAVE BEEN *MOVED* TO THE DETROIT FORTRESS, OR THE *SECRET SANCTUARY,* OR...

You don't know.

YEAH... IS THIS KIND OF THING GOING TO HAPPEN *EVERY* TIME I STAY HERE OVERNIGHT? DON'T ANSWER THAT...

LEMME SEE. *BATMAN?* NOPE, IT'S 3:30 AM. HE'LL BE AT WORK...

GOT IT!

HMMM. LET'S GO WAKE HIM UP.

NOT A *CLUE.*

Somebody must know.

WHO *ELSE* WAS IN THE OLD JLA...?

WHAT'S YOUR NAME?

ROSEMARY.

ROSEMARY... THAT'S FOR REMEMBERING...

SO WHAT SHOULD I CALL YOU?

I USED TO CALL MYSELF... DESTINY. DOCTOR DESTINY.

IT WASN'T MY NAME. MY MOTHER CALLED ME JOHN. JOHNNY BOY. DREAM BOY.

I WAS A REAL DOCTOR. NOT A MEDICAL ONE. A SCIENTIST ONE. NOW I'M JUST DR. DEE. DR... JOHN... DEE...

JOHN... I'VE GOT SOME SANDWICHES, IN A LUNCH-PAIL BEHIND MY SEAT, IF YOU'RE HUNGRY...?

NO. NO THANK YOU. I'M NEVER VERY HUNGRY ANY MORE...

LOOK, JOHN. I'M A NURSE. YOU CAN TELL ME, I WON'T FREAK. IS IT THE BIG A?

BIG A?

NIGHT OF THE LIVING DEAD
PLUS CO-HIT:
ZOMBY WOOF

AIDS.

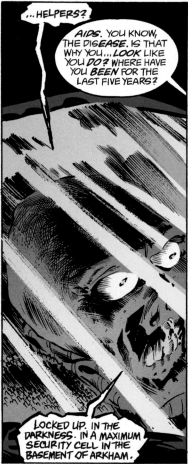

...HELPERS?

AIDS. YOU KNOW, THE DISEASE. IS THAT WHY YOU... LOOK LIKE YOU DO? WHERE HAVE YOU BEEN FOR THE LAST FIVE YEARS?

LOCKED UP. IN THE DARKNESS. IN A MAXIMUM SECURITY CELL IN THE BASEMENT OF ARKHAM.

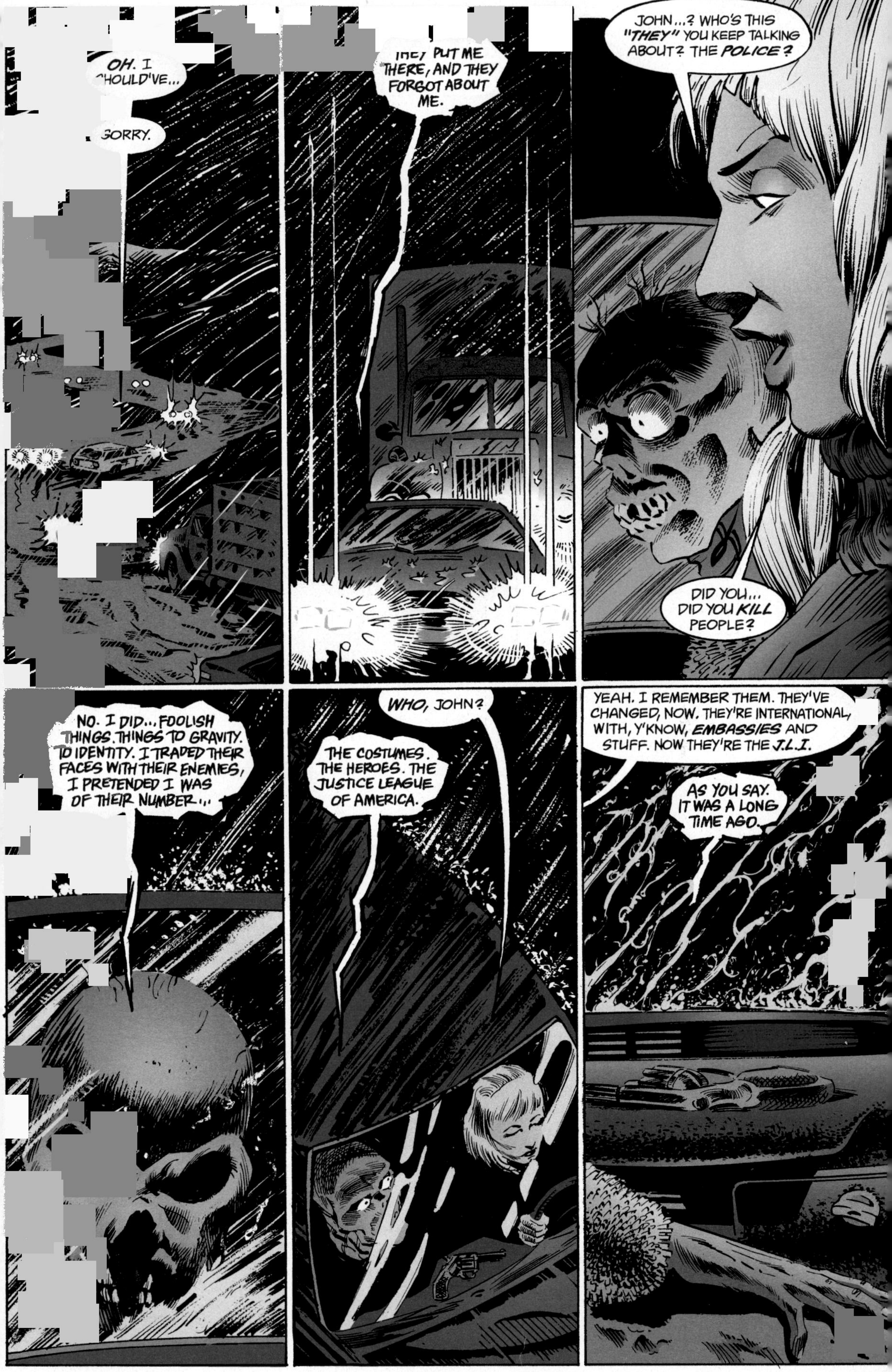
OH. I SHOULD'VE...
SORRY.
THEY PUT ME THERE, AND THEY FORGOT ABOUT ME.
JOHN...? WHO'S THIS "THEY" YOU KEEP TALKING ABOUT? THE POLICE?
DID YOU... DID YOU KILL PEOPLE?
NO. I DID... FOOLISH THINGS. THINGS TO GRAVITY. TO IDENTITY. I TRADED THEIR FACES WITH THEIR ENEMIES, I PRETENDED I WAS OF THEIR NUMBER...
WHO, JOHN?
THE COSTUMES. THE HEROES. THE JUSTICE LEAGUE OF AMERICA.
YEAH. I REMEMBER THEM. THEY'VE CHANGED, NOW. THEY'RE INTERNATIONAL, WITH, Y'KNOW, EMBASSIES AND STUFF. NOW THEY'RE THE J.L.I.
AS YOU SAY. IT WAS A LONG TIME AGO.

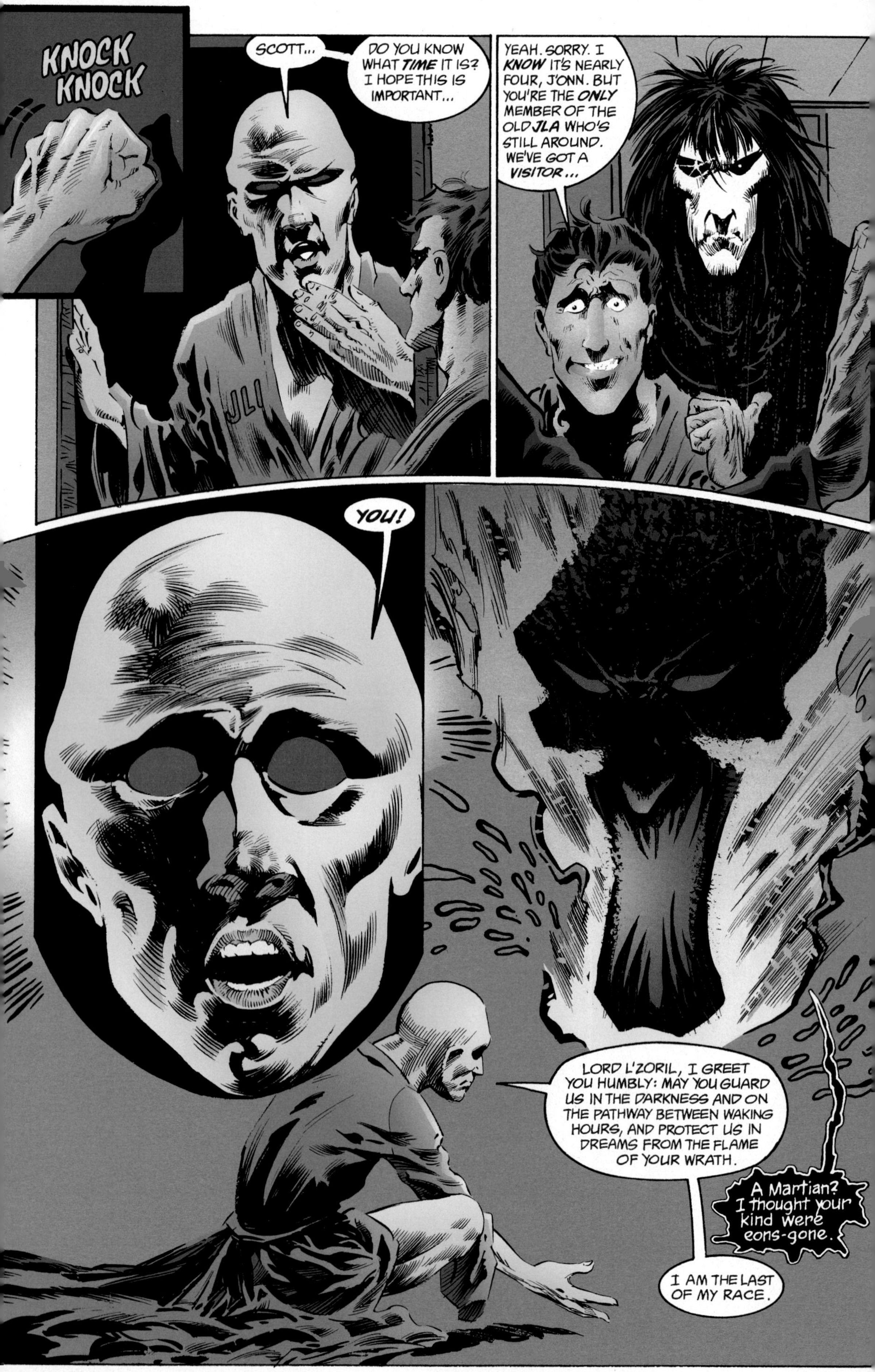
KNOCK KNOCK
SCOTT...
DO YOU KNOW WHAT TIME IT IS? I HOPE THIS IS IMPORTANT...
YEAH. SORRY. I KNOW IT'S NEARLY FOUR, J'ONN. BUT YOU'RE THE ONLY MEMBER OF THE OLD JLA WHO'S STILL AROUND. WE'VE GOT A VISITOR...
YOU!
LORD L'ZORIL, I GREET YOU HUMBLY: MAY YOU GUARD US IN THE DARKNESS AND ON THE PATHWAY BETWEEN WAKING HOURS, AND PROTECT US IN DREAMS FROM THE FLAME OF YOUR WRATH.
A Martian? I thought your kind were eons-gone.
I AM THE LAST OF MY RACE.

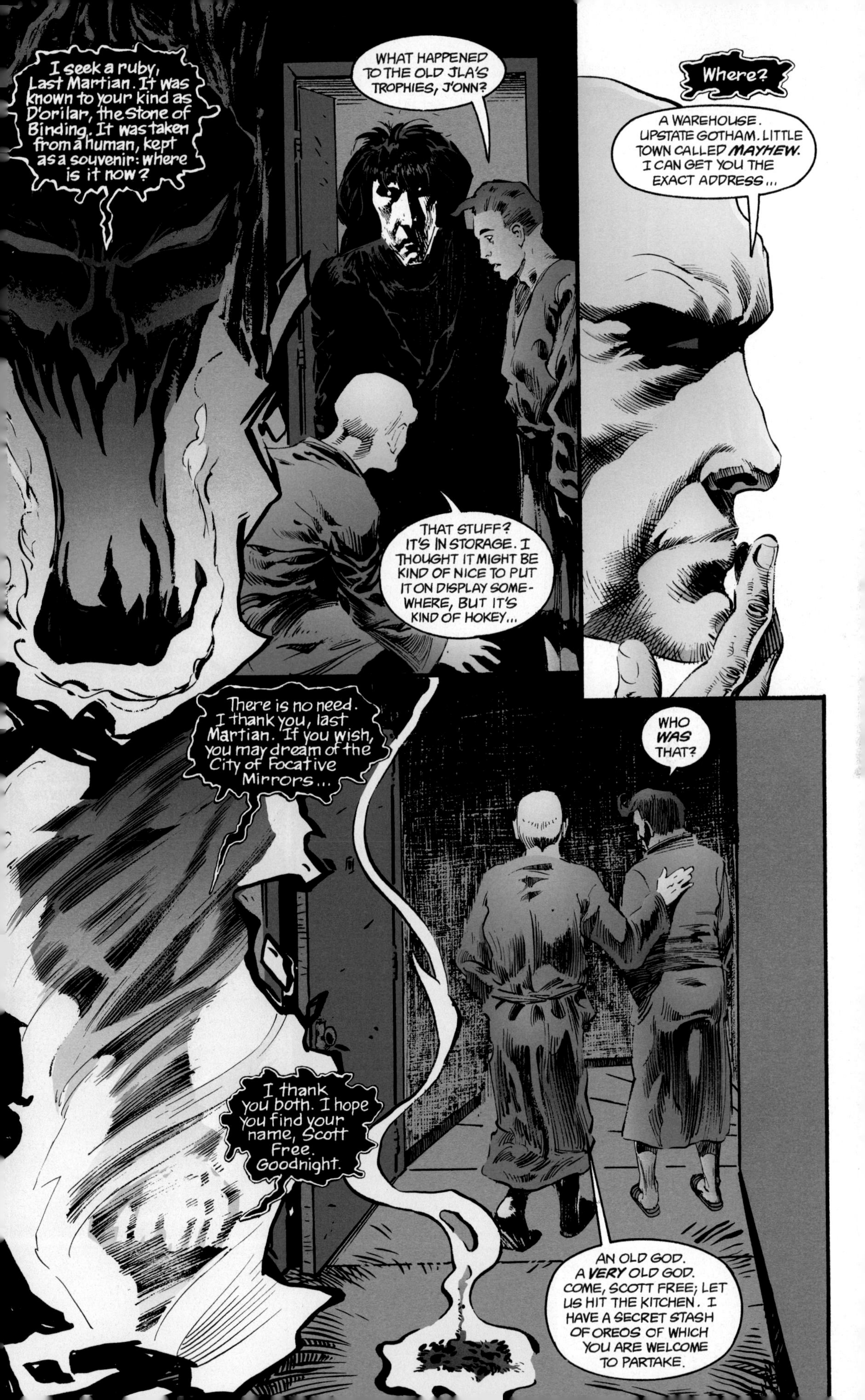
I seek a ruby, Last Martian. It was known to your kind as D'orilar, the Stone of Binding. It was taken from a human, kept as a souvenir: where is it now?
WHAT HAPPENED TO THE OLD JLA'S TROPHIES, J'ONN?
THAT STUFF? IT'S IN STORAGE. I THOUGHT IT MIGHT BE KIND OF NICE TO PUT IT ON DISPLAY SOMEWHERE, BUT IT'S KIND OF HOKEY...
Where?
A WAREHOUSE. UPSTATE GOTHAM. LITTLE TOWN CALLED MAYHEW. I CAN GET YOU THE EXACT ADDRESS...
There is no need. I thank you, last Martian. If you wish, you may dream of the City of Focative Mirrors...
I thank you both. I hope you find your name, Scott Free. Goodnight.
WHO WAS THAT?
AN OLD GOD. A VERY OLD GOD. COME, SCOTT FREE; LET US HIT THE KITCHEN. I HAVE A SECRET STASH OF OREOS OF WHICH YOU ARE WELCOME TO PARTAKE.

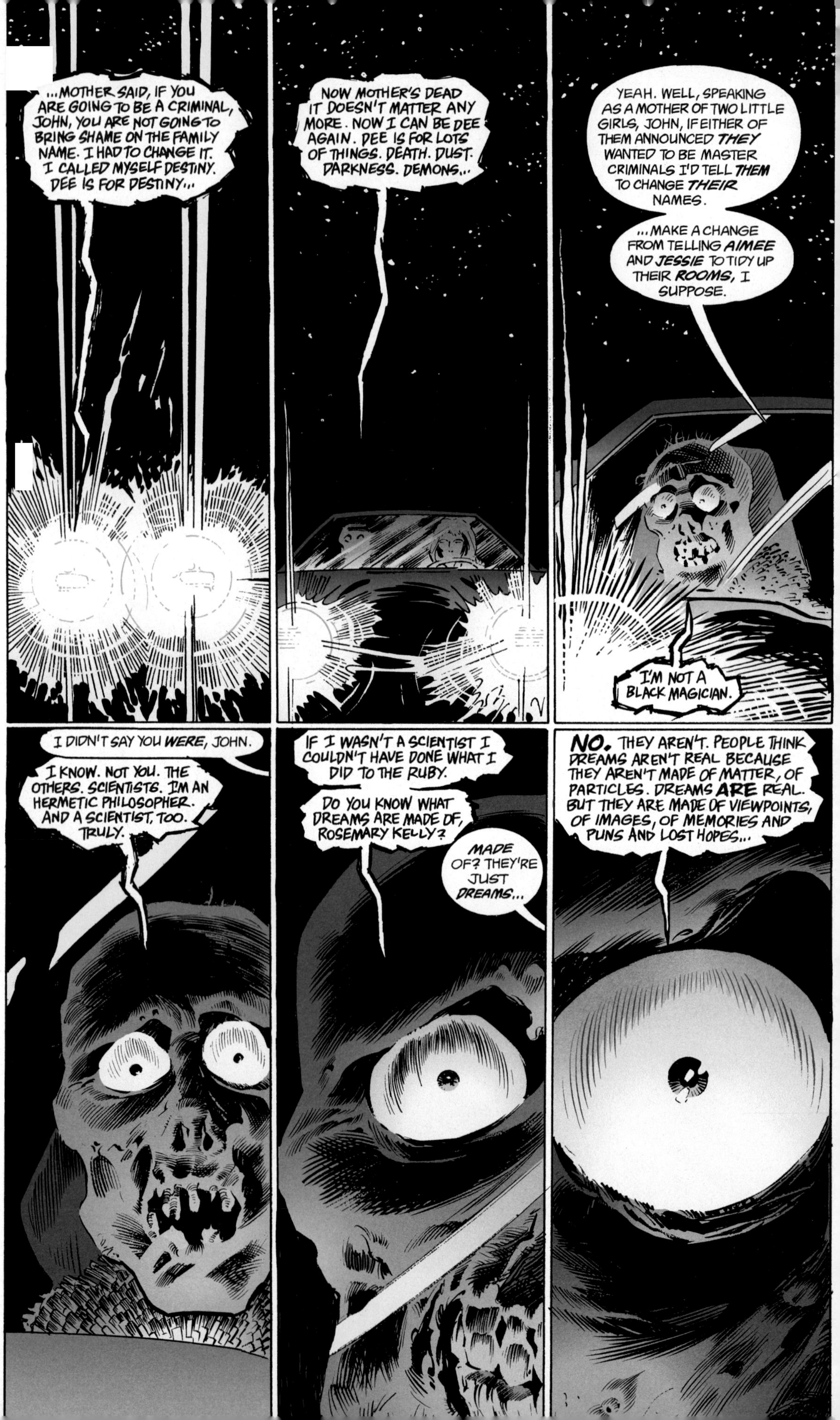
...MOTHER SAID, IF YOU ARE GOING TO BE A CRIMINAL, JOHN, YOU ARE NOT GOING TO BRING SHAME ON THE FAMILY NAME. I HAD TO CHANGE IT. I CALLED MYSELF DESTINY. DEE IS FOR DESTINY...
NOW MOTHER'S DEAD IT DOESN'T MATTER ANY MORE. NOW I CAN BE DEE AGAIN. DEE IS FOR LOTS OF THINGS. DEATH. DUST. DARKNESS. DEMONS...
YEAH. WELL, SPEAKING AS A MOTHER OF TWO LITTLE GIRLS, JOHN, IF EITHER OF THEM ANNOUNCED *THEY* WANTED TO BE MASTER CRIMINALS I'D TELL *THEM* TO CHANGE *THEIR* NAMES.
...MAKE A CHANGE FROM TELLING *AIMEE* AND *JESSIE* TO TIDY UP THEIR *ROOMS*, I SUPPOSE.
I'M NOT A BLACK MAGICIAN.
I DIDN'T SAY YOU *WERE*, JOHN.
I KNOW. NOT YOU. THE OTHERS. SCIENTISTS. I'M AN HERMETIC PHILOSOPHER. AND A SCIENTIST, TOO. TRULY.
IF I WASN'T A SCIENTIST I COULDN'T HAVE DONE WHAT I DID TO THE RUBY.
DO YOU KNOW WHAT DREAMS ARE MADE OF, ROSEMARY KELLY?
MADE OF? THEY'RE JUST *DREAMS*...
NO. THEY AREN'T. PEOPLE THINK DREAMS AREN'T REAL BECAUSE THEY AREN'T MADE OF MATTER, OF PARTICLES. DREAMS **ARE** REAL. BUT THEY ARE MADE OF VIEWPOINTS, OF IMAGES, OF MEMORIES AND PUNS AND LOST HOPES...

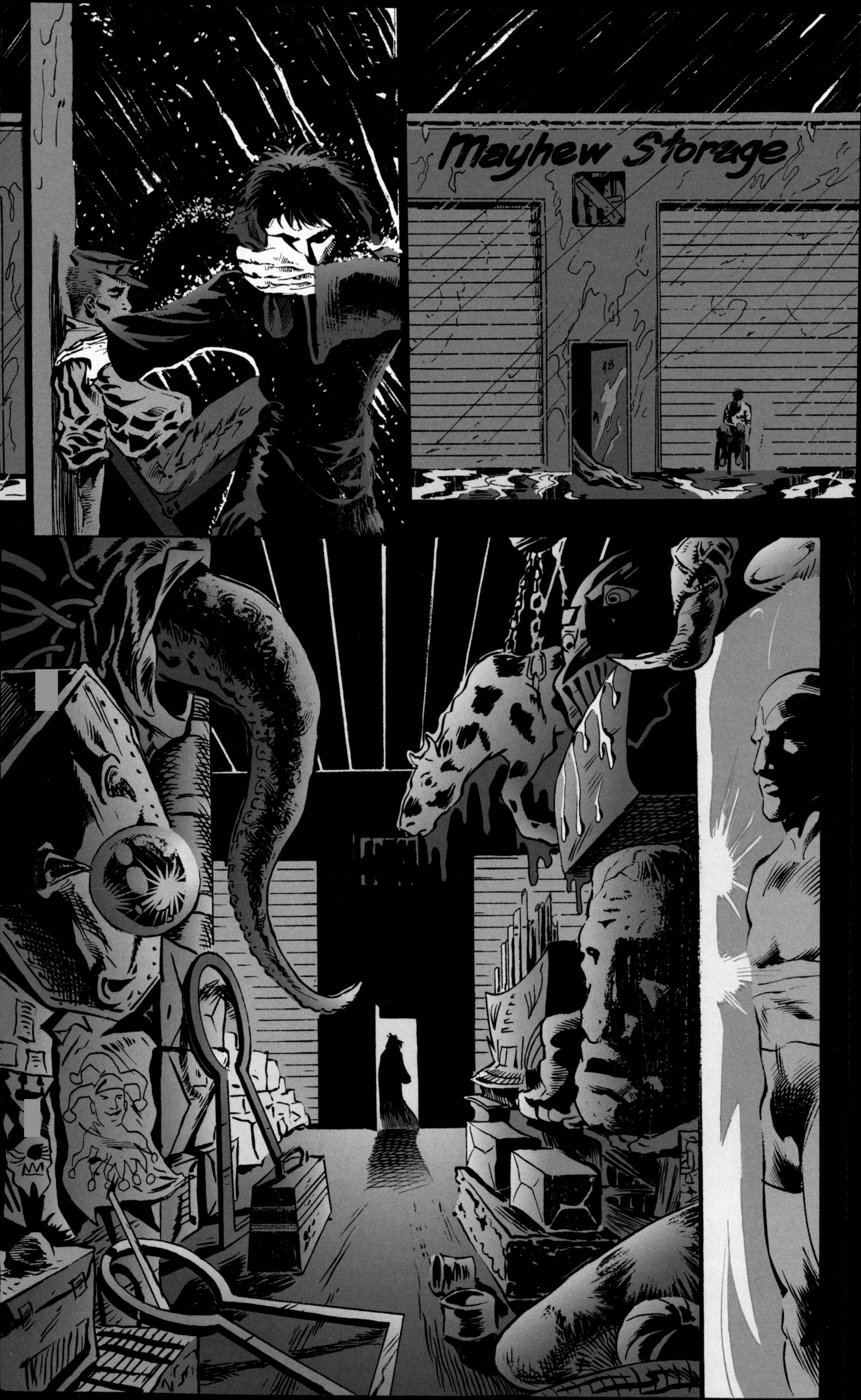
Mayhew Storage

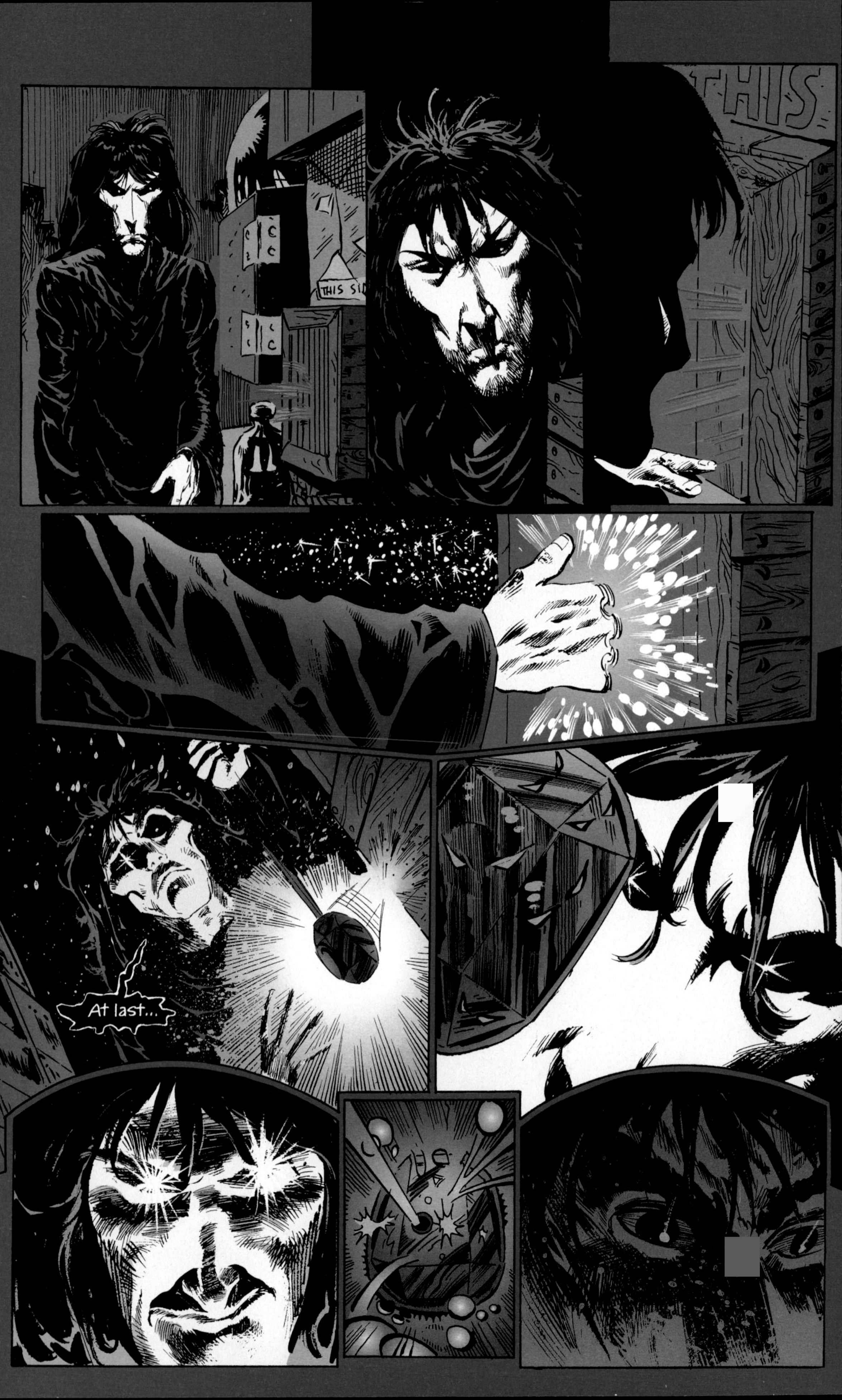
THIS
THIS SI
At last...

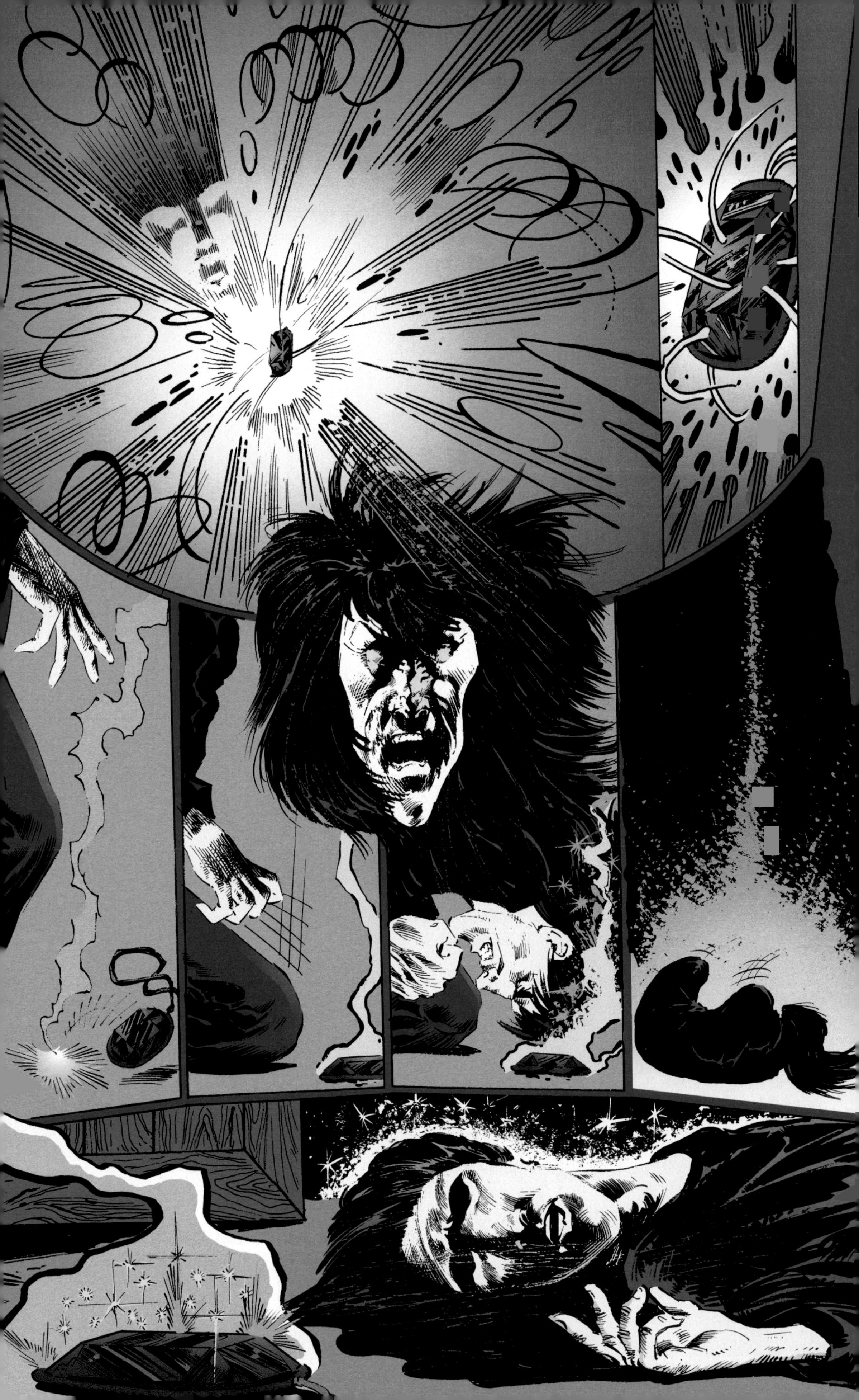

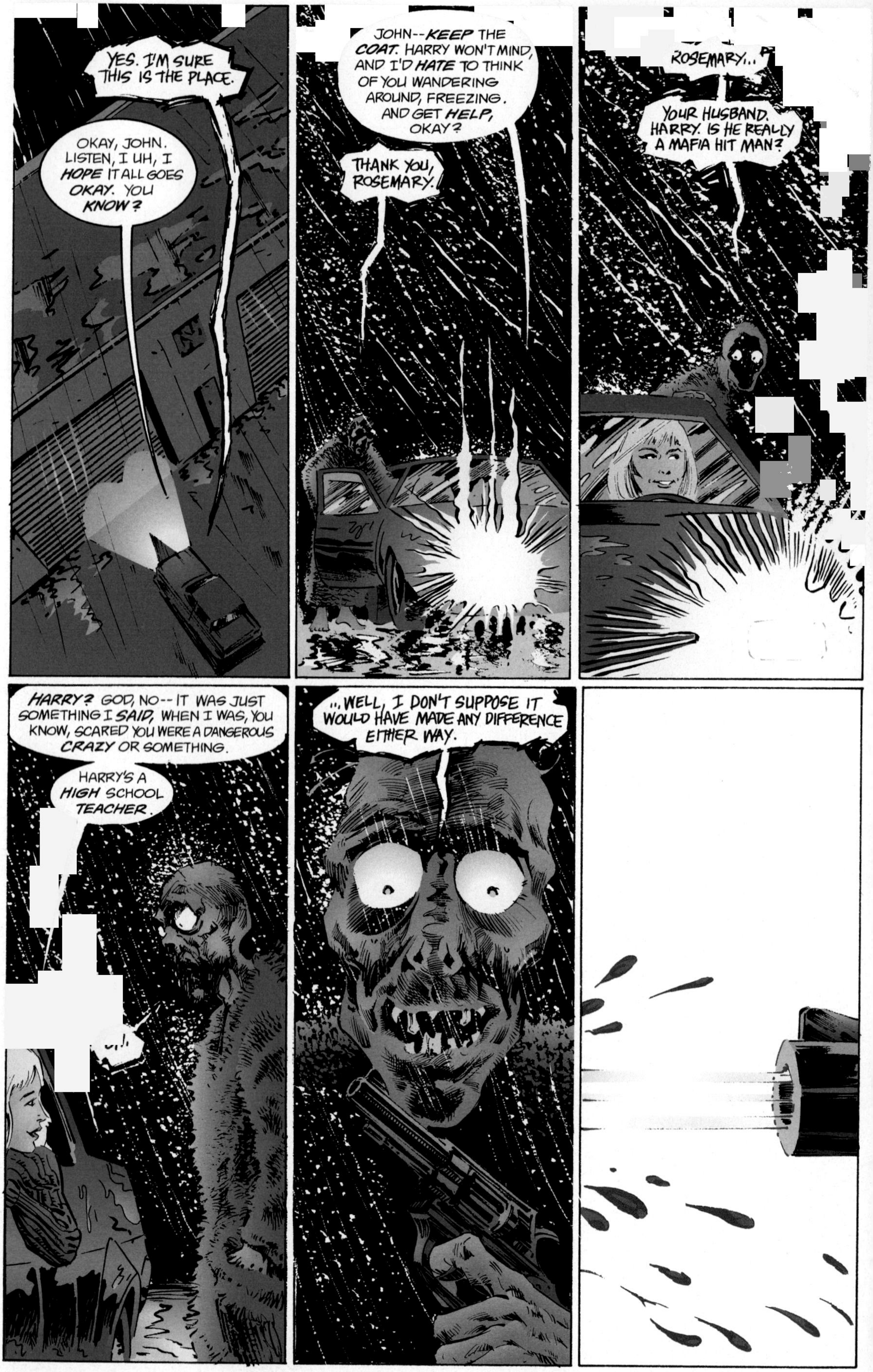
YES. I'M SURE THIS IS THE PLACE.
OKAY, JOHN. LISTEN, I UH, I HOPE IT ALL GOES OKAY. YOU KNOW?
JOHN--KEEP THE COAT. HARRY WON'T MIND, AND I'D HATE TO THINK OF YOU WANDERING AROUND, FREEZING. AND GET HELP, OKAY?
THANK YOU, ROSEMARY.
ROSEMARY...
YOUR HUSBAND. HARRY. IS HE REALLY A MAFIA HIT MAN?
HARRY? GOD, NO--IT WAS JUST SOMETHING I SAID, WHEN I WAS, YOU KNOW, SCARED YOU WERE A DANGEROUS CRAZY OR SOMETHING.
HARRY'S A HIGH SCHOOL TEACHER.
...WELL, I DON'T SUPPOSE IT WOULD HAVE MADE ANY DIFFERENCE EITHER WAY.

NEXT: WAITING FOR THE END OF THE WORLD...

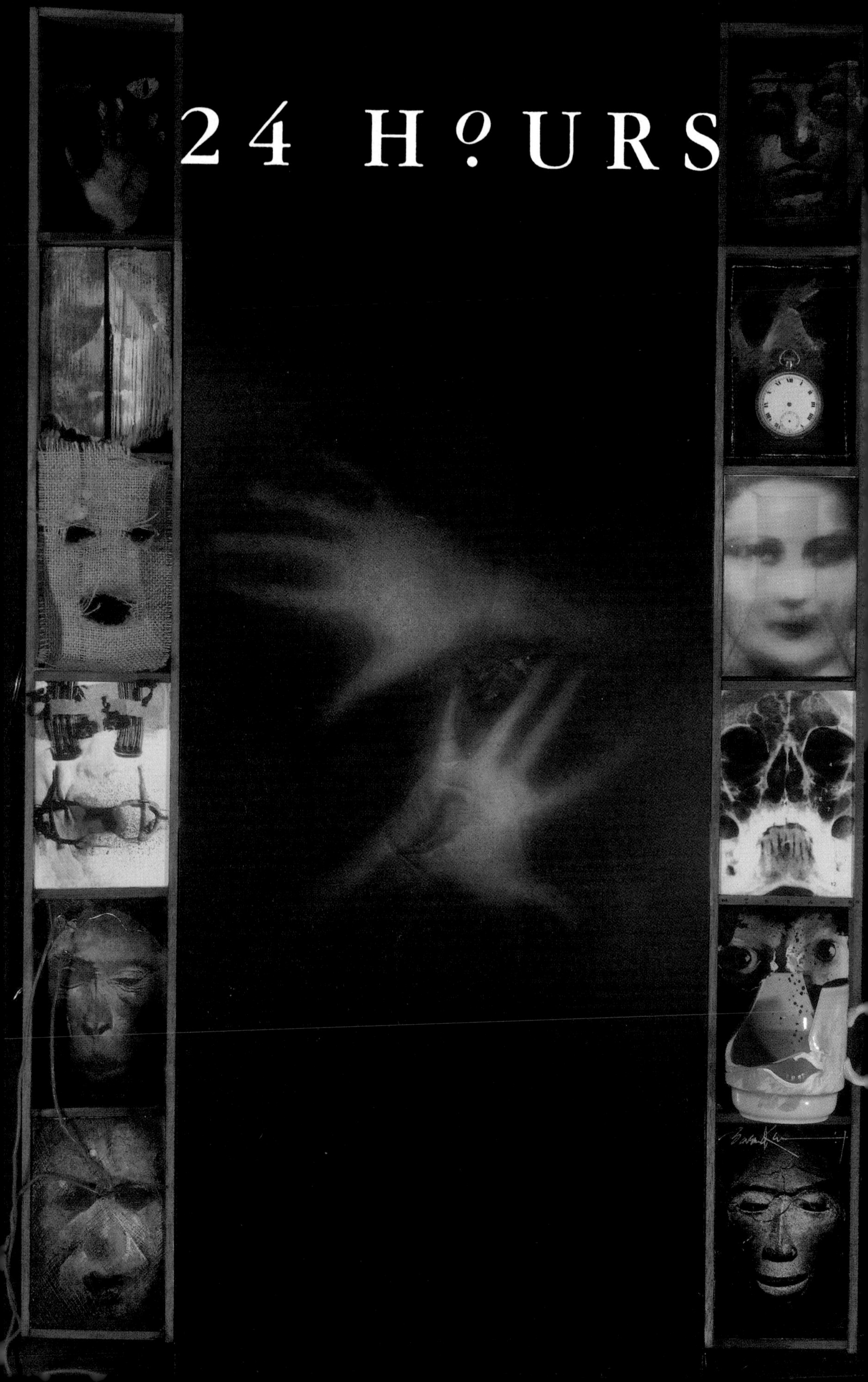
24 HOURS

HOUR 1: THE FLIES WALKED INTO THE WEB.

ART YOUNG, ASST. EDITOR
KAREN BERGER, EDITOR

DANIEL VOZZO, COLORIST

TODD KLEIN, LETTERS

NEIL GAIMAN, WRITER

MIKE DRINGENBERG & MALCOLM JONES III, ARTISTS & SPECIAL THANKS TO DOM CAROLA

OPEN

SPK SPK SPK

CIGARETTES

BETTE-- CAN I HAVE A COFFEE REFILL? AND A TUNA ON RYE?

SURE, HON.

ON HER DAYS OFF, AFTER SHE'S TIDIED THE HOUSE, BETTE MUNROE WRITES STORIES.

SHE WRITES THEM IN LONGHAND ON YELLOW LEGAL PADS.

HI! I'M BETTE

SOMETIMES SHE WRITES ABOUT HER EX-HUSBAND, BERNARD, AND ABOUT HER SON, BERNARD JR., WHO WENT OFF TO COLLEGE AND NEVER CAME BACK TO HER.

HI! I'M BETTE

SHE MAKES THESE STORIES END HAPPILY.

MOST OF HER STORIES, HOWEVER, ARE ABOUT HER CUSTOMERS.

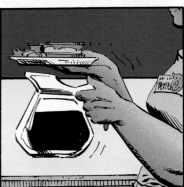

THEY LOOK AT HER AND THEY JUST SEE A WAITRESS; THEY DON'T KNOW SHE'S NURSING A SECRET.

A SECRET THAT KEEPS HER ACHING CALF-MUSCLES AND HER COFFEE-SCALDED FINGERS AND HER WEARINESS FROM DRAGGING HER DOWN...

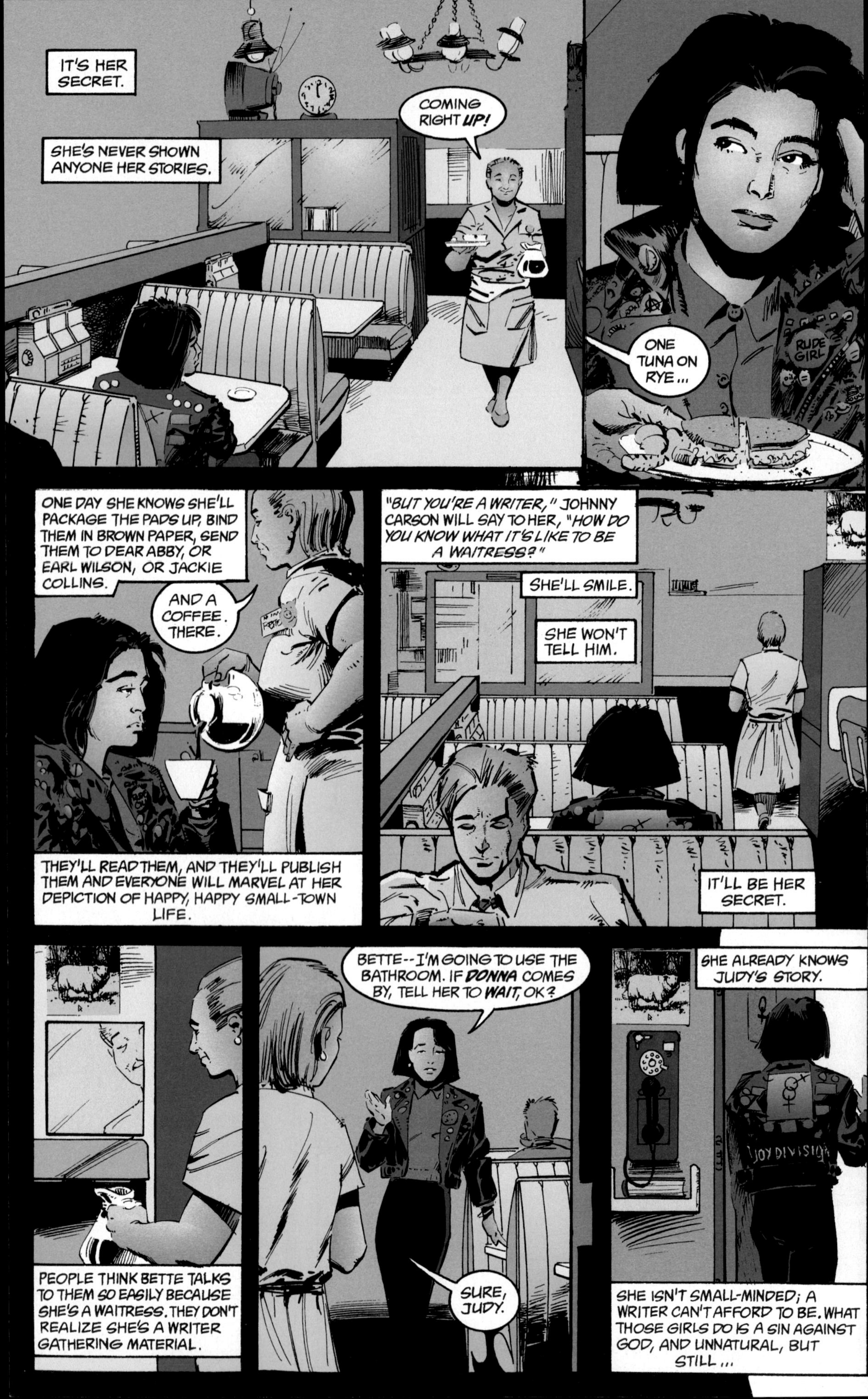
IT'S HER SECRET.
SHE'S NEVER SHOWN ANYONE HER STORIES.
COMING RIGHT UP!
ONE TUNA ON RYE...
RUDE GIRL
ONE DAY SHE KNOWS SHE'LL PACKAGE THE PADS UP, BIND THEM IN BROWN PAPER, SEND THEM TO DEAR ABBY, OR EARL WILSON, OR JACKIE COLLINS.
AND A COFFEE. THERE.
THEY'LL READ THEM, AND THEY'LL PUBLISH THEM AND EVERYONE WILL MARVEL AT HER DEPICTION OF HAPPY, HAPPY SMALL-TOWN LIFE.
"BUT YOU'RE A WRITER," JOHNNY CARSON WILL SAY TO HER, "HOW DO YOU KNOW WHAT IT'S LIKE TO BE A WAITRESS?"
SHE'LL SMILE.
SHE WON'T TELL HIM.
IT'LL BE HER SECRET.
BETTE--I'M GOING TO USE THE BATHROOM. IF DONNA COMES BY, TELL HER TO WAIT, OK?
SURE, JUDY.
PEOPLE THINK BETTE TALKS TO THEM SO EASILY BECAUSE SHE'S A WAITRESS. THEY DON'T REALIZE SHE'S A WRITER GATHERING MATERIAL.
SHE ALREADY KNOWS JUDY'S STORY.
JOY DIVISION
SHE ISN'T SMALL-MINDED; A WRITER CAN'T AFFORD TO BE. WHAT THOSE GIRLS DO IS A SIN AGAINST GOD, AND UNNATURAL, BUT STILL...

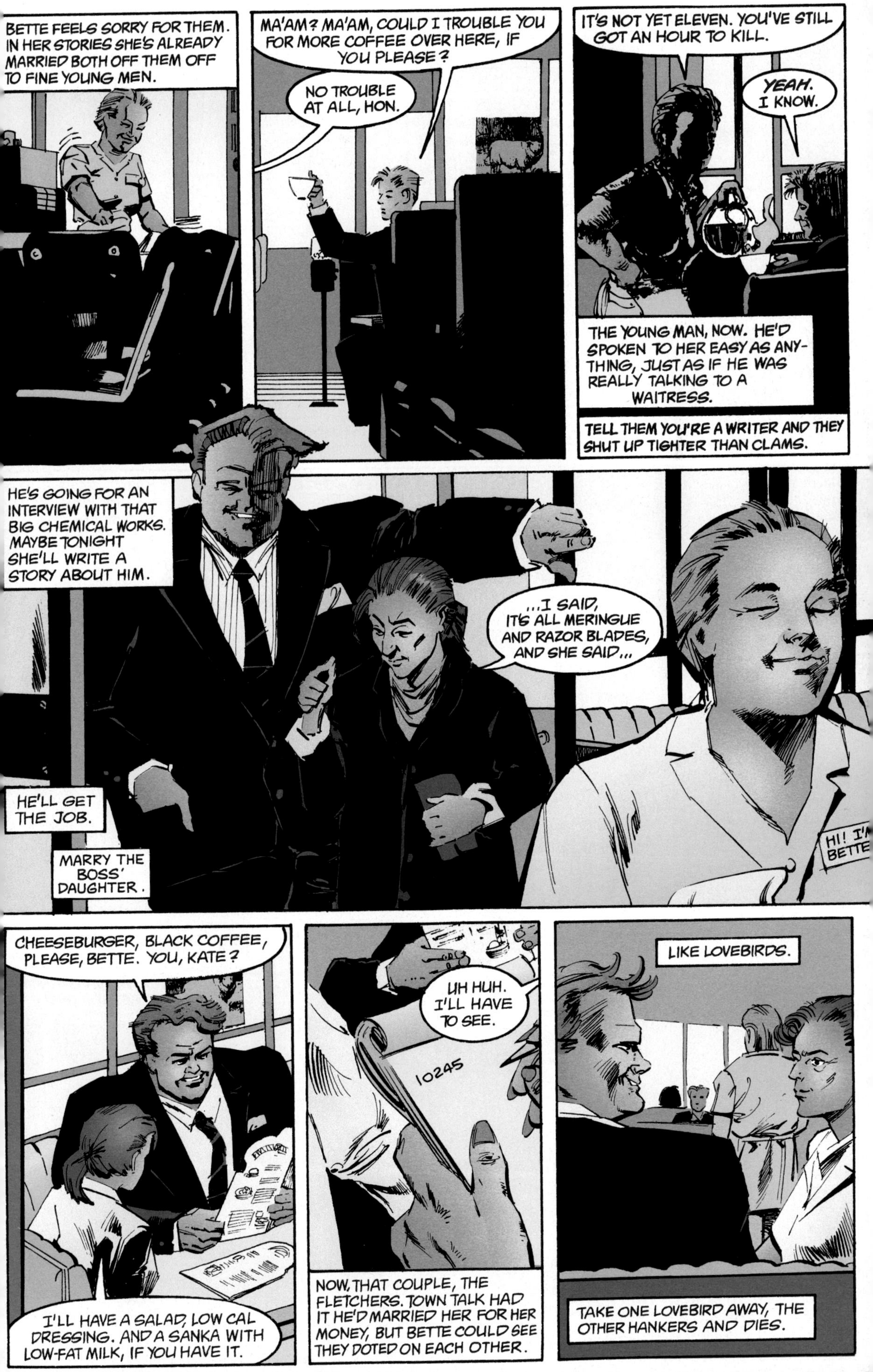
BETTE FEELS SORRY FOR THEM. IN HER STORIES SHE'S ALREADY MARRIED BOTH OFF THEM OFF TO FINE YOUNG MEN.
MA'AM? MA'AM, COULD I TROUBLE YOU FOR MORE COFFEE OVER HERE, IF YOU PLEASE?
NO TROUBLE AT ALL, HON.
IT'S NOT YET ELEVEN. YOU'VE STILL GOT AN HOUR TO KILL.
YEAH. I KNOW.
THE YOUNG MAN, NOW. HE'D SPOKEN TO HER EASY AS ANY-THING, JUST AS IF HE WAS REALLY TALKING TO A WAITRESS.
TELL THEM YOU'RE A WRITER AND THEY SHUT UP TIGHTER THAN CLAMS.
HE'S GOING FOR AN INTERVIEW WITH THAT BIG CHEMICAL WORKS. MAYBE TONIGHT SHE'LL WRITE A STORY ABOUT HIM.
...I SAID, IT'S ALL MERINGUE AND RAZOR BLADES, AND SHE SAID...
HE'LL GET THE JOB.
MARRY THE BOSS' DAUGHTER.
CHEESEBURGER, BLACK COFFEE, PLEASE, BETTE. YOU, KATE?
I'LL HAVE A SALAD, LOW CAL DRESSING. AND A SANKA WITH LOW-FAT MILK, IF YOU HAVE IT.
UH HUH. I'LL HAVE TO SEE.
10245
NOW, THAT COUPLE, THE FLETCHERS. TOWN TALK HAD IT HE'D MARRIED HER FOR HER MONEY, BUT BETTE COULD SEE THEY DOTED ON EACH OTHER.
LIKE LOVEBIRDS.
TAKE ONE LOVEBIRD AWAY, THE OTHER HANKERS AND DIES.

ZIPPEDEEDOODAH... ZIPPEDEE AYY...

ALL BETTE'S STORIES HAVE HAPPY ENDINGS. THAT'S BECAUSE SHE KNOWS WHERE TO STOP.

SHE'S REALIZED THE REAL PROBLEM WITH STORIES-- IF YOU KEEP THEM GOING LONG ENOUGH, THEY ALWAYS END IN DEATH.

HISSSSS

HI, BETTE. WHEN YOU'RE READY.

WITH YOU SOON, MARSH.

MARSH'S STORY SHE KNOWS ALREADY.

BETTE'S SORT OF LOOKED AFTER MARSH, SINCE MARSHA DIED. (MARSH AND MARSHA, THE WRITER IN HER WHISPERS, THEY WERE OBVIOUSLY MEANT FOR EACH OTHER.)

BUT MARSHA DRANK HERSELF TO DEATH, DIED YELLOW AND WHISPERING IN A SANITARIUM.

OH... THANKS.

HI I'M BETTE

MARSH, HE WENT SORT OF CRAZY AFTER THAT; A GOOD MAILMAN GONE BAD. STATE PEN, STEALING FROM THE MAILS. FIVE YEARS.

HE'S A TRUCKER THESE DAYS, WORKING OUT OF SOME UPSTATE TOWN THAT HAD NEVER HEARD OF HIM. BUT HE STILL LOOKS IN ON HER EVERY FEW WEEKS...

...FOR OLD TIME'S SAKE.

WHEN DO YOU GET OFF, HONEY?

YOU *KNOW,* MARSH, NOT UNTIL AFTER LUNCH.

S'OK. I'LL WAIT.

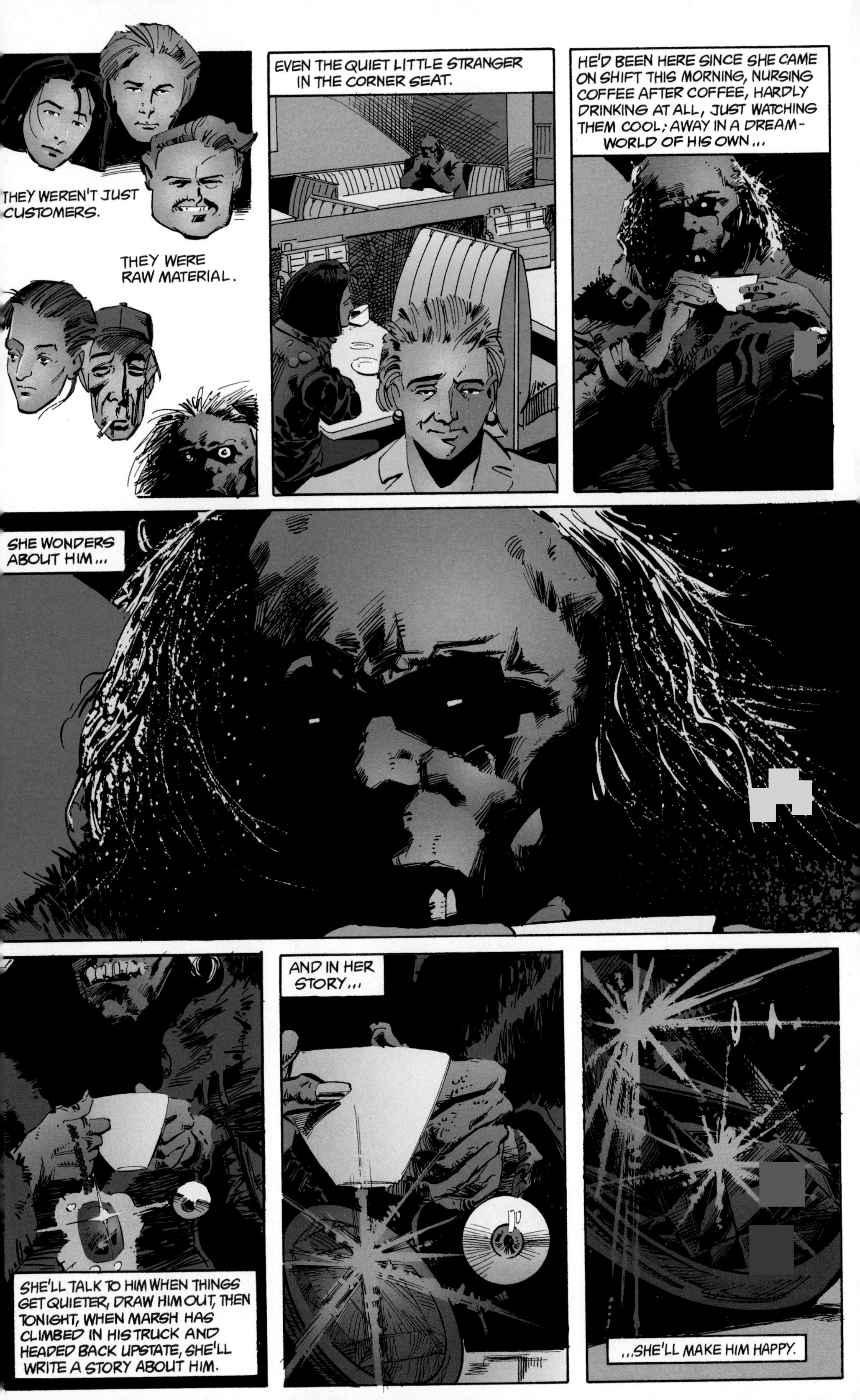
THEY WEREN'T JUST CUSTOMERS.
THEY WERE RAW MATERIAL.
EVEN THE QUIET LITTLE STRANGER IN THE CORNER SEAT.
HE'D BEEN HERE SINCE SHE CAME ON SHIFT THIS MORNING, NURSING COFFEE AFTER COFFEE, HARDLY DRINKING AT ALL, JUST WATCHING THEM COOL; AWAY IN A DREAM-WORLD OF HIS OWN...
SHE WONDERS ABOUT HIM...
SHE'LL TALK TO HIM WHEN THINGS GET QUIETER, DRAW HIM OUT, THEN TONIGHT, WHEN MARSH HAS CLIMBED IN HIS TRUCK AND HEADED BACK UPSTATE, SHE'LL WRITE A STORY ABOUT HIM.
AND IN HER STORY...
...SHE'LL MAKE HIM HAPPY.

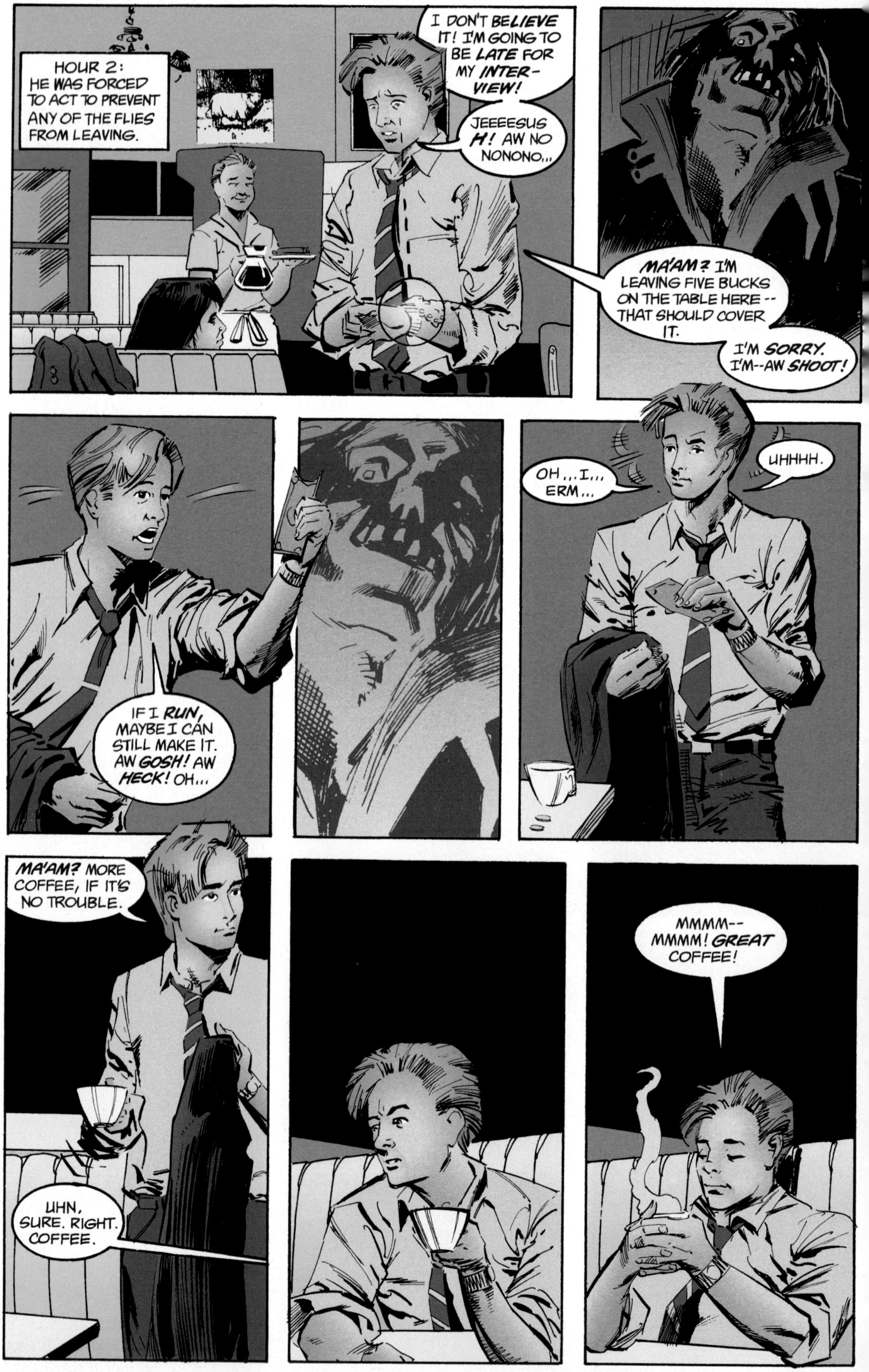
HOUR 2:
HE WAS FORCED TO ACT TO PREVENT ANY OF THE FLIES FROM LEAVING.
I DON'T BELIEVE IT! I'M GOING TO BE LATE FOR MY INTER-VIEW!
JEEEESUS H! AW NO NONONO...
MA'AM? I'M LEAVING FIVE BUCKS ON THE TABLE HERE -- THAT SHOULD COVER IT.
I'M SORRY. I'M--AW SHOOT!
IF I RUN, MAYBE I CAN STILL MAKE IT. AW GOSH! AW HECK! OH...
OH...I... ERM...
UHHHH.
MA'AM? MORE COFFEE, IF IT'S NO TROUBLE.
UHN, SURE. RIGHT. COFFEE.
MMMM-- MMMM! GREAT COFFEE!

HOUR 3: AFTERNOON SOAP OPERA

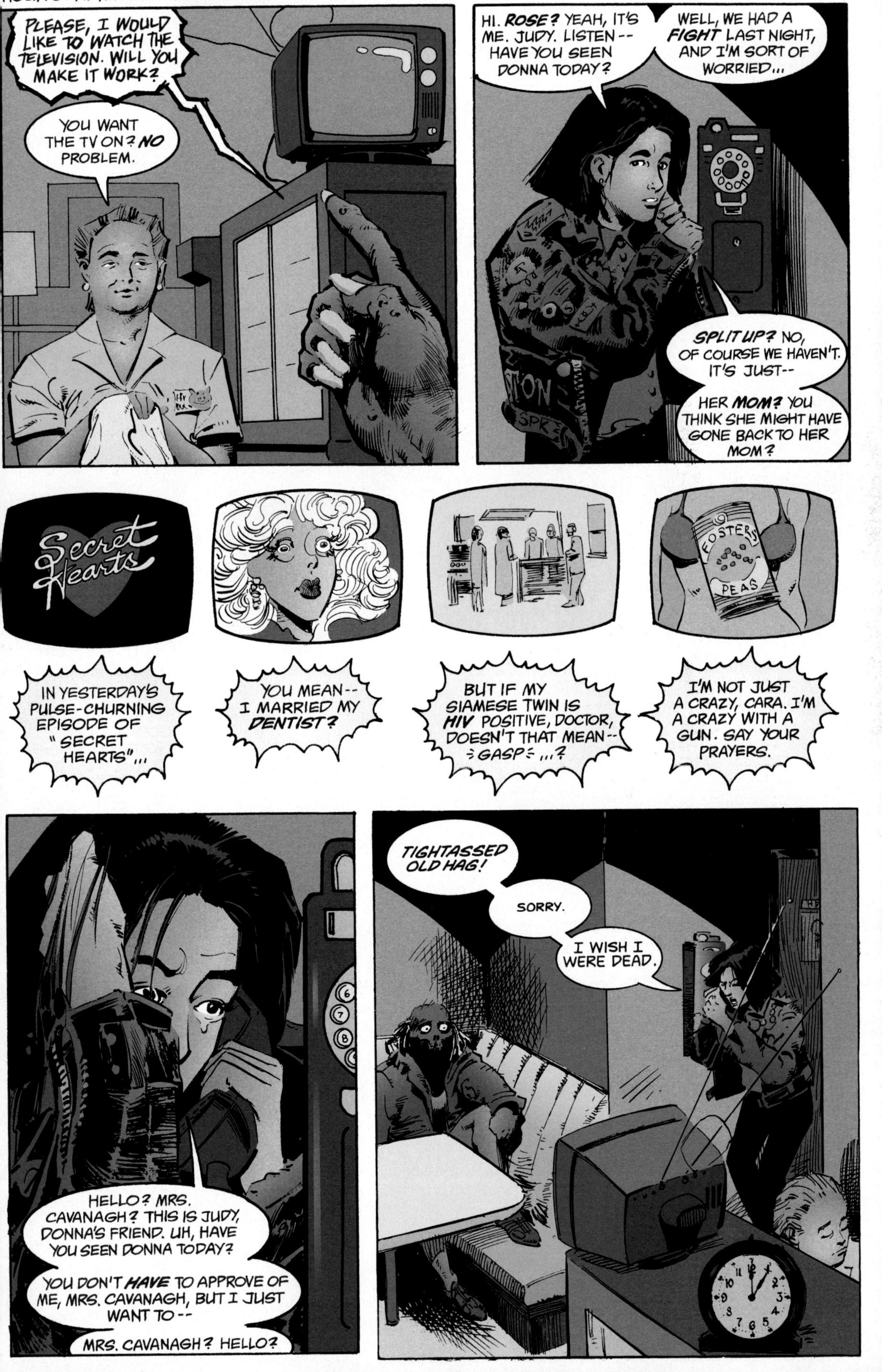
PLEASE, I WOULD LIKE TO WATCH THE TELEVISION. WILL YOU MAKE IT WORK?
YOU WANT THE TV ON? NO PROBLEM.
HI. ROSE? YEAH, IT'S ME. JUDY. LISTEN -- HAVE YOU SEEN DONNA TODAY?
WELL, WE HAD A FIGHT LAST NIGHT, AND I'M SORT OF WORRIED...
SPLIT UP? NO, OF COURSE WE HAVEN'T. IT'S JUST--
HER MOM? YOU THINK SHE MIGHT HAVE GONE BACK TO HER MOM?
Secret Hearts
FOSTERS PEAS
IN YESTERDAY'S PULSE-CHURNING EPISODE OF "SECRET HEARTS"...
YOU MEAN -- I MARRIED MY DENTIST?
BUT IF MY SIAMESE TWIN IS HIV POSITIVE, DOCTOR, DOESN'T THAT MEAN -- =GASP= ...?
I'M NOT JUST A CRAZY, CARA. I'M A CRAZY WITH A GUN. SAY YOUR PRAYERS.
HELLO? MRS. CAVANAGH? THIS IS JUDY, DONNA'S FRIEND. UH, HAVE YOU SEEN DONNA TODAY?
YOU DON'T HAVE TO APPROVE OF ME, MRS. CAVANAGH, BUT I JUST WANT TO --
MRS. CAVANAGH? HELLO?
TIGHTASSED OLD HAG!
SORRY.
I WISH I WERE DEAD.

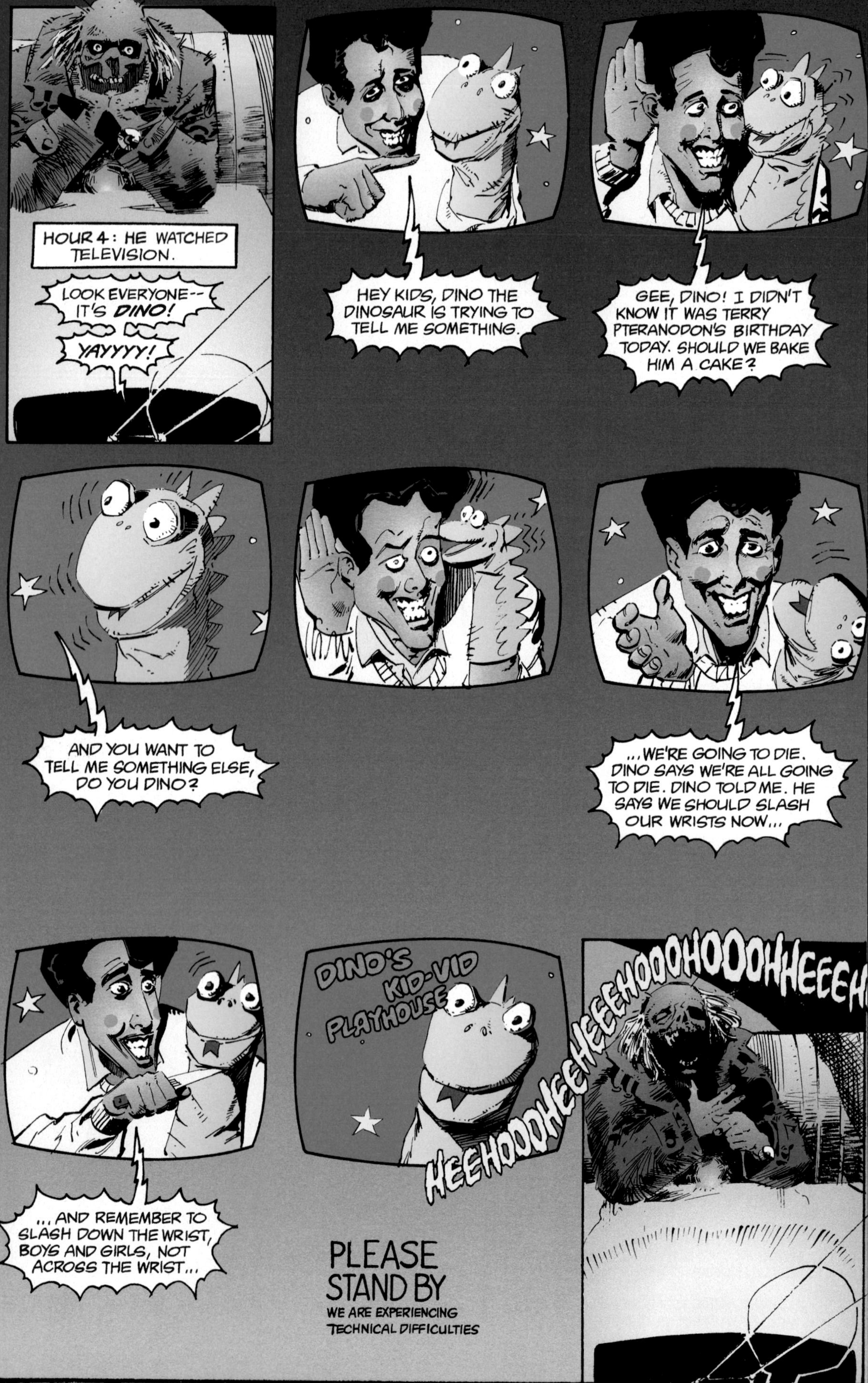
HOUR 4: HE WATCHED TELEVISION.
LOOK EVERYONE-- IT'S DINO!
YAYYYY!
HEY KIDS, DINO THE DINOSAUR IS TRYING TO TELL ME SOMETHING.
GEE, DINO! I DIDN'T KNOW IT WAS TERRY PTERANODON'S BIRTHDAY TODAY. SHOULD WE BAKE HIM A CAKE?
AND YOU WANT TO TELL ME SOMETHING ELSE, DO YOU DINO?
...WE'RE GOING TO DIE. DINO SAYS WE'RE ALL GOING TO DIE. DINO TOLD ME. HE SAYS WE SHOULD SLASH OUR WRISTS NOW...
...AND REMEMBER TO SLASH DOWN THE WRIST, BOYS AND GIRLS, NOT ACROSS THE WRIST...
DINO'S KID-VID PLAYHOUSE
PLEASE STAND BY
WE ARE EXPERIENCING TECHNICAL DIFFICULTIES
HEEHOOOHEEHEEEHOOOHOOOOHHEEEH

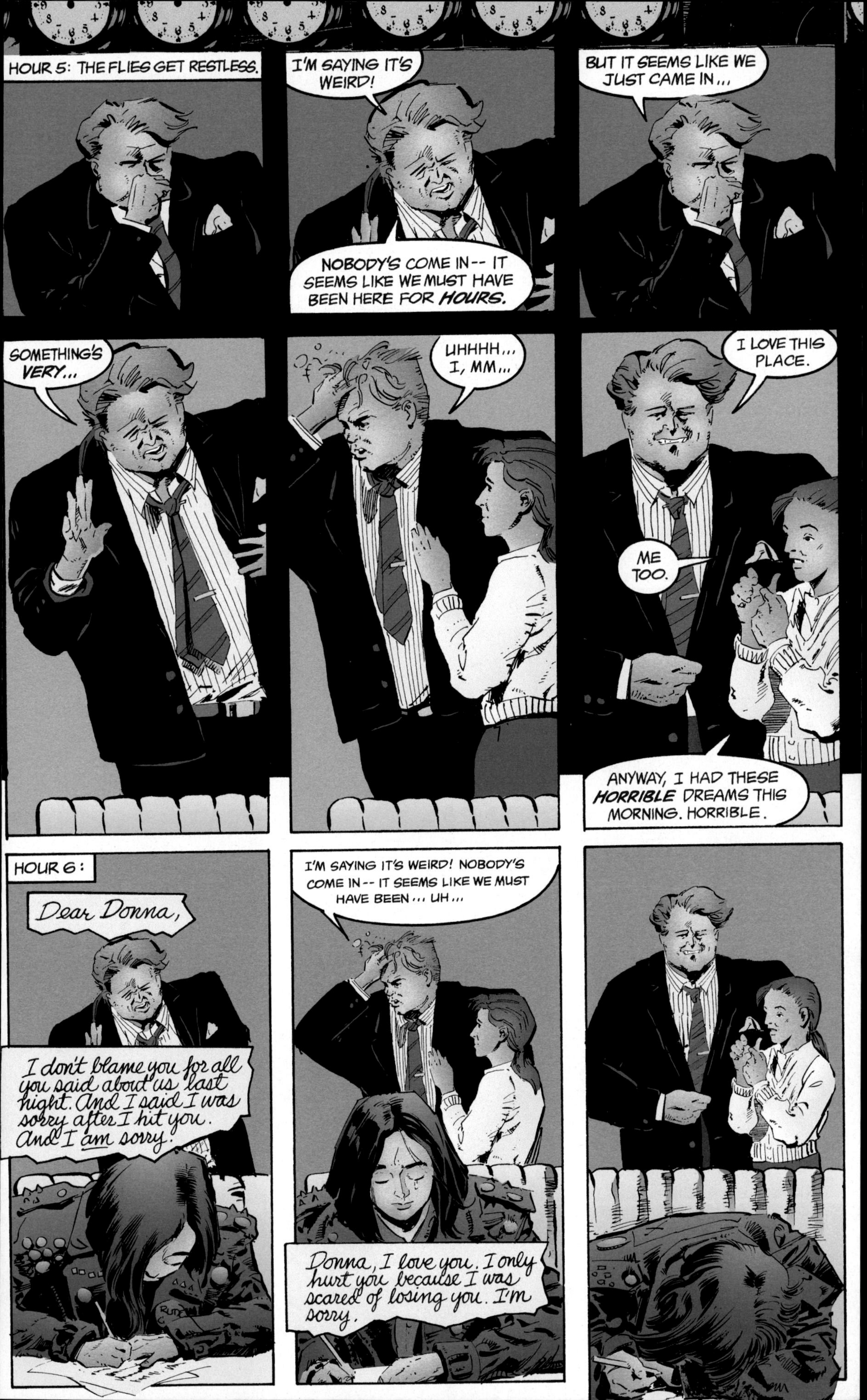
HOUR 5: THE FLIES GET RESTLESS.
I'M SAYING IT'S WEIRD!
NOBODY'S COME IN -- IT SEEMS LIKE WE MUST HAVE BEEN HERE FOR HOURS.
BUT IT SEEMS LIKE WE JUST CAME IN...
SOMETHING'S VERY...
UHHHH... I, MM...
I LOVE THIS PLACE.
ME TOO.
ANYWAY, I HAD THESE HORRIBLE DREAMS THIS MORNING. HORRIBLE.
HOUR 6:
Dear Donna,
I don't blame you for all you said about us last night. And I said I was sorry after I hit you. And I am sorry.
I'M SAYING IT'S WEIRD! NOBODY'S COME IN -- IT SEEMS LIKE WE MUST HAVE BEEN... UH...
Donna, I love you. I only hurt you because I was scared of losing you. I'm sorry.

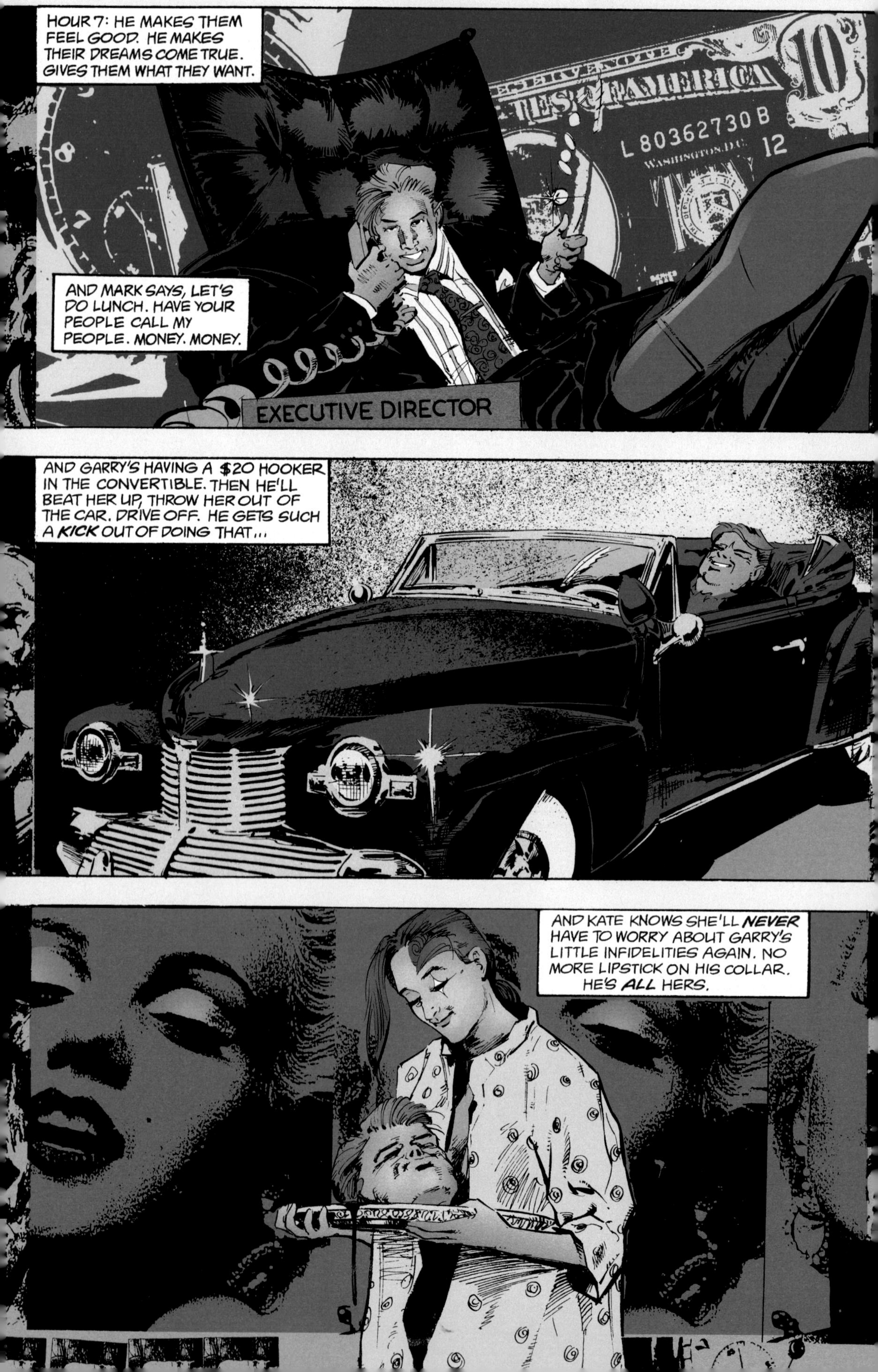
HOUR 7: HE MAKES THEM FEEL GOOD. HE MAKES THEIR DREAMS COME TRUE. GIVES THEM WHAT THEY WANT.
L 80362730 B
WASHINGTON, D.C.
12
10
AND MARK SAYS, LET'S DO LUNCH. HAVE YOUR PEOPLE CALL MY PEOPLE. MONEY. MONEY.
EXECUTIVE DIRECTOR
AND GARRY'S HAVING A $20 HOOKER IN THE CONVERTIBLE. THEN HE'LL BEAT HER UP, THROW HER OUT OF THE CAR. DRIVE OFF. HE GETS SUCH A KICK OUT OF DOING THAT...
AND KATE KNOWS SHE'LL NEVER HAVE TO WORRY ABOUT GARRY'S LITTLE INFIDELITIES AGAIN. NO MORE LIPSTICK ON HIS COLLAR. HE'S ALL HERS.

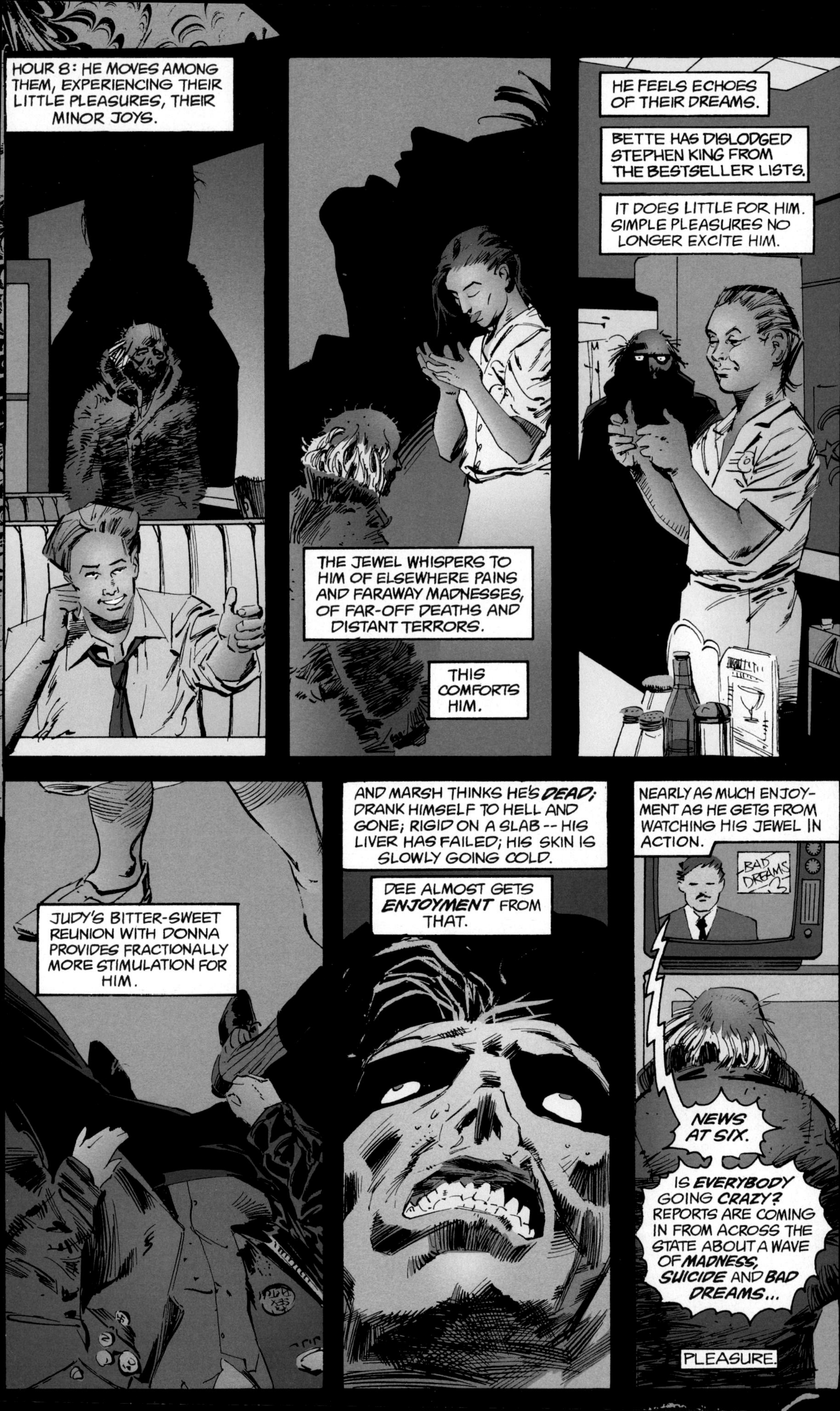
HOUR 8: HE MOVES AMONG THEM, EXPERIENCING THEIR LITTLE PLEASURES, THEIR MINOR JOYS.
THE JEWEL WHISPERS TO HIM OF ELSEWHERE PAINS AND FARAWAY MADNESSES, OF FAR-OFF DEATHS AND DISTANT TERRORS.
THIS COMFORTS HIM.
HE FEELS ECHOES OF THEIR DREAMS.
BETTE HAS DISLODGED STEPHEN KING FROM THE BESTSELLER LISTS.
IT DOES LITTLE FOR HIM. SIMPLE PLEASURES NO LONGER EXCITE HIM.
JUDY'S BITTER-SWEET REUNION WITH DONNA PROVIDES FRACTIONALLY MORE STIMULATION FOR HIM.
AND MARSH THINKS HE'S DEAD; DRANK HIMSELF TO HELL AND GONE; RIGID ON A SLAB -- HIS LIVER HAS FAILED; HIS SKIN IS SLOWLY GOING COLD.
DEE ALMOST GETS ENJOYMENT FROM THAT.
NEARLY AS MUCH ENJOYMENT AS HE GETS FROM WATCHING HIS JEWEL IN ACTION.
BAD DREAMS
NEWS AT SIX.
IS EVERYBODY GOING CRAZY? REPORTS ARE COMING IN FROM ACROSS THE STATE ABOUT A WAVE OF MADNESS, SUICIDE AND BAD DREAMS...
PLEASURE.

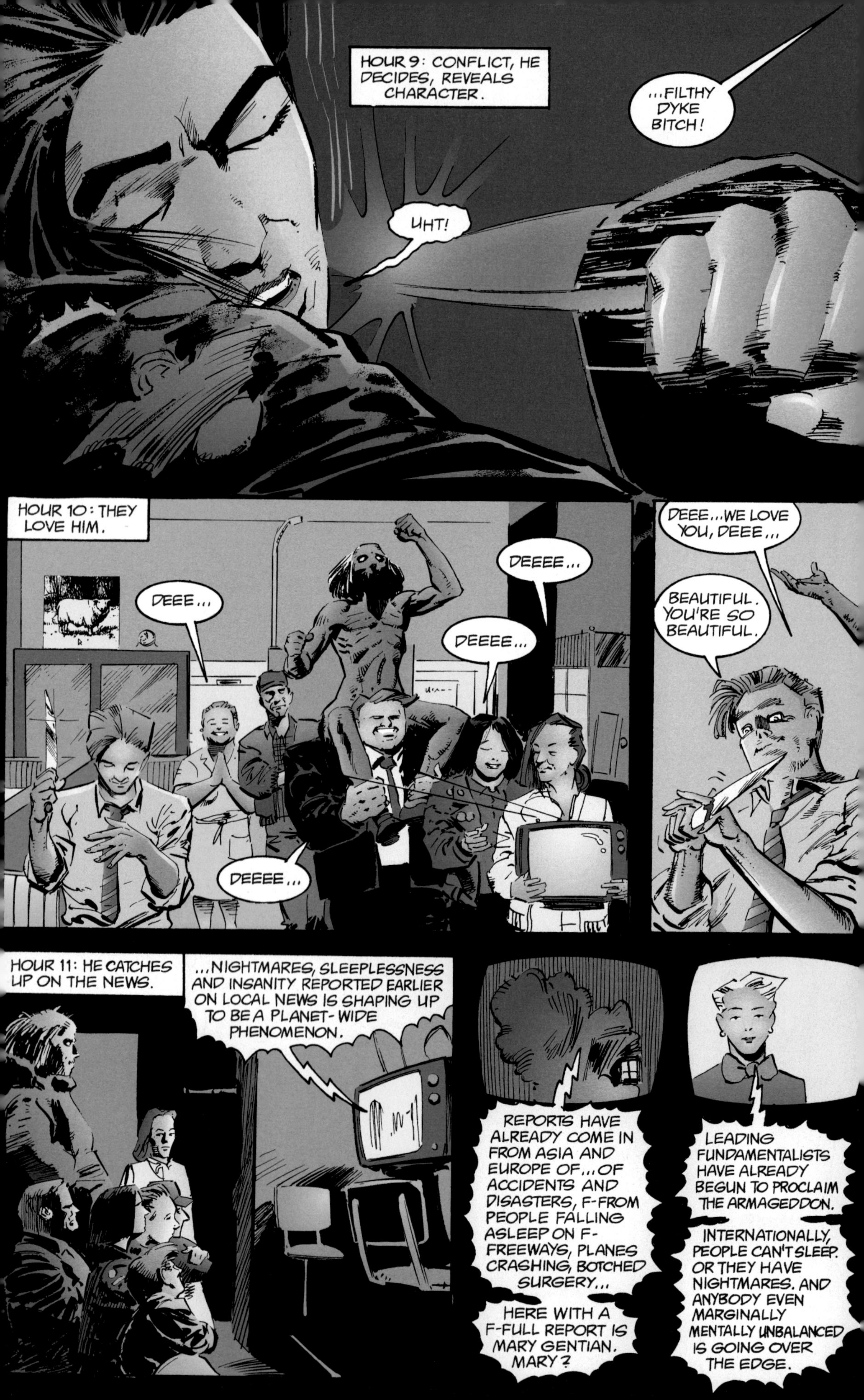
HOUR 9: CONFLICT, HE DECIDES, REVEALS CHARACTER.
...FILTHY DYKE BITCH!
UHT!
HOUR 10: THEY LOVE HIM.
DEEE...
DEEEE...
DEEEE...
DEEEE...
DEEE... WE LOVE YOU, DEEE...
BEAUTIFUL. YOU'RE SO BEAUTIFUL.
HOUR 11: HE CATCHES UP ON THE NEWS.
...NIGHTMARES, SLEEPLESSNESS AND INSANITY REPORTED EARLIER ON LOCAL NEWS IS SHAPING UP TO BE A PLANET-WIDE PHENOMENON.
REPORTS HAVE ALREADY COME IN FROM ASIA AND EUROPE OF... OF ACCIDENTS AND DISASTERS, F-FROM PEOPLE FALLING ASLEEP ON F-FREEWAYS, PLANES CRASHING, BOTCHED SURGERY...
HERE WITH A F-FULL REPORT IS MARY GENTIAN. MARY?
LEADING FUNDAMENTALISTS HAVE ALREADY BEGUN TO PROCLAIM THE ARMAGEDDON.
INTERNATIONALLY, PEOPLE CAN'T SLEEP. OR THEY HAVE NIGHTMARES. AND ANYBODY EVEN MARGINALLY MENTALLY UNBALANCED IS GOING OVER THE EDGE.

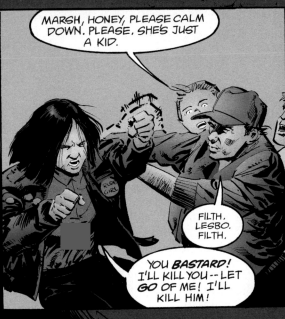

MARSH, HONEY, PLEASE CALM DOWN. PLEASE, SHE'S JUST A KID.

FILTH. LESBO. FILTH.

YOU *BASTARD!* I'LL KILL YOU -- LET *GO* OF ME! I'LL KILL HIM!

ALL YOU NEED. ALL YOU NEED IS A PROPER MAN. A REAL MAN. I'LL SHOW YOU, BITCH. I'LL GIVE IT TO YOU...

DOCTOR DEE. DOCTOR DEE.

GREAT AND WISE AND WONDERFUL...

DEE...

GOD

HE LICKS THE BLOOD FROM THE MAN'S FINGER. A GOD MUST NOT APPEAR UNGRACIOUS TOWARD A SACRIFICE; HOWEVER, HE DERIVES NO SATISFACTION FROM IT.

HE DOESN'T KNOW *WHAT* HE WANTS TO EAT. THERE MUST BE SOMETHING.

NO INTERNATIONAL SUPERHEROES WERE AVAILABLE FOR COMMENT, SO I SPOKE TO HERSCHEL OF LOCAL SUPER TEAM "THE AMAZING HERSCHEL AND BETTY":

HI. UH...AM I ON? IS THIS WORKING? YEAH...?

WELL, ME AND BETTY, WE FIGURE IT'S PROBABLY *RAYS*.

AND FINALLY, IN BALTIMORE, A WOMAN CLAIMS SHE'S TAUGHT HER DUCK TO TAP-DANCE. MORE ON THAT AFTER THE BREAK.

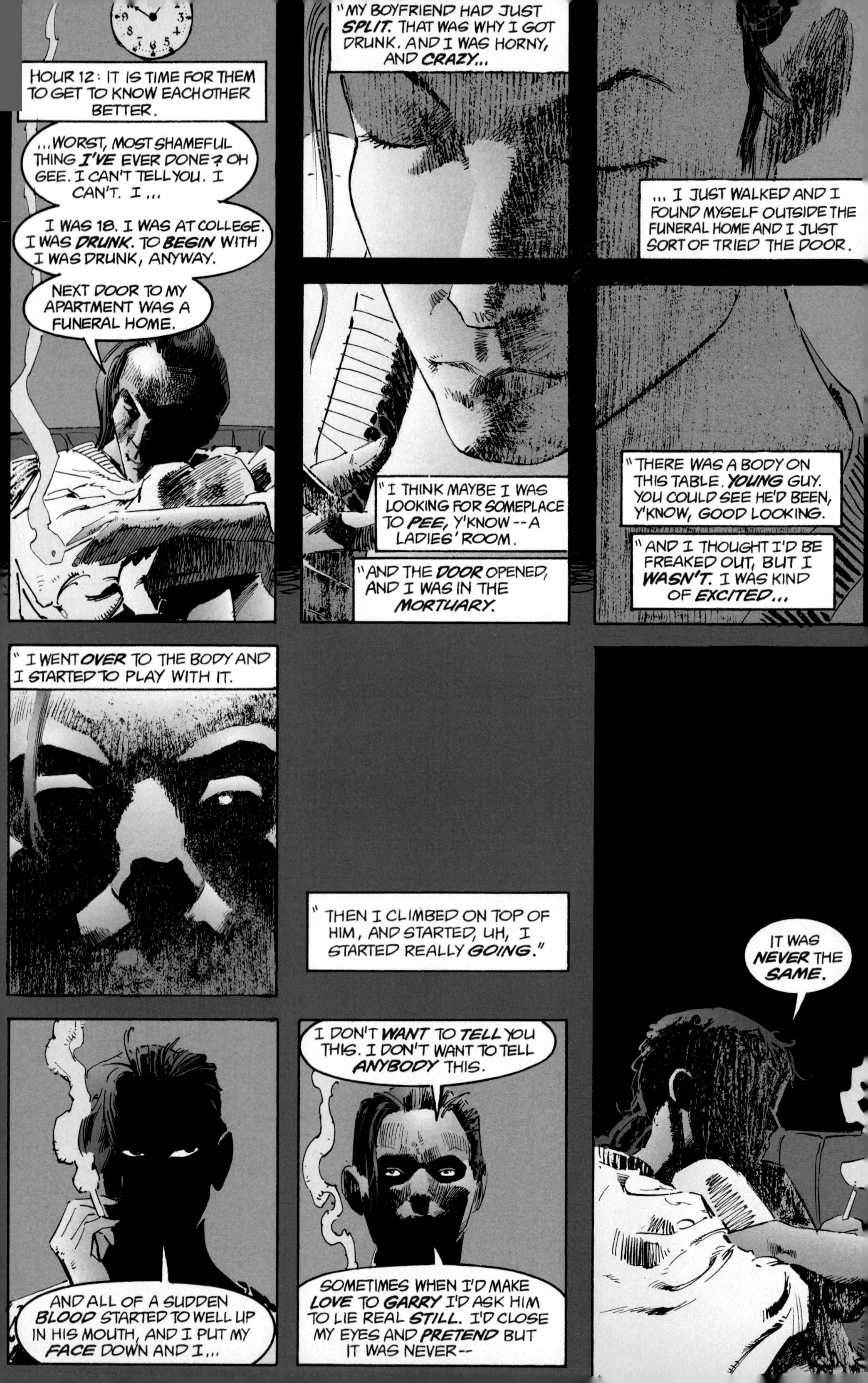
HOUR 12: IT IS TIME FOR THEM TO GET TO KNOW EACH OTHER BETTER.
...WORST, MOST SHAMEFUL THING I'VE EVER DONE? OH GEE. I CAN'T TELL YOU. I CAN'T. I...
I WAS 18. I WAS AT COLLEGE. I WAS DRUNK. TO BEGIN WITH I WAS DRUNK, ANYWAY.
NEXT DOOR TO MY APARTMENT WAS A FUNERAL HOME.
"MY BOYFRIEND HAD JUST SPLIT. THAT WAS WHY I GOT DRUNK. AND I WAS HORNY, AND CRAZY...
"I THINK MAYBE I WAS LOOKING FOR SOMEPLACE TO PEE, Y'KNOW -- A LADIES' ROOM.
"AND THE DOOR OPENED, AND I WAS IN THE MORTUARY.
... I JUST WALKED AND I FOUND MYSELF OUTSIDE THE FUNERAL HOME AND I JUST SORT OF TRIED THE DOOR.
"THERE WAS A BODY ON THIS TABLE. YOUNG GUY. YOU COULD SEE HE'D BEEN, Y'KNOW, GOOD LOOKING.
"AND I THOUGHT I'D BE FREAKED OUT, BUT I WASN'T. I WAS KIND OF EXCITED...
" I WENT OVER TO THE BODY AND I STARTED TO PLAY WITH IT.
" THEN I CLIMBED ON TOP OF HIM, AND STARTED, UH, I STARTED REALLY GOING."
AND ALL OF A SUDDEN BLOOD STARTED TO WELL UP IN HIS MOUTH, AND I PUT MY FACE DOWN AND I,...
I DON'T WANT TO TELL YOU THIS. I DON'T WANT TO TELL ANYBODY THIS.
SOMETIMES WHEN I'D MAKE LOVE TO GARRY I'D ASK HIM TO LIE REAL STILL. I'D CLOSE MY EYES AND PRETEND BUT IT WAS NEVER--
IT WAS NEVER THE SAME.

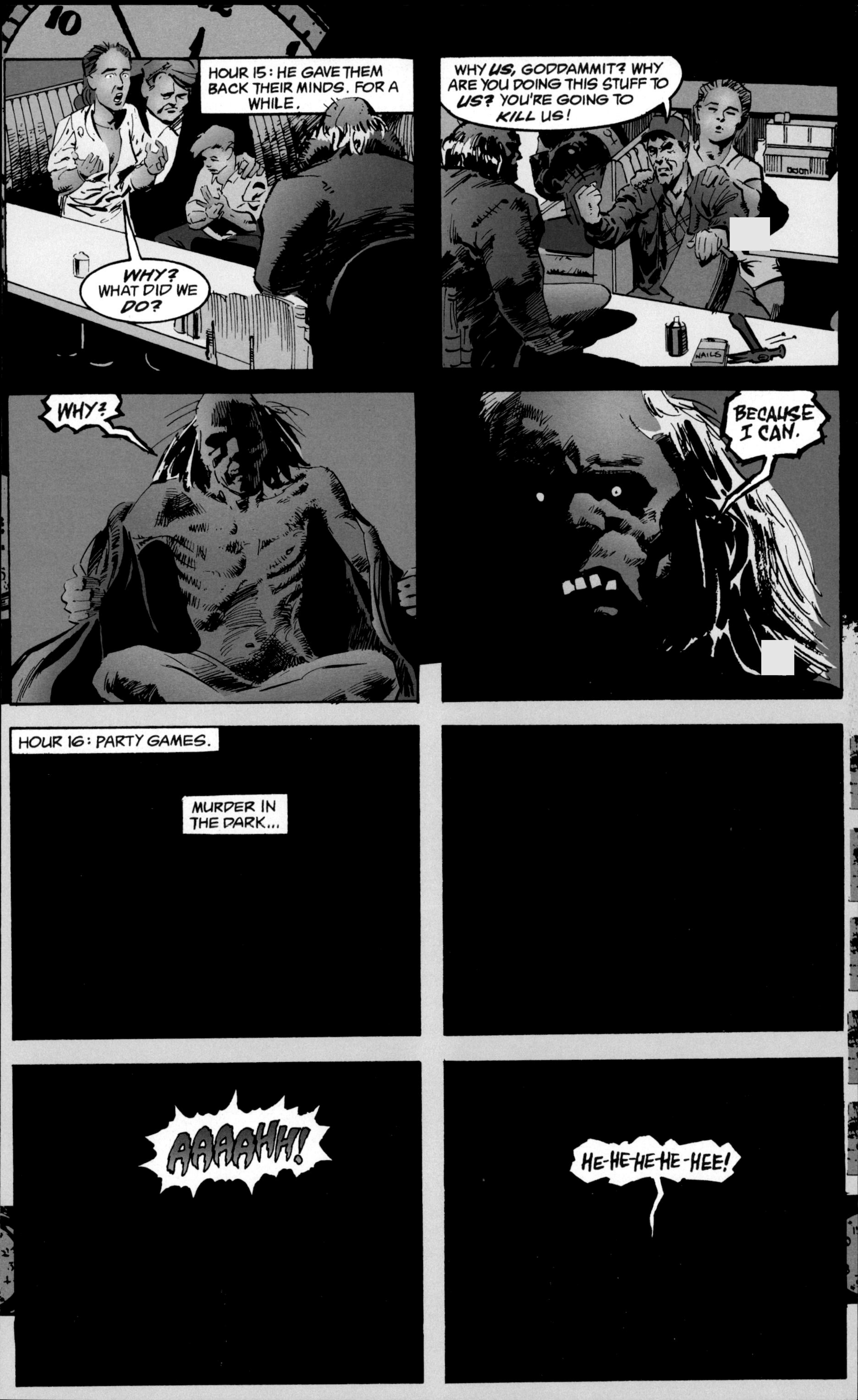
HOUR 15: HE GAVE THEM BACK THEIR MINDS. FOR A WHILE.
WHY? WHAT DID WE DO?
WHY US, GODDAMMIT? WHY ARE YOU DOING THIS STUFF TO US? YOU'RE GOING TO KILL US!
NAILS
WHY?
BECAUSE I CAN.
HOUR 16: PARTY GAMES.
MURDER IN THE DARK...
AAAAHH!
HE-HE-HE-HE-HEE!

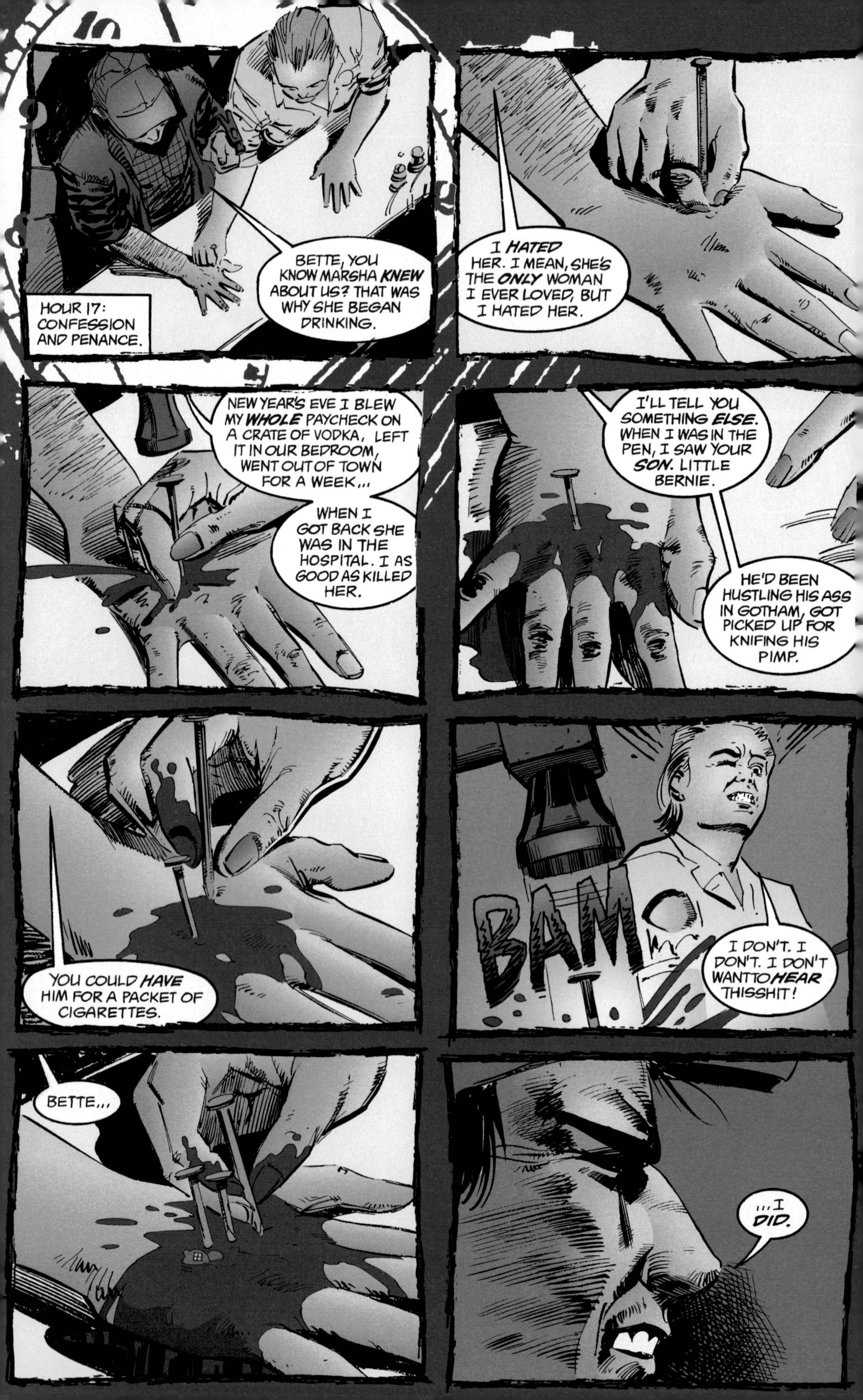
HOUR 17: CONFESSION AND PENANCE.
BETTE, YOU KNOW MARSHA KNEW ABOUT US? THAT WAS WHY SHE BEGAN DRINKING.
I HATED HER. I MEAN, SHE'S THE ONLY WOMAN I EVER LOVED, BUT I HATED HER.
NEW YEAR'S EVE I BLEW MY WHOLE PAYCHECK ON A CRATE OF VODKA, LEFT IT IN OUR BEDROOM, WENT OUT OF TOWN FOR A WEEK...
WHEN I GOT BACK SHE WAS IN THE HOSPITAL. I AS GOOD AS KILLED HER.
I'LL TELL YOU SOMETHING ELSE. WHEN I WAS IN THE PEN, I SAW YOUR SON. LITTLE BERNIE.
HE'D BEEN HUSTLING HIS ASS IN GOTHAM, GOT PICKED UP FOR KNIFING HIS PIMP.
YOU COULD HAVE HIM FOR A PACKET OF CIGARETTES.
BAM
I DON'T. I DON'T. I DON'T WANTTO HEAR THISSHIT!
BETTE...
...I DID.

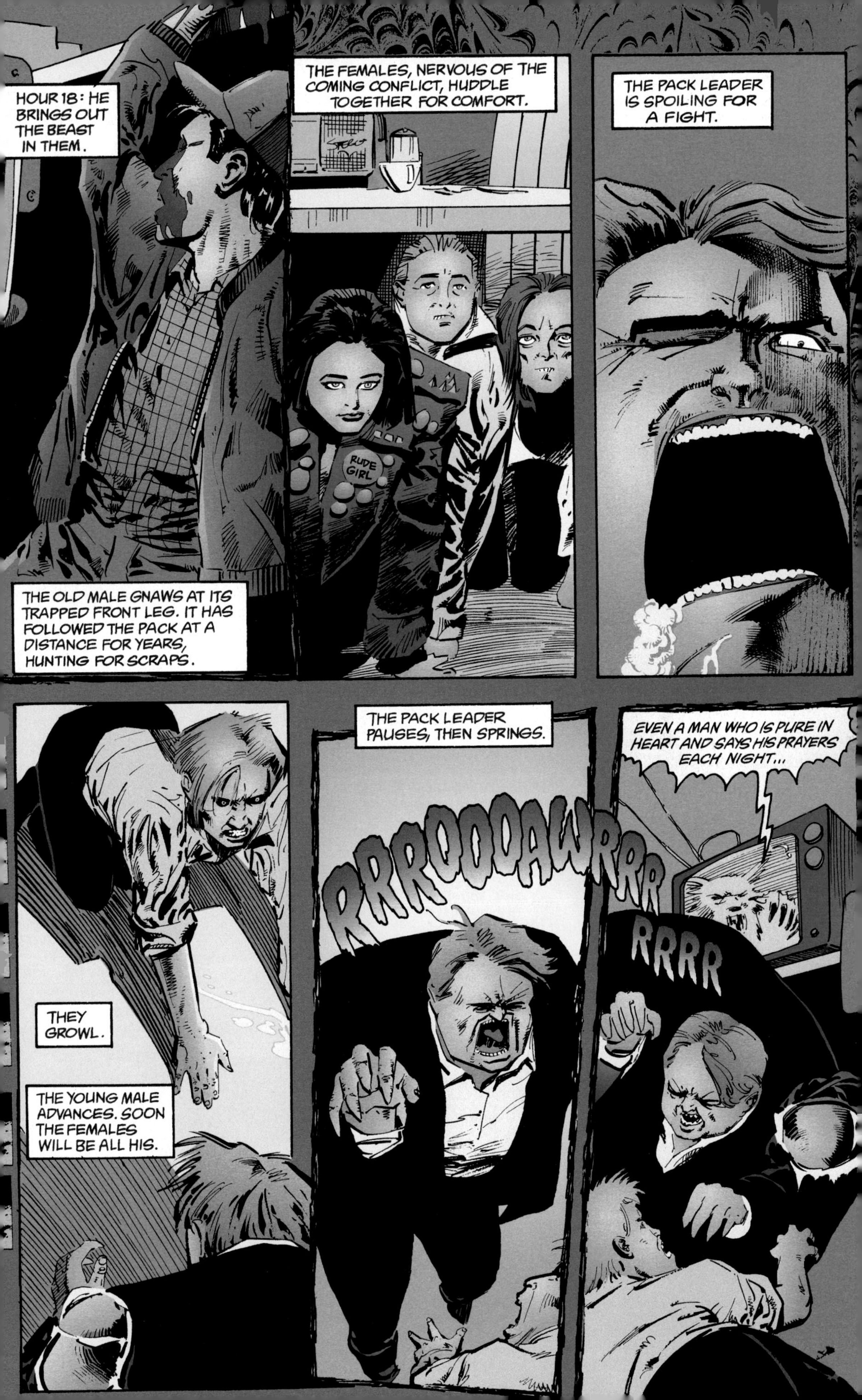
HOUR 18: HE BRINGS OUT THE BEAST IN THEM.
THE OLD MALE GNAWS AT ITS TRAPPED FRONT LEG. IT HAS FOLLOWED THE PACK AT A DISTANCE FOR YEARS, HUNTING FOR SCRAPS.
THE FEMALES, NERVOUS OF THE COMING CONFLICT, HUDDLE TOGETHER FOR COMFORT.
RUDE GIRL
THE PACK LEADER IS SPOILING FOR A FIGHT.
THEY GROWL.
THE YOUNG MALE ADVANCES. SOON THE FEMALES WILL BE ALL HIS.
THE PACK LEADER PAUSES, THEN SPRINGS.
RRROOOAWRRR
EVEN A MAN WHO IS PURE IN HEART AND SAYS HIS PRAYERS EACH NIGHT...
RRRR

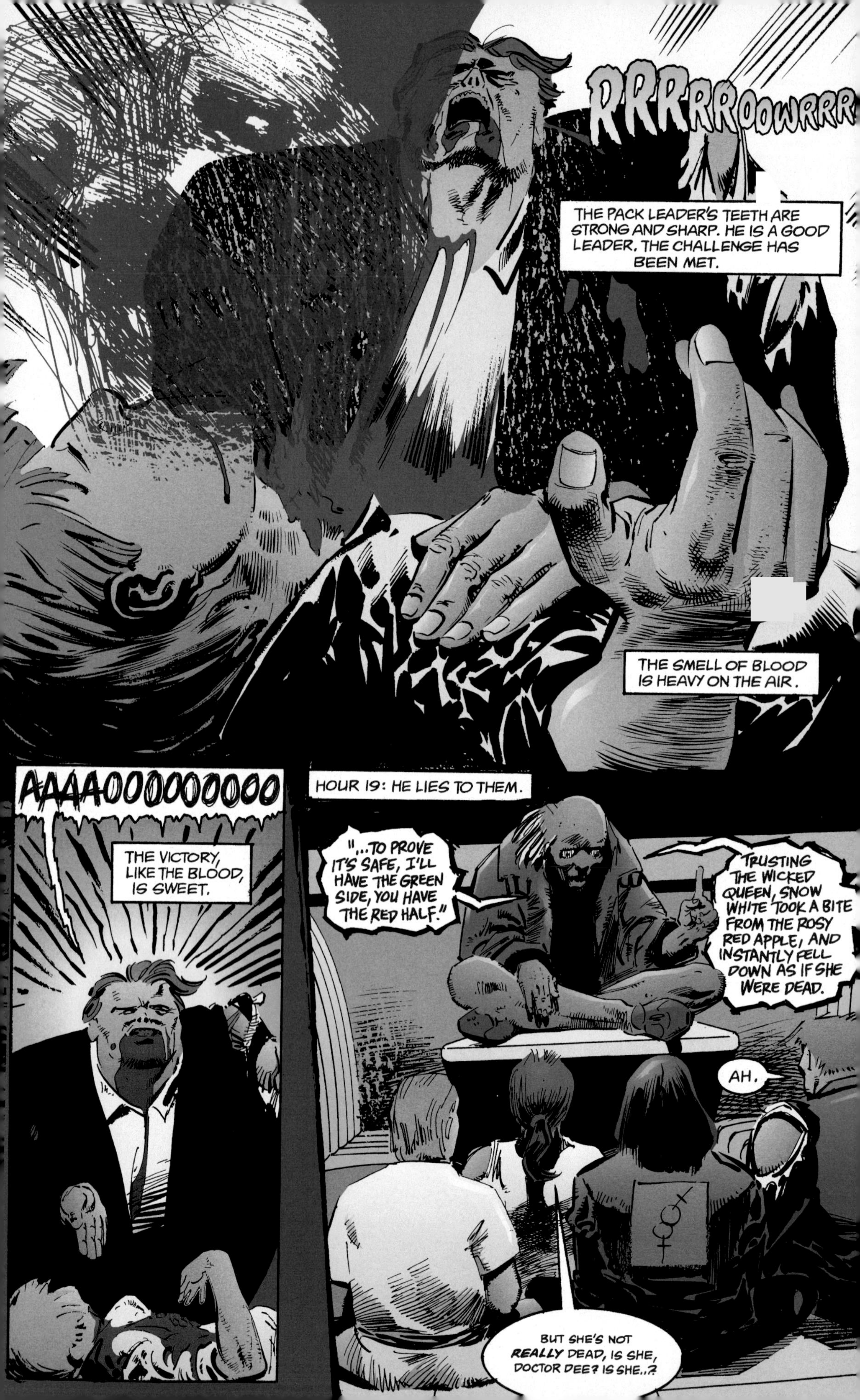
RRRRROOWRRR
THE PACK LEADER'S TEETH ARE STRONG AND SHARP. HE IS A GOOD LEADER. THE CHALLENGE HAS BEEN MET.
THE SMELL OF BLOOD IS HEAVY ON THE AIR.
AAAAOOOOOOOOO
THE VICTORY, LIKE THE BLOOD, IS SWEET.
HOUR 19: HE LIES TO THEM.
"...TO PROVE IT'S SAFE, I'LL HAVE THE GREEN SIDE, YOU HAVE THE RED HALF."
TRUSTING THE WICKED QUEEN, SNOW WHITE TOOK A BITE FROM THE ROSY RED APPLE, AND INSTANTLY FELL DOWN AS IF SHE WERE DEAD.
AH.
BUT SHE'S NOT *REALLY* DEAD, IS SHE, DOCTOR DEE? IS SHE..?

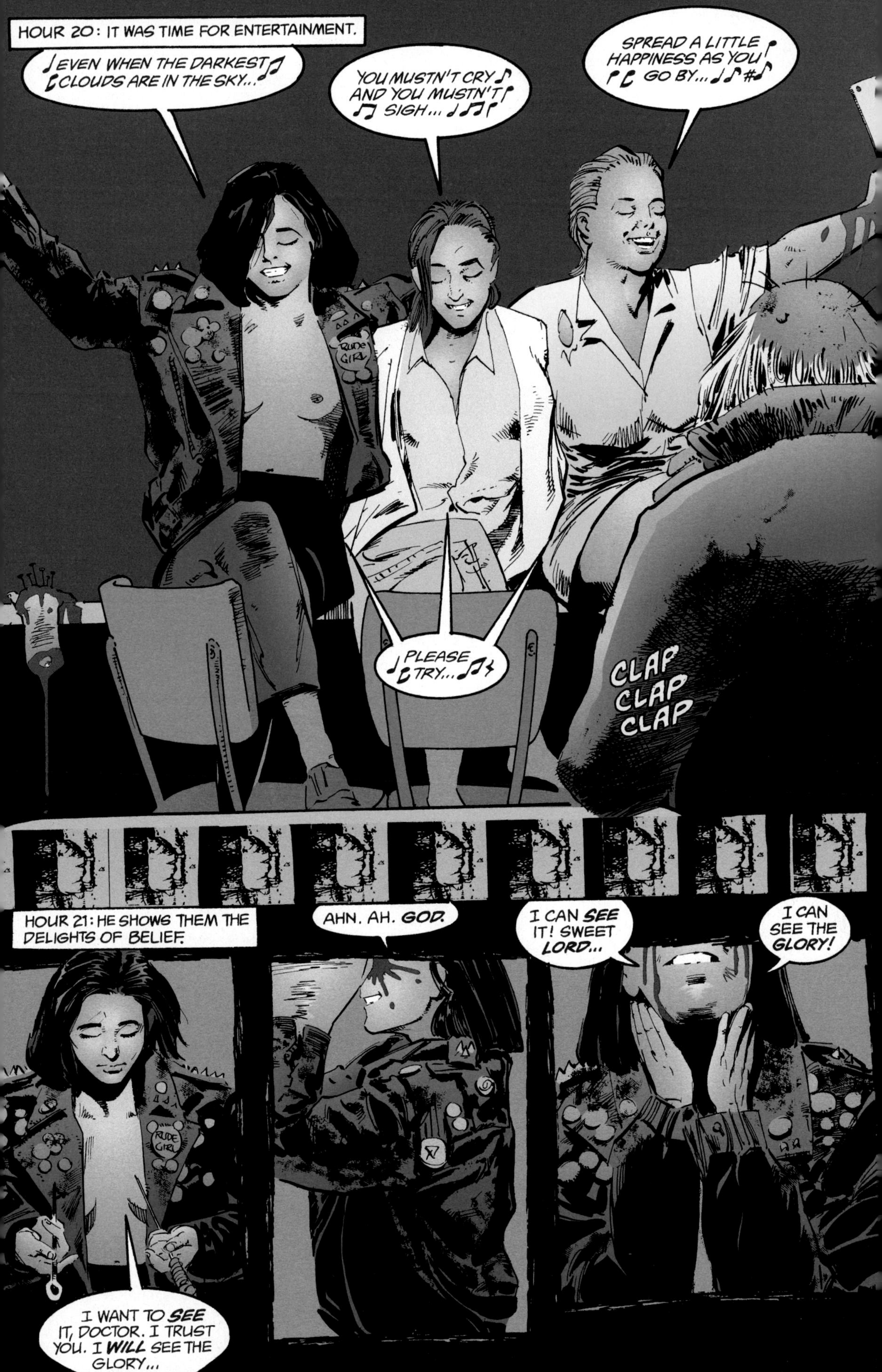
HOUR 20: IT WAS TIME FOR ENTERTAINMENT.
EVEN WHEN THE DARKEST CLOUDS ARE IN THE SKY...
YOU MUSTN'T CRY AND YOU MUSTN'T SIGH...
SPREAD A LITTLE HAPPINESS AS YOU GO BY...
PLEASE TRY...
CLAP CLAP CLAP
RUDE GIRL
HOUR 21: HE SHOWS THEM THE DELIGHTS OF BELIEF.
RUDE GIRL
I WANT TO SEE IT, DOCTOR. I TRUST YOU. I WILL SEE THE GLORY...
AHN. AH. GOD.
I CAN SEE IT! SWEET LORD...
I CAN SEE THE GLORY!

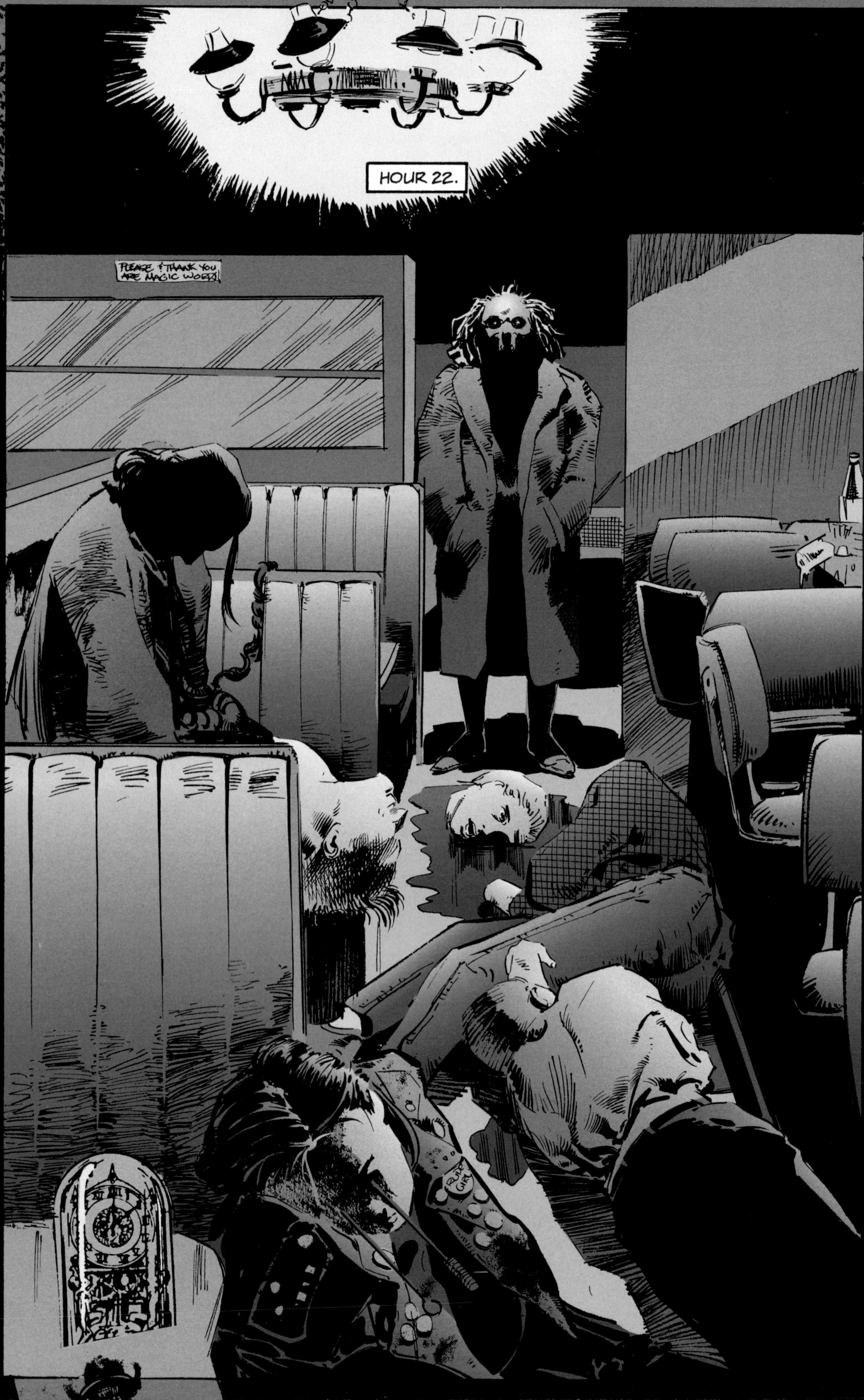
HOUR 22.
PLEASE & THANK YOU ARE MAGIC WORDS!

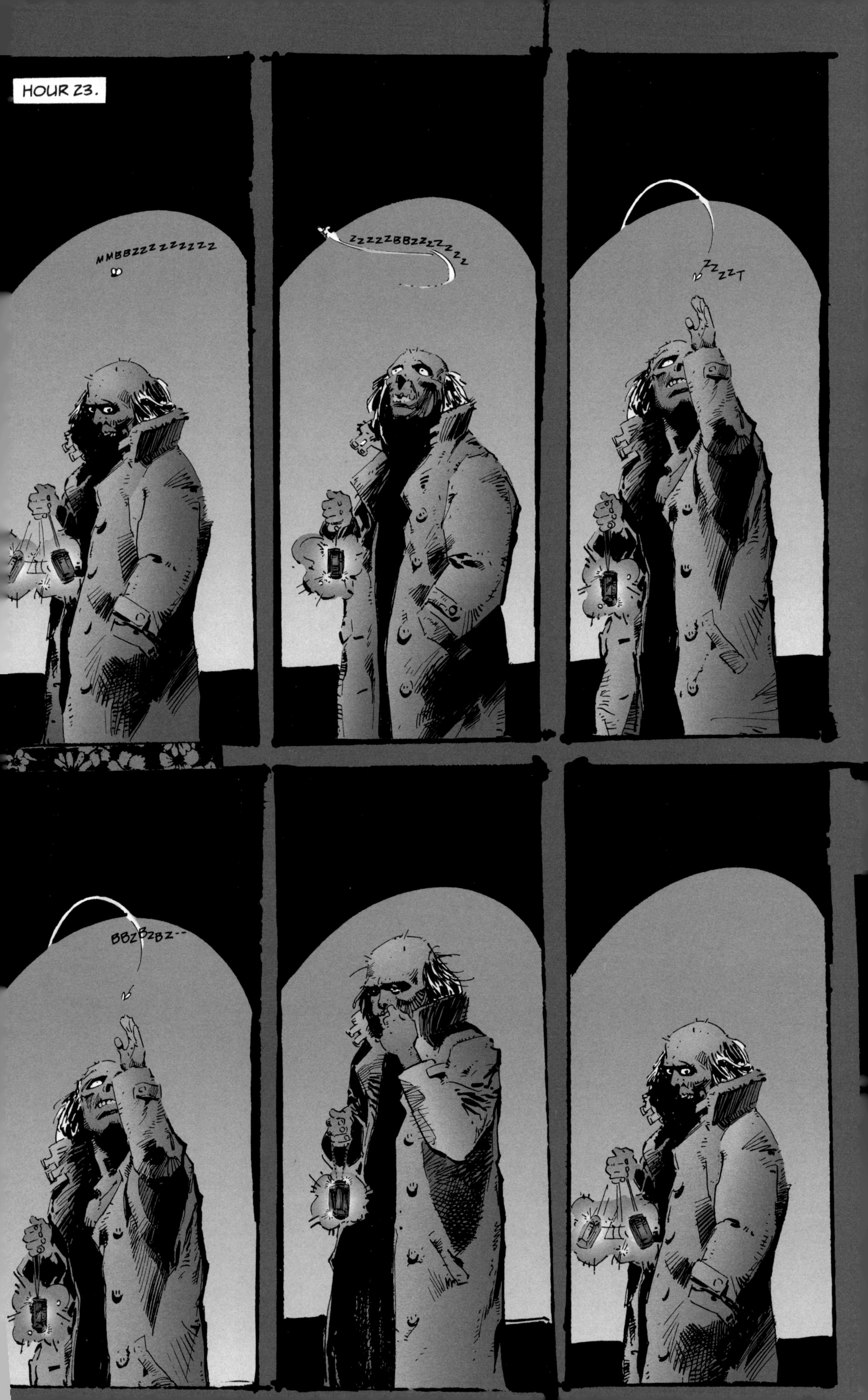
HOUR 23.
MMBBZZZZZZZZZZZ
ZZZZZBBZZZZZZZ
ZZZZT
BBZBZBZ--

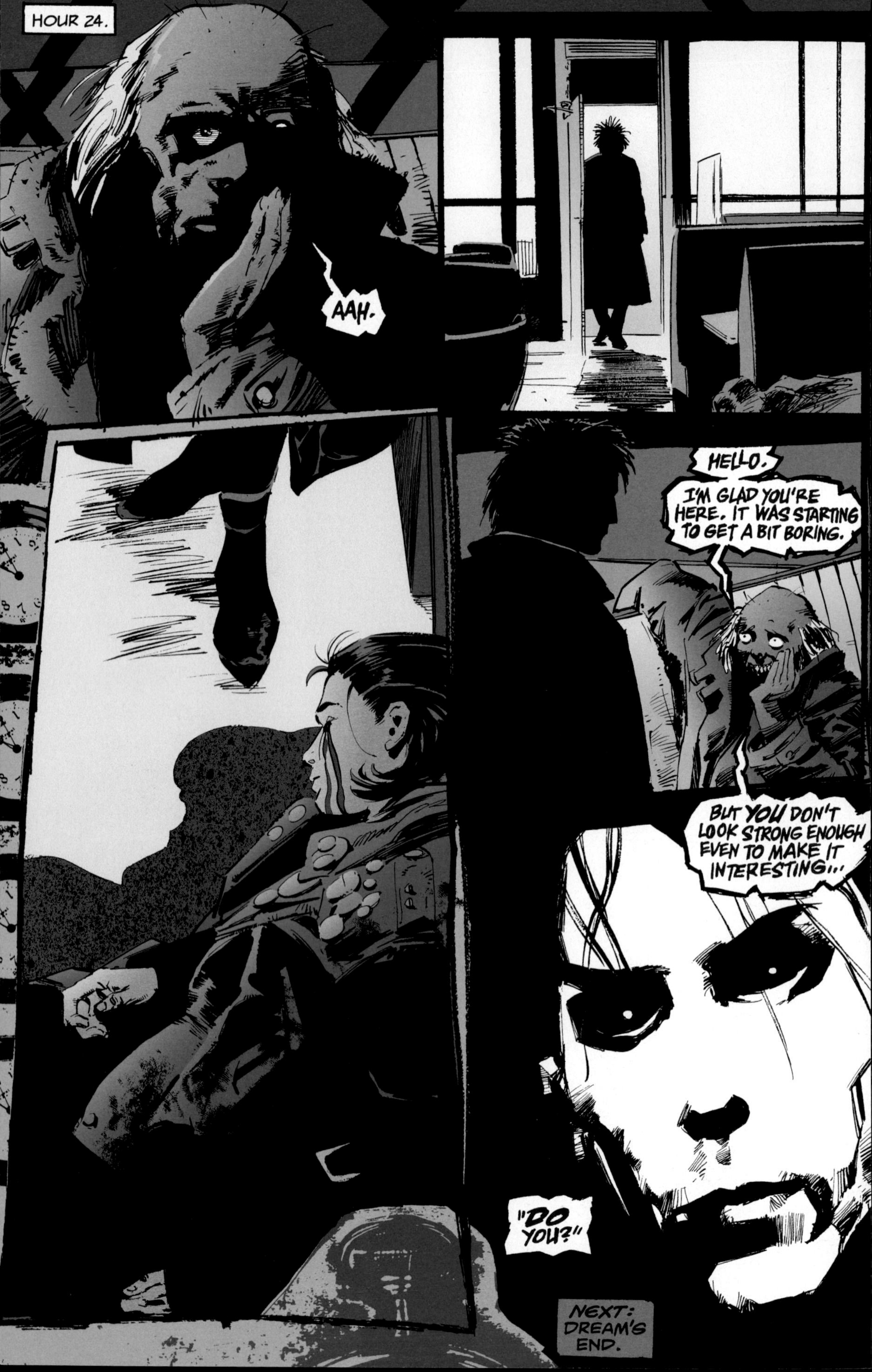
HOUR 24.
AAH.
HELLO.
I'M GLAD YOU'RE HERE. IT WAS STARTING TO GET A BIT BORING.
BUT YOU DON'T LOOK STRONG ENOUGH EVEN TO MAKE IT INTERESTING...
"DO YOU?"
NEXT: DREAM'S END.

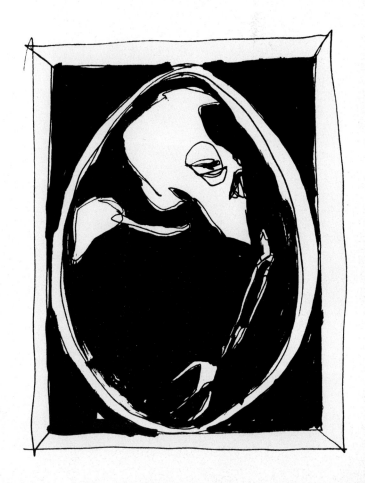

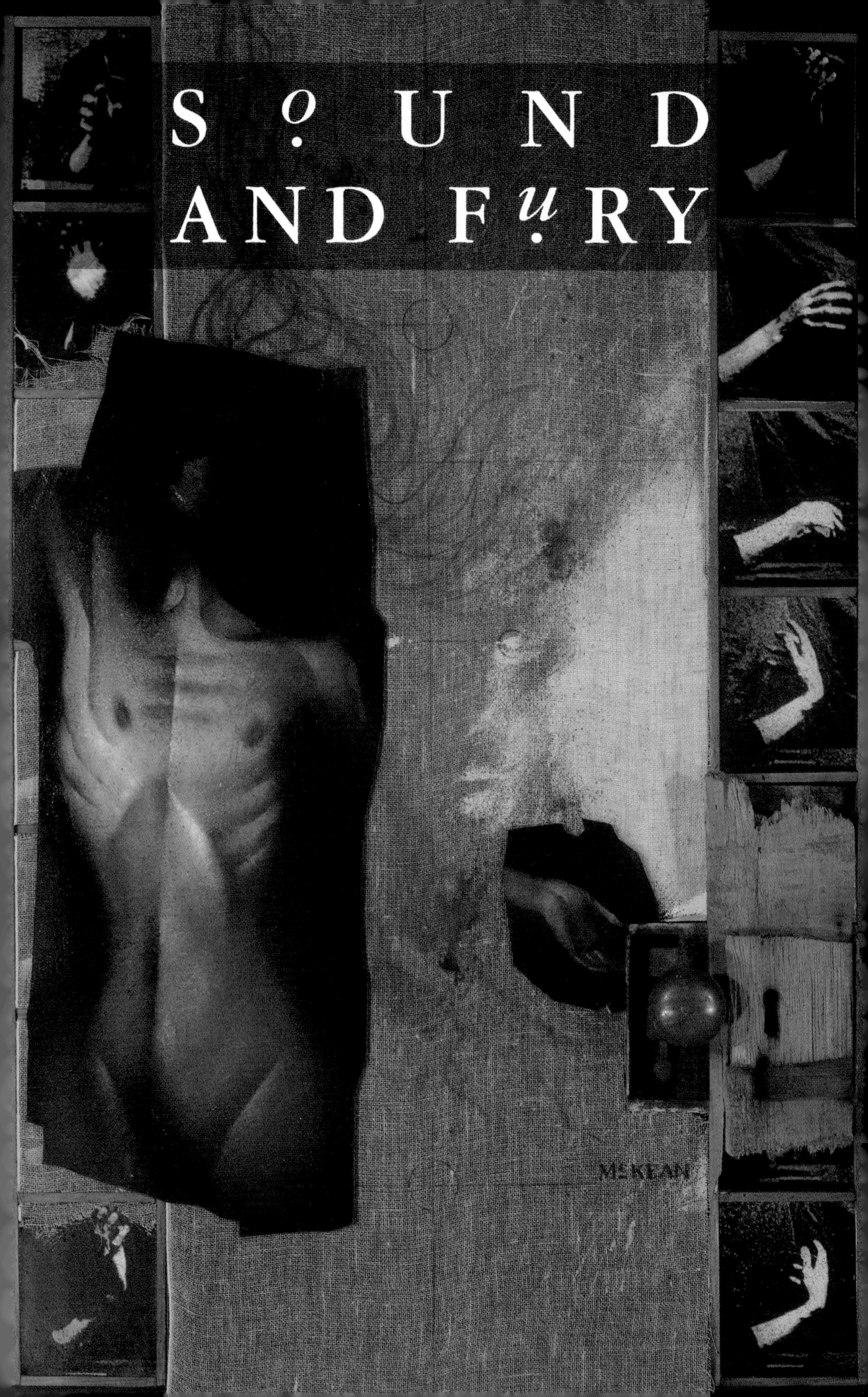
SOUND
AND FURY
McKEAN

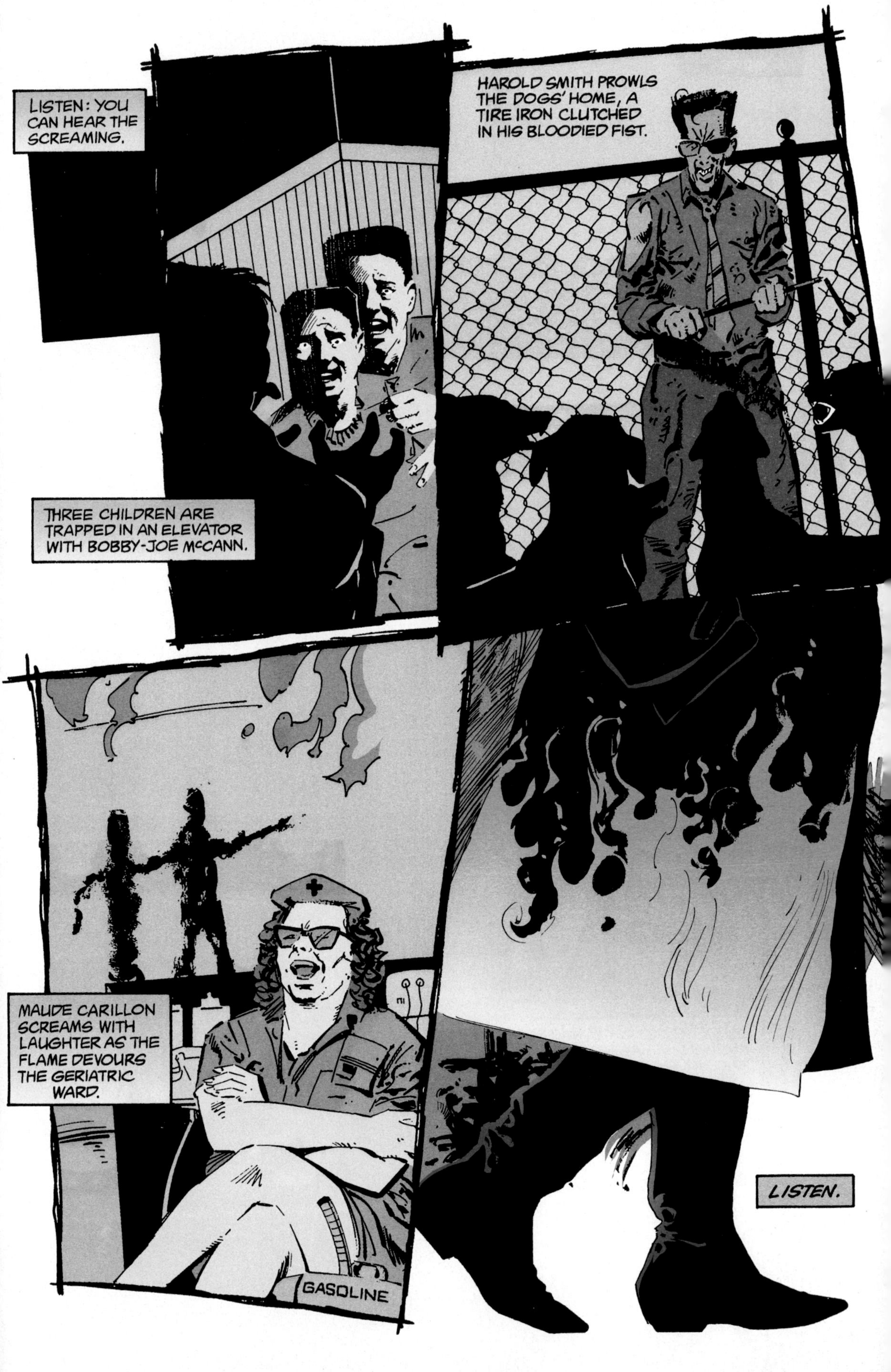

LISTEN: YOU CAN HEAR THE SCREAMING.
THREE CHILDREN ARE TRAPPED IN AN ELEVATOR WITH BOBBY-JOE McCANN.
HAROLD SMITH PROWLS THE DOGS' HOME, A TIRE IRON CLUTCHED IN HIS BLOODIED FIST.
MAUDE CARILLON SCREAMS WITH LAUGHTER AS THE FLAME DEVOURS THE GERIATRIC WARD.
GASOLINE
LISTEN.

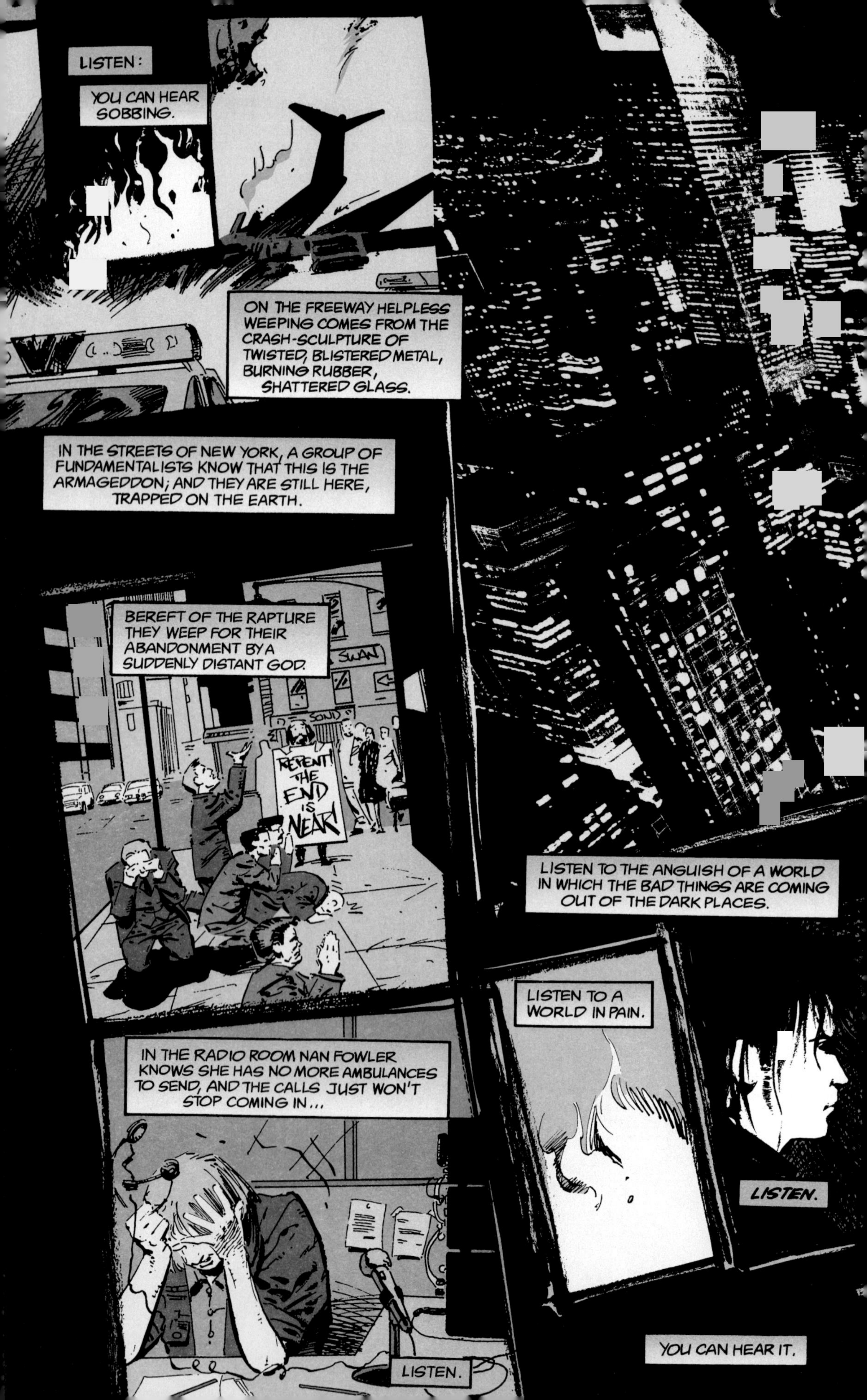

LISTEN:
YOU CAN HEAR SOBBING.
ON THE FREEWAY HELPLESS WEEPING COMES FROM THE CRASH-SCULPTURE OF TWISTED, BLISTERED METAL, BURNING RUBBER, SHATTERED GLASS.
IN THE STREETS OF NEW YORK, A GROUP OF FUNDAMENTALISTS KNOW THAT THIS IS THE ARMAGEDDON; AND THEY ARE STILL HERE, TRAPPED ON THE EARTH.
BEREFT OF THE RAPTURE THEY WEEP FOR THEIR ABANDONMENT BY A SUDDENLY DISTANT GOD.
SWAN
REPENT THE END IS NEAR!
IN THE RADIO ROOM NAN FOWLER KNOWS SHE HAS NO MORE AMBULANCES TO SEND, AND THE CALLS JUST WON'T STOP COMING IN...
LISTEN.
LISTEN TO THE ANGUISH OF A WORLD IN WHICH THE BAD THINGS ARE COMING OUT OF THE DARK PLACES.
LISTEN TO A WORLD IN PAIN.
LISTEN.
YOU CAN HEAR IT.

SOUND

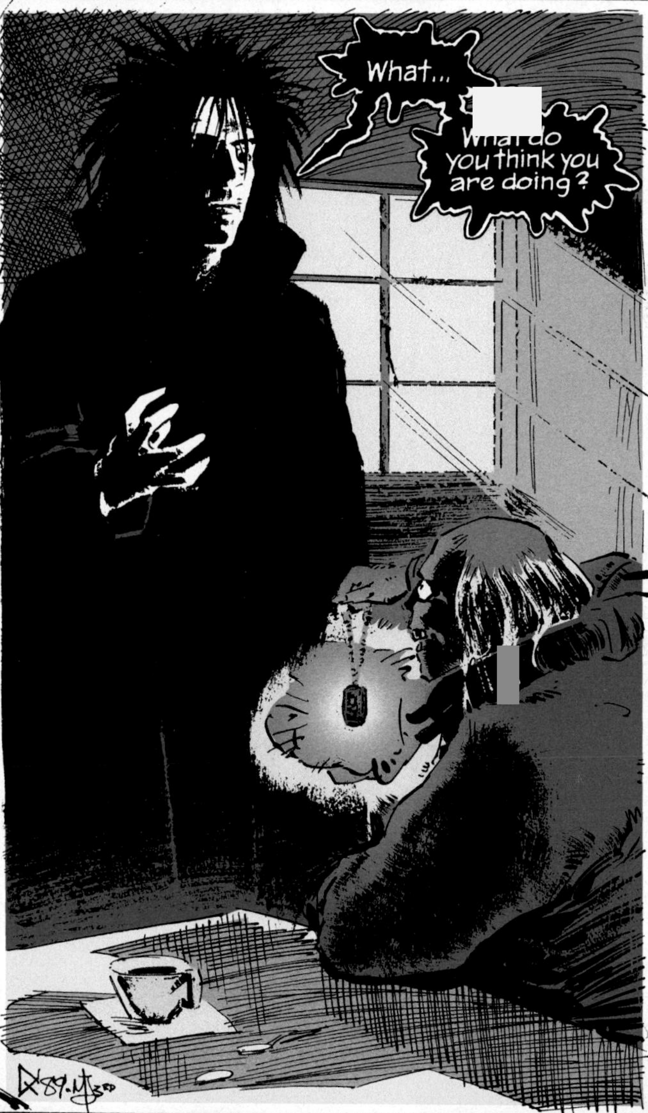
What...
What do you think you are doing?

AND FURY

NEIL GAIMAN, WRITER * MIKE DRINGENBERG AND MALCOLM JONES III, ARTISTS * DANIEL VOZZO, COLORIST TODD KLEIN, LETTERER * ART YOUNG, ASSOC. EDITOR KAREN BERGER, EDITOR

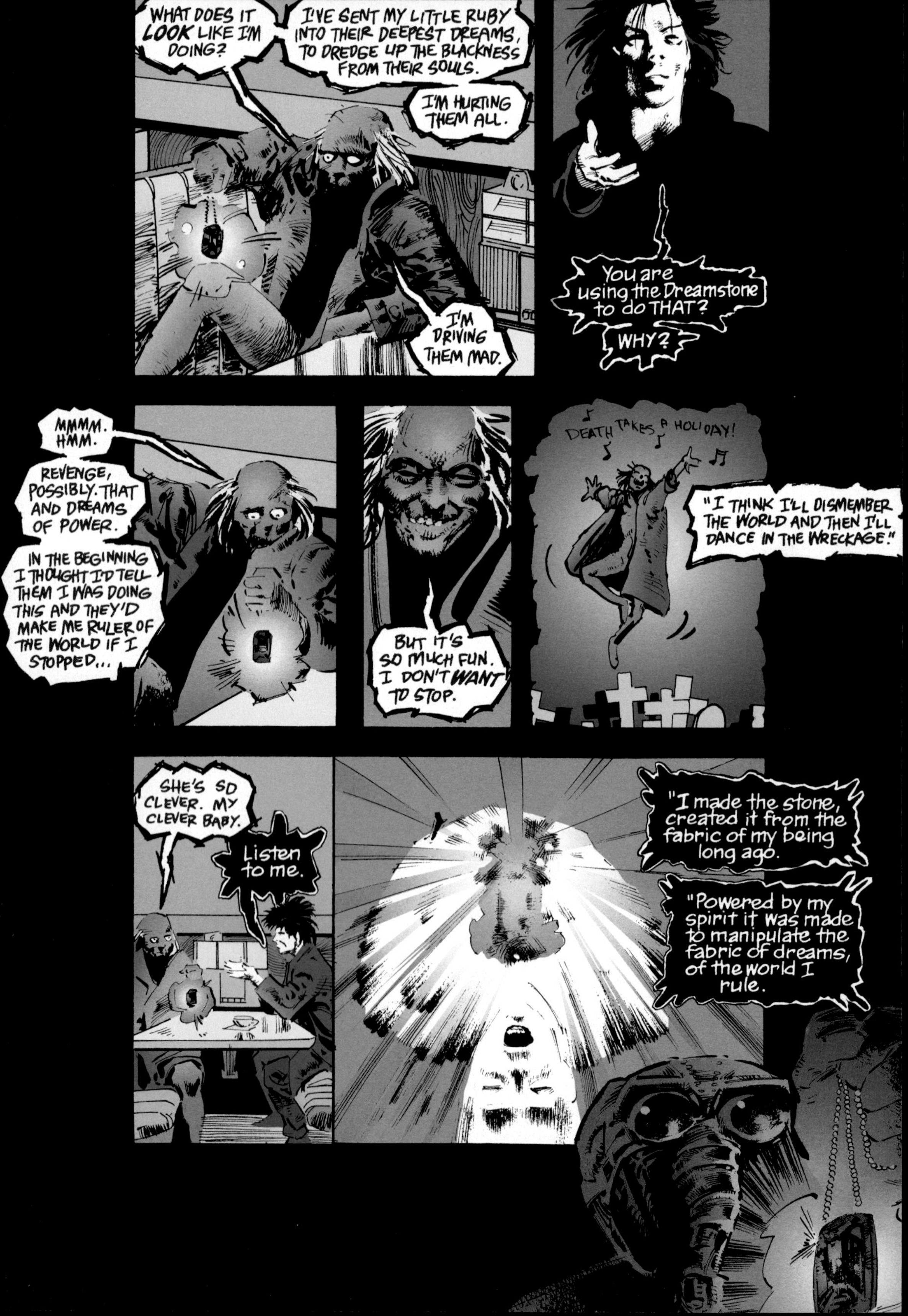
WHAT DOES IT LOOK LIKE I'M DOING?
I'VE SENT MY LITTLE RUBY INTO THEIR DEEPEST DREAMS, TO DREDGE UP THE BLACKNESS FROM THEIR SOULS.
I'M HURTING THEM ALL.
I'M DRIVING THEM MAD.
You are using the Dreamstone to do THAT?
WHY?
MMMM. HMM.
REVENGE, POSSIBLY. THAT AND DREAMS OF POWER.
IN THE BEGINNING I THOUGHT I'D TELL THEM I WAS DOING THIS AND THEY'D MAKE ME RULER OF THE WORLD IF I STOPPED...
BUT IT'S SO MUCH FUN. I DON'T WANT TO STOP.
DEATH TAKES A HOLIDAY!
"I THINK I'LL DISMEMBER THE WORLD AND THEN I'LL DANCE IN THE WRECKAGE!"
SHE'S SO CLEVER. MY CLEVER BABY.
Listen to me.
"I made the stone, created it from the fabric of my being long ago.
"Powered by my spirit it was made to manipulate the fabric of dreams, of the world I rule.

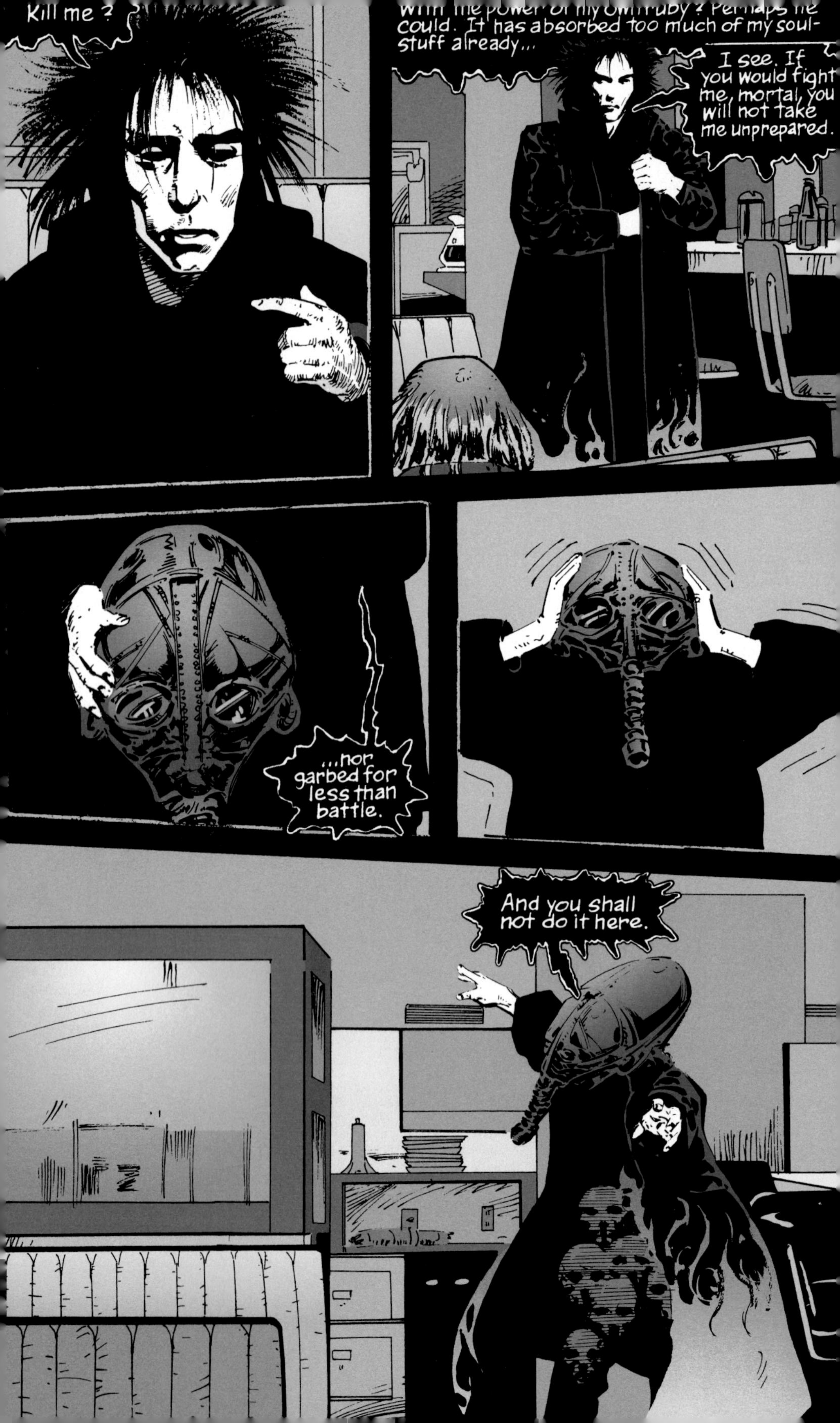

Kill me?
could. It has absorbed too much of my soul-stuff already...
I see. If you would fight me, mortal, you will not take me unprepared.
...nor garbed for less than battle.
And you shall not do it here.

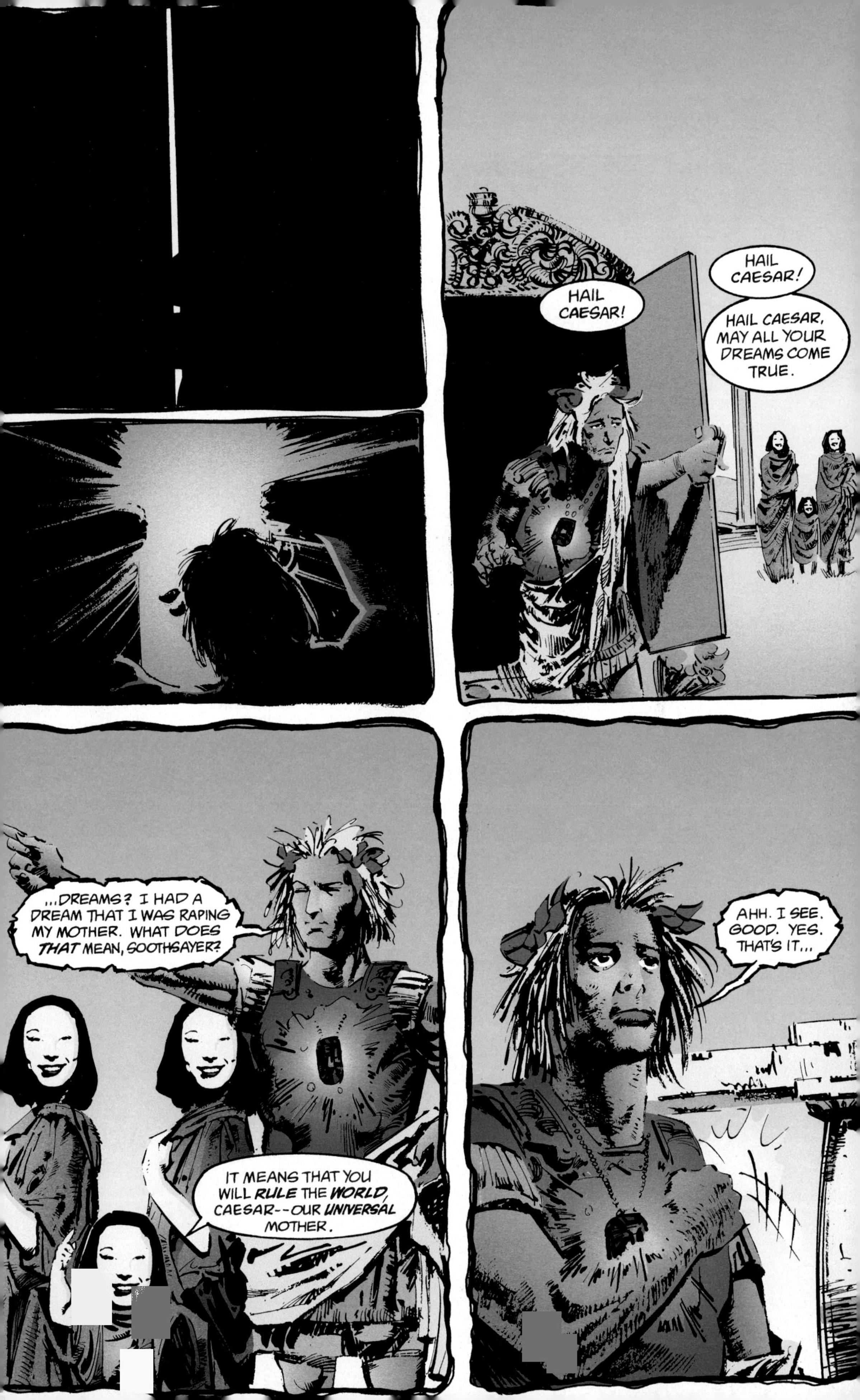
HAIL CAESAR!
HAIL CAESAR!
HAIL CAESAR, MAY ALL YOUR DREAMS COME TRUE.
...DREAMS? I HAD A DREAM THAT I WAS RAPING MY MOTHER. WHAT DOES *THAT* MEAN, SOOTHSAYER?
IT MEANS THAT YOU WILL *RULE* THE *WORLD*, CAESAR--OUR *UNIVERSAL* MOTHER.
AHH. I SEE. GOOD. YES. THAT'S IT...

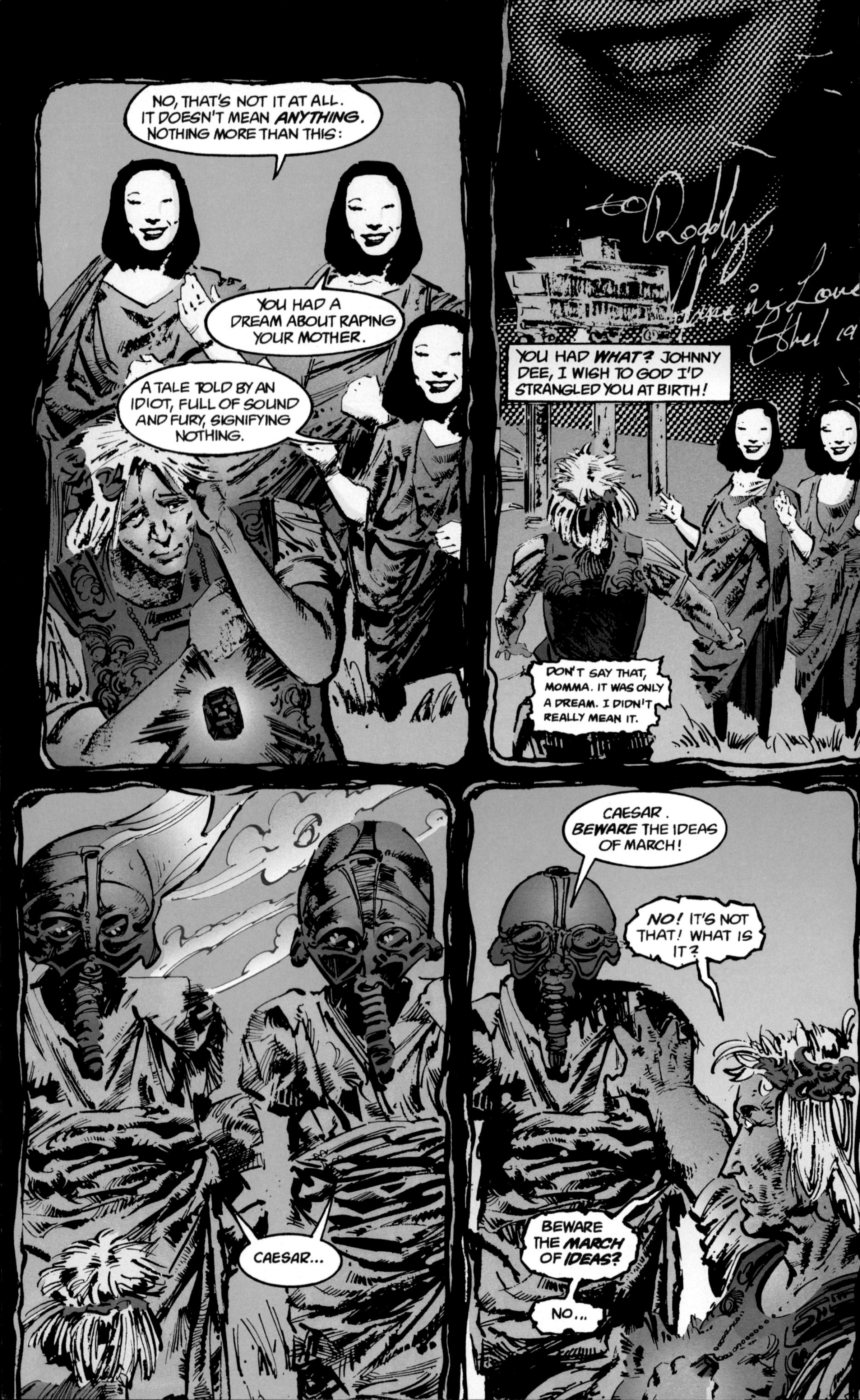
NO, THAT'S NOT IT AT ALL. IT DOESN'T MEAN ANYTHING. NOTHING MORE THAN THIS:
YOU HAD A DREAM ABOUT RAPING YOUR MOTHER.
A TALE TOLD BY AN IDIOT, FULL OF SOUND AND FURY, SIGNIFYING NOTHING.
to Roddy,
YOU HAD WHAT? JOHNNY DEE, I WISH TO GOD I'D STRANGLED YOU AT BIRTH!
DON'T SAY THAT, MOMMA. IT WAS ONLY A DREAM. I DIDN'T REALLY MEAN IT.
CAESAR...
CAESAR. BEWARE THE IDEAS OF MARCH!
NO! IT'S NOT THAT! WHAT IS IT?
BEWARE THE MARCH OF IDEAS?
NO...

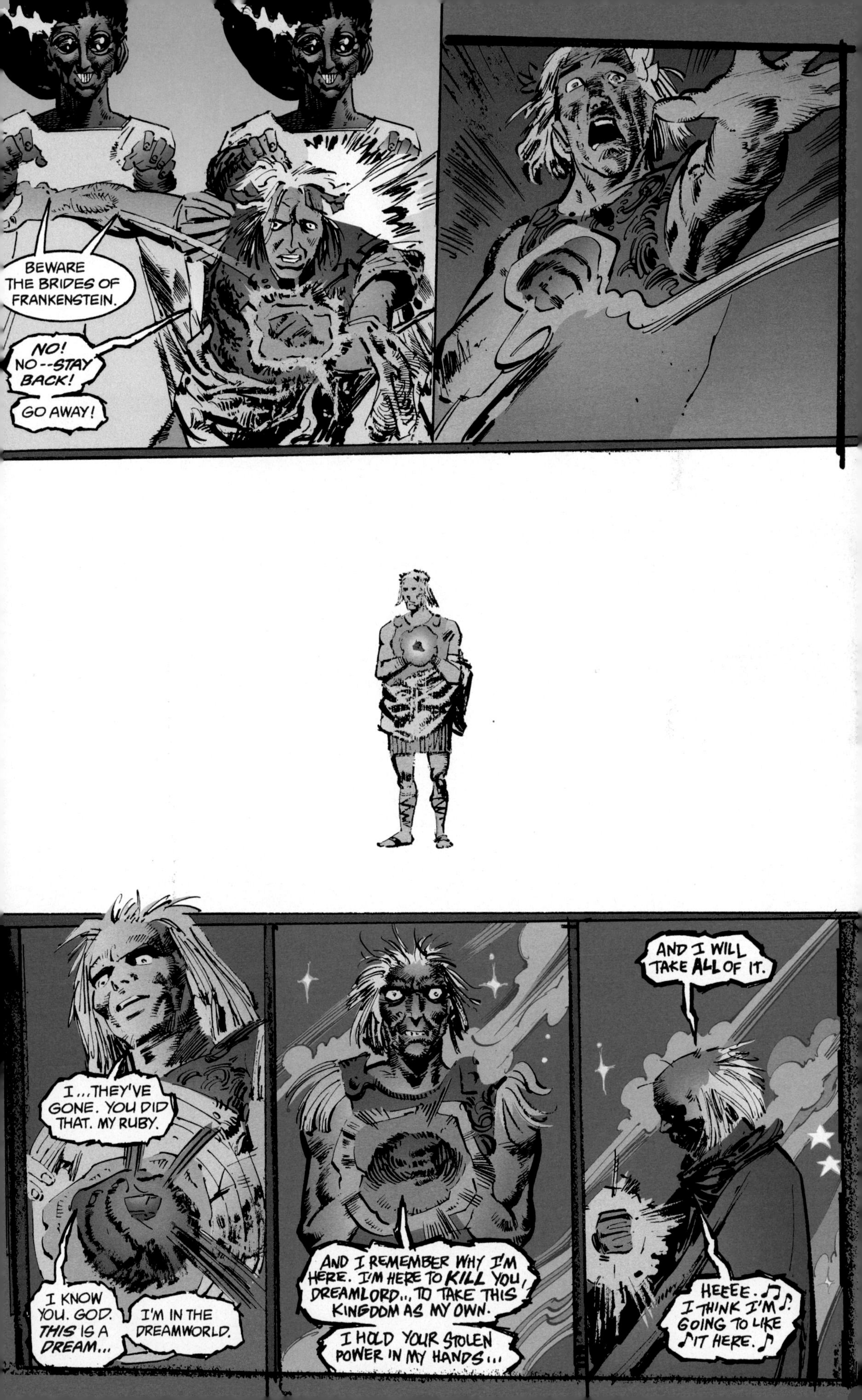
BEWARE THE BRIDES OF FRANKENSTEIN.
NO! NO--STAY BACK!
GO AWAY!
I...THEY'VE GONE. YOU DID THAT. MY RUBY.
I KNOW YOU. GOD. THIS IS A DREAM...
I'M IN THE DREAMWORLD.
AND I REMEMBER WHY I'M HERE. I'M HERE TO KILL YOU, DREAMLORD.., TO TAKE THIS KINGDOM AS MY OWN.
I HOLD YOUR STOLEN POWER IN MY HANDS...
AND I WILL TAKE ALL OF IT.
HEEEE. ♪ I THINK I'M ♪ GOING TO LIKE ♪ IT HERE. ♪

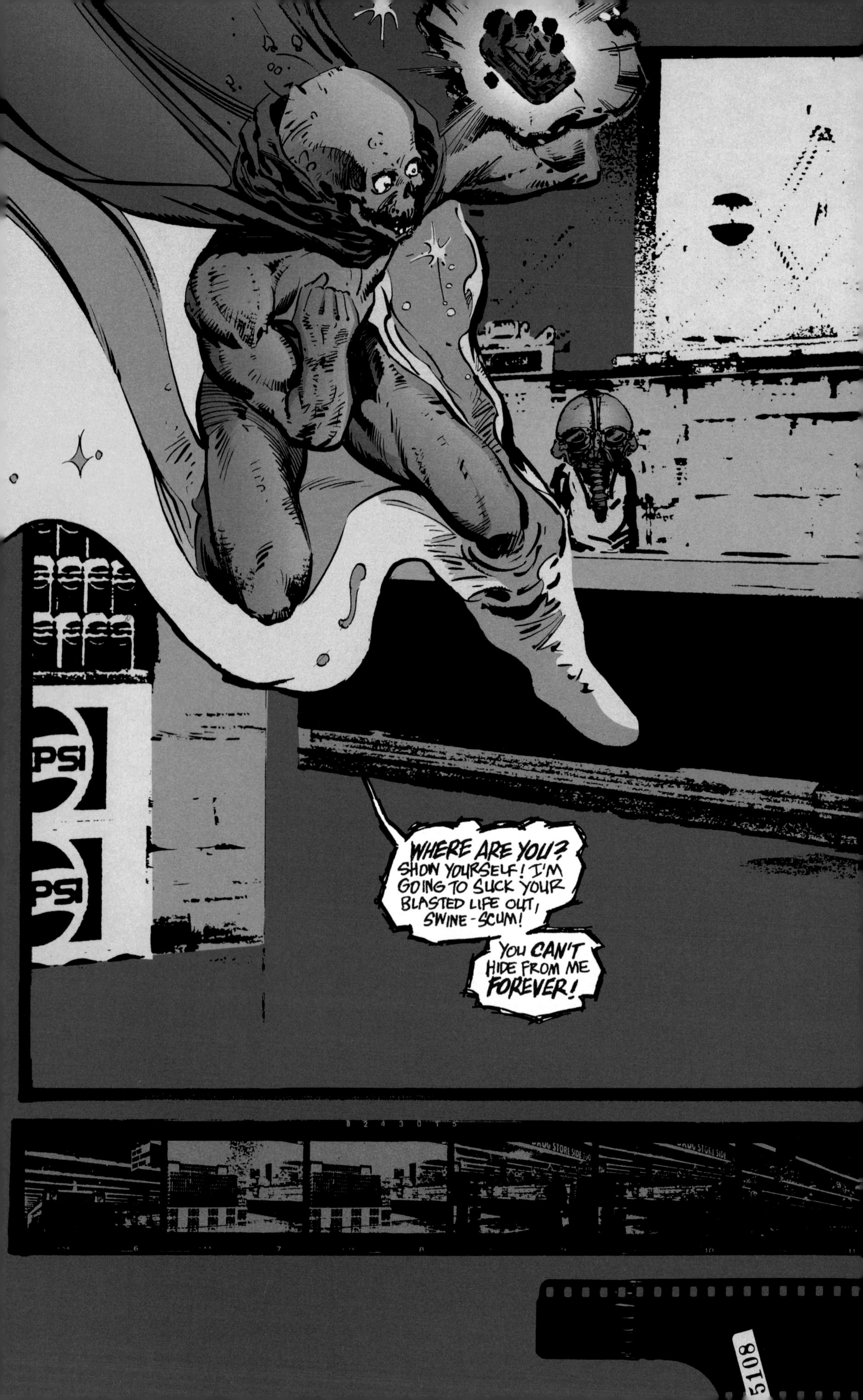
WHERE ARE YOU? SHOW YOURSELF! I'M GOING TO SUCK YOUR BLASTED LIFE OUT, SWINE-SCUM!
YOU CAN'T HIDE FROM ME FOREVER!
PEPSI
PEPSI

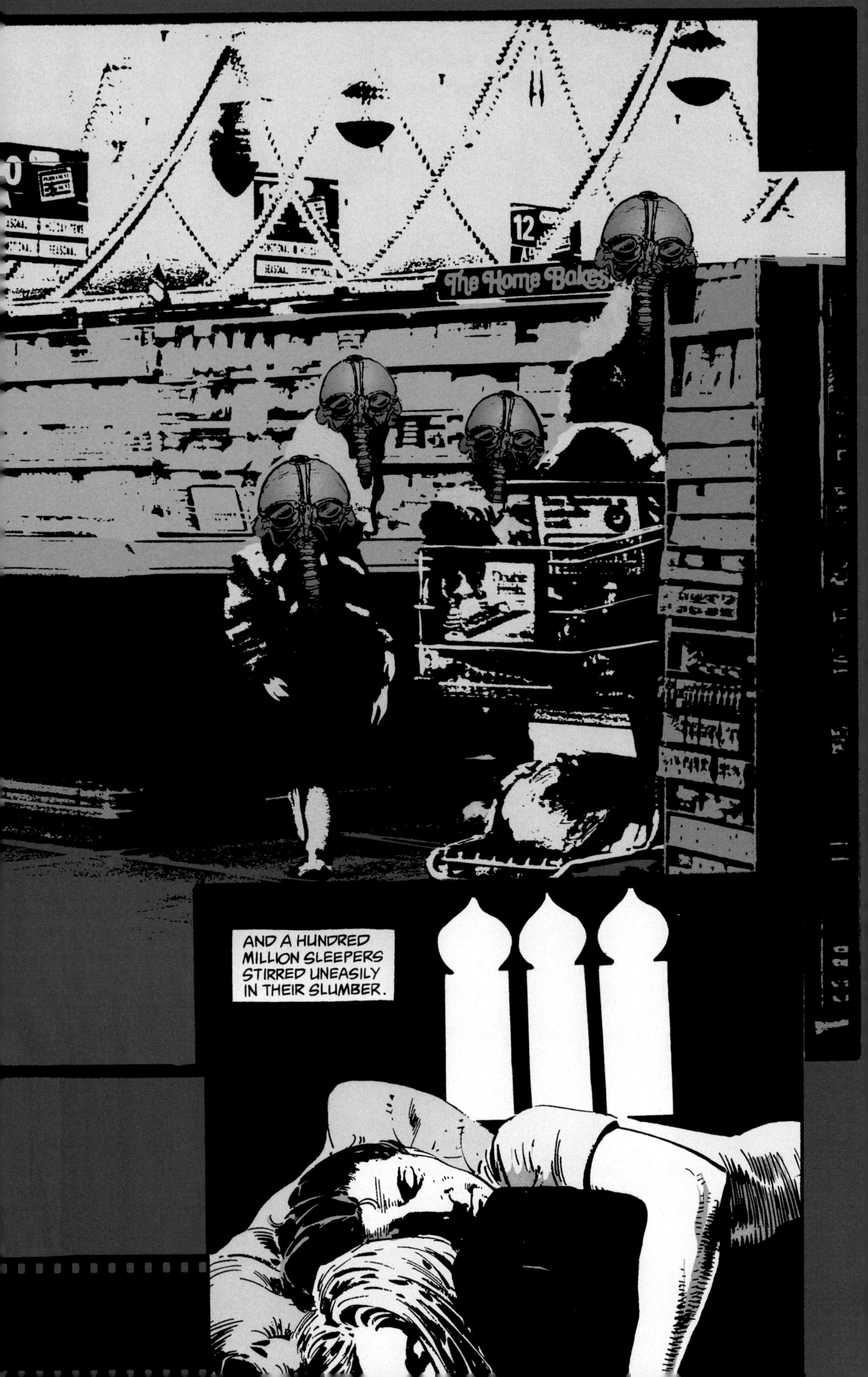
The Home Bakes
12
AND A HUNDRED MILLION SLEEPERS STIRRED UNEASILY IN THEIR SLUMBER.

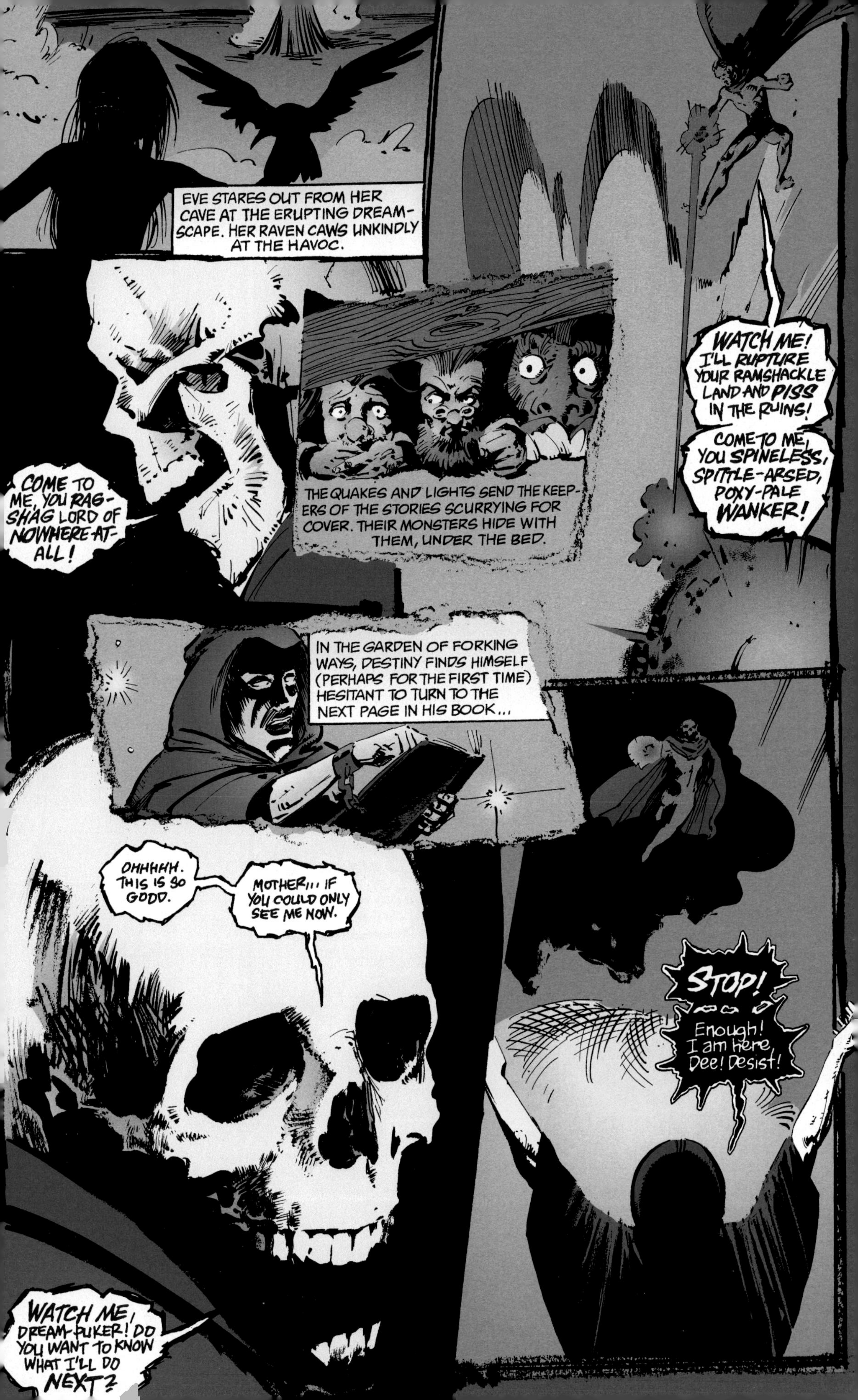
EVE STARES OUT FROM HER CAVE AT THE ERUPTING DREAM-SCAPE. HER RAVEN CAWS UNKINDLY AT THE HAVOC.
COME TO ME, YOU RAG-SHAG LORD OF NOWHERE-AT-ALL!
THE QUAKES AND LIGHTS SEND THE KEEPERS OF THE STORIES SCURRYING FOR COVER. THEIR MONSTERS HIDE WITH THEM, UNDER THE BED.
WATCH ME! I'LL RUPTURE YOUR RAMSHACKLE LAND AND PISS IN THE RUINS!
COME TO ME, YOU SPINELESS, SPITTLE-ARSED, POXY-PALE WANKER!
IN THE GARDEN OF FORKING WAYS, DESTINY FINDS HIMSELF (PERHAPS FOR THE FIRST TIME) HESITANT TO TURN TO THE NEXT PAGE IN HIS BOOK...
OHHHHH. THIS IS SO GOOD.
MOTHER... IF YOU COULD ONLY SEE ME NOW.
WATCH ME, DREAM-PUKER! DO YOU WANT TO KNOW WHAT I'LL DO NEXT?
STOP!
Enough! I am here, Dee! Desist!

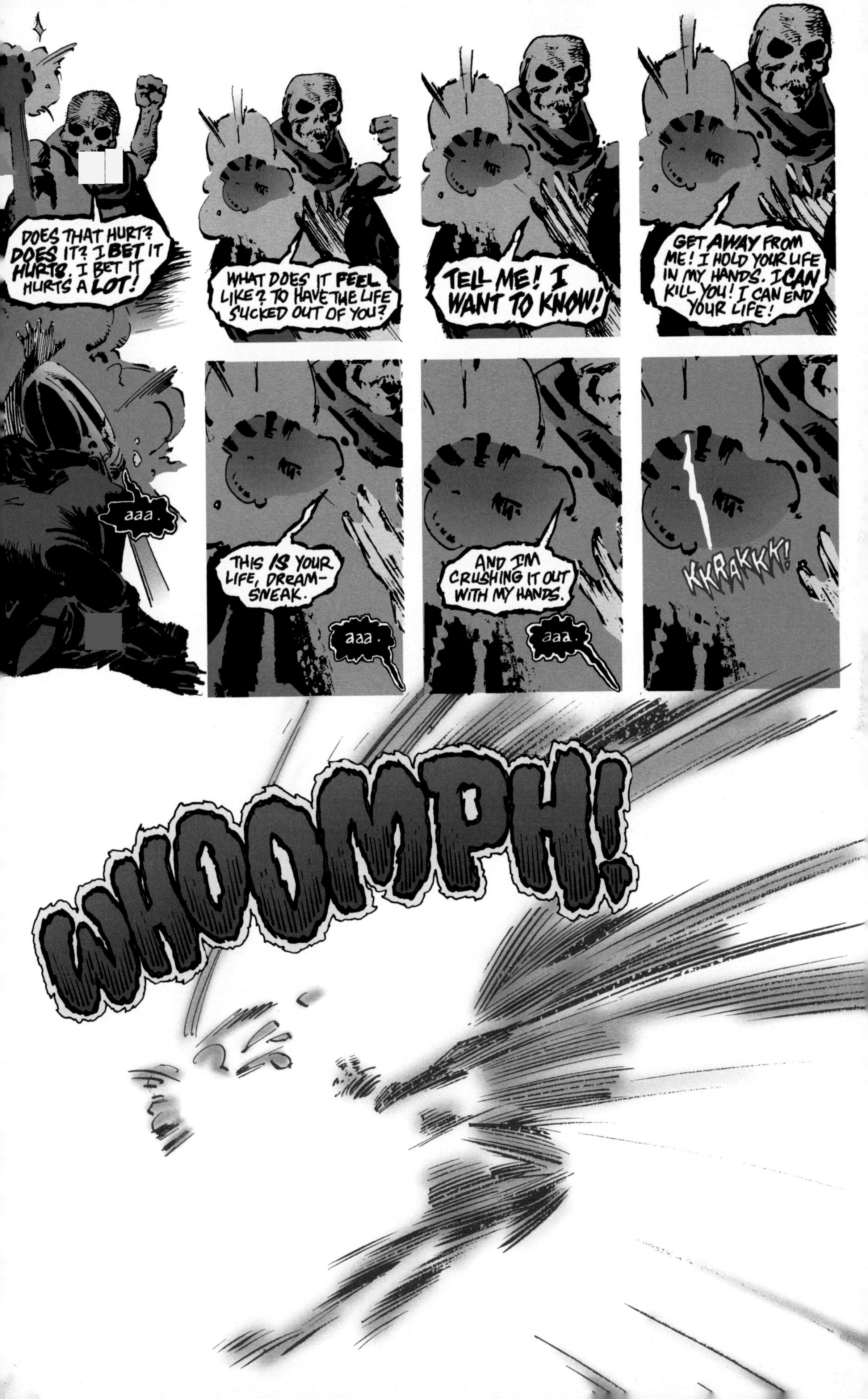
DOES THAT HURT? DOES IT? I BET IT HURTS. I BET IT HURTS A LOT!
WHAT DOES IT FEEL LIKE? TO HAVE THE LIFE SUCKED OUT OF YOU?
TELL ME! I WANT TO KNOW!
GET AWAY FROM ME! I HOLD YOUR LIFE IN MY HANDS. I CAN KILL YOU! I CAN END YOUR LIFE!
aaa.
THIS IS YOUR LIFE, DREAM-SNEAK.
aaa.
AND I'M CRUSHING IT OUT WITH MY HANDS.
aaa.
KKRAKKK!
WHOOMPH!

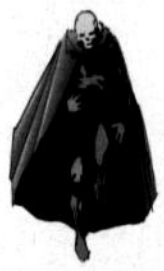

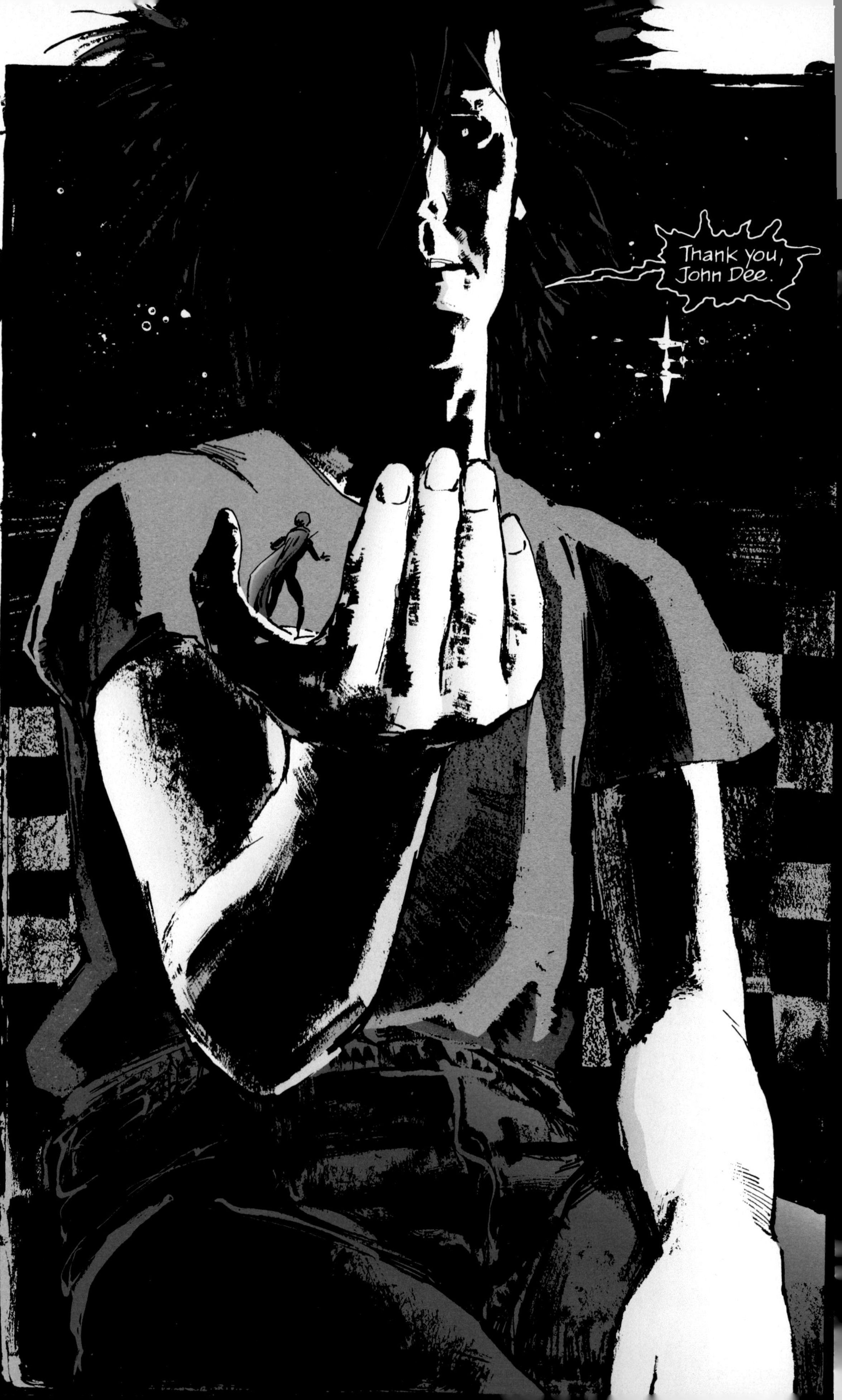
Thank you, John Dee.

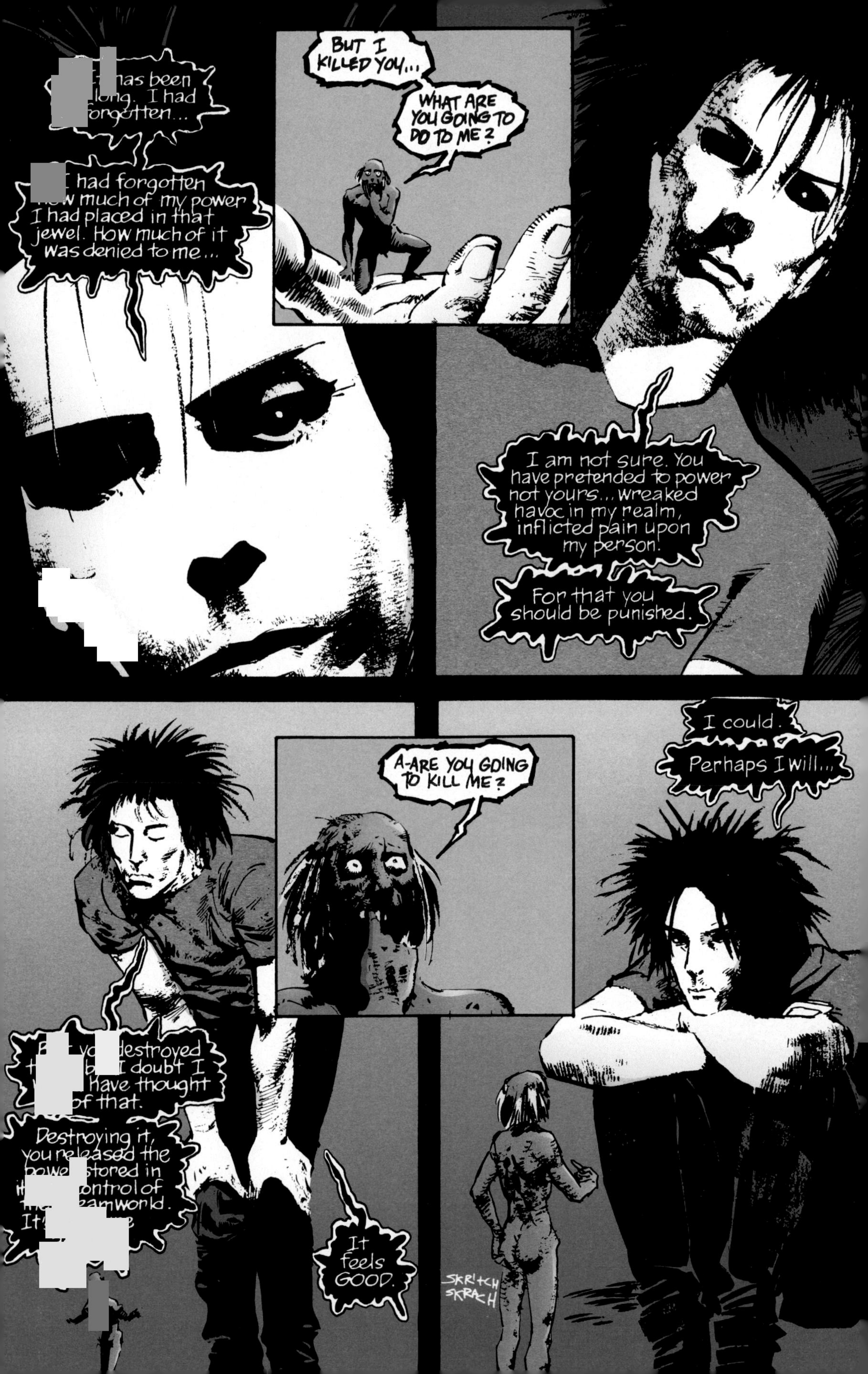

has been
long. I had
forgotten...
I had forgotten
ow much of my power I had placed in that jewel. How much of it was denied to me...
BUT I KILLED YOU...
WHAT ARE YOU GOING TO DO TO ME?
I am not sure. You have pretended to power not yours... wreaked havoc in my realm, inflicted pain upon my person.
For that you should be punished.
A-ARE YOU GOING TO KILL ME?
I could.
Perhaps I will...
destroyed
I doubt I
have thought
of that.
Destroying it,
stored in
ontrol of
eamworld.
It feels GOOD.
SKR'TCH SKRACH

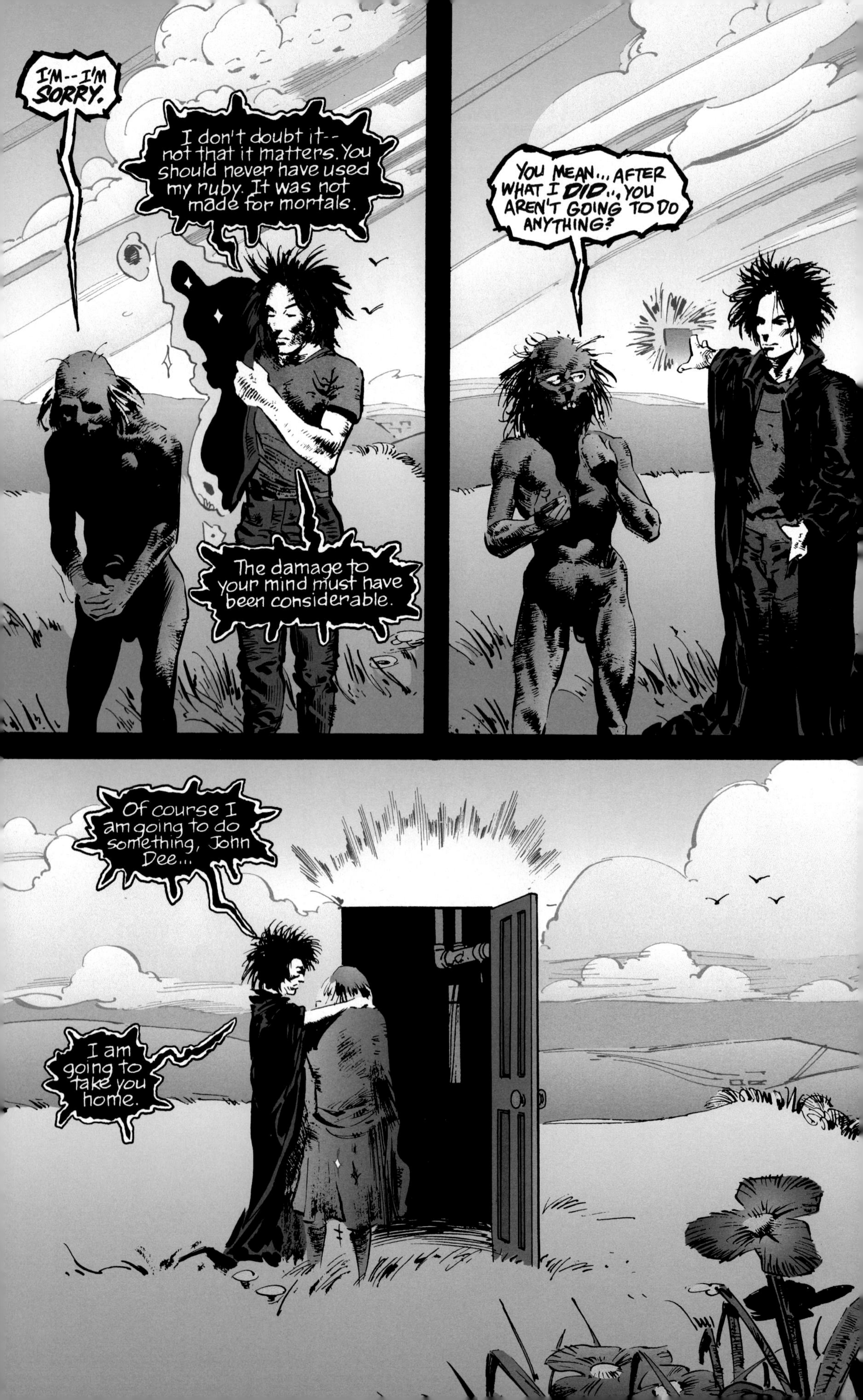
I'M-- I'M SORRY.
I don't doubt it-- not that it matters. You should never have used my ruby. It was not made for mortals.
The damage to your mind must have been considerable.
YOU MEAN... AFTER WHAT I DID.., YOU AREN'T GOING TO DO ANYTHING?
Of course I am going to do something, John Dee...
I am going to take you home.

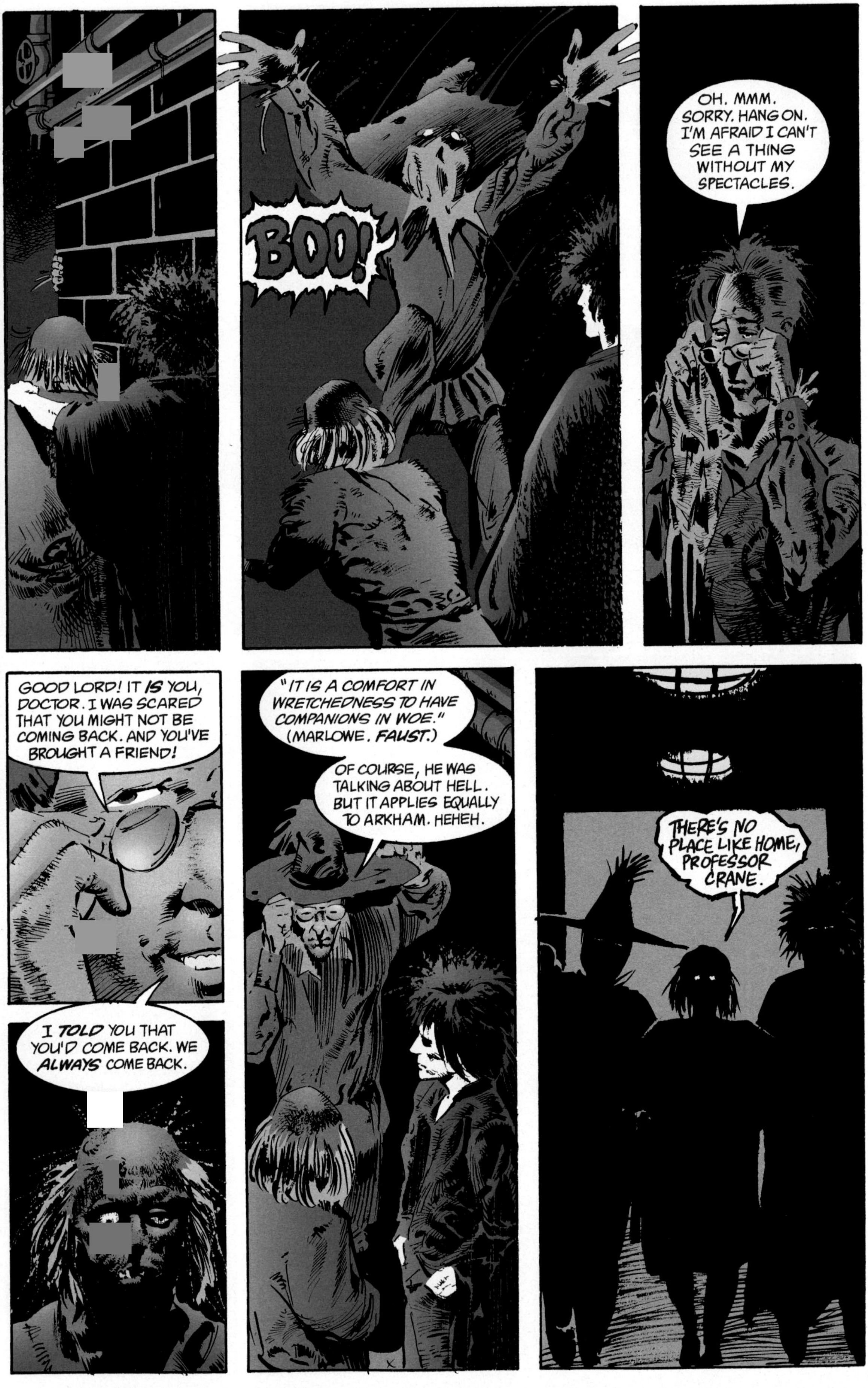
BOO!
OH. MMM. SORRY. HANG ON. I'M AFRAID I CAN'T SEE A THING WITHOUT MY SPECTACLES.
GOOD LORD! IT IS YOU, DOCTOR. I WAS SCARED THAT YOU MIGHT NOT BE COMING BACK. AND YOU'VE BROUGHT A FRIEND!
I TOLD YOU THAT YOU'D COME BACK. WE ALWAYS COME BACK.
"IT IS A COMFORT IN WRETCHEDNESS TO HAVE COMPANIONS IN WOE." (MARLOWE. FAUST.)
OF COURSE, HE WAS TALKING ABOUT HELL. BUT IT APPLIES EQUALLY TO ARKHAM. HEHEH.
THERE'S NO PLACE LIKE HOME, PROFESSOR CRANE.

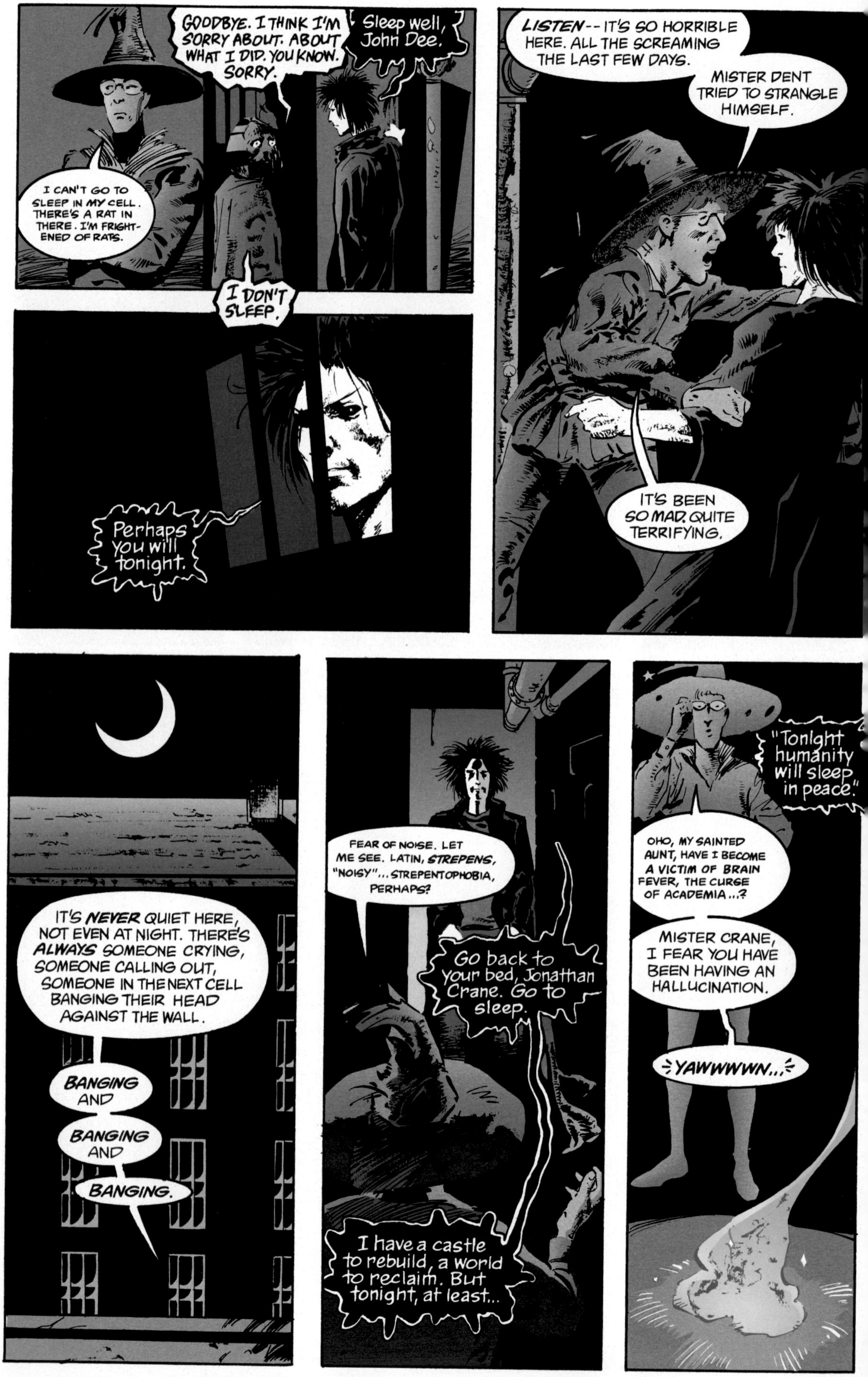
GOODBYE. I THINK I'M SORRY ABOUT. ABOUT WHAT I DID. YOU KNOW. SORRY.
Sleep well, John Dee.
I CAN'T GO TO SLEEP IN MY CELL. THERE'S A RAT IN THERE. I'M FRIGHT-ENED OF RATS.
I DON'T SLEEP.
Perhaps you will tonight.
LISTEN-- IT'S SO HORRIBLE HERE. ALL THE SCREAMING THE LAST FEW DAYS.
MISTER DENT TRIED TO STRANGLE HIMSELF.
IT'S BEEN SO MAD. QUITE TERRIFYING.
IT'S NEVER QUIET HERE, NOT EVEN AT NIGHT. THERE'S ALWAYS SOMEONE CRYING, SOMEONE CALLING OUT, SOMEONE IN THE NEXT CELL BANGING THEIR HEAD AGAINST THE WALL.
BANGING AND
BANGING AND
BANGING.
FEAR OF NOISE. LET ME SEE. LATIN, STREPENS, "NOISY"... STREPENTOPHOBIA, PERHAPS?
Go back to your bed, Jonathan Crane. Go to sleep.
I have a castle to rebuild, a world to reclaim. But tonight, at least...
"Tonight humanity will sleep in peace."
OHO, MY SAINTED AUNT, HAVE I BECOME A VICTIM OF BRAIN FEVER, THE CURSE OF ACADEMIA...?
MISTER CRANE, I FEAR YOU HAVE BEEN HAVING AN HALLUCINATION.
YAWWWWN...

AS FAST AS THEY DAWNED, THE CRAZY TIMES ARE OVER.

NAN FOWLER IS ASLEEP ON HER DESK. SHE IS BREATHING SLOWLY, DEEPLY.

AND THE PATIENTS BROUGHT IN THAT DAY, CUT AND SMASHED AND BROKEN, ALL SLEEP LIKE ANGELS, NEEDING NO MORPHINE.

THEY BREATHE IN, OUT, IN, OUT, IN UNBROKEN AND QUIET RHYTHM.

AND IN BEDLAM JOHN DEE SLEEPS WITHOUT DREAMING, BUT HIS SLEEP IS SOUND AND RESTFUL.

SILENCE WASHES LIKE A RIVER OVER ARKHAM. NO SOUNDS OF SCREAMING, NO SOBBING, NO NOISES OF PAIN OR MADNESS.

JUST PEACE.

THE ONLY NOISE IS THE GENTLE, EVEN CADENCE OF PEOPLE ASLEEP. IN, OUT, IN, OUT.

LISTEN.

YOU CAN HEAR IT.

ARKHAM ASYLVM

NEXT:
A DEATH IN THE FAMILY

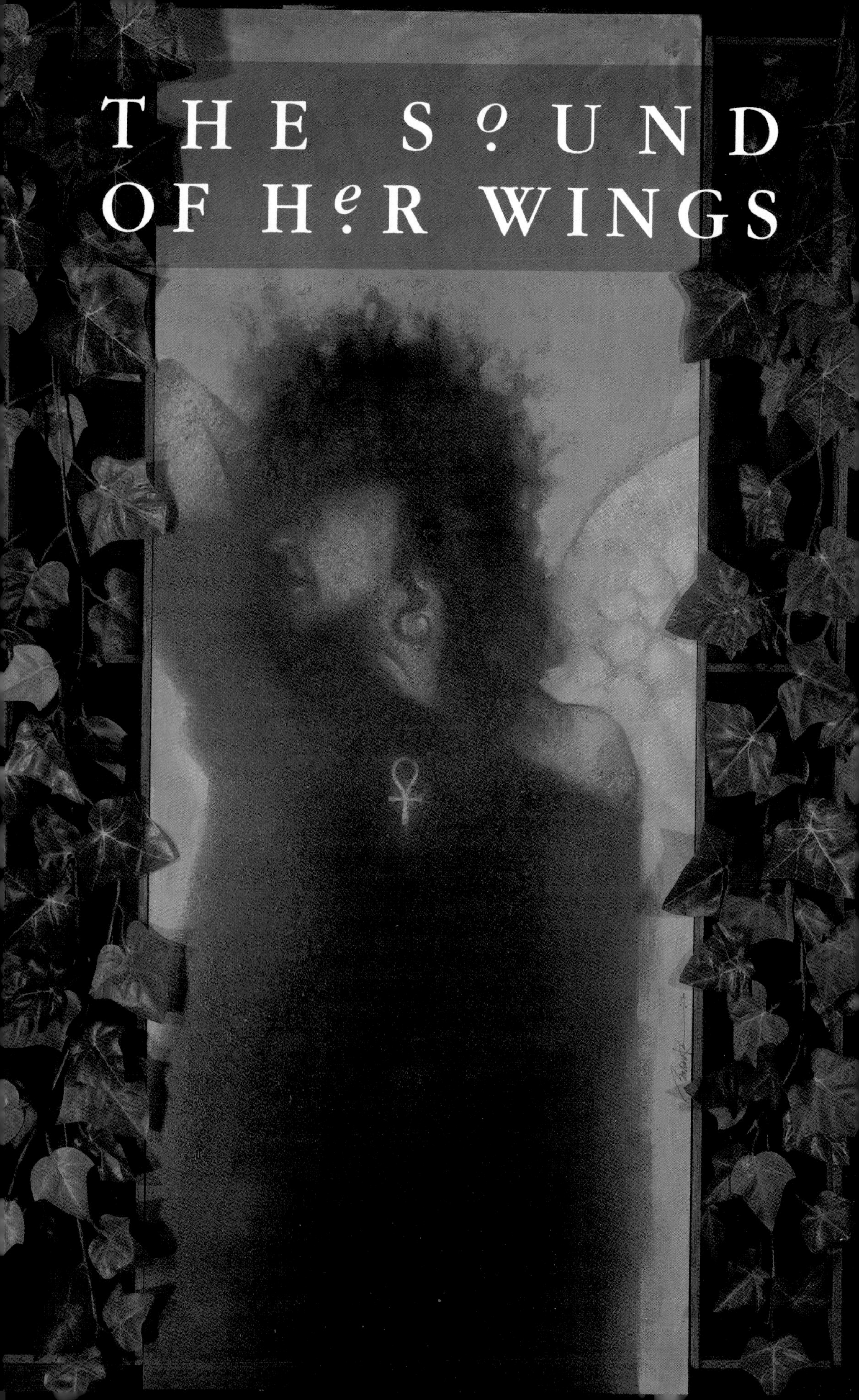
THE SOUND
OF HER WINGS

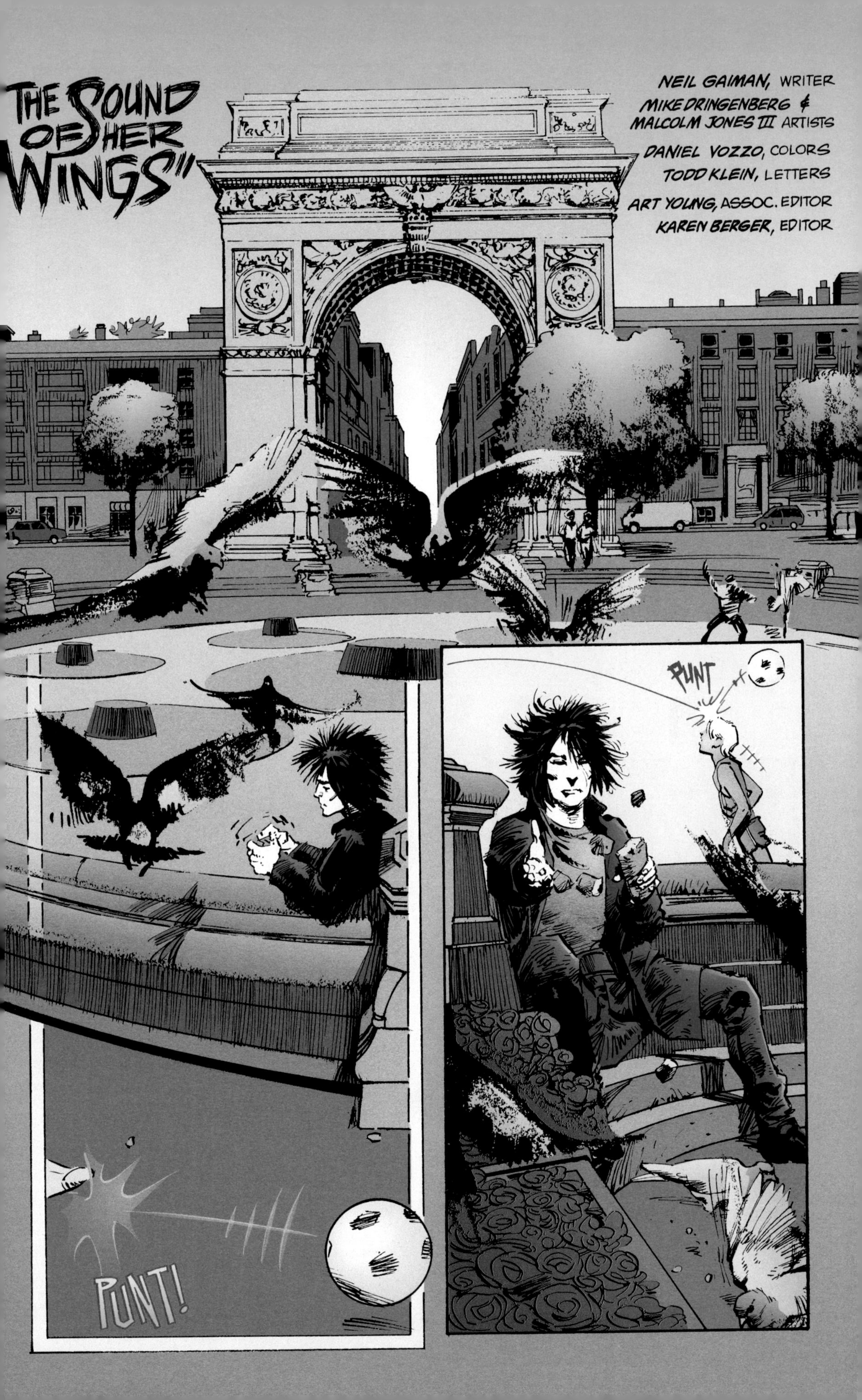
"THE SOUND OF HER WINGS"
NEIL GAIMAN, WRITER
MIKE DRINGENBERG & MALCOLM JONES III ARTISTS
DANIEL VOZZO, COLORS
TODD KLEIN, LETTERS
ART YOUNG, ASSOC. EDITOR
KAREN BERGER, EDITOR
PUNT!
PUNT

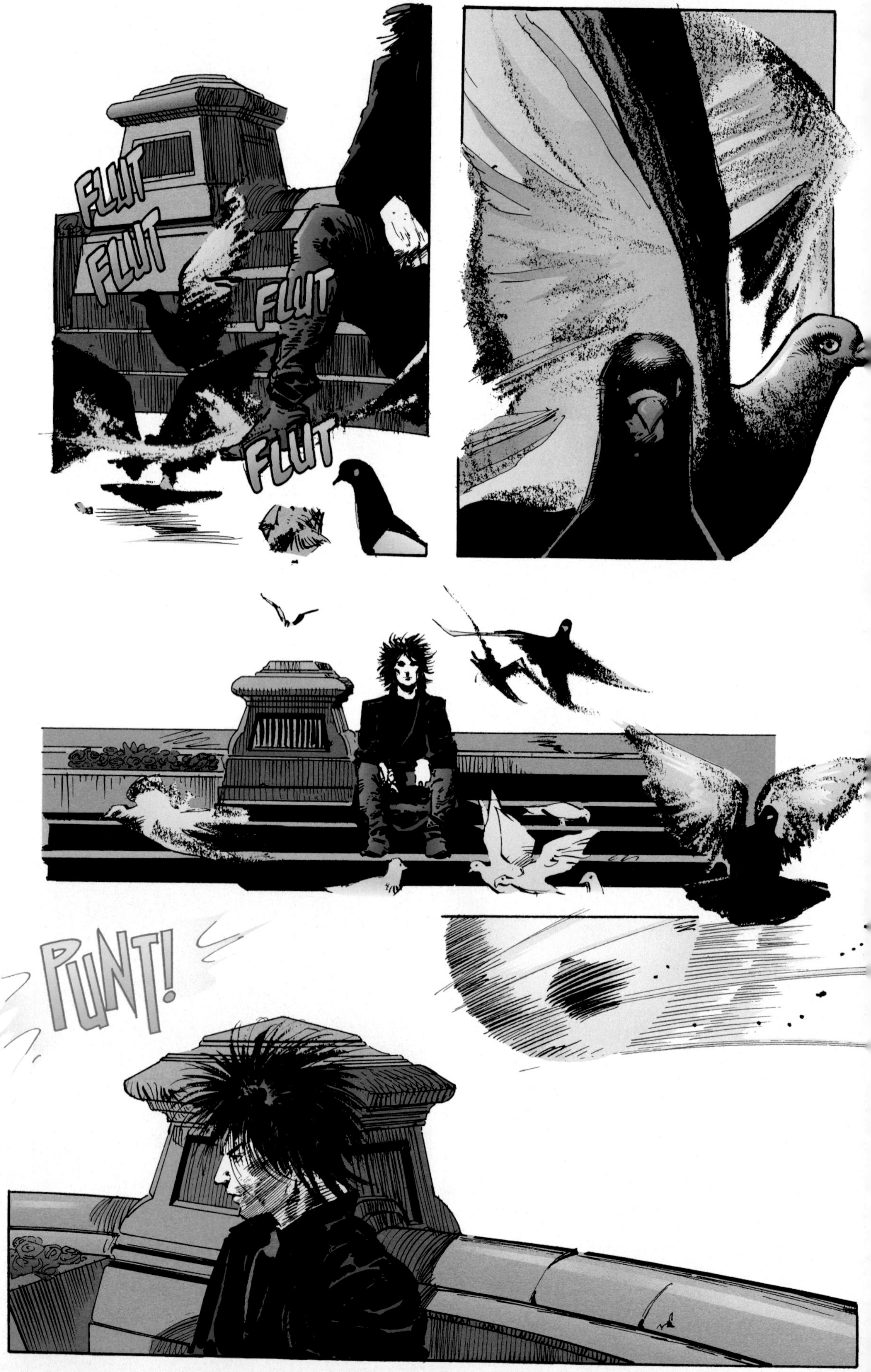
FLUT
FLUT
FLUT
FLUT
PUNT!

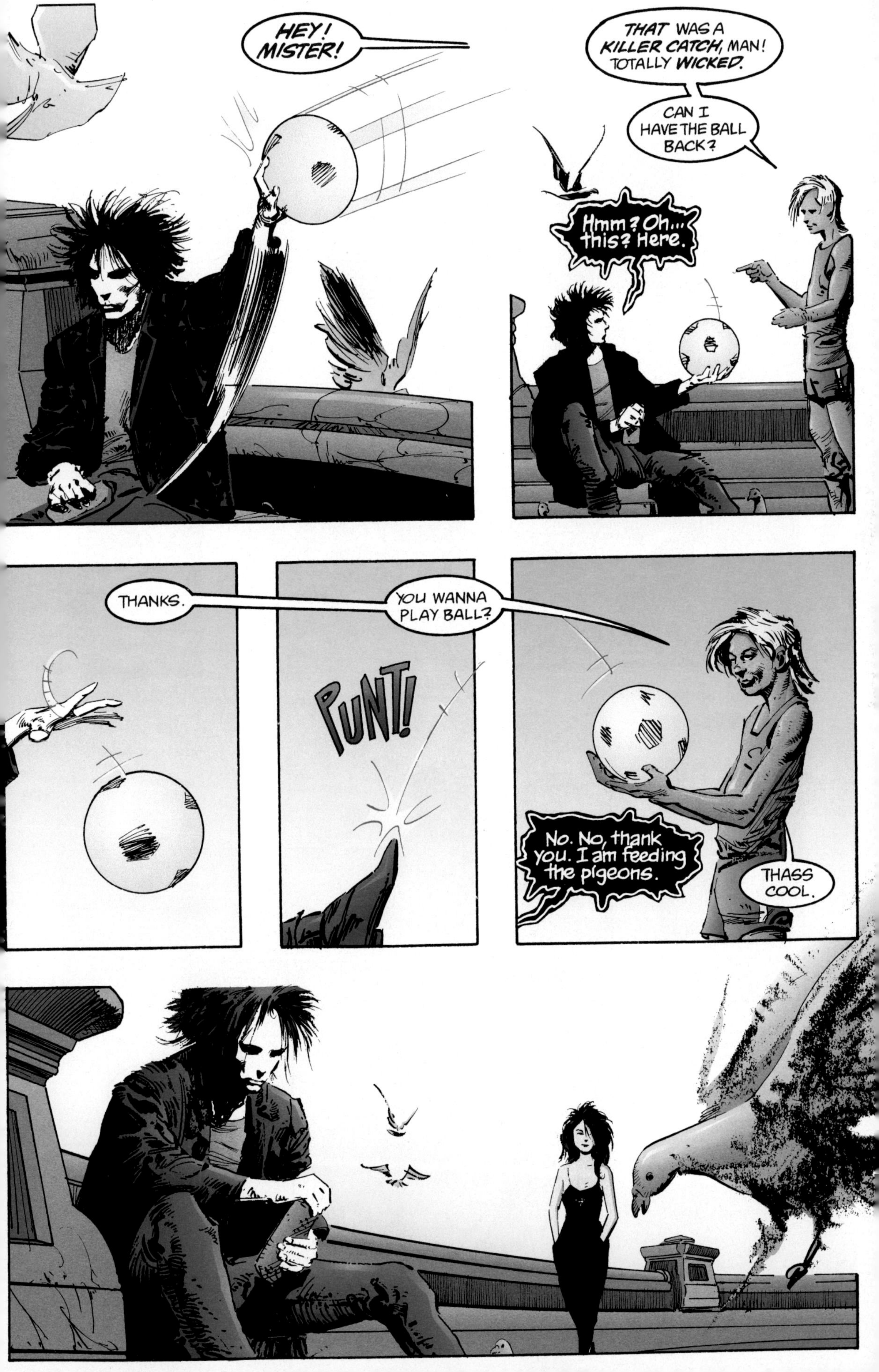
HEY! MISTER!
THAT WAS A KILLER CATCH, MAN! TOTALLY WICKED.
CAN I HAVE THE BALL BACK?
Hmm? Oh... this? Here.
THANKS.
YOU WANNA PLAY BALL?
PUNT!
No. No, thank you. I am feeding the pigeons.
THASS COOL.

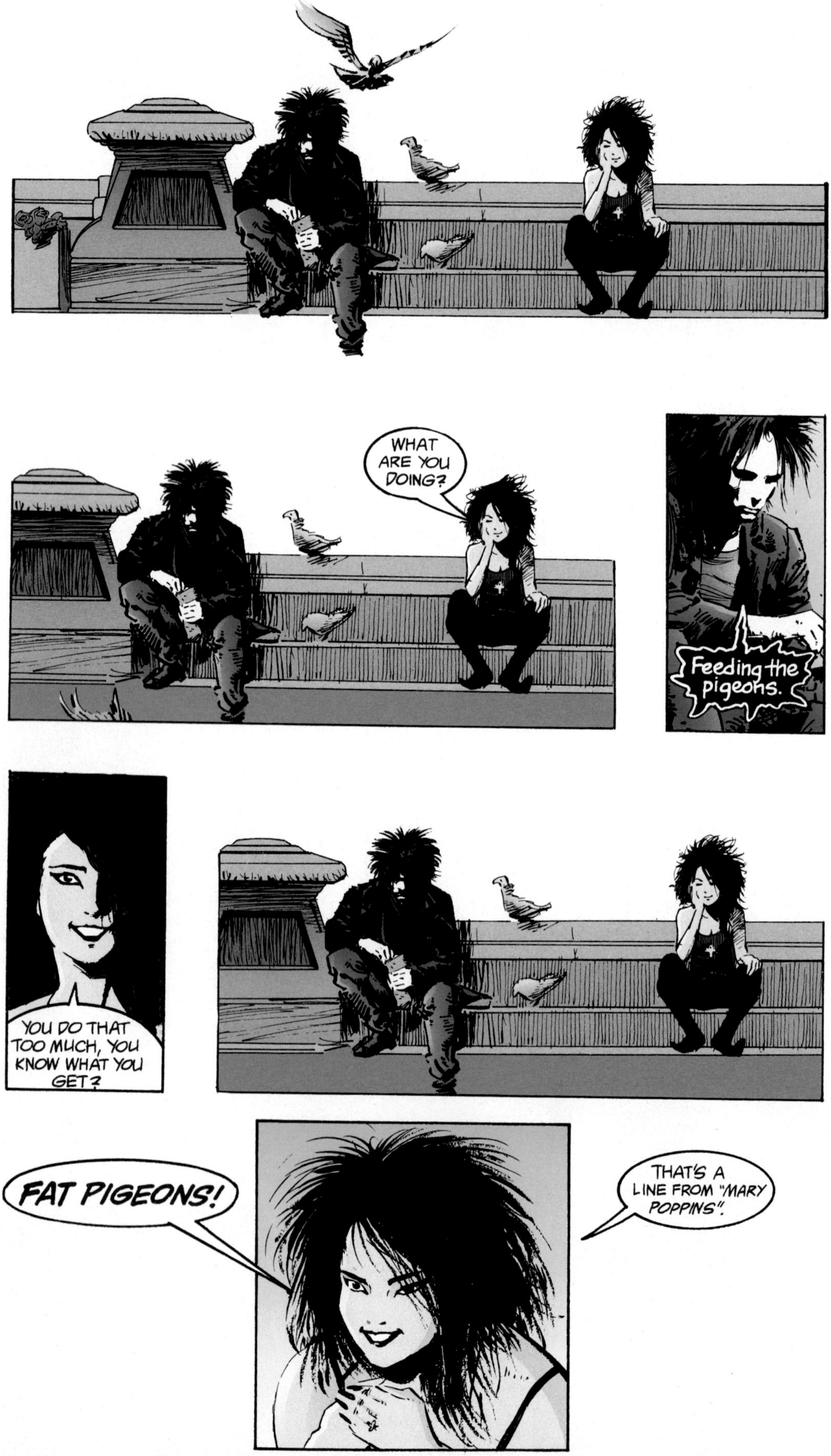
WHAT ARE YOU DOING?
Feeding the pigeons.
YOU DO THAT TOO MUCH, YOU KNOW WHAT YOU GET?
FAT PIGEONS!
THAT'S A LINE FROM "MARY POPPINS".

I *LOVE* THAT MOVIE. YOU EVER SEE IT?

No.

THERE'S THIS GUY WHO'S *UTTERLY* A BANKER, AND HE DOESN'T HAVE *TIME* FOR HIS FAMILY, OR FOR *LIVING*, OR ANYTHING.

AND MARY POPPINS, SHE COMES DOWN FROM THE CLOUDS, AND SHE SHOWS HIM WHAT'S *IMPORTANT*.

FUN. FLYING *KITES*, ALL THAT STUFF.

SUPERCALIFRAGILISTICEXPIALIDOCIOUS!

What?

SUPER-*CALI*-FRAGIL-*IST*IC-EXPI-*ALI*-DOCIOUS. *UTTERLY* FAN*TAB*ULOUS WORD, HUH? IT MEANS, Y'KNOW, GREAT.

WONDERFUL

GINCHY. GNARLY.

PEACHY KEEN!

WOOGA-WOOGA-WOOGA! VROOOOOM! YIIIIIIIII!!

Ah.

IT'S A *CUTE* MOVIE. MAYBE NOT *EVERYBODY'S* THING, BUT, Y'KNOW...

DICK VAN DYKE'S BRITISH ACCENT DEFIES *BELIEF*. "HOH 'HITS A JOLLY 'OLIEDYE WIV YEW, MAIREE PAWPINS!"

Y'KNOW. *CUTE.*

FLIT FLIT

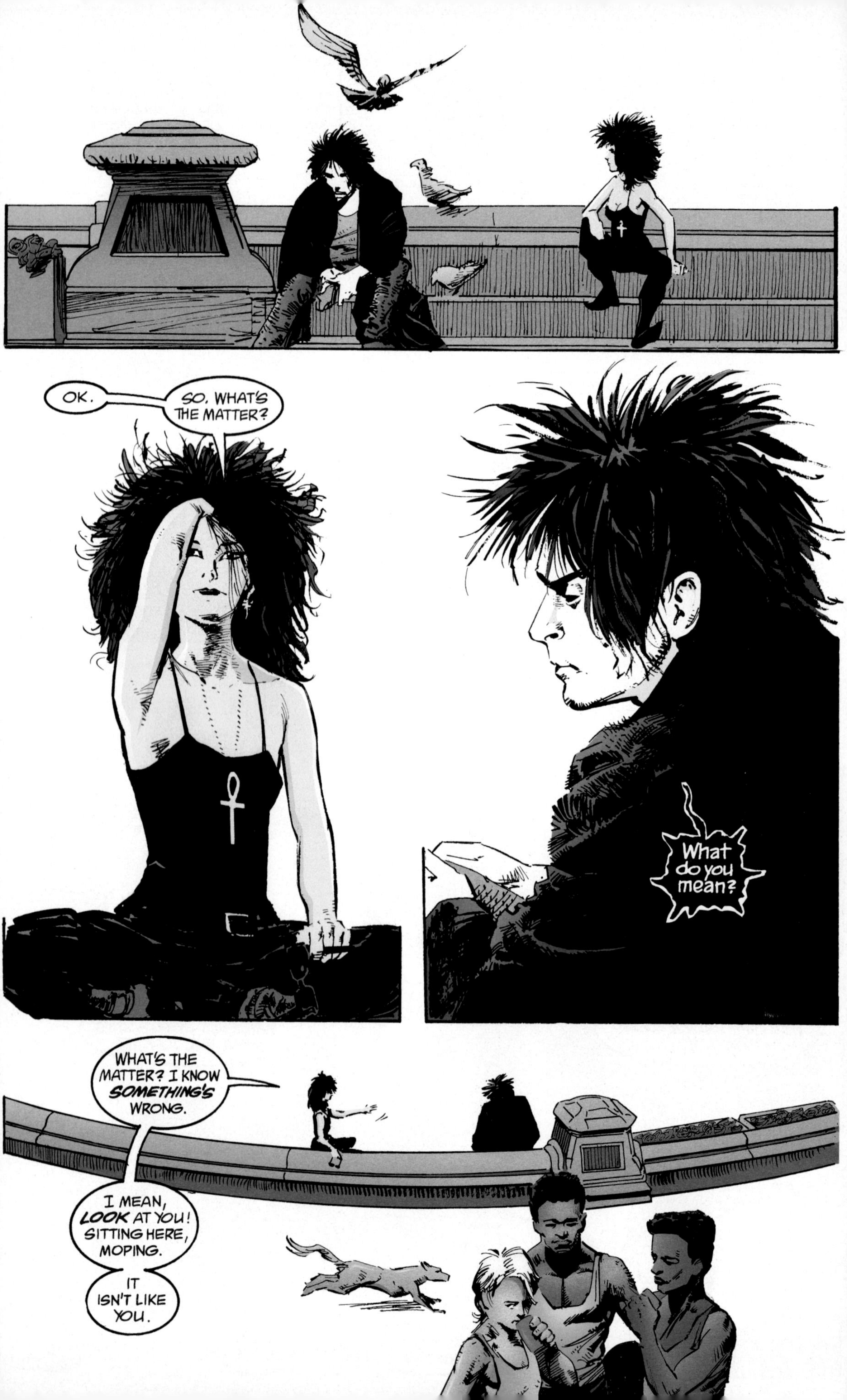
OK.
SO, WHAT'S THE MATTER?
What do you mean?
WHAT'S THE MATTER? I KNOW SOMETHING'S WRONG.
I MEAN, LOOK AT YOU! SITTING HERE, MOPING.
IT ISN'T LIKE YOU.

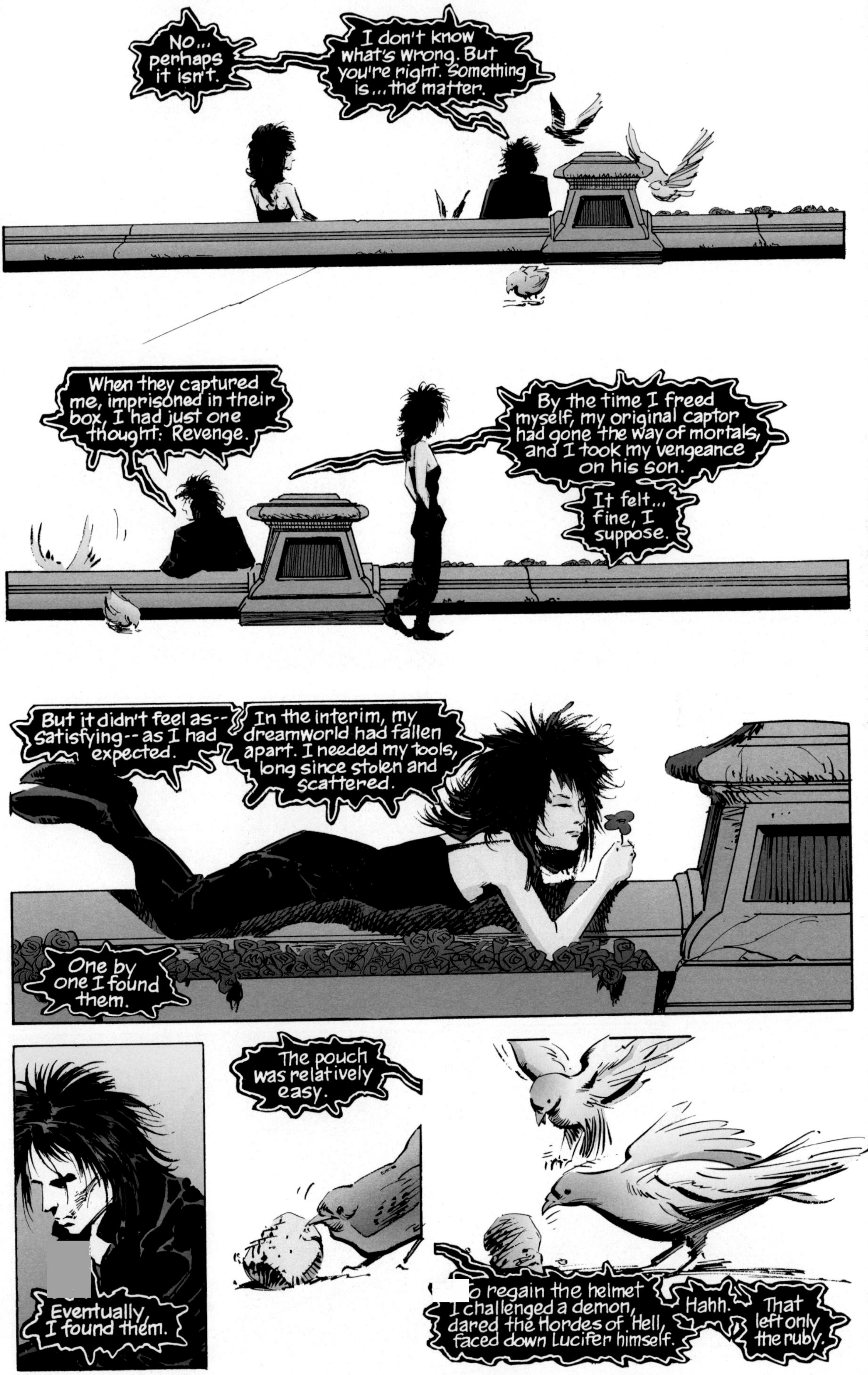
No... perhaps it isn't.
I don't know what's wrong. But you're right. Something is... the matter.
When they captured me, imprisoned in their box, I had just one thought: Revenge.
By the time I freed myself, my original captor had gone the way of mortals, and I took my vengeance on his son.
It felt... fine, I suppose.
But it didn't feel as-- satisfying-- as I had expected.
In the interim, my dreamworld had fallen apart. I needed my tools, long since stolen and scattered.
One by one I found them.
Eventually, I found them.
The pouch was relatively easy.
o regain the helmet I challenged a demon, dared the Hordes of Hell, faced down Lucifer himself.
Hahh.
That left only the ruby.

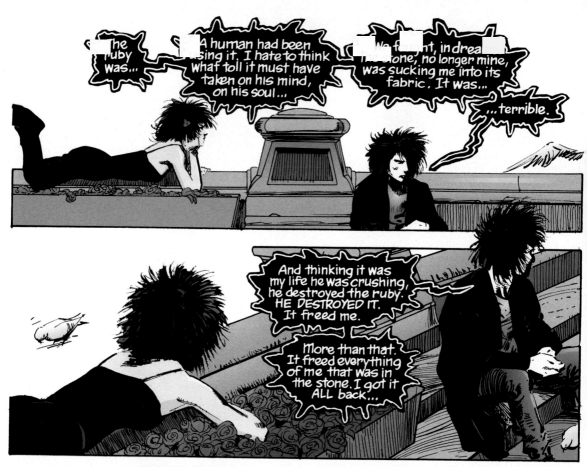

...he ruby was...

A human had been using it. I hate to think what toll it must have taken on his mind, on his soul...

We fought, in dream. The stone, no longer mine, was sucking me into its fabric. It was...

...terrible.

And thinking it was my life he was crushing, he destroyed the ruby. HE DESTROYED IT. It freed me.

More than that. It freed everything of me that was in the stone. I got it ALL back...

I was more powerful than I had been in eons. I returned the human to the madhouse...

You see, until then I'd been driven. I'd had a true quest, a purpose beyond my function--and then, suddenly, the quest was over.

I felt...drained. Disappointed. Let down.

Does that make sense? I had been sure that as soon as I had everything back I'd feel good. But inside I felt worse than when I started.

I feel like... nothing.

There. You asked.

I'm sorry. Maybe I don't have an answer.

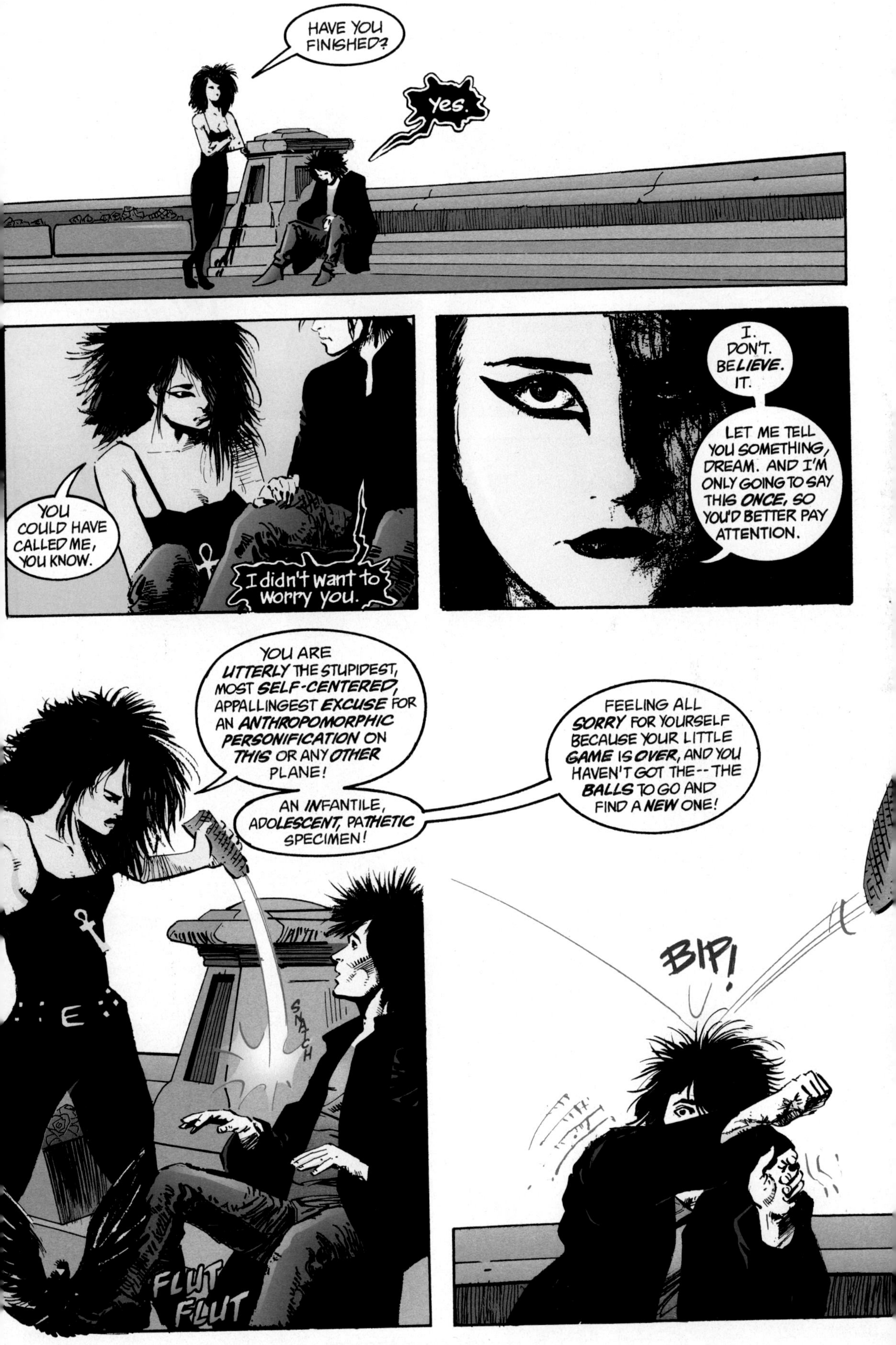
HAVE YOU FINISHED?
Yes.
YOU COULD HAVE CALLED ME, YOU KNOW.
I didn't want to worry you.
I. DON'T. BELIEVE. IT.
LET ME TELL YOU SOMETHING, DREAM. AND I'M ONLY GOING TO SAY THIS ONCE, SO YOU'D BETTER PAY ATTENTION.
YOU ARE UTTERLY THE STUPIDEST, MOST SELF-CENTERED, APPALLINGEST EXCUSE FOR AN ANTHROPOMORPHIC PERSONIFICATION ON THIS OR ANY OTHER PLANE!
AN INFANTILE, ADOLESCENT, PATHETIC SPECIMEN!
FEELING ALL SORRY FOR YOURSELF BECAUSE YOUR LITTLE GAME IS OVER, AND YOU HAVEN'T GOT THE-- THE BALLS TO GO AND FIND A NEW ONE!
SNATCH
FLUT
FLUT
BIP!

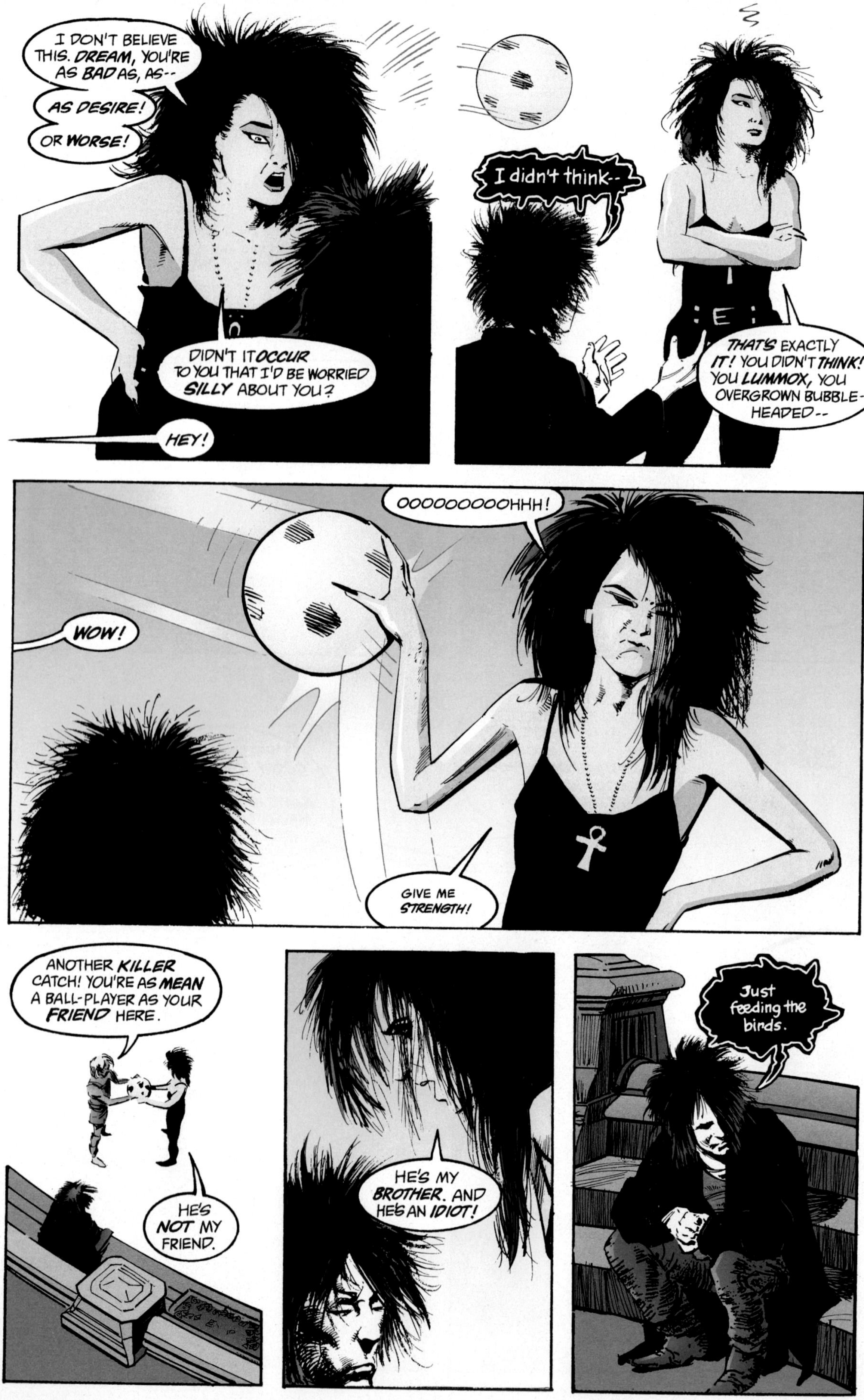
I DON'T BELIEVE THIS. DREAM, YOU'RE AS BAD AS, AS--
AS DESIRE!
OR WORSE!
DIDN'T IT OCCUR TO YOU THAT I'D BE WORRIED SILLY ABOUT YOU?
HEY!
I didn't think--
THAT'S EXACTLY IT! YOU DIDN'T THINK! YOU LUMMOX, YOU OVERGROWN BUBBLE-HEADED--
OOOOOOOOOHHH!
WOW!
GIVE ME STRENGTH!
ANOTHER KILLER CATCH! YOU'RE AS MEAN A BALL-PLAYER AS YOUR FRIEND HERE.
HE'S NOT MY FRIEND.
HE'S MY BROTHER. AND HE'S AN IDIOT!
Just feeding the birds.

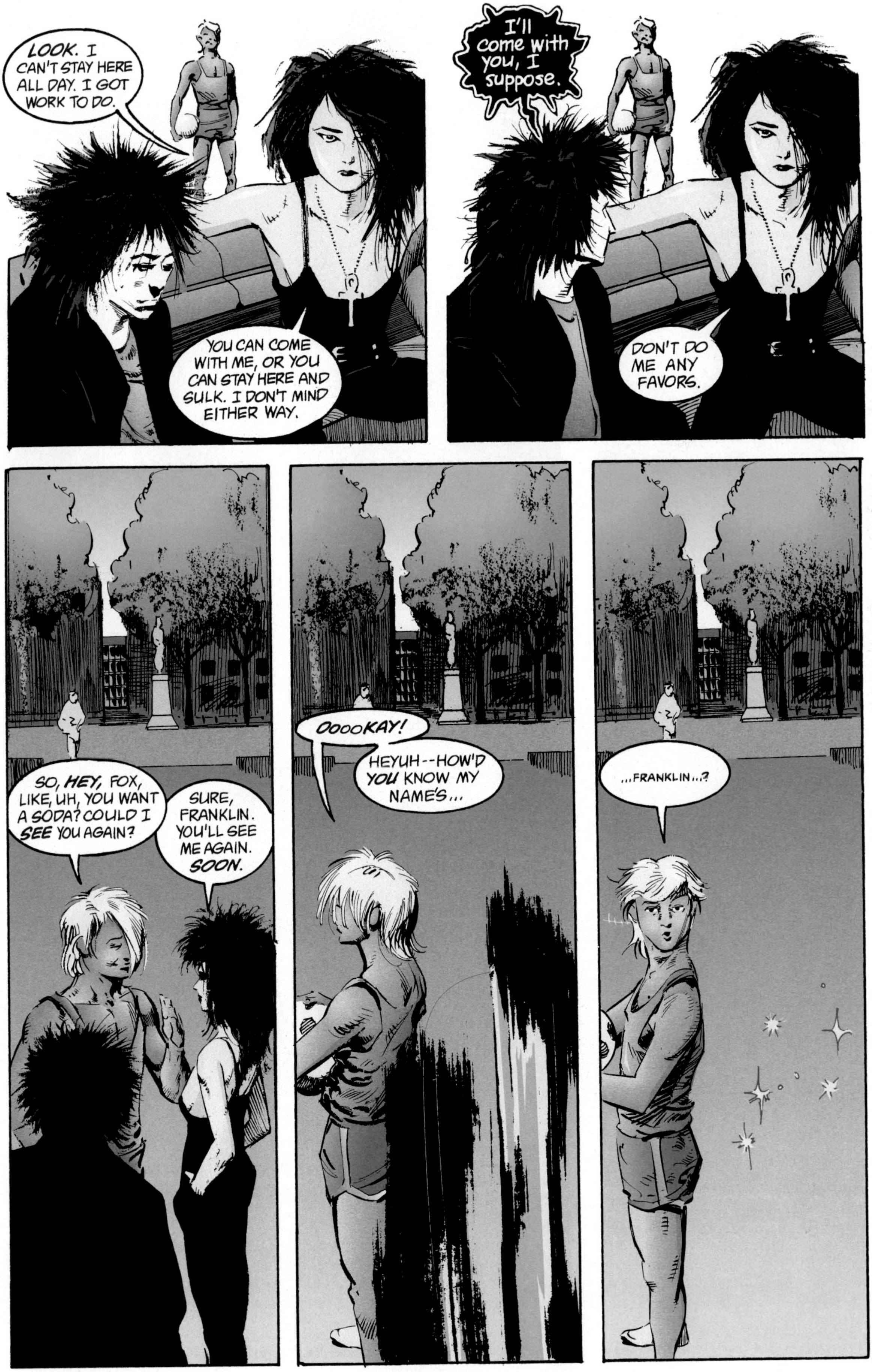
LOOK. I CAN'T STAY HERE ALL DAY. I GOT WORK TO DO.
YOU CAN COME WITH ME, OR YOU CAN STAY HERE AND SULK. I DON'T MIND EITHER WAY.
I'll come with you, I suppose.
DON'T DO ME ANY FAVORS.
SO, HEY, FOX, LIKE, UH, YOU WANT A SODA? COULD I SEE YOU AGAIN?
SURE, FRANKLIN. YOU'LL SEE ME AGAIN. SOON.
OOOOKAY!
HEYUH--HOW'D YOU KNOW MY NAME'S...
...FRANKLIN...?

CAN YOU ROCKER ROMANY? CAN YOU PATTER FLASH? ♪ ♩ ♪ ♪ ♫

CAN YOU ROCKER ROMANY? CAN YOU FAKE A BOSH? ♫ ♩ ♪ ♩ ♩

YES. I CAN PATTER ROMANY, HARRY. CAN YOU?

HUNH? I DIDN'T HEAR NOBODY COME IN ...

CAN *I* PATTER ROMANY?

NOT SO GOOD. BUT I CAN FAKE A BOSH. MEANS T' PLAY THE FIDDLE. I'M NOT REAL ROMANY...

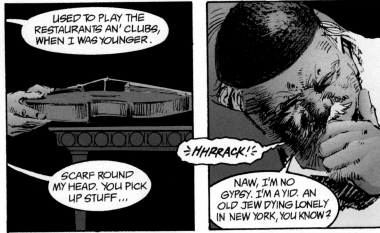

USED TO PLAY THE RESTAURANTS AN' CLUBS, WHEN I WAS YOUNGER.

SCARF ROUND MY HEAD. YOU PICK UP STUFF...

⁓HHRRACK!⁓

NAW, I'M NO GYPSY. I'M A YID. AN OLD JEW DYING LONELY IN NEW YORK, YOU KNOW?

YES, I KNOW WHO YOU ARE, HARRY. DO YOU KNOW WHO I AM?

YOU? YOU'RE... NO! NOT *YET!* ...PLEASE?

YEAH, I KNOW WHO YOU ARE.

HRRUCCK!

'SCUSE ME. SOMETHING I GOT TO SAY. ALWAYS USED TO WONDER IF I WOULD, BUT, Y'KNOW, WHAT TH' HEY...

SH'MA YISROEL.

ADONAI ELOHAYNU, ADONAI E'HOD.

HEAR, O ISRAEL...

THE LORD OUR GOD...

THE LORD IS ONE.

✶

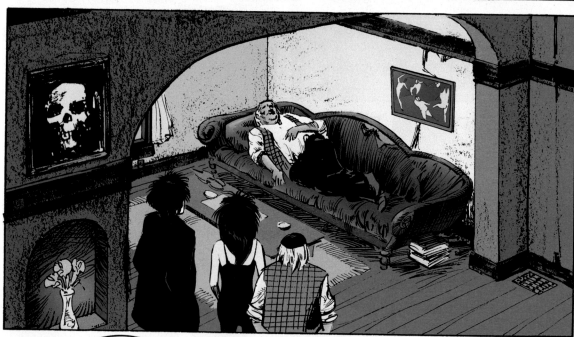

I LOOK SO EMPTY. I LOOK SO OLD.

IT'S GOOD THAT I SAID THE SH'MA. MY OLD MAN ALWAYS SAID IT GUARANTEED YOU A PLACE IN HEAVEN. IF YOU BELIEVE IN HEAVEN...

SO. I'M DEAD.

NOW WHAT?

NOW'S WHEN YOU FIND OUT, HARRY.

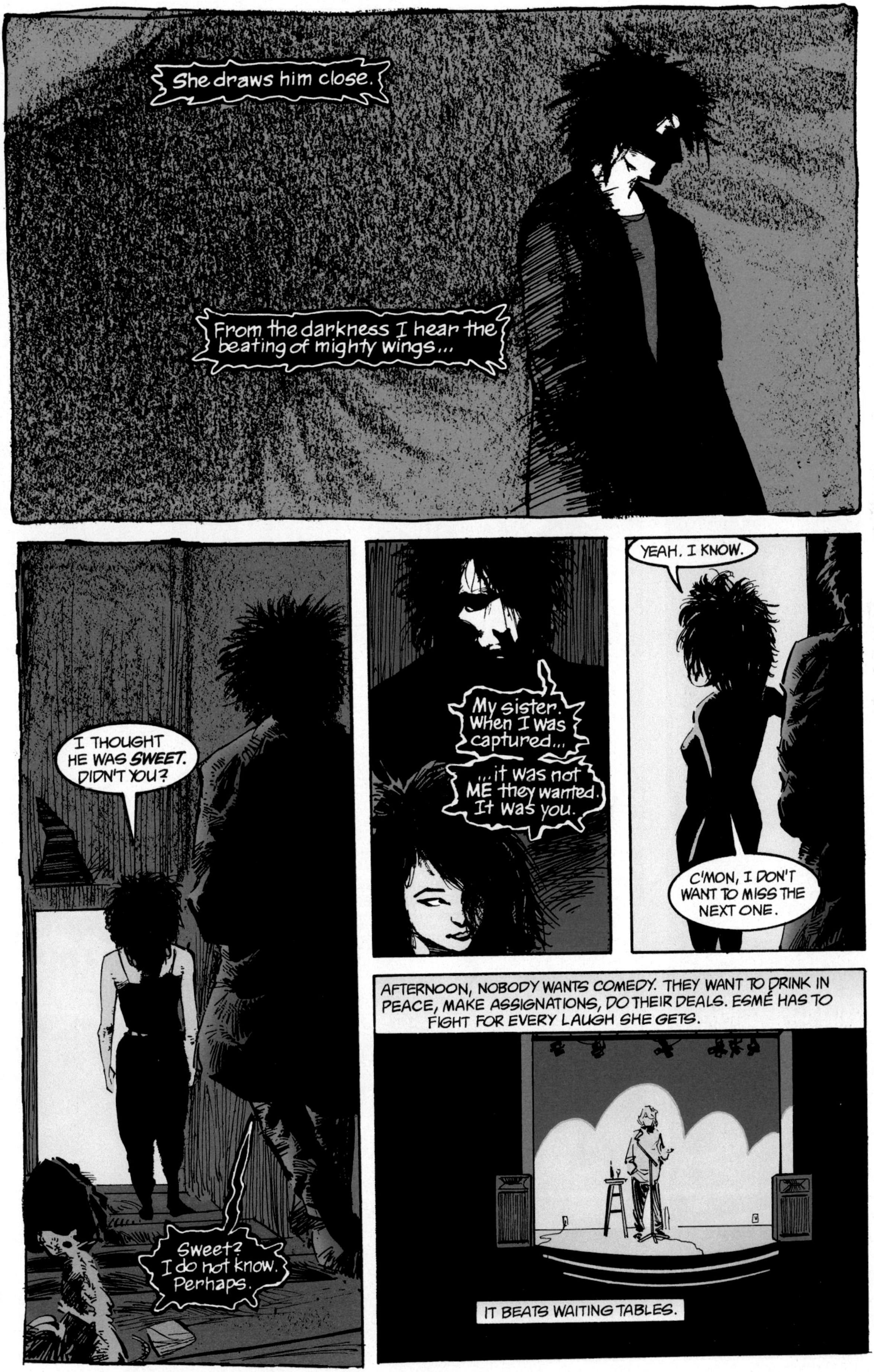
She draws him close.
From the darkness I hear the beating of mighty wings...
I THOUGHT HE WAS SWEET. DIDN'T YOU?
Sweet? I do not know. Perhaps.
My sister. When I was captured...
...it was not ME they wanted. It was you.
YEAH. I KNOW.
C'MON, I DON'T WANT TO MISS THE NEXT ONE.
AFTERNOON, NOBODY WANTS COMEDY. THEY WANT TO DRINK IN PEACE, MAKE ASSIGNATIONS, DO THEIR DEALS. ESMÉ HAS TO FIGHT FOR EVERY LAUGH SHE GETS.
IT BEATS WAITING TABLES.

HER HANDS ARE SWEATING.

...SERIOUSLY, DON'T YOU EVER *WONDER* ABOUT BATMAN? HOW HE GOT STARTED? I CAN SEE HIM OVER BREAKFAST SAYING TO HIS WIFE:

"MORNING, HON. LISTEN, I GOT SOMETHING TO TELL YA. I UH, I *QUIT* THE JOB AT THE *AD AGENCY*."

"SO WHADAYA GOING TO DO *NOW*, RALPHIE? *HUH*?"

"I GOT IT *ALL* FIGURED OUT. I'M GONNA DRESS UP LIKE A *BAT* AND FIGHT *CRIME*."

"YOU'RE GONNA *WHAAT?* RALPHIE, HAVE YOU TALKED THIS OVER WITH YOUR ANALYST?"

AND WHAT ABOUT *ROBIN?* NOW THAT KID WAS...

But if they HAD captured you, the consequences--

HA HA HA HA

SHH! I WANT TO HEAR THIS.

HAHAHAHAHA

"HEY, MA BELL-- REACH OUT AND *KILL* SOMEONE!" AND THIS DEEP VOICE SAYS, "WELL, THERE'S MORE WHERE THAT CAME FROM!"...

THEY LIKE HER. WAVES OF APPROVAL, OF SWEET LAUGHTER, WASH OVER HER.

NOW SHE'S GOING PLACES.

YEEEEAGK!

SHE'S A SCREAM.

THOSE *ASSHOLES!* I DON'T BELIEVE IT--THAT SCREWIN' MIKE WAS *LIVE!* THOSE *CHEAP,* NO GOOD...

WHO *ARE* YOU?

I JUST REALIZED. THAT'S EVERY COMEDIAN'S *NIGHTMARE,* HUH? *DYING* ON STAGE. HEHH... I THOUGHT YOU WERE REALLY FUNNY.

NO. BUT I WOULD HAVE BEEN...

WHY COULDN'T I HAVE HAD A *FEW* MORE LOUSY *YEARS?* I WOULD HAVE MADE IT TO THE *TOP. WHY?*

I'M SORRY, ESMÉ. YOUR TIME WAS UP. COME HERE, HONEY.

I hear the sound of her wings.

...GETS ME DOWN, TOO. MOSTLY THEY AREN'T TOO KEEN TO SEE ME. THEY FEAR THE SUNLESS LANDS. BUT THEY ENTER *YOUR* REALM EACH NIGHT WITHOUT FEAR.

NO ONE HERE GETS OUT ALIVE!

And I am far more terrible than you, my sister.

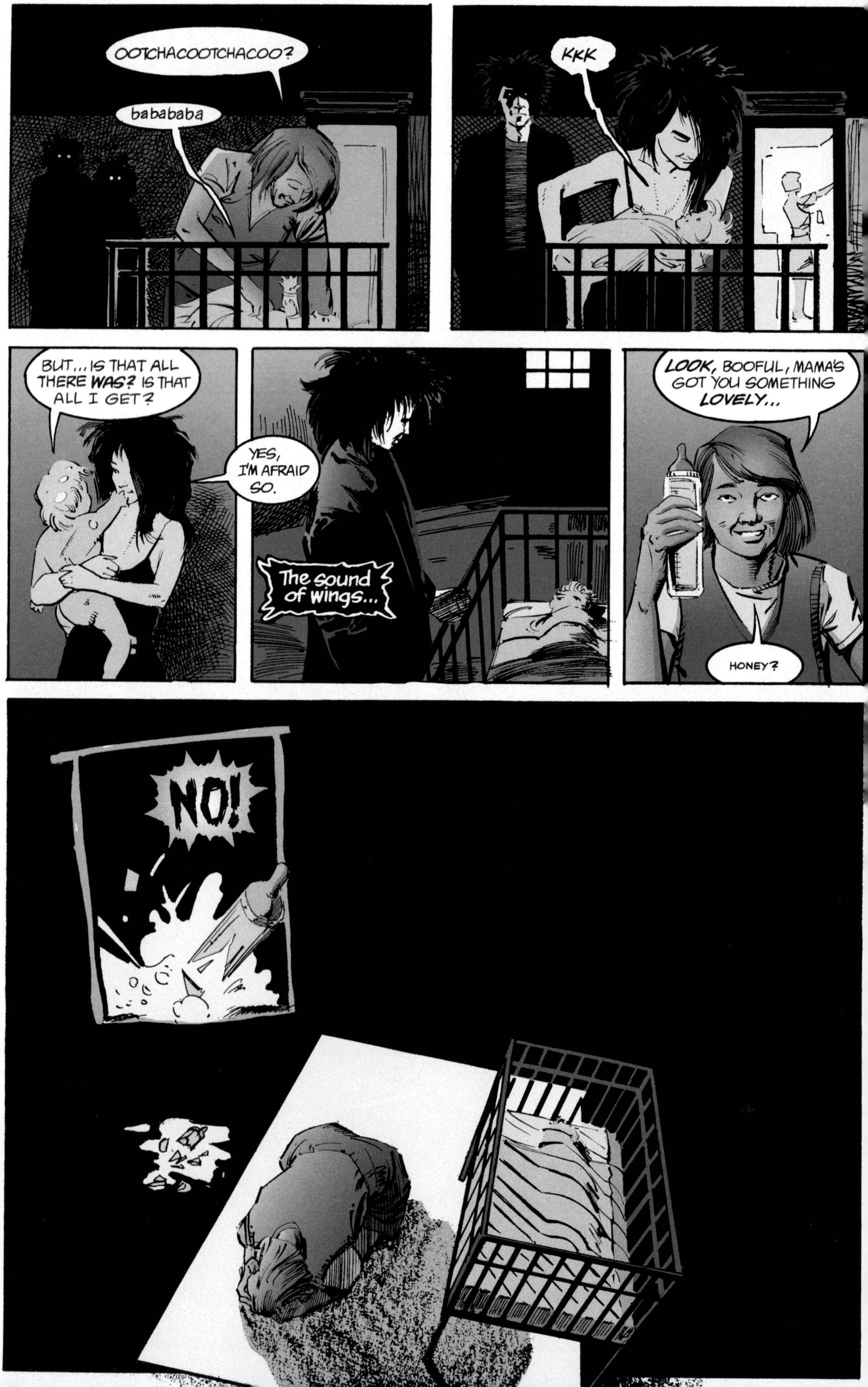
OOTCHACOOTCHACOO?
bababababa
KKK
BUT... IS THAT ALL THERE WAS? IS THAT ALL I GET?
YES, I'M AFRAID SO.
The sound of wings...
LOOK, BOOFUL, MAMA'S GOT YOU SOMETHING LOVELY...
HONEY?
NO!

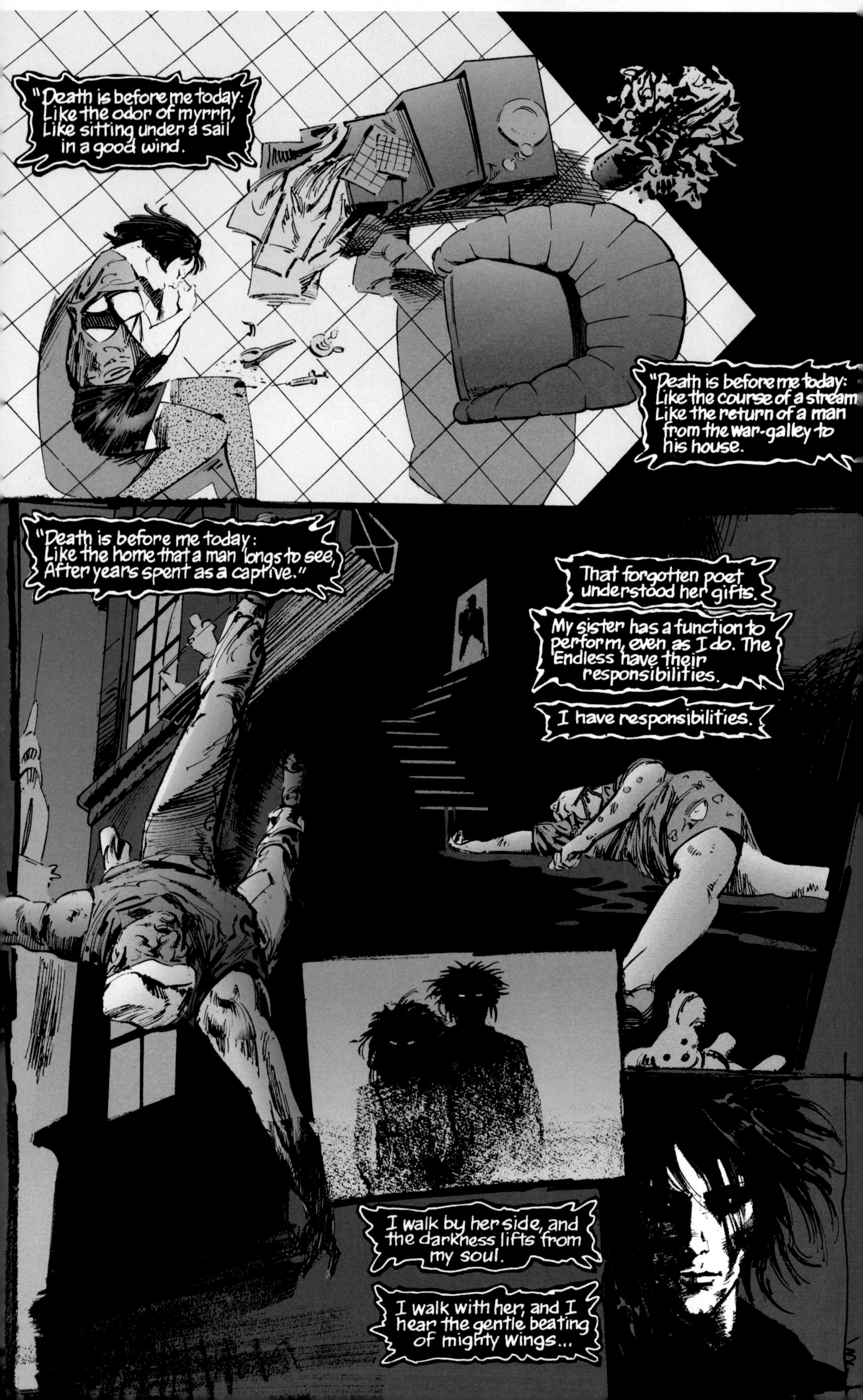
"Death is before me today: Like the odor of myrrh, Like sitting under a sail in a good wind.
"Death is before me today: Like the course of a stream Like the return of a man from the war-galley to his house.
"Death is before me today: Like the home that a man longs to see, After years spent as a captive."
That forgotten poet understood her gifts.
My sister has a function to perform, even as I do. The Endless have their responsibilities.
I have responsibilities.
I walk by her side, and the darkness lifts from my soul.
I walk with her, and I hear the gentle beating of mighty wings...

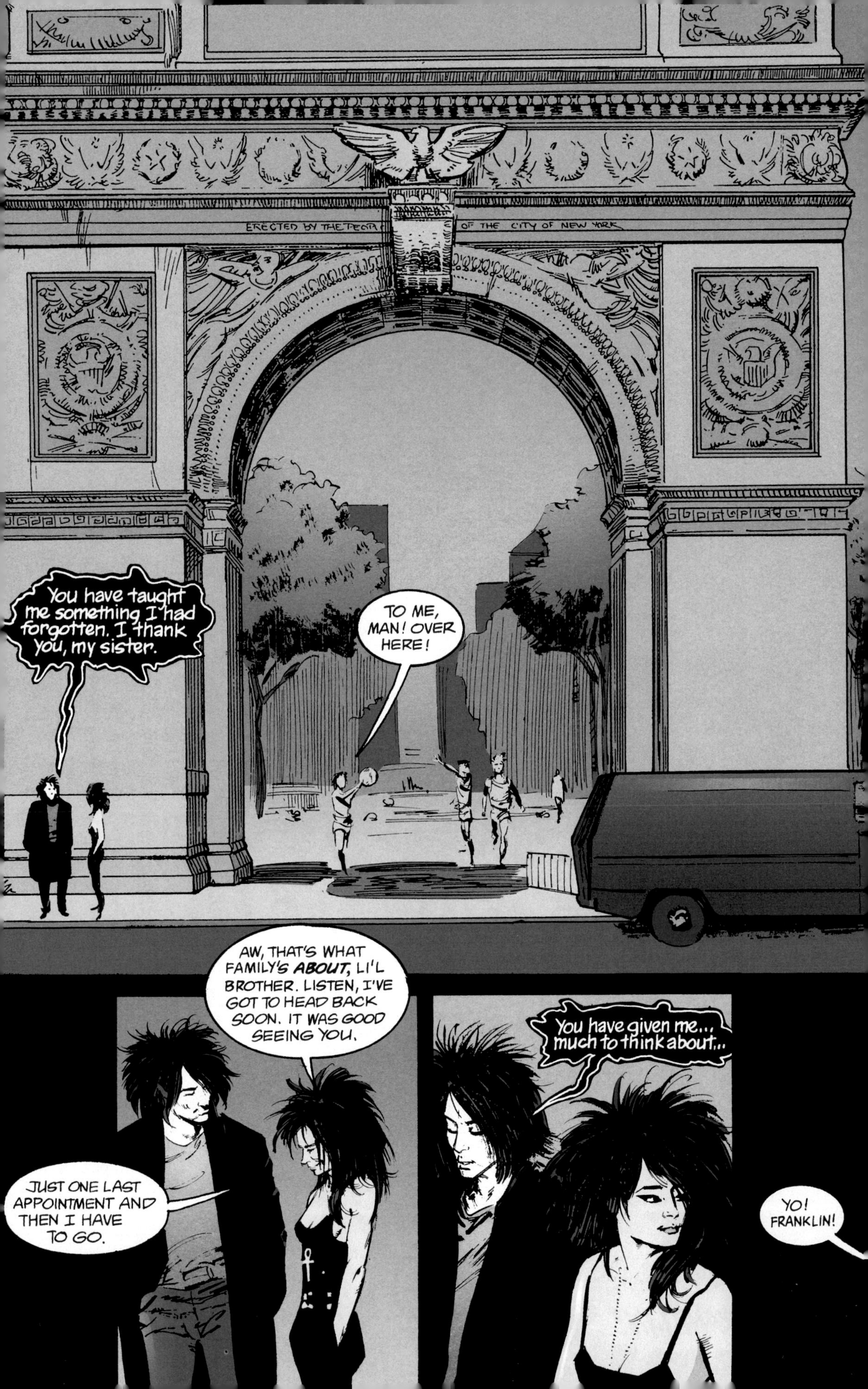
ERECTED BY THE PEOP... OF THE CITY OF NEW YORK
You have taught me something I had forgotten. I thank you, my sister.
TO ME, MAN! OVER HERE!
AW, THAT'S WHAT FAMILY'S **ABOUT**, LI'L BROTHER. LISTEN, I'VE GOT TO HEAD BACK SOON. IT WAS GOOD SEEING YOU.
JUST ONE LAST APPOINTMENT AND THEN I HAVE TO GO.
You have given me... much to think about...
YO! FRANKLIN!

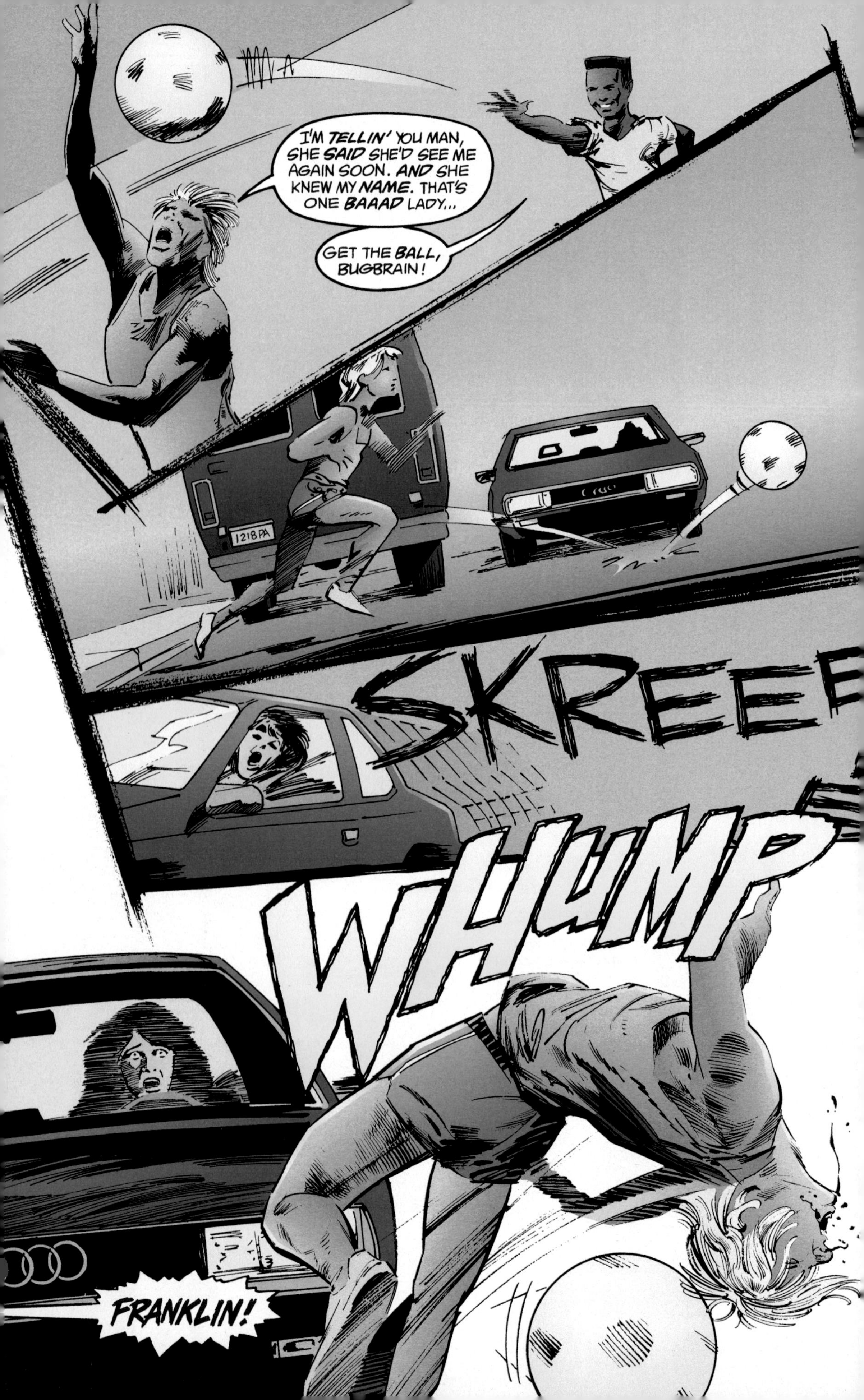
I'M TELLIN' YOU MAN, SHE SAID SHE'D SEE ME AGAIN SOON. AND SHE KNEW MY NAME. THAT'S ONE BAAAD LADY...
GET THE BALL, BUGBRAIN!
1218 PA
SKREEE
WHUMP
FRANKLIN!

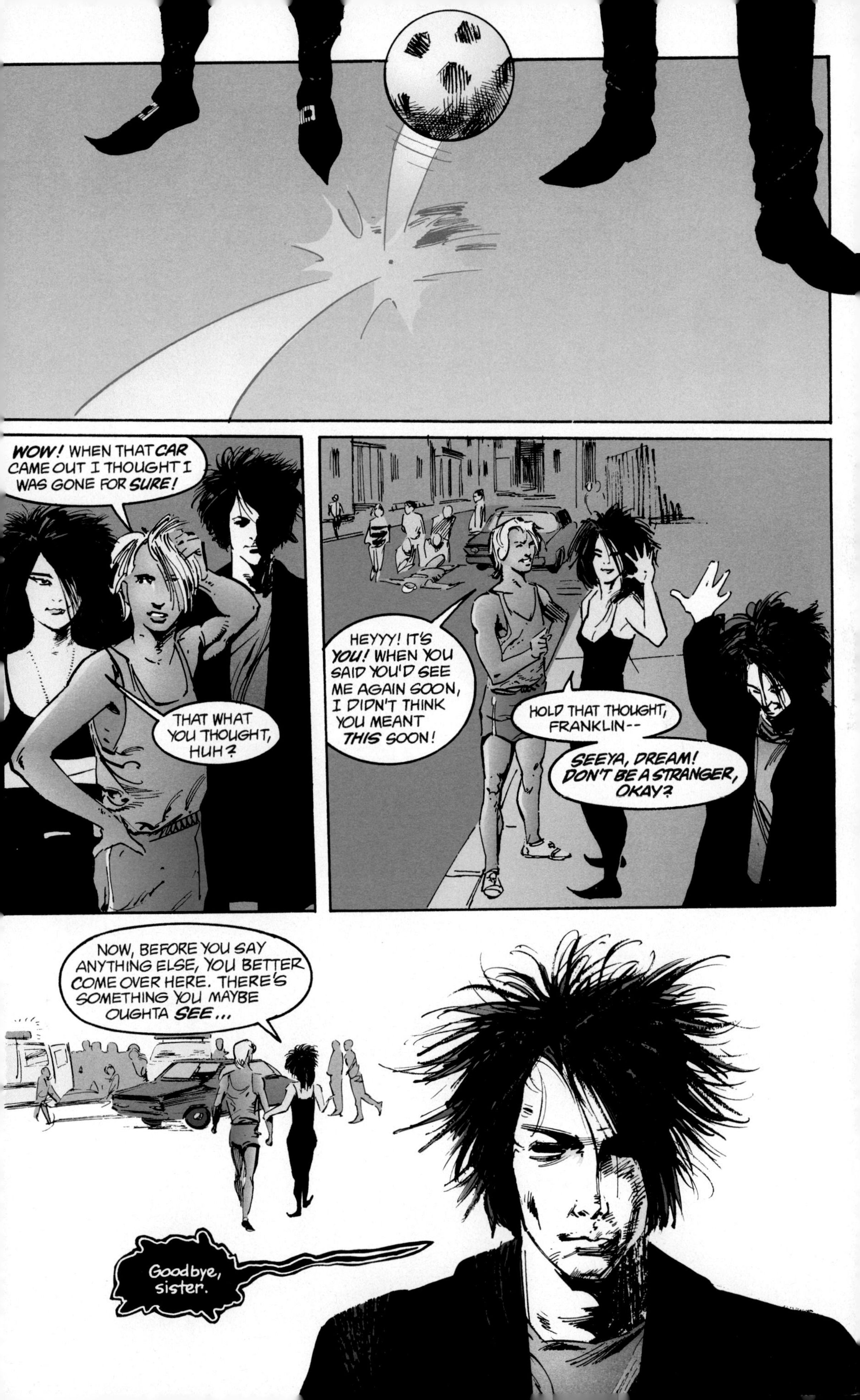
WOW! WHEN THAT CAR CAME OUT I THOUGHT I WAS GONE FOR SURE!
THAT WHAT YOU THOUGHT, HUH?
HEYYY! IT'S YOU! WHEN YOU SAID YOU'D SEE ME AGAIN SOON, I DIDN'T THINK YOU MEANT THIS SOON!
HOLD THAT THOUGHT, FRANKLIN--
SEEYA, DREAM! DON'T BE A STRANGER, OKAY?
NOW, BEFORE YOU SAY ANYTHING ELSE, YOU BETTER COME OVER HERE. THERE'S SOMETHING YOU MAYBE OUGHTA SEE...
Goodbye, sister.

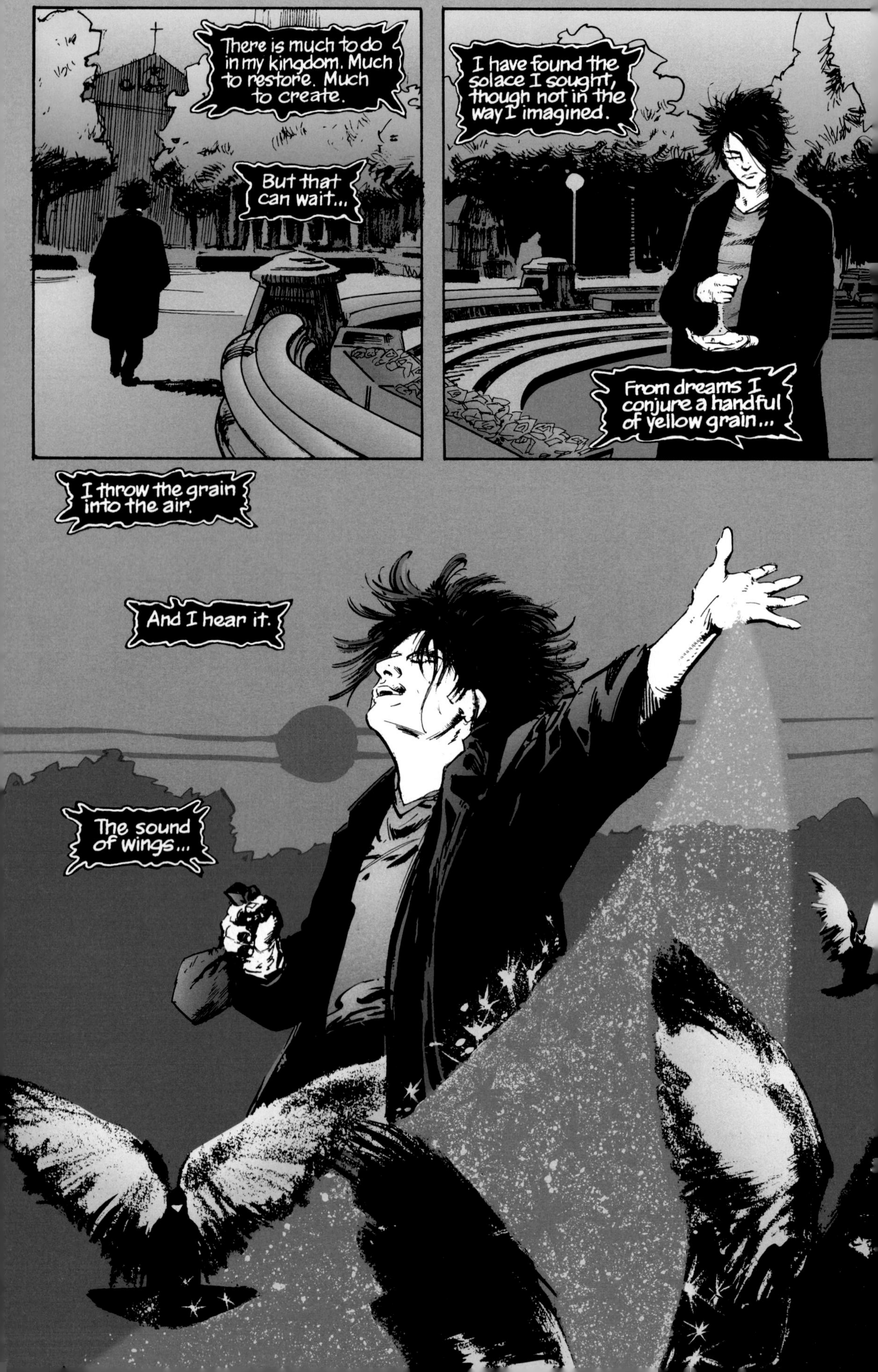
There is much to do in my kingdom. Much to restore. Much to create.
But that can wait...
I have found the solace I sought, though not in the way I imagined.
From dreams I conjure a handful of yellow grain...
I throw the grain into the air.
And I hear it.
The sound of wings...

AFTERWORD

In September 1987 Karen Berger phoned me up and asked me if I'd be interested in writing a monthly title for DC. That was how it all started.

Karen was already my editor on a book called BLACK ORCHID, and was DC's British liaison.

She rejected all my initial suggestions (sundry established DC characters I thought it might be fun to revive from limbo), and instead reminded me of a conversation we'd had the last time she was in England—a conversation I'd almost forgotten—in which I'd suggested reviving an almost forgotten DC character, "The Sandman," and doing a story set almost entirely in dreams.

"Do it. But create a *new* character," she suggested. "Someone no one's seen before."

So I did. A year later the first issue of THE SANDMAN appeared in the stores. Put like that, it all sounds so simple.

I don't think it could have been, though. Not really.

Looking back, the process of coming up with the Lord of Dreams seems less like an act of creation than one of sculpture: as if he were already waiting, grave and patient, inside a block of white marble, and all I needed to do was chip away everything that wasn't him.

An initial image, before I even knew who he was: a man, young, pale and naked, imprisoned in a tiny cell, waiting until his captors passed away, willing to wait until the room he was in crumbled to dust; deathly thin with long dark hair, and strange eyes: *Dream*. That was what he was. That was who he was.

The inspiration for his clothes came from a print in a book of Japanese design, of a black kimono, with yellow markings at the bottom which looked vaguely like flames; and also from my desire to write a character I could have a certain amount of sympathy with. (As I wouldn't wear a costume, I couldn't imagine him wanting to wear one. And seeing that the greater part of my wardrobe is black [It's a sensible color. It goes with anything. Well, anything black.], then his tastes in clothes echoed mine on that score as well.)

I had never written a monthly comic before, and wasn't sure that I would be able to. Each month, every month, the story had to be written. On this basis I wanted to tell stories that could go anywhere, from the real to the surreal, from the most mundane tales to the most outrageous. THE SANDMAN seemed like it would be able to do that, to be more than just a monthly horror title.

I wrote an initial outline, describing the title character and the first eight issues as best I could, and gave copies of the outline to friends (and artists) Dave McKean and Leigh Baulch: both of them did some character sketches and I sent the sketches along with the outline to Karen.

Fast forward to January 1988. Karen's back in England for a few days. Dave McKean, Karen and I met in London and wound up in The Worst French Restaurant In Soho for dinner (it had a pianist who knew the first three bars of at least two songs, the ugliest paintings you've ever seen on the wall, and a waitress who spoke no known language. The food took over two hours to come, and was neither what we had ordered, nor warm, nor edible). Then Dave went off to try to negotiate the release of his car from an underground car park, and Karen and I went back to her hotel room, devoured the complimentary fruit and nuts, and talked about Sandman.

I showed her my own notebook sketches of the character, and we talked about artists, throwing names at each other. Eventually Karen suggested Sam Kieth. I'd seen some of Sam's work, and liked it, and said so.

We rang Sam. Karen barely managed to convince him it wasn't a practical joke (and I completely failed to convince him I had actually seen his work and liked it), and she sent him a copy of the outline. He did a few character sketches, one of which was pretty close to the face I had in my head, and we got started.

Mike Dringenberg, whose work I'd seen and liked on *Enchanter*, came in to ink Sam's pencils. Dave McKean, my friend and frequent collaborator, agreed to paint (and, frequently, build) the covers. Todd Klein, possibly the best letterer in the business, agreed to letter, and Robbie Busch came in on coloring. We were in business.

The first few issues were awkward—neither Sam, Mike, Robbie nor myself had worked on a mainstream monthly comic before, and we were all pushing and pulling in different directions. Sam told us that he didn't want to carry on while drawing the third issue ("I feel like Jimi Hendrix in the Beatles," he told me. "I'm in the wrong band." I was sorry to see him go.) and with "24 Hours" Mike Dringenberg took over on pencils. The remarkable Malcolm Jones was now our regular inker.

Together we finished the first SANDMAN storyline, collected in this book.

There was a definite effort on my part, in the stories in this volume, to explore the genres available: "The Sleep of the Just" was intended to be a classical English horror story; "Imperfect Hosts" plays with some of the conventions of the old DC and E.C. horror comics (and the hosts thereof); "Dream a Little Dream of Me" is a slightly more contemporary British horror story; "A Hope in Hell" harks back to the kind of dark fantasy found in *Unknown* in the 1940s; "Passengers" was my (perhaps misguided) attempt to try to mix superheroes into the SANDMAN world; "24 Hours" is an essay on stories and authors, and also one of the very few genuinely horrific tales I've written; "Sound and Fury" wrapped up the storyline; and "The Sound of Her Wings" was the epilogue and the first story in the sequence I felt was truly mine, and in which I knew I was beginning to find my own voice.

Rereading these stories today I must confess I find many of them awkward and ungainly, although even the clumsiest of them has something—a phrase, perhaps, or an idea, or an image I'm still proud of. But they're where the story starts, and the seeds of much that has come after—and much that is still to come—were sown in the tales in this book.

Preludes and nocturnes; a little night music from me to you.

I hope you liked them. Good night.

Pleasant dreams.

—Neil Gaiman
June 1991

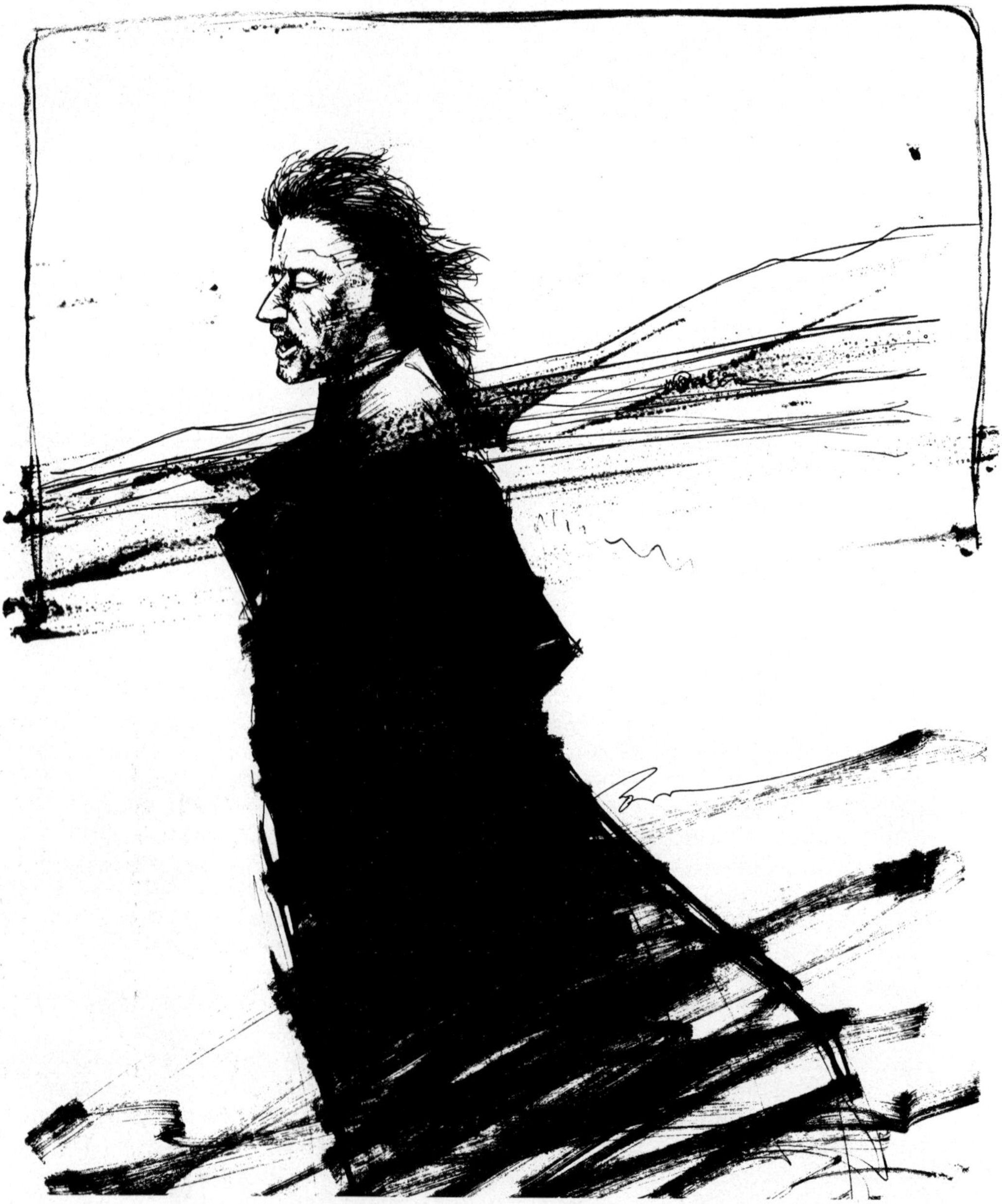

BIOGRAPHIES

Neil Gaiman is the creator and writer of the internationally acclaimed comics masterpiece THE SANDMAN, which was the first comic book to receive mainstream literary recognition when issue #19 ("A Midsummer Night's Dream") won the World Fantasy Award for Short Fiction in 1991. His most recent installment in the series, THE SANDMAN: OVERTURE, won the Hugo Award for Best Graphic Fiction in 2016.

He is also a *New York Times* best-selling author of books, short stories, films and graphic novels for all ages. Some of his most notable titles include *American Gods*, for which he received the Hugo, Nebula, Bram Stoker and Locus awards; *The Graveyard Book*, which was the first book to ever win both the Newbery and Carnegie medals; and *The Ocean at the End of the Lane*, which was named Book of the Year in 2013 by the UK's National Book Awards. His most recent title, *Norse Mythology*, is a retelling of the stories of the Norse gods and giants from the *Prose* and *Poetic Eddas*, and he is currently adapting *Good Omens*, the novel he co-wrote with Sir Terry Pratchett, into a six-part television series with the BBC and Amazon Studios.

In addition to his work on the page and screen, Gaiman is a professor in the arts at Bard College. He has four children and is married to the writer and performer Amanda Palmer.

Sam Kieth has drawn other people's characters, including the Sandman and Batman for DC Comics and Wolverine and the Hulk for Marvel Comics. He's also written and drawn for titles featuring characters of his own creation, the best known of which are probably THE MAXX, ZERO GIRL and FOUR WOMEN. He's currently creating a series of books for Oni Press involving a trout, magical creatures, toilet seats and (of course) dysfunctional relationships. Kieth also makes small weird movies in his garage that no one sees, but he enjoys.

Michael Dringenberg was born in France and grew up in Germany before emigrating to America in the early 1970s. He studied illustration and graphic design at the University of Utah and began illustrating books and comics before leaving college.

He met Neil Gaiman in 1988 and with him co-created the hugely popular and critically successful series THE SANDMAN.

Dringenberg's work as an illustrator continues, focusing on book jackets and, more recently, CD covers, exploring the relationship of sound and vision.

He still likes cats and rain.

Malcolm Jones III attended the High School of Art and Design and the Pratt Institute in New York City before making his comics debut in the pages of DC's YOUNG ALL-STARS. In addition to his celebrated work on THE SANDMAN, Jones contributed work to many other titles from both DC and Marvel, including BATMAN, THE QUESTION QUARTERLY, *Dracula* and *Spider-Man*. He died in 1995.

Dave McKean has illustrated over 80 books and graphic novels, including *Signal to Noise, The Wolves in the Walls, Coraline* and *The Graveyard Book*, all written by Neil Gaiman, *The Magic of Reality* by Richard Dawkins, *The Fat Duck Cookbook* by Heston Blumenthal and *What's Welsh for Zen* by John Cale. He has written and illustrated the multi-award-winning *Cages, Pictures That Tick 1* and *2* and *Black Dog: The Dreams of Paul Nash*. He has also directed several short films and three features: *MirrorMask, The Gospel of Us* with Michael Sheen and *Luna*, which premiered at the Toronto Film Festival in 2014. He lives on the Isle of Oxney in Kent, UK.

Daniel Vozzo was born and raised in Brooklyn, New York. After spending most of the 1980s drumming for several rock-and-roll bands, he landed a job working in DC Comics' production department, where he helped develop a computer coloring department in 1989. He soon began to work freelance, coloring a number of titles for DC's Vertigo line.

He sings great in the shower and always holds the door open for people. Currently living in northern New Jersey, Vozzo continues to color comics and is once again playing music. He has also been working on fine-tuning his writing skills. When asked if he thinks he's good at writing, he insists that he has always had very good penmanship.

One of the industry's most versatile and accomplished letterers, **Todd Klein** has been lettering comics since 1977 and has won numerous Eisner and Harvey awards for his work. A highlight of his career has been working with Neil Gaiman on nearly all the original issues of THE SANDMAN, as well as BLACK ORCHID, DEATH: THE HIGH COST OF LIVING, DEATH: THE TIME OF YOUR LIFE and THE BOOKS OF MAGIC.

THE SANDMAN™

PRELUDES & NOCTURNES